THE CONQUERORS
THE PAGEANT OF ENGLAND

ENGLAND
at the Time
of the Conquest

THE PAGEANT OF ENGLAND

The
Conquerors

THOMAS B. COSTAIN

GARDEN CITY, N.Y., 1949

DOUBLEDAY & COMPANY, INC.

To
MY WIFE

CONTENTS

Contents

Introduction

I T MUST be said at the outset that there is no need for another history of England unless it can be given popular appeal.

History, on which people depended once for enlightenment and entertainment in reading, is now little read except in classrooms, and this is due to the stern limits which historians have set for themselves. Thomas Babington Macaulay, one of the very greatest of them but a rebel in the matter of the traditions of the craft, had this to say in his definition: "The writers of history seem to entertain an aristocratical contempt for the writers of memoirs. . . . The most characteristic and interesting circumstances are omitted, or softened down, because, we are told, they are too trivial for the majesty of history." He quarreled with the theory which brushed aside biography and the technique of biographers, and which sternly decreed that history must remain within narrow bounds. He was not content that the annals of mankind should deal with public affairs so much and with life so little. And, of course, he was right. If the high ideals and conceptions which Macaulay laid down could be followed, history would regain some at least of its lost position.

To evolve a popular record of the period covered in this volume is not an easy task. The chronicles of the century and a half which followed the Norman Conquest were written by monks who toiled in cloistered withdrawal and depended on hearsay evidence. Much of what they produced is legend and fable on the face of it; still more is, at least, suspect. Industrious historians have found in the scant records room for much divergent theory. A single speech often has been translated in a dozen forms. It is hard, therefore, to keep the pen from wandering off into imaginative bypaths when dealing with material into which fancy has already entered so largely. But the greatest difficulty lies in the fact that the plodding fingers of the monks wrote with one-dimensional brevity.

How, then, may a history of the period be written which will have drama, color, and visual substance? I have always been convinced that it could be done and that various methods are available for the writer who undertakes the task.

First, there is the additional material which may readily be obtained by carrying research into unusual channels, ransacking old and forgotten histories, searching through memoirs and diaries and church documents and the proceedings of local historical societies, above everything else by reading what is available on such subjects as currency, minting, monastic life, sheep raising, weaving, heraldry, architecture, archery. In this way great quantities of fresh fact may be secured; enough, certainly, to clothe quite amply the loose-jointed frame of monkish chronicle.

Even more important is to act upon the suggestion of Macaulay and turn to biography. History, which has dealt with kings and statesmen and soldiers, may be broadened profitably by dealing adequately with the men and women of lesser stature who deserve so much of memory and are accorded so little, the monk and the schoolmaster, the architect and the builder, the thinker and the inventor, the poet and the painter.

There is need for something more, however, if history is to be made up, not of dry bones and locks of hair which crumble at a touch, but of blood and muscle and flesh with the tint of life. Obviously no stories may be invented, no speech may be put into the mouth of a historic character which cannot be authenticated. If the main actors have few scenes to play and brief lines to speak, how may a full-bodied drama be achieved? The answer is, by giving more scope to the players of minor roles (rewarding fellows, they always prove themselves) and by being lavish with scenery and sound effects and by having brisk drummers in the orchestra pit. It is my belief, as it has been that of many historians, that dramatization of certain non-essentials is within the right of the recorder of

history. For instance, when it is known that Henry II met Thomas
à Becket for the first time at Westminster on Christmas, it is surely
not wrong to picture the holiday revelry in the royal palace that
day, nor to say that Henry indulged his habit of sticking his thumbs
in his belt when confronting the man who would become his
chancellor and archbishop and would die under the axes of his
knights. When it is known that Good Queen Mold introduced the
fashion of letting the hair hang free, is it not permissible to depict
her as wearing her golden locks down her back on the occasion
when she rode to Lambeth Palace? This method I have adopted, but
without invention of fact or incident or the putting of fictional
speech in any mouth, believing it to be the only way of making
the story of the period live for the casual reader. If this is a crime
against the sacred code, then I must plead guilty. In that case,
however, I must plead also that the time has come to amend the
code.

The picture which emerges is, in my opinion, an honest and complete one. There has been no distortion of events to prove a point,
and a sincere attempt has been made to study the men and women
of those distant days through the mists which cloud them and to
present them as human beings.

I have not weighted the saddle of every page with the lead of
footnotes, and old Ibid., that ubiquitous Man Friday of the historian, has not been allowed to stick his long nose in once. The
reader, I am sure, will welcome the omission of credit notes and
the departure from historical precedent.

The present volume, complete in itself because of the rounding
out of the period of the Conquest and its results, is offered with
some hesitation, being my first venture into this field. It is my
desire and hope, however, to go on with the story of the men and
women who have played parts in the pageant of England, the noteworthy, the fantastic, the brave, the too often forgotten great
people who made the island empire great. In succeeding volumes,
which will deal with periods where the records are more full, it
will be easier to accomplish the purpose with which I have begun.

THOMAS B. COSTAIN

THE CONQUERORS
THE PAGEANT OF ENGLAND

CHAPTER I

Three Strong Men

IT WAS late in September, the year was 1066, and that section of the great north highway which crosses the Aire and the Wharfe and rolls on to the city of York was black with marching soldiers. In the van were the Thingmen, the trained troops who formed the King's bodyguard, proudly carrying the Standard of the Fighting Man, the personal flag of Harold. The King marched with them, this great son of Earl Godwine who had been elected by the Witanagemot to succeed Edward the Confessor, the first man of the people to wear a crown. His presence lent strength to stiffening muscles and persuaded the racing squadrons to pour forth from not too melodious throats the battle songs of Assanduan in full confidence that victory lay ahead of them.

They marched on foot, these space-devouring Anglo-Saxons, battle-ax on shoulder and kite-shaped shield on arm, their knee-length tunics gray with dust, their legs bare (only the leaders wore the *bracco* or cross-gartering), their gauntlet-topped buskins cut to ribbons of leather. They were of medium height and inclined to a squareness of build. Under their caps, which curved to hornlike points, they had bristling manes of fair hair. Their faces were broad and stolid in expression. But look at them well, these dusty warriors who have marched from London in less than five days. In spite of their cloddish appearance and their obvious lack of learning, these men and their fathers before them had been groping toward an understanding of two great principles; first, that kings are the

[1]

servants and not the masters of men, and, second, that in all things the will of the majority expressed through a properly constituted assemblage must prevail.

They did not know it, but it was to defend these beliefs that the soldiers of England were marching on sore and blistered feet up the great north highway.

2

Three strong men were fighting for the crown of England: Harold, the choice of the people; Duke William of Normandy, who pretended to have a claim based on a promise of the deceased King, and Harold Hardrada, ruler of Norway, whose only claim lay in his heavy two-handed sword.

The succession had become involved when Edward, called the Confessor, took the crown. Edward was the sole surviving son of Ethelred the Unready, that incapable monarch who earned the hatred of the people to such a degree that they welcomed the Danish invaders who chased him from the throne. His mother was Emma, a beautiful Norman woman of gentle birth and fiercely acquisitive instincts. She later married Canute, the leader of the Danes, and so became Queen of England a second time. She loved Canute devotedly and gave little thought to her son Edward, who had fled the country and was living in Normandy. After the death of Canute and his sons, Edward was summoned back to England by the Witanagemot. His choice had been brought about by the influence of Godwine, Earl of the South and West. A speaker of persuasive eloquence, Godwine was able to win men over to his way of thinking, and his sagacity was such that he should rank with the greatest of the kingmakers who have played parts in English history.

Edward came to the throne with a reputation for saintliness which flickered during his reign but steadied into a strong flame after his death; which grew and grew, in fact, into a legend nothing could shake. It must be said, however, that if he had been left to rule by himself he would almost certainly have been as great a failure as his weak father. That would have been a sorry thing indeed for the country. Fortunately the pious Edward had Godwine to direct him and later the earl's son, Harold, who was quite as able as his father and less devious.

[2]

Three Strong Men

Edward was a strange individual. He had white hair and a long white beard and a pinkish complexion which made him look almost albino. His hands were long and thin and white to the point of transparency. He had a curious way of staring and he was given to sudden fits of unexplained speech and laughter. He won his reputation for piety by spending hours each day at his devotions. After emerging from his oratory, however, he would go off on hunting orgies during which he slaughtered the poor beasts of the forest with singular bloodthirstiness. When trouble arose in any part of the kingdom, it was Edward's first thought to send troops with orders to burn and slay; and only the influence of Harold kept him from acting on his sanguinary impulses. After his death people compared the peacefulness of his reign with the terrible years which followed and began to think of him as a saint; a tendency strengthened by the fact that miracles were reported at his tomb.

But the blame for the terrible years, nearly two centuries of cruelty and oppression, can be laid squarely on the doorstep of this second unready King. Although married to Edytha, the beautiful daughter of Godwine, he showed no inclination to beget an heir. In addition he brought Normans over in droves and made bishops of them and earls and court stallers, and he gave lands and great wealth to them; and so created in Norman minds the belief that England was a rich plum for Norman plucking. What is more, when William of Normandy paid him a visit, he promised that intensely ambitious man (or so William swore) the throne of England.

The throne of England was not a prize to be scrambled for by ambitious men or disposed of by weak kings. It was an office which the people conferred through the Witanagemot, the first ancestor of the modern Parliament. Although sons generally followed their fathers, it was understood that this was by the will of the people and not because of any divine right to succeed. The people could dethrone a bad king, and sometimes (but not often enough) they did. If ascetic Edward made such a promise to Norman William, it could not be considered a valid claim.

But William ruled over a land where the people had no rights at all. From that day forward he regarded himself as Edward's legal successor. He was, however, a longheaded and farseeing man and he took every precaution. When Harold was shipwrecked on the coast of Normandy, William had him brought before a chest covered with a cloth of gold thread on which a missal had been placed. He then demanded that his involuntary guest swear to support his claim. Harold, having no alternative, swore to do so, and the Norman barons, who had been summoned to hear, repeated sonorously, *May God be thy Help!* The cloth was then whisked off, and it was seen that the chest was filled with the bones and relics of saints. Norman chroniclers say that Harold turned pale when he thus realized the profundity of the oath he had sworn. This was the first evidence that England had of the deep craft of Duke William, but proofs of it would multiply over the years.

When the thin hands of the weak old King had been folded on his breast and his body had been laid away in the great church he had built at Westminster (his one real personal achievement), the Witanagemot faced a problem. England needed a strong man at the head of the state and there was no prince of the blood left with enough resolution to administer a knight's fee. Harold had not a drop of royal blood in his veins but he had governed England for Edward with wisdom, firmness, and a degree of forbearance which was most unusual in those cruel days. He was, moreover, a general of proven skill and the only man capable of defending the kingdom against the designs of that great schemer across the Channel. Finally, Edward on his deathbed had seen the accession in the right light and had voiced his preference for Harold.

So Harold was chosen. Counting his oath to William wiped out by the nation's need of him, and considering it invalid because given under duress, he accepted. He was anointed with the holy oil, the *Veni, Creator Spiritus* was sung over him, he placed the crown of England on his own head, and the country rejoiced at the prospect of a continuation of enlightened rule.

The day after his coronation Harold began to prepare for the blow he knew was coming.

He might perhaps have beaten the forces of William if the issue had been confined to them, but it developed that he had two invading armies to fight. Sometime before the death of the Confessor, Harold had acquiesced in the deposing and banishment of his brother Tostig because of the oppressive way the latter ruled his earldom of Northumberland. Tostig, burning with rage and spite, had since been plotting against Harold. He had been in Normandy, urging William (who needed no urging at all) to assert his right to

NORMANDY
at the Time
of the Conquest

N ENGLAND

Hastings

ENGLISH CHANNEL

(THE SLEEVE)

Alderney

Barfleur

Guernsey

Jersey

Bayeux

Caen

NORMANDY

Falaise

Rouen

SEINE

Avranches

Mont St. Michel

the throne. From there he went to Denmark and asked King Sweyn for aid against his brother. Meeting refusal here, he went finally to Norway and found a ready listener in Harold, called Hardrada, the King of that country.

A word about this viking King, the third of our three strong men. Harold Hardrada was a blond giant, Thor come down to earth in the guise of a man. He had spent his life in search of adventure, and legends had gathered about him. He was called sometimes Harold the Varanger, sometimes Harold the Lionslayer. He was supposed to have led a small personal crusade against the Saracens (an unsuccessful one, needless to state). He had sailed haughtily through the Bosporus, breaking the chain across it with the prow of his flagship and laughing at Eastern might. He had put out the eyes of the Byzantine Emperor Constantine Monomachos and had enjoyed (but not exclusively) the passionate favors of the Empress Zoë. Strange wild songs came into his head when he went into battle, and he sang them exultantly as he hacked his opponents to pieces. No living man had ever been able to stand against him. His fame was even putting the memory of the truly great Olaf Trygvisson into temporary shade, and such lesser heroes as Thorkill the Tall and Swen Forkbeard were being forgotten.

So much for legend. This much is certain: Harold Hardrada was a hard-bitten champion who was never happy without his sword in his hand and the head of a foeman to cleave. He was not wise enough to perceive the weaknesses in the proposition Tostig brought him. He listened to that glum traitor and decided he would like to steal the throne of England for himself.

English Harold had been King for a few months only when he learned of the double danger facing him. Harold Hardrada and Tostig had sailed up the Humber River with a large army of invasion. They landed at Riccall and defeated an English force commanded by Edwin and Morkar, earls of the north.

Knowing that he must beat off the Norsemen before the Normans landed, English Harold collected his army and led it on its breakneck march up the north highway.

3

Harold Hardrada had come to stay. He had sailed from Norway with a fleet of extraordinary size and a large army. Some reports have

Three Strong Men

it that he took a thousand ships to transport his troops. However, the remnants of the invading force returned to Norway in twenty-three ships, so it may safely be assumed that the chroniclers have been guilty in this instance of one of the gross exaggerations in which all early annals abound. But the gigantic Norseman had brought his wife, a Russian princess to whom he seems to have been much attached, some at least of his many mistresses, a drove of his children, an ingot of gold so large that twelve men were needed to get it on board, his household goods, his wardrobe, all his shining armor and his prized weapons and his bewinged helmets. He intended to remain and to rule over England.

After beating the English earls at Fulford, he established his headquarters near the village of Aldby in what had once been the home of the kings of Northumberland. This, no doubt, he considered the fit habitation for a conqueror. By settling himself here, he allowed his vanity to get the better of his strategic sense. His army had to be assembled loosely nearby along the banks of the Derwent. It was flat country and offered no advantages at all to defenders.

The truth of the matter is that the powerful Norseman had not expected his English namesake so soon. He would have disposed his troops with greater care had he thought he would be attacked here. It is recorded that he was a much surprised man when he saw a cloud of dust on the road from York and realized that the English were coming to Stamfordbridge. He must have known a moment of panic when it came home to him that a large part of his army was with the ships at Riccall and that still more were encamped on the other side of the river. Harold Hardrada sent off messengers to summon the absent troops and then drew up what forces he had in battle array.

In spite of the poor position of the invaders, they looked formidable enough to the tired English as they crossed the river. The viking King had formed his men in the traditional shield wall which made a complete circle. Little was to be seen save the fierce eyes of the Norsemen above the interlocked shields and the dread flag of the King, his standard, the Land-waster, curling and uncurling in the wind above them. Harold Hardrada rode out to inspect his forces, looking very handsome and martial on his huge black horse. It may have been that the weight in the saddle was too much for even so strong a mount. The black steed stumbled, at any rate, and the King pitched forward to the ground.

[7]

The Conquerors

English Harold, assembling his men for the attack, saw what had happened. He smiled grimly.

"Who is the tall man who fell from his horse?" he asked those about him.

"It is King Harold of Norway."

The English King, cupping a hand over his eyes, watched his crestfallen enemy return to the Norwegian ranks on foot. "A tall man, and a goodly," he is reported to have said. "Methinks his luck has left him."

But the English leader, who was almost as hardheaded and realistic as Duke William, put no reliance in that possibility. Thinking of the Norman army which was being assembled across the channel and the need he had of every English soldier, he made an effort to effect a settlement. A herald was sent forward, accompanied by twenty armed horsemen.

The herald stopped and called, "Where is Tostig, the son of Godwine?"

The traitor, carrying his English battle-ax over his shoulder, stepped out from the ranks. "He is here."

"Thy brother sends word by my mouth that he salutes thee and offers thee peace, friendship, and thy former honors."

"Those are fine words," said Tostig. "But if I accept, what will there be for my ally, the noble King Harold, son of Sigurd?"

"Seven feet of English earth," answered the herald. "As he is taller than other men, perhaps a little more."

"Go then," cried the brother of the English King, "and tell your master to make ready for the battle!"

It is reported further that Harold Hardrada, having recovered from his mishap, searched eagerly for a sight of English Harold. When his quest was rewarded, he remarked with all the condescension of a man of extra inches that "the King of England is a small man." Then he added with a generous gesture, "He stands well in his stirrups."

Harold was small only when compared with a man of the stature of the Norse leader. He led the first charge against the shield wall, brandishing his battle-ax. His men followed close after him, shouting eagerly, "The Rood! The Rood!" It was apparent from the first that the advantage was with the English. Men fight their hardest when the feet of invaders press on their native soil. If the Norsemen won, they would ravage England from coast to coast. No man's life, no woman's honor, would be safe. The need of the homeland inspired every English thrust, it put edge to the sword and weight to the mace, it sped on the tip of every English arrow.

Harold Hardrada, standing beneath the Land-waster, held the English at bay long after they had broken the shield wall. The hero of a hundred legends, the victor of a thousand fights, he fought his last battle like the God of War himself. Singing the battle songs of the north, his eyes blazing with the madness of conflict, he fought until a mound of his dead surrounded him. No man lived who knew the edge of his terrible two-handed sword. But one man cannot win a battle by himself (the records of chivalry to the contrary) and in time the royal gladiator and troubadour went down, an arrow in his throat. He died with his bloodstained kirtle over his face and so was spared the spectacle of the victorious English breaking through.

The battle still went on. Tostig, who was brave in spite of his faults, commanded after the death of the King and fell in turn by the Land-waster. The reinforcements from the ships arrived under the leadership of a soldier named Eystein Orre, but the battle was lost when they reached the field and all they could do was die as their fallen comrades had done.

Harold Hardrada's amazing career had ended in the seven feet of earth promised him. Most of his men had died with him. Those who survived made their peace and sailed back to Norway, with their women and their household goods and a small remnant of their pride.

But it had been a costly victory. Five days later, when presiding at a victory banquet in York, Harold received word that the Normans had landed on the south coast. Brandishing a bull in his favor which the Pope had sent, William had proclaimed England his and Harold a perjured thief.

The victor of Stamfordbridge rose from his seat and went out to begin preparations for a second battle. Perhaps, as he thought of his weary and shrunken army, he realized that his two dead foes had won after all. Their adventure had so depleted the English ranks that Harold had small chance now of prevailing against the mounted and superbly equipped forces of Norman William. The mad whim of Harold Hardrada and Tostig, which had cost them their own lives, was to clamp a yoke of steel on the neck of England!

4

William's army was camped around Hastings, facing a spur of the Downs which provided a formidable horizon northward. The rising ground ahead of them was in reality a clutter of choppy hills, through which ran deep ravines with bottoms of broken stone and trickling streams called in those days *becks*. Strategically placed in the midst of this tumbled confusion of levels was the ridge of Senlac, with high hills from behind which a glimpse might be had of the sea, its flanks well guarded by nature. This ridge was large enough to contain an army; and here on October 14 was fought one of the most discussed and most written about, certainly the most wept over, and most deeply deplored battle in English history.

Harold, not waiting for the tardy earls from the north to arrive with their forces (and not sure even that they would come) because the savage wasting of the countryside was forcing his hand, showed his skill as a general by disposing his hastily assembed and ill-equipped army along Senlac. It was perfect for his purpose. Here he commanded all the roads. Here he could watch the Normans like the eagle from its lofty perch, and pounce if there was any attempt at diversion of forces. Here he had a strong defensive position which he proceeded to improve with trenches and barricades of stakes and osier hurdles. Here he waited.

William had two alternatives, to fight a pitched battle on Harold's terms or take to his ships. He chose, of course, the former. On the morning of the battle he exhorted his troops at great length, making clear to them that victory meant glory and wealth, but defeat was death for every Norman on English soil. Then the charge began, a fearsome spectacle of steel-clad men on madly plunging chargers, standards swaying wildly above the ranks, covering the rolling ground like a rising tide. A minstrel named Taillefer was in front, tossing his battle-ax in the air and singing the Song of Roland. The defenders on the ridge ahead responded with the deep-throated Saxon invocation to the Rood. A few raised for the first time the cry which was to be employed in clashes so often later, that pathetic shout of men in chains, "No Normans! No Normans! No Normans!"

Between the English center and right a spur ran out and down from the ridge. The chief Norman attack was along this spur, wheel-

TO LONDON

Malfosse

SENLAC

BROOK

BATTLE of SENLAC
(HASTINGS)
Oct 14, 1066

ENGLISH
□ Light Armed
◨ Housecarls
▣ Outpost
NORMAN
▬ Heavy Armed
⚑ Cavalry
⠿ Archers

TO HASTINGS
6½ MILES

Scale of Yards
0   500   1000   1500   1Mile

palacios

ing at the top to attack the English center; certainly not a favorable situation for the assailants. The interlocked shields of the English were a greater obstacle, however, than anything nature had provided. The Normans were thrown back time and again. Taillefer was killed, William was unhorsed, the hopes of the invading forces reached a low ebb. Then William set his mind to finding other methods than the shock of frontal assault. Twice he had his men simulate retreat, drawing the inexperienced Saxons after them in undisciplined and exuberant pursuit, then turning and cutting the ill-armed peasants to pieces. Even in the face of these losses and the consequent weakening of his flanks, Harold still stood firmly in the center, his brothers Gyrth and Loefwin beside him, the Standard of the Fighting Man as defiantly erect as ever.

The shield wall of the center held as though the men behind it knew that a break would mean not only their deaths and the subjugation of England but also the extinction for centuries of a light which they, the Anglo-Saxons, had kindled, the light which was to guide men in their long quest for freedom. How bravely they stood!

If the archers of Crécy and Agincourt had stood on Senlac with their mighty longbows, the Normans would have been cut to pieces as they charged up the slope. But the English had not yet any great addiction to the bow. They relied on the battle-ax, which was a doughty weapon at close range and one they understood. The Normans had more archers than Harold, and it was a wily use of the weapon which William employed as his final effort to break that stubborn wall.

"Shoot your arrows into the air!" he ordered.

His hired crossbowmen dropped back far enough to enjoy ease of aim. The arrows began to rain into the circle of English resistance. This lethal hail was so thick that the losses seemed unbearable; unbearable, indeed, for one lodged in the eye of the brave Harold. He fell to the ground and writhed in the most intense agony before death came. The heart went out of the defense as soon as this terrible news spread through the ranks.

The wall broke and the battle became a confused tangle of personal fighting. The sun went down and with it the hopes of men for individual freedom.

CHAPTER II

The Strongest Man Rules

T HE STRONGEST of the three men had won.

Never in history, perhaps, have the qualities which make a successful dictator been combined more perfectly and completely in one vigorous frame and one keen brain. William was a great warrior as well as an astute general. No other man, according to legend, had the strength to bend his bow. But this perfect fighting machine was topped by a forehead of splendid proportions, and behind that fine brow a brain was at work. He was shrewd, sagacious, farseeing. He planned everything out in advance like a chess champion who figures seven or eight moves ahead. During the years that he reigned as King of England he did many things which verged on genius. His was a stern and thorough rule, but this must be said: he imposed it on his own followers as well as on the conquered Anglo-Saxons.

Like all dictators, he kept the reins in his own hands. He could be just, but he never allowed justice to stand in the way of expediency. Any hint of opposition or double-dealing drove him into tempestuous rages, and when in these fits of anger he was like a mad boar. Revenge was a strong motive with all Normans; with William the Conqueror it was a black urge which drove him to the most horrible cruelties.

When Robert, the first-born son, began to quarrel with William, the Queen was much disturbed and sent to a German hermit who was supposed to have the gift of prophecy, asking advice as to how the dissension could be cured. The hermit replied in part: "The Most High has made known to me in a dream the things you desire to know. I saw in my vision a beautiful pasture, covered with grass and flowers, and a noble charger feeding therein. A numerous herd gathered round about, eager to enter and share the feast, but the fiery charger would not permit them to approach near enough to crop the flowers and herbage. But, alas! The majestic steed, in the midst of his pride and courage, died, his terror departed with him, and a poor silly steer appeared in his place as the guardian of the pasture. . . ."

The hermit had struck the nail squarely on the head. The Conqueror would not share the beautiful pasture which was England with anyone, not even his first-born. He wanted to keep to himself all the responsibilities and the power, and all the glory.

No one can study the life of William without being amazed at his genius and in equal degree appalled by his ruthlessness and cruelty.

2

Nearly twenty years before the Conquest there was at the court of Count Baldwin of Flanders a very beautiful girl, his sister Matilda. Young Duke William of Normandy fell in love with her at first sight. He did not manifest his devotion, however, in the usual ways. There was none of the mooning of adolescence, no shy dancing of attendance, on the part of the determined Norman. He courted Matilda in a forthright way, making it clear that he intended to marry her, come what may. Matilda met his advances coldly.

Her reluctance may have been due to the fact that William's mother had been Herleva, the pretty daughter of a tanner, and that his father had taken no steps to legitimatize his birth, thereby condemning him for life to the appellation of Bastard. Most likely, however, her coldness was because the image of a handsome Saxon still filled her mind.

Brihtric Meau, the son of Alfgar, lord of the honor of Gloucester, had been sent to Flanders on a diplomatic mission. He was a handsome fellow, tall and straight of back and leg and with such a fairness of skin that he had been nicknamed Snow. One look at the blue-eyed stranger and Matilda fell as deeply in love with him as

William had on his first glimpse of her. She took no pains to hide her infatuation for the blond Saxon but followed him everywhere and tried every expedient to win his attention. When the ladies had retired from the Great Hall (which was so large that three hundred people could dine there at once) and the men had settled down to their wine swilling, she would hide on the minstrels' gallery and watch Brihtric from behind a tapestry hanging on the railing. Finally she took matters into her own hands and went to him with a suggestion. Why must he return to England, which was a poor and barbarous land? Why not remain in Flanders and take a wife? It would not be hard to find one.

Brihtric knew what she meant, of course. Just how he answered her is not on record. He was flattered, no doubt, by the devotion of the highborn Flemish beauty, but he was also a man of firm principles. There was a lady of his choice in England and he meant to marry her on his return. Whatever his manner of phrasing it, his answer to Matilda was a firm no. Soon after, his mission completed, he sailed back to England.

William's courting of Matilda lasted seven years in all. At the end of that time, in the year 1047, he became so enraged at her continued refusals that he waited outside a church in the city of Bruges, where she was hearing mass, and attacked her when she emerged. He knocked her down, rolled her in the dirt of the street, tore her fine cloak, upbraided her furiously, and then sprang into the saddle and rode away. Perhaps he should have adopted this method of courtship earlier. It produced, at any rate, the desired effect. Matilda gave in.

They were married in William's castle of Angi, and it was a grand occasion. If the bride retained any regrets for the handsome Englishman who had rebuffed her, she did not show it. She and William, in fact, were quite happy in their marriage. They had a large family, including four sons, Robert, Richard (who died in his youth), William, and Henry. The last two became kings of England. William saw to it that Matilda was the first wife of an English king to have the title of Queen. The consort of a Saxon ruler had been called "lady companion of the King," but this was not good enough for Matilda. William had a special coronation for her and had a crown placed on her fine dark locks. When she died in 1083 he mourned her the rest of his days. He built a great tomb for her at Caen in Normandy, covered with gems and with an epitaph lettered in gold.

But the story has a sequel. Brihtric survived the Conquest. He was married and had a family and he had become a very wealthy man with lands in Gloucestershire and Devonshire and Cornwall. He had many manor houses, and to the manor of Hanley, where he spent most of his time, a new chapel had been added. Wulfstan, the saintly old Bishop of Worcester, had come to hallow it, and the ceremony was under way when a troop of Norman soldiers put in an appearance. They took Brihtric in charge and threw him into a cell in Winchester. The cell was so deep underground that it had no window and the only sound its occupants ever heard was the ironshod foot of a jailer on the stone stairs. It was damp and cold and filled with rats and toads.

Matilda was not in England when this occurred, and it might have been due to the jealousy of William, who had never ceased to resent her early preference for the handsome Saxon. There is nothing in her record to hint at a strain of vindictiveness in her character, and the fact, moreover, that Brihtric's punishment was conceived with a thoroughness typical of the Conqueror lends further substance to that view. The unfortunate thane, whose only fault had been his constancy, was kept in his deep, dank cell until he died. His possessions were all confiscated. The city of Gloucester was deprived of its charter and all its civic liberties were taken away because Brihtric was a Gloucester man. His family, penniless, were turned away, to live or die.

But Matilda cannot be cleared as easily as that. It is recorded in Domesday Book that all Brihtric's possessions were given to her and that she held them as her personal property until her death, when they reverted to the Crown. It seems reasonable to believe, therefore, that this remarkable woman stood at William's shoulder and whispered in his ear. Certainly she acquiesced in the despoiling and death of the fair-haired stranger she had once watched with worshiping eyes from the minstrels' gallery.

3

But the fate of Brihtric was exceptional only because of the personal reason for the severity shown him. All over England the Saxons were being dispossessed. William had recruited his army by offering to make rich men of all who would follow him to England. He had won and now he had to find rewards for hundreds of clamoring Norman nobles and their followers. The Norman nature was hard, acquisitive, exacting. Nothing was going to satisfy the FitzOsborns, the Mortimers, the Laceys, short of land grants in keeping with his most lavish promises. William had proceeded slowly after his victory at Hastings. He had not advanced at once on London but had waited while the distraught Saxon leaders tried all kinds of desperate expedients, even going to the extreme of crowning Edgar the Atheling of the royal line as successor to Harold. It was not until they had time to realize there was nothing they could do, that their army had been almost exterminated in the lost battle, that he advanced to the English capital. The princeling fled, London opened its gates without striking a blow, and William was crowned King on Christmas Day. A grim present for the people of England.

William had been thinking as he paced in front of the pavilion he had raised on the bloodstained soil of Senlac, and an idea had been born in that shrewd head which he proceeded to put into effect. He had realized that, in order to justify what he was now going to do, he must declare what had happened in England since the death of Edward the Confessor an interlude of confusion and misrule. He, William, was the rightful successor to the Confessor. On arriving with his men to take possession of the throne, he had found the country in the hands of an archrobber. Harold had never been King of England, he had been a usurper. The Battle of Hastings had not been a meeting of the armies of two nations but one in which a rebellion had been suppressed. It followed that the men who had fought under Harold were rebels and were to be treated as such. This ingenious piece of casuistry was the weapon he would now use to satisfy his clamoring mercenaries.

He decreed that the property of every man who had fought at Hastings be confiscated to the Crown. Not a Saxon landowner who could get there had failed to fight under the banner of Harold, and most of them had died in the shield wall. It was no longer difficult now to meet the demands of the Norman knights, for William had all of the south of England to give away. He proceeded to do so.

One case will serve to illustrate how generously the Conqueror sweetened the palms of the robber barons. The town of Nottingham had stood out against the invaders, and when it fell he built a typical Norman citadel there to prevent any further attempts at resistance. The citadel was then given to a Norman knight named Guillaume Peveril. But this was a small part only of what he received. It is on record that he was given no fewer than fifty-five manors thereabouts and that in the town he became the owner of sixty-eight houses. He did not need one hundred and twenty-three homes for his own use, and so it is to be assumed that Guillaume Peveril portioned out these properties to the men under him. For himself he built a castle on a very high rock, so high that the place became known as the Peak. To this day some remnants of the original masonry are to be seen.

Guillaume de Garonne was given eighteen villages and Guillaume de Percy eighty manors. Ives de Vesey was awarded the town of Alnwick and the granddaughter of the former owner as his wife. When the wife of Eudes de Champagne, who had been allotted the island of Holderness, gave birth to a son, the father complained to William that the island was capable of growing oats only and that the new heir would die for lack of wheat. This problem was easily solved. William picked out the town of Bytham and gave it over to the anxious father so that the revenues could be applied to securing better land. It is probable that the boy grew up strong and hearty, but it is certain that the unfortunate children of Bytham paid for his health in misery and malnutrition.

William, canny Norman that he was, did not neglect his own interests while thus carving up England like a Christmas turkey. It is recorded that he kept fifteen hundred manor houses, and all the lands attached thereto, for himself; which seems a handsome share. Occasionally he would hand one of these estates away as a special reward. When Matilda was given a coronation of her own, the King was so pleased with a dish of dilligrout (a kind of oatmeal soup) which his cook Tezelin made for the banquet that he there and then conferred the manor of Addington on the lucky chef. Because of this the owners of Addington continued to send a great container of dilligrout to the kings of England on their coronations for many centuries. The bones of the real owner of Addington were moldering on the hill of Senlac, so all this made little difference.

But even through these excesses of liberality William kept a cool and calculating head. He saw to it that the new lands of his knights were scattered. They received a village in one shire, a tract of land in another. He did not want them to grow so powerful with great compact holdings that they would be a menace to royal authority. As the Normans married among themselves, the country soon became a curious crisscross of scattered inheritances. Some nobles held bits of property in nearly all the counties of England!

It was not even necessary for a Frenchman to have fought with William's army to receive a share. Take the case of a ferocious fellow named Hugues-de-Loup who had succeeded in putting down resistance in the county of Chester. As a reward he was made an earl and had the disposal of the land in his hands. Hugues-de-Loup lost no time in taking advantage of this. He sent at once for all his friends and relatives to come over and get a share of the rich booty. Five brothers named Houdard, Edward, Volmar, Horswin, and Volfan were among the first to arrive. None of them had fought for William, but each received two bovates of land (a bovate being as much as a team of oxen could plow in a year) except Volfan, who was a priest. The Saxon incumbent of the church at Runcone was turned out and Volfan was put in his place.

The people of England were able to retain some sense of humor even in the face of this kind of treatment. They watched the mad scramble of the land-hungry Normans and sometimes they would sing under their breaths a song which was going the rounds:

> *William of Coningsby*
> *Came out of Brittany,*
> *With his wife Tiffany*
> *And his maid Manfas,*
> *And his dog Hardigras.*

They were so bitter in their hearts, however, that they called any Englishman who fell into Norman ways or showed a tendency to conform to the new authority "thrall of the Mamzer [bastard]." The Mamzer! They never referred to the self-made King by any other name among themselves. Sometimes they did it openly, without fear of the punishment the Mamzer might inflict.

In order to keep the conquered people in proper subjection, the new masters of England began to erect castles. William entrusted the task of converting a small Roman tower on the Thames into a London stronghold and home for himself to an ingenious monk who had followed victory into England and had been rewarded with the bishopric of Rochester. Gundulph the Weeper, as he became known, was a good builder, and soon Caesar's Tower was changed into a formidable structure called the White Tower. Here the new King set himself up in the business of governing. He located the mint here and courts of justice and the royal wardrobe. In it were grouped the royal banqueting hall and around it the Queen's gardens. What the lachrymose Gundulph was building was not intended at first as a prison, but in later reigns it became known as the Tower of London, the most famous prison the world has ever seen.

All the great nobles followed his example by putting up castles of stone, surrounded by deep moats and with battlements from which hot pitch and burning brands and a rain of arrows could be directed at attackers. In all, one hundred strongholds were built during the reign of the Conqueror and that of his son, William Rufus.

This was something new for England. The homes of the thanes had been low wooden houses surrounded by moats and with palisades of pointed beams, strong enough to repel robbers but not to serve the ends of aggression. Now these grim Norman structures, with their glowering keeps, loomed up on every horizon and commanded every strategic point, as proof that the English were a subject race.

4

William had to lead two armies as far as Cumberland and even to the Roman Wall before stamping out resistance in the north, but by the end of the year 1070 the task had been accomplished. When the last Saxon had hidden his ax or his brown bill under the thatch of his cottage and given in, the country was subjected to systematic ravaging. The Normans, who had proved masters of the art of theft and murder and rape, outdid themselves here. A French historian says that more than one hundred thousand died of want in York and thereabouts after William was through and that those who survived had to live on the bodies of dead Norman horses, even on human flesh. From the Humber north, not a farmhouse stood except in charred ruins. For nine years thereafter no effort was made to till the land. Wild beasts had sole possession of what had once been thriving towns and villages.

The Strongest Man Rules

All England had given in by this time save for the Isle of Ely, where a brave Englishman named Hereward, sometimes called the Wake, was holding out with a comparatively small band of followers. It may not seem at first thought that the flat fen lands along the eastern coast were as well suited for defense as, say, the rugged mountains of Wales or the highlands of Scotland, where so often successful stands had been made against invasion. But beyond the wolds of the fen country were marshy stretches which developed into a crisscross of open water where horsemen could not ride and which stopped armed men in their tracks, even when equipped with special aids called "leaping poles." The vikings had sometimes been called "creekers" because of their liking for fighting on this kind of terrain. Hereward, a trained soldier, knew how to take full advantage of the sometimes lovely, sometimes ghostly country which surrounded the Isle of Ely.

A word about Hereward. If a fraction of what has been written about this stout fighter were true, he must have been a greater warrior even than any of the three strong men who contested the throne of England. He had been living in France in exile, having been led by youthful high spirits into certain excesses, and had married a Frenchwoman named Torfrida, who is charged with practicing witchcraft by some chronicles of the period. They came back to England after Hastings. It was a custom with the fighters of that day to find names for their weapons as they would for their horses and dogs. Hereward's name for his great sword was Brain-biter; and as he plunged ashore Brain-biter flapped against his thighs with what might have seemed an eagerness to be at the task of cutting through Norman skulls. It did not take Hereward long to see how serious was the plight of the land of his birth, and he proceeded to break the war arrow and send pieces of it around, up and down the land of Ermine Street, as far west as the Welsh Marches, and even down into Kent, where the Norman hold was tight and hard. Men answered the summons with a willingness which made it clear they had been waiting for such a signal. They came trooping in, dispossessed men, sons who had lost fathers, fathers who had lost families, desperate men, all of them, who had lost the right to call themselves free. They built as the core of their operations a wooden fort on Ely, which was a small island rising well above the fens but not high enough to escape the misty exhalations which come up from the rank water in the fall and in which the people of the lowlands believed they could read the future.

Here they stayed for five years, playing hide-and-seek with the Normans all through the fen country, issuing out to attack a castle, disappearing, flashing out again to strike at a land convoy or to harry the estates of the interlopers. Brain-biter was often red with Norman blood when the resourceful leader of the little band holding the Camp of Refuge returned from their forays. He was such a thorn in the flesh of the Mamzer that it became necessary for the latter to make a major effort to end the resistance. William, in fact, was so determined to stamp out the last embers of rebellion that he himself directed the shrewd scheme decided upon. He began to build a causeway across the quaking sands and the interminable bogs, getting closer daily to Ely, where the defenders, their ranks sharply thinned, waited the inevitable assault.

Finally the Normans thought they were near enough to begin storming operations and they shoved forward a wooden tower of the kind used to screen attacking forces and which for some reason is called a sow. Not content with his vastly superior strength, William allowed himself to be persuaded into stationing a very old witch atop the sow who was to check resistance by the use of incantations and the casting of spells. Hereward waited until the tower had been shoved well out over the last bit of water and then set fire to the dry reeds along the banks of the stream. The blaze soon swept over the tower, and hundreds of Norman soldiers were trapped and died in the flames. The gibbering old witch had no chance of escaping from her elevated post on the top of the sow and she abandoned her absurd ritual to heap maledictions on the Normans who had brought her to such an unpleasant end.

After this fiasco William decided to depend on engineering principles without any further effort to benefit by abracadabra, and the land was cleared before the causeway was shoved out over the stagnant waters. Soon it was close enough to the beleaguered isle for an attack in force. The struggle which ensued was a desperate one, but in the end numbers told and the Camp of Refuge was overrun by the Norman mercenaries. The defenders were killed or captured almost to a man. Some records have it that Hereward the Wake was killed; in others it is asserted that he escaped and later made his submission and that he lived peacefully at his home in Bourne until his death.

All resistance was over. The leopards of Normandy floated above every keep in England, over the gates of the towns, on the ships of the royal navy. The conquest was complete.

5

To say that so many hundreds of Saxons were killed in this county or so many thousands in that shire conveys no idea of the tragic conditions which prevailed or of the bitterness of the struggle between the two races. The Normans, contemptuous of the English and impatient of any obstacles to the taking of what they wanted, did not spare the conquered people. If a Norman bishop needed materials for a new chantry, he tore down whole sections of a town to provide them and laughed at the clamor of the unhappy owners. If any part of the country showed itself mutinous, the troops sent in to restore order never made an effort to obtain the facts. They killed or mutilated every man they could catch, innocent or guilty, and they burned every house to the ground.

Of all the terrible things which happened, nothing is more tragic than the fate of the monks of Glastonbury. It might have seemed that Glastonbury, the most historic of all ecclesiastical institutions in England, would have been left alone. Here Joseph of Arimathaea, the rich merchant who befriended Christ and the Disciples, was supposed to have come in his old age, bringing the Holy Grail with him; here he had planted the Glastonbury thorn. Here Dunstan, first of the kingmakers, had lived and ruled and, presumably, it was in one of the cells that he caught the nose of the devil in a pair of red-hot pincers and twisted it until the cloistered arches of the chapel reverberated with the agonized screams of His Satanic Majesty. Sanctity brooded over its long halls; tradition set it apart.

But it was not to be exempt from the general upheaval. The native head of the monastery was removed and a Norman named Toustain was put in his place. Toustain proved himself an aggressive tyrant. It was clear that he wanted to be rid of the English monks and to fill the abbey with men of his own country, for his first step was to reduce the amount of food allowed them (it was meager enough to begin with) so that they would become more amenable to discipline. The poor fellows bore everything in silence until Toustain insisted that Norman music be used. The love they had for the old Gregorian chants led them to refuse. He insisted. They continued, respectfully but firmly, to refuse. One day in full chapter they declared that they would rather die than use the new music.

Toustain, white with rage, rose from his seat and left. When he returned he had a file of armed soldiers with him. "You have made your choice!" he declared, motioning the soldiers to follow out the orders he had given them.

The terrified monks fled to the church and took possession of the choir, locking the gates after them. The troops were on their heels, shouting and laughing, their armed feet ringing loudly on the flagged floor. Finding it impossible to get through the gates, some of them climbed the pillars, wriggling their way up even to the clerestory. From this point of vantage they began to shoot arrows into the choir, roaring boisterously over the results of their marksmanship. The monks skurried to the altar, where they huddled together in a frightened group. If they believed they would be safe there, they had no true conception of the temper of their tormentors. The bowmen might have been practicing at the targets for all the concern they showed. Their arrows pierced the crucifix above the altar and destroyed the monstrance and played havoc with the altar cloths. Some found human marks, and blood began to run in red streams down the steps into the nave.

In the meantime the rest of the soldiers had succeeded in breaking the gates. They poured into the choir with drawn swords, shouting as gleefully as spectators at a bear-baiting. The monks, realizing that their lives were at stake, ripped the backs off the choir seats and fought stoutly with them. One of them betrayed his Danish blood by chanting *Yuch-hey-saa-saa,* the war song of the vikings, as he swung an oak plank as effectively as though it were a battle-ax. But the poor fellows could offer little real resistance. Eighteen of them were butchered before the attacking party desisted.

The English people did not accept such treatment without any effort at retaliation. It became unsafe for Normans to go out alone; they were likely to be found with their throats cut if they did. There were so many killings of this kind that William finally passed a law which read in part, "When a Frenchman is killed, the men of the hundred shall seize and bring up the murderer within eight days; otherwise they shall pay, at their common cost, a fine of forty-seven marks."

It is not on record that the people of any section produced an assassin as stipulated in this law. At the same time, however, they found the fines too great a burden to bear. They were so poor to begin with and so ground down by excessive taxes that a single fine was enough to reduce a whole community to penury. In cases where bodies were discovered, therefore, it became the custom to remove all marks of identification and to mutilate the body so that the nationality of the victim could not be determined.

This worked for a short time only. William was too shrewd to be balked and he promptly passed another law. It was now assumed that every victim of murder was French and that the community fine must be collected unless the people could prove the dead man to be of native birth. It was stipulated that four relatives should be produced to swear to the identity of the victim.

It was never possible to outwit William the Conqueror. His keen mind was equal to any situation which might arise, as surely as his heart was hard enough to stamp out any form of opposition without mercy.

It should be added that this ingenious and cruel law continued in force for centuries. At murder inquests the first step was to prove the victim English. In legal parlance this was called *Presentment of Englishry.*

6

William had shown conspicuous ability all the years of his life, and near the close he was to demonstrate that what he possessed in reality was genius. At a midwinter assembly of the Witanagemot held at Gloucester twelve years after the Battle of Hastings, the King made a long speech. He was concerned, he said, about the condition of the country, the confusion brought about by so many wars, the lack of knowledge which existed of population and wealth. "By the splendor of God!" exclaimed William at the conclusion of his address, using his favorite oath. "We must know all about this land and what it contains. Today we know nothing."

He stumbled for words as he began later to explain what was in his mind. The years had taken their toll and the great man who had never tasted defeat was as round as a barrel and slow in all his movements. But fat and old though he might be, he dominated the assembly so completely that no one raised an objection to the idea he was setting forth, although few of them had any conception of what it meant. This was not surprising, for certainly not more than a dozen of them could read or write. The mind of William had leaped centuries ahead to arrive at a method of restoring order in the land.

The King, needless to state, had his way. The nation was divided into nine districts, and a special commission was appointed for each, consisting of a bishop and a man of noble birth to govern the proceedings and a staff of clerks and scriveners to do the actual work. Each commission moved about the territory assigned to it, and all landowners and tenants were summoned to attend their meetings. Every man was questioned minutely, and the information he gave was later checked to insure honesty and accuracy. How much land did he hold? Who held it before he became the owner? How many people resided on it, and what was their condition? How many horses did he have, how many cows, sheep, goats? It was a slow and tedious proceeding. The old records had fallen into total confusion. Each county seemed to possess its own methods of land reckoning. The commissions dealt with trithings here, with wapentakes there. Elsewhere it would be ridings, hundreds, lathes, rapes, or leets Some estates had never been surveyed; many had been fought over and burned and the matter of valuation was almost in the realm of guesswork. It was a complicated undertaking and took several years in the completion.

The result was Domesday Book, the document from which more than from any chronicle or history the truth about England at the start of Norman rule has been gleaned. It substituted facts and figures for the mass of vague information which had existed before. It marked the beginning of accuracy in deeds and registration, the commencement of statistical documentation which is a basis of historical truth. If William had done nothing else, his reputation as an able ruler and a man of vision could have rested on this one achievement.

William's keen mind had gone as straight as an arrow to the proper method of establishing property order, but the motive which impelled him to act had more than a hint of selfishness. He had been realizing that inasmuch as his followers had been rewarded with practically all the land in England they must now bear the burden of government and defense out of the wealth thus acquired. But how could the necessary taxes be collected unless he knew what each man possessed and the size of his income? Domesday Book was the answer. As soon as it was completed, he levied an impost of six shillings on each hide of land (a vague measurement which took into account wasteland and water and was meant to represent what a free family needed for subsistence) and, as the Normans held most of the land, it meant that the newcomers paid the bulk of the tax. The royal revenues were increased as a result of Domesday to the extent of four hundred thousand pounds a year! It was a truly stupendous sum for those days. The barons groaned and gritted their teeth and expostulated bitterly, but William, studying the tax papers with a keen eye, paid no attention. The dispossessed Saxons found it a joke to their liking.

7

William died in Normandy, a violent death as was entirely fitting. It was in the summer of 1087 and he had gone to the duchy to set things in order. While there he quarreled with Philip of France over the ownership of the town of Mantes on the Seine. The man who had conquered England was himself in the grip of a conqueror to whom all men, kings and commoners alike, must yield in the end. He had grown so corpulent that people laughed behind his back and whispered jokes at the size of his belly. While the dispute was being waged, with great bitterness on each side, William was confined to his bed in Rouen, and the French monarch was injudicious enough to make a joke at his expense.

"King William has as long a lying-in as a woman behind her curtains," declared Philip in the full hearing of his court.

When word of it reached William, he rose from his couch, his face contorted with rage. "By the resurrection and the splendor of God!" he declared. "I will go to mass in Philip's land and bring a rich offering for my churching. I will offer a thousand candles for my fee—flaming brands, each of them—and steel shall glitter over the fire they make!"

His vengeance was not vented on the French King, for that monarch was safely beyond his reach. Whenever the anger of the great Norman was aroused, however, someone had to pay, and more often than not the brunt of his violent rages was borne by persons entirely innocent. When the garrison of a French town he was besieging hung hides over the walls as a reminder of his humble origin, he had the eyes of prisoners torn out and thrown over the fortifications. He had a servant blinded who carried money from Queen Matilda to their rebellious eldest son Robert, but he did not raise his hand against the wife who alone had disobeyed him.

And now it was the whole town of Mantes which was to pay for the French King's jest. William waited until the time of harvest, when the crops were being gathered and the people of the district were happy over the plenteous yield. Then he struck. His cavalry rode over the fields of grain, setting fire to the crops. His foot soldiers tore up the vines. The orchards were destroyed and even the shade trees were cut down. This accomplished, and his rage against Philip still burning deeply in his passionate soul, William set fire to the town itself. So thorough was the work of demolition carried out that it might have been supposed he was back in poor England and administering a sample of Norman justice to his unhappy subjects.

It was surely an instance of divine justice that the Conqueror, while riding through the conflagration, should sustain a fall when his horse stepped on a burning plank. He was carried out of the blazing ruins and back to a monastery under the walls of Rouen. Here he lingered for six weeks, suffering greatly and becoming weaker with each day. When it was certain he was going to die, the violent man called in two of his sons, William and Henry, and made a verbal will. He left Normandy to Robert, in spite of the eldest son's mutinous record. Then he looked at William, his favorite, who also was strong and cruel and who was called the Red because of his coloring.

"As for the kingdom of England," he said, struggling for breath, "I bequeath it to no one, for it was not bequeathed to me. I acquired it by force and at the cost of blood. I leave it in the hands of God— only wishing that my son William, who has been submissive to me in all things, may obtain it if he please God and prosper."

Thus in his last moments he acknowledged the truth, that he had no right to the throne of England, that it had been a conquest by force of arms, and that all his acts of oppression had been doubly wrong on that account. What could his thoughts have been as he lay there in pain, knowing that soon he must face his Maker and answer for all his violence on earth? Did he give thought to the countless thousands of people who had died because of his passionate will and ambition? Did the weeping of a nation in chains reach his dying ears? Did he see a huddle of frightened monks about Glastonbury altar and Norman archers climbing the pillars to shoot them down? What were his thoughts of Harold, who would have made England a just and able king, lying dead on the field of Hastings with an arrow in his eye?

CHAPTER III

A Dangerous King, a Saint, and a Rogue

HERE is only one good thing to be said about the reign of William II, called Rufus or the Red. It was brief.

It was thirteen years of fighting with the Scots and the French, of crushing rebellions, of incarcerating political prisoners in deep dungeons (Robert de Mowbray, Earl of Northumberland, was kept for thirty years in a cell so far under the ground that the church counted him dead and granted his young wife a divorce), of extending the royal forests, of drawing more and more power and wealth into the royal maw.

William Rufus was cruel, false, avaricious, and with no sense of the responsibilities of a ruler. He had a good share of his father's fighting quality but he lacked perseverance in the face of obstacles. When Peter the Hermit carried the fiery cross over Europe and stirred men to join in the First Crusade, the new English King saw in the religious zeal thus aroused nothing but a chance of profit for himself. He gave his brother Robert, who was a clod but the possessor of soldierly qualities, the sum of ten thousand marks to equip a force and join in the march to the Holy City, accepting the duchy of Normandy as security; a deal which cost poor Robert dear before he was through, and the people of England also, as a special tax was levied to raise the money.

He quickly undid the generous things his father had done. The political prisoners who had been released when the Conqueror was dying and trying to establish a credit entry in the books of the

A Dangerous King, a Saint, and a Rogue

Recording Angel were promptly seized and sent back to their dungeons. The Conqueror had abolished the death penalty (but not the habit of blinding and mutilating wrongdoers), and his fiery-faced son restored it and proceeded to hang men for killing a rabbit or for other small offenses. The father had believed in keeping his word, but the son considered a promise worth observing if it had been pledged on some concern of chivalry (that iron code which was just beginning to take hold of bloodthirsty imaginations) but under no other circumstances. On his hurried arrival in England to claim the throne he had been supported by the native people against the barons and knights who thought the first-born Robert should have the preference, but when he had prevailed with their aid, he broke all the fair pledges he had made them. He quickly proceeded to show them, in fact, what oppression could mean. "No man can keep all his promises," declared this knightly King.

The one great quality in which all men of that rough age shared was religious faith. All men, seemingly, but William the Red. "I have suffered too much at God's hands," he declared openly, "to be a good man." He remained a bachelor king, and it is not on record that he begat any illegitimate children. Historians whisper primly of *Eastern vices!* The word bestial can most fittingly be employed to describe his court, a nest of favorites and catamites.

He was a big man and a striking figure when he rode out to show himself to the people with nothing on his flowing blond curls (his nickname was derived solely from his high complexion) but a narrow circlet of gold. He liked gay plumage and was generally seen in a rich green tunic with broad and elaborately embroidered bands. Over this he wore a cloak of light blue held at the shoulder with a jeweled clasp, its folds artfully arranged to conceal the fact that he had inherited his father's tendency to a protuberance of stomach. His handsome legs were cross-gartered with cloth of gold, and his shoes were of rich green leather with toes which curled up. A squire rode behind him with his sword, a continental custom. William was always looking for new things like that, and it tickled his fancy to set a fashion. A final word of description: his high complexion was partly due to the fact that he drank with his favorites continuously, deeply, quarrelsomely, soddenly.

Perhaps no other king has ever shared William II's conception of absolute rule. Countless tyrants have believed themselves the embodiment of the law and the sole arbiter of the lives and destinies of their subjects. William went beyond that. He believed that all England belonged to him, the land, the woods, the waters, the beasts of the field, the people, the revenues. He did not believe in private property. A man might be the holder of land, but only as a favor from him, William Rex. He even dipped his greedy hands into church funds.

One incident tells as much of the character of the Red King as a complete record of his reign. He accepted a fee of sixty silver marks from a wealthy Jew to persuade the latter's son that he should not become a convert to Christianity; and this in the days of the First Crusade! His pleading had no effect. The young man, who had adopted the name of Stephen, remained firm in his purpose, and the interview ended with a wild outburst of profanity, the undignified King shouting at him, "Son of the dunghill!"

2

The thirteen years of the Red King's rule produced two figures worth telling about, the one a saint, the other a clever and sly villain.

The saint came into prominence through a happy chance. William had acquired the habit of not filling the ecclesiastical posts which fell vacant and of coolly scooping in the revenue to fatten his own purse. At this time there were two claimants to the Holy See, each proclaiming the other anti-Christ, and so the greedy king had a ready-made excuse. If he allowed English gold to go to one of the contenders, how could he be sure he had sent it to the right one, the real Vicar of God?

After the death of Lanfranc, the Norman who had been made Archbishop of Canterbury by the Conqueror, William Rufus allowed the see to remain vacant for four years and, of course, appropriated its huge revenues to himself. An Italian named Anselm, who had given up a good station in life and the prospects of substantial inheritance to become a monk at the famed Norman abbey of Bec and had risen to be abbot, paid a visit to England. He was a gentle, pious, learned man and he made a deep impression wherever he went. The feeling became general that here was a God-sent candidate for the vacant see. William heard what was being said and declared flatly, "Other archbishop than me, there shall be none!"

A Dangerous King, a Saint, and a Rogue

The pressure continued, nevertheless, and the kingly temper flared. "No man's prayer," he shouted, "will do anything to shake my will!"

But a way was found to shake his will. The Red King became ill, so ill that he feared he was going to die. As he tossed feverishly on his couch the first hint of remorse entered his mind. What could he do to show repentance before the dread summons came? Perhaps if he appointed an archbishop the Lord would look more leniently on him. Anselm was still in the country, fortunately, and a hasty call was sent for him to attend the royal sickbed.

When Anselm heard he was to be given the pastoral staff of Canterbury he had deep misgivings. He was sure he lacked the physical stamina and perhaps the resolution to carry such a responsibility. "The plow of England should be drawn by a team of equal strength," he said piteously to the churchmen who had come to escort him into the royal presence. "Would you yoke a feeble old sheep with a wild young bull?"

The wild young bull was so tamed by his illness, however, that he begged Anselm to accept. "My salvation is in your hands," he said weakly.

The abbot's pleas to be spared were not heeded and so, most reluctantly and with a conviction that trouble would come of it, Anselm agreed. The churchmen who were present, overjoyed at having the matter settled, hurried the new archbishop out of the room and to the nearest shrine, where the *Te Deum* was chanted.

Trouble did come of it, and William was the chief sufferer. The gentle old man he had compelled to accept this onerous post became as strong and as bold as a lion in opposing the King's exactions. He refused to allow the head of the state to touch church funds and he lectured him on the sad condition into which the land had fallen since he took the throne. They quarreled sharply and bitterly over which of the two popes should give the *pallium* to Anselm. This was a scarf made from the wool of the lambs the Pope blessed on St. Agnes's Day and always sent to a new archbishop. Anselm wanted it from the hands of Urban II, who had been elected by the cardinals in the traditional manner. William stood out for Guibert, perhaps because the latter had been selected by the German emperor, the Red King being a believer in royal power in all things. When the archbishop refused to give in, the ruddy-faced occupant of the throne fell into the most violent tantrum of his whole bad-tempered life. "Tell him," he cried, "that as I hated him yesterday I hate him more today, and will hate him more and more with every day we both shall live!"

The kingly hatred did not swerve Anselm as much as an inch from the path of duty. He had Urban send a papal legate with the *pallium* in spite of the blustering of William. The latter tried to appropriate the scarf for himself and, when the Pope's representative refused, he endeavored to persuade the legate that he should depose Anselm. The legate, apprehensive of the royal temper, did not dare proceed with the customary ceremony. Instead he laid the *pallium* on the altar at Canterbury and left it to Anselm to drape it about his own neck.

The stage was reached finally where the King could no longer brook the presence of the archbishop in England. Anselm was banished. He left England with his pilgrim's staff and, when he was searched for gold on going aboard ship, it was found that he had no money. He went to Rome and begged Urban to allow him to resign. The Pope refused, and so Canterbury was again without an occupant. It remained vacant until William's death, after which Anselm, tired and feeble but as stoutly resolved in his duty as ever, returned to England and occupied the post until his death.

The record of this splendid old man does not contain any special achievements. His greatness lay in the attitude he adopted, in his unbending resistance to the encroachments of royal power. He became before his death, and increasingly so as time rolled on, the symbol of hope to the downtrodden people. Before Anselm, there had been no one to curb the bitter Norman tyranny. The stand of the gentle old priest who dared to say NO was as welcome to the English as the sight of the dove to the despairing eyes at the rail of the Ark. Small wonder that even to this day the memory of a kind Italian monk is kept green and that he is generally acclaimed the leader of the long muster roll of those who have held the pastoral staff.

The villain was also a priest, a Norman named Ralph or Randulph, who was made Bishop of Durham and who soon won for himself the nickname of Flambard (the Torch) or, as it was sometimes spelled, Passemflambard. There is considerable mystery as to the antecedents of Ralph Flambard. He is variously said to have been a footman in the service of the Norman ducal family, the son of a poor priest of the Bessin and a woman who was given to witchcraft and had lost an eye through a mischievous poke of the satanic forefinger, and an adventurer who had arrived in England in the early days when Edward the Confessor was inviting Normans to come over and help themselves. There is doubt also as to how he attracted the attention of William Rufus, but on this point it may safely be assumed that the King, his head crammed with greed and the determination to make himself master of everything, was looking for an instrument and found the perfect one in the suave, handsome, genial, and diabolically clever Ralph. A prominent historian has written of this early exponent of machiavellian principles as "a subtle and malignant brain" and also as "the lawgiver of feudalism." These phrases are quoted because they describe William's minister perfectly.

Ralph Flambard was clever enough to find ways in which William could disregard the laws and flout tradition without seeming to do so. So ingenious was he, in fact, that it was made to appear as though the covetous King was always within the law. What a picture they conjure up, William and his familiar spirit, the puffy, ruddy King, the suave Ralph whispering in the royal ear of the devices he had found in moldy statutes!

Consider now some of the things which Ralph proposed and which William acted upon with invariable success. First, it was declared that the King *was the heir of every man.* This meant that the ownership of land was a privilege granted by the King in return for military service and that, on the death of the holder, the land reverted to the Crown to be reassigned on the same understanding. In other words, all land was *loanland* (a term coined perhaps by the ingenious Flambard) and could not be willed to the members of a man's family. Inheritance on this basis could be ratified only by the King; with, no doubt, the payment of a substantial share into the royal treasury.

In the light of present-day tendencies it will be seen that the unholy team had hit upon a principle which could be applied in a socialistic state. All it did in that distant day, however, was to increase the power of the throne and fatten the royal treasury. It was, in fact, one of the most effective aids to tyranny ever devised.

Less sweeping in its implications but actually more productive was Flambard's theory of wardship. When the heir to an estate was a minor, the control of the property was vested in the King and all revenue came to him. When a daughter was left to succeed, the King had the right of selling her hand to the highest bidder or, at any rate, of bestowing it on any suitor he might prefer.

Thus for the first time was introduced the principle which for many centuries thereafter resulted in the gutting of estates, the robbery of widows and orphans by officers of the ruler sworn to protect their interests, the unhappiness of children left to the neglect of crown officials, the heartbreaks of heiresses sold into matrimonial slavery.

When Rufus gave royal authority to the theory that the King was the heir of every man, he had no thought of exempting the clergy. The heads of the Church were among the largest landowners and so were ripe for plucking. The new scheme was made to apply even more damagingly to the bishop and the abbot than to the baron and the alderman. It was postulated that when a bishop died, or any lesser church appointee, it was the same as when a landholder left heirs below the legal age. As there was no successor ready to step into the shoes of the deceased churchman, all properties and revenues of the see or abbey reverted to the Crown until such time as the King was ready to sanction the appointment of a successor. Flambard applied this startling rule, which set all Christendom by the ears, with such efficiency and dispatch that as soon as a lord of the Church passed away a royal clerk was sent in to make an inventory of all the worldly possessions of the dead man. The highwayman with mask and pistol was no more dishonest than the minister who conceived this method of wholesale robbery or the King who backed him in the execution thereof. When William died in his turn there were three bishoprics without incumbents (Canterbury, Winchester, and Salisbury) and eleven abbeys; and the revenues of all of them were pouring, flowing, jingling, into the royal pockets!

But Ralph the Torch did not confine himself to laying down the principles of systematic looting. He was full of ingenious tricks for special occasions. Whenever he sat by the King and whispered into the reddish porcine ear, it could be taken for granted that he had thought of something choice to please his master and plague everyone else. One instance of his ingenuity will suffice. During the second war that William waged against the King of France and his brother Robert of Normandy, he sent back word that he needed reinforcements. An army of twenty thousand was recruited, each earl and baron and lord of manor sending a specified number of fighting men. This large army had assembled back of Hastings and was waiting to sail for France. They were all willing enough to go, for the whisper had spread that there would be plenty of booty and that even the lowliest foot soldier or archer would come back with gold and rich tapestries and silver vessels and French feather beds on his back. Each man had in his pocket while he waited ten shillings which, on orders direct from the King, had been given to him by his liege lord or by the shire from which he hailed to pay for his maintenance abroad.

The ships were lying in the roadstead and ready to take the troops aboard when the smiling Flambard arrived with what looked like an army of clerks. They went down the ranks and took from every reluctant recruit the ten shillings. Then the King's order was given to disband and go home! The King, by this almost unbelievable ruse, took ten thousand pounds out of the pockets of his subjects!

Master Ralph the Torch was full of tricks like this.

3

All this time Gundulph the Weeper had continued his work on the White Tower. He had built it ninety feet high, and it frowned over London like the threat of tyranny, as indeed it was. The walls, which were fifteen feet thick, were filled with stairways and corridors and even small bedchambers. The Weeper had been so careful to make it secure that the Tower had one door only, and that a narrow one. The vaults beneath, which were vast and dark and cavernous, had one means of communication with the ground floor, a narrow and winding stairway. Around the grim structure a high wall had been erected. The Tower, in fact, was hard to get into and even harder for anyone who wanted to get out.

And now it was completed and ready for its first unwilling occupant.

When his master died (to cast ahead of our story for a moment) Ralph Flambard was promptly laid by the heels by Henry, the new King. All the people who had suffered from his policy of unlaw and unright, which meant every landed man in the kingdom, clamored for his punishment. Henry did not need any urging in this matter. He had a bone to pick with Master Ralph himself, the wily churchman having by some devious means robbed the prince of land willed him by his mother. So the once powerful bishop was marched to the Tower and lodged in rooms on the third story, which was known as the Banqueting Floor.

He was allowed to live in comfort and even state, with a suite of large, light rooms, his own servants and chaplains, a fine fireplace, two shillings a day for his food from the royal funds (and the right to send out for extras), and even the Constable of the Tower, one William de Mandeville, to act as his special keeper. But Ralph Flambard had been the most powerful man in England after the King and was still one of the wealthiest, and he did not like the confinement of his prison. He pulled every conceivable string to secure his freedom, even appealing to Anselm, who had just returned to resume his duties as archbishop, pointing out that he, Flambard, was a priest and above secular law. When this appeal reached him, the noble old man ceased to be a saint and for one moment was completely human. "Out on this caitiff!" he cried. "I know him not, neither as brother nor as priest!"

So the prisoner turned to a surer means of escape, his own abundant wits. He studied his guards and found them without exception a dull lot, fond of good wine and a well-filled trencher and a jolly song. He began to have them at his table regularly, using as excuse his desire for company. One winter night (it was in February 1101, and very cold) the wine served at the bishop's table was particularly ample and potent. It is just possible that it contained a drug as well, for soon the untended candles revealed all the guards sprawling across the table or sleeping on the floor. One of the servants then took a long rope which had been smuggled in (it had to be long, for the windows of the Banqueting Floor were sixty-five feet above the ground) and tied one end to an iron bar in the bishop's window. The bishop had become fat and short of breath and he descended the rope painfully and with as much wheezing and puffing as came from the slumbering guards in the rooms above.

The rope, it developed, was not long enough. When Ralph Flambard reached the end of it, he saw yawning black space beneath and no more support for his feet than if he were a condemned prisoner dangling at the end of a rope. It took him some time to get his courage up for the drop, but finally he said a prayer and let himself go. He landed heavily, one leg doubled up under him.

He was picked up by his confederates and carried to a boat which took him across the Channel to France.

The Tower, in spite of all the Weeper's care and ingenuity, had failed to hold its first prisoner. Many centuries were to pass, however, before another got away.

Ralph's victims had been the landholders, the men of wealth, and so the common people had not disliked him. It is probable, in fact, that they were glad when he made his escape. All the jackals who followed him down the centuries, to serve as extortioners for their kings, were men of a sinister taint. They were miserly in type, with the long claw, the heavy-lidded eye, the grim mien. Ralph Flambard was a genial rogue, full-bellied and fond of good living and a coarse joke. But make no mistake about him. Here was the sliest, the most capable, and the most dangerous rogue in English history. He was so clever and his methods were so deeply rooted in legal chicanery that it was hard to tear them out. The evil he brought into the world did not end that cold night when he landed on his fat rump in the Tower ditch. It lived after him, and it took six centuries to exorcise the last trace of it.

4

The Norman kings were fiercely addicted to the chase, and one of the first acts of William the Conqueror had been to seize all of the forest land in Hampshire known as the Jettenwald, or Giant's Wood, and turn it into a royal preserve. Some of the early chronicles say that he drove the people out of fifty-two villages and tore down twenty-two churches to obtain what he wanted in the way of private hunting grounds, but this obviously is an exaggeration. He did, however, appropriate nearly one hundred thousand acres between the Solent and the Avon and he fixed the most rigid restrictions. It became known as the New Forest.

The people resented the preserve laws so bitterly that a superstition grew in their minds about the New Forest. They believed it would prove unlucky for the Norman breed. The first evidence in support of this belief was the death there of William's young son Richard, who was gored by a stag.

On the second day of August in the year 1100 William Rufus and a party from the court were at Brockenhurst in the New Forest. Henry, his brother, was one of the party, the rest being William's special cronies and, no doubt, a rude and dissolute lot. The King's sleep had been broken the night before by dreams of death, his own death, and in the morning word reached him from an Abbot Serlo in Normandy that one of his monks had been troubled by similar dreams and had reported them so that the King might have due warning. At first the Red King had doubts about going on with his plans for the day. It was a warm day, however, and perfect for hunting. Whenever William was in the woods he expanded with pride. The forests were his and every living thing therein. He was so pre-emptive of the privileges of the chase that it could easily be believed he said to himself, Every tree in England is mine, every stream and glade, every deer and bear and fox and rabbit is mine, mine, mine!

He spent the morning over state papers, which had to be read to him because he had never gone to the trouble of learning his letters. After a heavy dinner in the middle of the day he made up his mind. "Do they take me for an Englishman," he muttered, "that I pay heed to their dreams and go out of my way when an old woman sneezes?"

He called for six of the special arrows he always used. Three he gave to his usual hunting companion, Walter Tyrrell, lord of Poix. "Take them, Wat," he said. "A good marksman should have good arrows."

The party divided up. Prince Henry proceeded in one direction. The others made up groups of threes and fours. The King and Walter Tyrrell went off alone, plunging deep into the woods which, to anyone who believed in the curse, might have seemed to beckon. William Rufus was never seen alive again.

His body was found later in the afternoon in a glade near Stoney Cross Knoll, stretched out at full length, an arrow in his heart. The ruddy tone had left his cheeks, his eyes were fixed. He had been dead for some hours.

Walter Tyrrell was not to be found. Whether or not he was responsible in any way for the violent death of the violent King, he knew that he would be blamed. To be blamed for the death of a

A Dangerous King, a Saint, and a Rogue

king might mean being kept for life in one of those deep dungeons, or the loss of one's eyes through the application of iron bars heated white, or the tightening of a hempen rope around the neck. The lord of Poix wanted none of this. It was learned later that he had turned and ridden at breakneck speed for the coast. He reached France and went off crusading; and, wise man that he was, never came back to England.

The manner of the Red King's death remained a complete mystery. Someone with a grievance may have shot the fatal arrow from behind a tree as William and his solitary companion rode by. It may have been an accident, and this seems the likeliest explanation. But the people of England had no doubts about it whatever. The curse was still working, and it had brought another of the royal line to his death.

The men who discovered the body seemed as anxious to get away as Wat Tyrrell had been. They scattered in all directions, and the remains of the King lay untended until nightfall, when a charcoal burner named Purkis came along. In a matter-of-fact way he dumped the body in his cart and carried it to Winchester. Here it was taken to the minster of St. Swithin and it was buried in a black stone coffin under the central tower. No bells were rung, no masses said. The man who had thought he owned all England and all Englishmen was deposited in consecrated ground, but it was a hurried and apprehensive laying away, as though they feared that evil still lingered about the inanimate clay.

Several years after the burial the tower collapsed and a mass of broken masonry and rubble covered the bones of the dead King. This, needless to state, was accepted almost universally as a Sign.

5

Prince Henry had been hunting in a different part of the forest. The story is told that he snapped the string of his bow and stopped at the hut of a forester in hopes of getting it repaired. The hut, however, was occupied by an old woman who went into a trance as soon as she realized who her visitor was and delivered him a message which began as follows:

> *Hasty news to thee I bring,*
> *Henry, thou art now a king.*

Henry seems to have believed the message. At any rate, he made off at once, going direct to Winchester where the royal treasure was kept. Here he found William de Breteuil, the royal treasurer, who refused to hand over the keys.

Breteuil scowled at the anxious Henry. "Would you rob your brother Robert who is fighting for the cross?" he demanded.

Henry drew his sword. The treasurer, who seems to have been a stout fellow, drew his. They stormed at one another, and soon there was a crowd about them. Henry, it was clear, was going to have plenty of support in his pretensions to the throne. He had been born in England after the Conquest, and the people, who were ready to grasp blindly for any kind of consolation, had begun to think of him as one of themselves. A great deal of sympathy was felt for him also as a result of his ill luck. He had been willed five thousand pounds and no land by his father, and the lands he had purchased in Normandy had been taken away from him by his two older brothers. He was now a handsome man of thirty-two, unmarried, a scholar, and to the people he seemed infinitely more desirable as King than the distant Robert, who had already displayed his lack of capacity to rule in his duchy of Normandy.

The available members of the nobility gathered in the council chamber of the royal castle to debate what was to be done. Most of them favored Robert, knowing that he would make a weak ruler, and at first a few only were ready to speak up for the landless prince. While they debated, however, a crowd was collecting in the streets who threatened to tear the castle down stone by stone if they were given any other King but Henry. Prudent counsel finally prevailed and the nobles voted for the younger brother. The church bells rang and the criers went through the streets shouting, "Long live King Henry!"

With the keys to the treasury safely in his pocket, the new incumbent of the throne rode to London and on Sunday, August 5, he was crowned in Westminster Abbey by Maurice, Bishop of London. He swore solemnly "to annul the unrighteous acts which took place in my brother's reign."

The death of William II left much to be annulled.

CHAPTER IV

Good Queen Mold and the Charter

OOD NEWS travels fast, even in a land where most of the roads are no better than cow trails. The word which swept over England immediately after the accession to the throne of the youngest son of William the Conqueror was so good that it set the whole countryside ablaze with joyful expectations. Henry wanted to take a Saxon princess as his bride.

It was quite true. Henry had openly stated his desire to wed Edytha, daughter of the late King Malcolm of Scotland and Queen Margaret, who had been a sister of Edgar the Atheling and was one of the few descendants left of King Alfred. The English people knew all about the lovely little princess. They had talked about her wherever they met, at entrances to church, on village greens, in clay-floored taverns, most particularly in the evenings when the doors and windows of the wattled huts were barred against the devil, who roamed the earth in the hours of darkness. Her hair was like gold and she was as sweet as sugar roset and as good as her mother, who had been like a saint. No wonder the young King had fallen in love with her! No wonder he had waited all these years until he was in a position to claim her!

But Henry had not remained unwed until his thirty-second year out of a deep passion for the daughter of the Scottish King. It is not even certain that he had seen her. He knew of her beauty and her fine qualities (three men of high degree, including Warren, Henry's cousin, had sought her hand) and he was wise enough to perceive the advantages of marriage with a princess of the old royal line. Unfortunately the highly romantic picture of a landless prince languishing for love of a princess and winning her in the end was much too good to be true.

When he ascended the throne Henry had already acknowledged twenty illegitimate children!

Before proceeding with the story of the King's courtship, it will be necessary to tell something about the Princess Edytha and her family. Two years after the Battle of Hastings, Edgar the Atheling left England, taking his sisters Margaret and Christina with him. Their objective was Hungary, where they had relatives, but a storm came up and drove their ship so far out of its course that they landed finally on the Firth of Forth. Malcolm Canmore (Bighead) had just succeeded in recovering his kingdom from the usurper Macbeth and he came down to the shore to welcome the fugitives. One glance at the Princess Margaret was enough. Her sweet and lovely face so enthralled him that he proposed for her hand at once. He seems to have been a fine fellow, this young King Malcolm. His nickname belied him, for he could neither read nor write, but he was loyal and honest and a good soldier. The match was arranged (what exile could refuse the hand of a king?), and Malcolm remained devoted to his Queen for the rest of his life.

During the reign of William Rufus, Malcolm Canmore was killed in an invasion of the north of England. Queen Margaret died soon after, and the throne was seized by Donald Bane, an illegitimate brother of Malcolm. Fearing for the safety of the orphaned family, Edgar the Atheling hurried north and took all of the royal brood back with him, five young princes and two daughters, the older of the pair being Edytha. He placed the girls in the nunnery of Rumsey, where the Princess Christina had been made abbess, and here they were brought up. Rumsey belonged to the Black Benedictines, and the royal abbess was determined that both girls should join the order. As a result Edytha wore the regulation head covering of coarse black cloth when she received visitors.

To say that all England hung on the news of Henry's preference would be no exaggeration. It meant (or so the downtrodden people believed) the difference between remaining a conquered race and attaining some degree of equality with the Normans. It meant, at least, that the blood of great King Alfred would again flow in the veins of the rulers of the land! There was dismay, therefore, when it became known that the Norman nobility were against the match, that they were determined to stop it and had started to laugh scornfully at the King's expense, calling the couple Gaffer Godric and Goody Godiva. The dismay changed to despair when it developed that a serious obstacle had been encountered. The Abbess Christina had lodged a protest to the effect that "her niece was a veiled nun and that it would be an act of sacrilege to remove her from the convent."

Henry realized that the objection raised by the abbess would have to be passed on by the Church. Archbishop Anselm, who had gone into exile as a result of his quarrel with William Rufus, was still living in Lyons. The new King sent an urgent summons, asking the old man to come back at once and settle the question. Anselm assented, but he was so old that he traveled very slowly and it took a long time for him to reach England again. His first step on arriving was to convoke the Council of the Church to Lambeth to hear the evidence. Edytha herself was summoned to appear.

London streets were black with people the day the princess rode in from Wilton. They were almost a different race, the Londoners, with their guilds, their laws, their special rights, their portgraves and aldermen. They were shrewd, commercial, a little arrogant of their privileges, a little selfish in matters of gain. Many of them were Norman and all were taking on some of the outward semblance of Normanism. The tailor Baldwin, who came over with the invading army and who set up his booth on the very edge of the bloodstained turf of Senlac, had moved to London as soon as William had been crowned King. Gilbert the Weaver, Mauger the Smith, Benet the Steward had all done the same. Other Norman tailors had come to London since, and now they had their own little settlement in the busy city on the Thames. Some of the citizens had fallen into the habit of going there for their clothes. They had been showing a weakness for the more luxurious type of costume which had come in with the vain Red King, the long sleeves, the cuffs embroidered inside and out, the ankle garters of fine leather. A few even were combing and curling their beards, and their wives were wearing gowns of costly materials, richly diapered and embroidered. London was more Norman than any other part of England, but in matters of racial importance or racial conflict the people left no doubt as to where they stood.

On this day they waited for the arrival of the princess in anxious groups all the way from the western entrances to London Bridge. Their faces reflected a mood of the deepest gloom. Was this one great chance for rehabilitation to be taken away from them?

Despite their misgivings they tossed their pointed caps high into the air when a party of horsemen appeared with the princess riding in their midst, and they cheered madly when it was seen that she had not followed the Norman custom of keeping her hair wrapped and coiffed in heavy veilings but was wearing no headdress of any kind, so that her long golden locks fell down over her shoulders in the good old English manner. Her eyes were a bright blue and she was, in fact, so beautiful that many of them fell to their knees as she rode by and prayed that nothing might stand in the way of the marriage. Even the name of Goody Godiva seemed lovely when applied to her, and those who remained on their feet used it with affectionate fervor. Lovely Goody Godiva, when had her equal been seen! No other queen would they have but this slender Saxon girl who smiled to them as she rode by and raised her gloved hand in greeting!

All the princes of the Church had gathered in the dingy episcopal palace at Lambeth. It was fortunate that Anselm was there, for it was certain that the kind old archbishop would see the case was fairly tried. It was fortunate also that a Saxon priest named Edmer sat at the old man's elbow and took copious notes of the proceedings, scribbling feverishly on a pad of parchment which he held on his knee. Years later, when he had been given a high post and could spare himself the time, Edmer set down the events of this turbulent period in a series of useful chronicles. He alone gives a full report of the hearing in his *Historia Novorum.*

Edmer does not describe the scene, but it is not difficult to summon from the imagination a picture of the long room: Anselm seated at the end, his back bent with the weight of years but his eye as resolutely clear as ever; the bishops in a half circle about him, wearing their miters and their gleaming pectoral crosses; Edytha seated alone in front of them, hands clasped nervously in her lap; the officials of the court bustling about and passing documents one to another. It is certain that the girl, straight from the calm life of a nunnery, stirred uneasily as she faced this circle of stern faces.

The Council of the Church was exclusively Norman, and it can be taken for granted that each bishop and abbot there felt as disapproving as the barons of this match on which Henry had set his heart. The record makes it clear, however, that they found their doubts dwindling as they listened to her answers.

Anselm conducted the questioning himself.

Had she embraced a religious life by her own choice?

She raised her voice until it could be heard in all parts of the high-arched hall. "No, my lord."

Had she done so at the wish of her parents or to fulfill a parental vow?

"Neither, my lord."

Had she worn the black veil of the votaress at her father's court?

There was a moment's delay, and then she answered in a lower tone: "It cannot be denied that I wore the veil at my father's court. When I was a child my aunt Christina put black cloth over my head, but the King my father tore it off in a rage and blamed my aunt."

She had worn it once only, then?

"No, my lord. On other occasions I made a pretense of wearing it to excuse myself from unsuitable marriages. Once my father tore it off again and said to Alan of Bretagne," naming one of her three suitors, a man of high rank but decidedly mature years, "that he intended to give me in marriage and not devote me to the Church."

Had she worn the veil in the nunnery at Rumsey?

"Yes, my lord bishop." A long pause followed. The reason she must give would not please Norman ears. "I wore it as a protection from the violence of—of the Norman nobles." She went on to say that she had continued to wear it on the stern insistence of her militant aunt. "She would torment me with blows and reproaches and so I wore it in her presence, but always, when I was out of her sight, I took the veil off." She did not put it into words, but it was clear there had been no love lost between herself and the determined Christina.

Two archdeacons were then heard, William of Canterbury and Humbold af Salisbury. They had been sent to Rumsey and had questioned the sisters, bringing back the impression that neither princess had ever been considered by the rank and file as *Dei sponsa*.

The Council then went into secret session to arrive at a verdict. The princess continued to sit quietly in her chair, where every pair

of eyes remained fixed on her. It might have been seen that her
hands were clasped still more tensely together in her lap and that
she watched the door through which the princes of the Church
would return with the words on which her future depended. If they
said she could not marry the King, then she could never marry at all
but would be sent back to the nunnery under her stern and disapproving aunt. She would wear the stiff headdress of the Black
Benedictines for the rest of her life.

Anselm himself announced the decision. The Princess Edytha, he
said, had been found free to contract marriage with the King.

The archbishop proceeded to read a curious clause of justification. It ran as follows: "When King William conquered this land,
many of his men, elated by the greatness of the victory, not only
seized the possessions of the conquered but invaded the honor of
their wives and daughters whenever they had the opportunity. This
forced many ladies to preserve their honor by putting on the veil."
A strange admission indeed from a body of high-placed Normans!
This was the first clear evidence that it was now possible for people
on both sides to look back at the events of the Conquest with some
degree of detachment.

The delight of the native population was so intense that even the
announcement of the change of the bride's name to Matilda in honor
of the King's mother (and perhaps to appease the still unreconciled
barons) did not blunt its edge. They now had a king born on English soil and he was taking to himself a wife of the sacred line of
great Alfred. Surely better days were ahead for England!

2

The life into which the princess entered after her marriage with
Henry at Westminster on November 11, St. Martin's Day, was not as
exalted and brilliant as might be supposed. In those days even rulers
existed in the most complete discomfort. It may be advisable to
pause at this stage for a quick glimpse at the times.

The castles of the nobility were towering piles of frowning masonry which had been designed for one purpose and one only,
security. The living quarters were bare apartments behind thick,
cold walls. The Great Hall was always of imposing proportions,
stretching up into realms of darkness in which drafts set banners

and tapestries to a ghostly rustling and flapping. It had a raised dais on which a table was set impressively with silver ewers and standing cups and tall candlesticks for the meals of the family and guests. Below this were trestle tables which were brought out at each meal for the retainers, who consumed their food, with much noise, below the salt. The floors were never cleaned, and the continual adding of fresh rushes over the bones left by the household dogs created heavy and sickening odors. From a gallery opposite the dais, minstrels played and sang while the great people dined. There was a stateliness about all this, but it must be said at once that it was deceptive. Manners were not good. Forks had not yet been invented, and so food was conveyed to the mouth by the hand. The food was very plain. The Crusaders had not yet introduced the spices of the East which later brought such delight to the palate of the Middle Ages (the cinnamon, cloves, pepper, galangal, fennel), and to make up for its flatness food was served in enormous quantities. The monks at Canterbury were accustomed to sixteen courses and they objected fiercely when the number was reduced to twelve. Heavy drinking was, of course, a part of every meal. Wines were imbibed on the dais, mead and pigment along the creaking trestles.

The homes of the smaller nobility were bare and sparsely furnished. Some contained not more than one bed, an enormous affair in which the lord of the manor and his lady slept, in company with the dowager, perhaps, an uncle or two, and almost certainly a venerable aunt. The bed would be vacated for special occasions, such as a wedding or the arrival of distinguished guests, and its usual occupants would then betake themselves to the straw pallets on which less important members of the household rested at all times. The servants slept on skins or rags or heaps of straw wherever they could find an untenanted corner, in winter as close to the fire as they could get. More rarely the lower orders slept on raised wooden platforms with beams for pillows, the early forerunner of what later was called the barrack bed.

The larger castles boasted more than one bed, of course, but they possessed most of the discomforts of the lesser. The bathhouse, a steamy hole in which there were hogsheads of water and raised planks on which bathers could sit while sloshing themselves, was most often one of the outbuildings which clustered in the inner bailey, in company with the bakehouse, the malthouse, the salthouse, and the squillery, and so it was inconveniently conspicuous and hard to reach without advertising a ladylike addiction to soap and water. The garderobe (if there is doubt as to the meaning of this word, consider that it was a polite term for the department vulgarly called the jakes) was usually on an upper floor and as far removed from the stately entrance as possible. This cold and acrid chamber was at least equipped with pipes which ran to the outer surface of the wall and allowed the filth to ooze down the masonry to the moat, fouling the water and creating an odor which filled the air in both inner and outer bailey and could be depended on to assail the nostrils of visitors as they rode in over the drawbridge.

The castles of the kings were on a higher level than this, it is hardly necessary to state, but they contained no luxuries which the nobility lacked. Henry and his bride lived at first in the two royal homes, Westminster and Winchester. A little later they began to fit up a part of the Tower of London, which was safe and dry and could be kept warm in winter, and the conversion of this grim-appearing pile to domestic occupation was an achievement of the Queen. Later still, perhaps with the desire of making his wife more comfortable, Henry decided to build a castle of his own at a place called Windsor. It stood high up above the Thames on steep clay bluffs, and there had always been a Saxon hunting lodge there. William the Conqueror had seen other possibilities in the site and had erected a keep there to serve as a prison, a circular tower of such strength that escape from it was impossible. Henry decided to have his new castle as much apart from the keep as possible. He built it outside the walls, a long and narrow structure with a tower at one end and a chapel at the other, named St. Edward's. What later became the Jousting Grounds lay between it and the river. It was not large and it could not have stood any kind of siege, but it had plenty of windows and a delightful view of the greenest and loveliest countryside, dotted with thick patches of wood and at intervals the spires of churches and the bell towers of monasteries. On a still day the bells could be heard and the distant lowing of cattle. Three years were taken in the building, and the pretty Queen on her first visit found it filled with sunshine, the rooms large and airy, the walls warm with tapestries.

Matilda became attached to her new home (in after years it was called the First King's House) and spent much of her time there.

Good Queen Mold and the Charter

It was to Windsor that the German ambassadors came to ask for the hand of little Ethelric for their master, the Emperor. The child was married by proxy in St. Edward's Chapel.

The Queen may not have been aware that she had a most unhappy neighbor at Windsor, Robert de Mowbray, who had rebelled against William Rufus and who was still living deep down in his dungeon at the very bottom of the keep. The former earl's young wife, who had been much attached to him, had been given her divorce on the strength of the inexorable nature of his confinement and had married another man. Her second husband left the country and found another wife, so the countess had the unique distinction of being in a sense the widow of two men, both of them alive. It could hardly be said that the once arrogant Earl of Northumberland, who had refused to take off his hat in the presence of the King of Scotland, was still alive. The half-crazed thing, existing in the darkness in rags and filth, had ceased to have a name with the jailers. She would not have done anything for him had she known who he was. Her countrymen, remembering his cruel exactions, would not have thanked her for the release of Robert de Mowbray.

When the royal couple came to Windsor they must have been hard pressed to find quarters for the whole court. Royal abodes were always hives of activity. All the high officials of the government and the members of the Council lived with the monarch. The place was overrun with bishops, confessors, and chantry priests; justiciars, clerks, and scriveners. It was a rule that members of the nobility should visit the King three or four times a year, and this kept the halls filled with loud talk and loud laughter and the rustling of rich robes from dawn to dark (people went to bed soon after the setting of the sun and rose with the first cockcrow, kings and queens and nobles alike), and an army of servants was needed to look after them. There were stallers and sewers, squires of the horse, yeomen of the ewery and the bedchamber, hordes of cellarers and larderers and almoners, not to mention such humble denizens as cooks and drawers and maids.

There had been many shifts and changes in such matters from Anglo-Saxon days. The staller had been an important fellow at the court of the Confessor, even having the rank of constable, but now he had been cut down to something in the nature of a household officer. The sewer, on the other hand, had gone up in the world. His responsibility was the table, even extending to the seating of guests and the first tasting of food and wine. Henry, however, had a sewer named Eudes who was much more than that. Eudes seems to have been always at his master's elbow and he witnessed most of the writs issued during the reign. A writ which did not contain his attesting signature was one granting to himself and his wife Rohaise the city of Colchester with keep and castle. This seems an excessive reward for a man who, no matter how much he pleased the King, was only a sewer. Henry and Matilda, however, seem to have liked the officials about them and were so prone to give rewards that they laid themselves open to charges of favoritism. Following through one series of appointments will demonstrate how often creatures of the court were sent out to important posts. The see of Hereford fell vacant and the King appointed as new bishop—Roger, his larderer! This unexpected grandeur and responsibility may have weighed too heavily on the larderer. At any rate, he died soon after and the bishopric then fell to Reinhelm, the Queen's physician. Reinhelm held it for several years before passing on, and it was then the turn of Geoffert, the King's physician. This was very generous and democratic, but doubts cannot be suppressed as to how this series of appointments affected the spiritual welfare of the people of Hereford.

Queens were always provided with extensive apartments for themselves and their ladies. It must have been the rule to locate these in the sunniest parts, for how otherwise could such masterpieces of historical recording as the Bayeux tapestry, made by William the Conqueror's Matilda and her ladies, have been possible? English Matilda was equally diligent, but she did not accomplish anything to rank with the enduring work of her deceased mother-in-law. Perhaps she was too busy. She was undoubtedly one of the busiest queens England ever had. In addition to the supervision of the royal household and the part she played in the councils of the King (she must have been consulted continually, for her signature appears on more writs even than that of Eudes, the sewer), she was left with state responsibilities for many long stretches when Henry crossed the Channel to fight a never-ending series of wars with his brother Robert of Normandy and the French King. She was as pious as her sainted mother had been, spending much time at her prayers and going each day in Lent to Westminster Abbey with bare feet and dress of the coarsest haircloth to pray and wash the feet of the poor. And of course she brought several children into the world.

She was fond of dress, as all beautiful women are, and was responsible for many innovations, as is always true of queens, beautiful or not. After her ride through London to the Council at Lambeth, all women began to wear their hair loose instead of having it in tight braids. The Anglo-Saxons were a saving people and made their cloth of such enduring strength that costumes often passed through three generations of wearers. Matilda, as Saxon as her bright hair, did not bring these frugal notions to the court of her King and husband. She loved gay colors, and the skirts in which she swished happily through her stately apartments were blue and red and green, and made of the costliest materials. She was one of the first, if not the first, to wear the full circular skirt which fell to the feet in voluminous folds, and to make use of cords and tassels under the cloak to hold that necessary article in place. She may or may not have been responsible for banning the attempts at lacing which had been noticed during the peacock era of William Rufus. It had been no more than a mild attempt to draw in bodices to a nicety of fitting, and it could not have been prejudicial to the health. However, the fact remains that lacing went out completely, and loose-fitting bodices came back into favor at court. There had been much preaching on the subject and much predicting of torments in hell, and so it seems certain that the devout queen had been the one to put down a foot.

Chivalry was just beginning to take hold of knightly imaginations. It was a code with some fine points but forever to be condemned because it was rooted in a fanatical system of caste. A knight had to be fair and generous with equals and superiors, but he need have no consideration for those under him. If ill-born men were killed in the keeping of knightly vows, if children were crushed under the hoofs of galloping horses, it did not matter. What did matter was carrying out the vow to the letter. With chivalry, however, came minstrelsy and the holding of absurd Courts of Love where knights vied in the trolling of ballads, and all this stilted posturing and trumpeting of praise to a lady's eyebrow had one beneficial effect. Ladies were the judges in the Courts of Love, and for almost the first time they had power in their hands. Men had not been prone to give much thought or consideration to their wives after the first enraptured days of marriage consummation. Now they began to treat them almost as equals.

It is recorded that Queen Matilda had a pleasant voice and that she encouraged the visits of minstrels and poets at court. Henry was fond of them also. It is certain, however, that in his absence many a gallant waxed unusually eloquent as he sought to please with his *sirventes* the queen whose delicate features reflected none of the coarseness of the Saxon face. It is even more certain, however, that her interest was confined to the quality of the voices and the poetic merit of the lines and never in the singers themselves. Matilda was a good wife as well as a queen above reproach. Even in the spiteful atmosphere of the court, where a word spoken in haste would be seized up and repeated and warped, and the flutter of an eyelash could be magnified into proof of infidelity, the English Queen held herself above all criticism.

3

The real story of Henry and Matilda is still to be told. The princess made a stipulation. Before she would leave the convent and become his wife, he must sign a charter which Englishmen had been praying for, a guarantee of the rights of individuals and a promise to relinquish some at least of the dictatorial practices of his father and brother; in other words, a return to constitutional rule as understood in the time of Edward the Confessor.

Henry agreed and the Charter was duly signed. It was a great historic document from many standpoints. Not only did it repudiate the concept of absolute rule which William I had imposed on the people, a necessity of conquest, but it named and denounced the evils of William II—all the ingenious ideas on inheritance and wardship which Ralph Flambard had invented, and most particularly the delay in appointments to church posts which had been the Red King's favorite misdemeanor. It specified that certain taxes only should be levied on the baronage and other landowners instead of the oppressive opportunism of exaction which had been the method of the first two Norman kings. It went further than that and established some exemptions for the common man from the ruthless tyranny of the nobility. "And I also command," it read, "that my barons conduct themselves in this manner toward the sons, daugh-

ters, and wives of their tenants." It promised, openly and unequivo-
cally, to return to the laws which had existed in the time of Edward,
which carried the implication of government with the consent of the
governed.

The Charter of Henry I was the forerunner of Magna Charta and
as such should be ranked high among the historic documents of all
time. What farseeing mind conceived the Charter? What hand
worded its clauses? It could not have been Henry's work. No king,
at least not one who combined with a highly developed capacity for
government the calculating selfishness which Henry was to display
later, would thus forge shackles for his own wrists. It was not the
work of a Norman. Most of the aristocracy were for Robert at the
start, and none was close enough to the landless prince to lend him
advice at the time of his seizure of the throne; and had there been
such, the advice would not have been in this direction. There is no
hint in the chronicles of the day of a leader among the Anglo-Saxons
of the stature to dictate terms to the new King.

One early authority at least attempted to give the credit to
Matilda: Robert of Gloucester, who wrote a history of Norman
times in limping verse. In one place he declares:

Many were the good laws that were made in England,
Through Maude the good queen, as I understand.

It would be absurd to assume that a girl who had lived most of
her life in the seclusion of a nunnery would reach this realization of
the needs of the nation. The laws referred to in the doggerel record
of Master Robert of Gloucester must have been the writs issued
throughout Henry's reign in which individual injustices were righted
at the Queen's behest. The means by which Henry was induced to
sign is a different matter, and here it is not hard to detect the hand
of the bride who was to become known as the Good Queen. Who
else was in a position to force his consent? Henry was dependent at
this stage on the support of the people, but so also had been William
Rufus, and for the same reason (the superior right of Robert, the
first-born son, and the tendency of the Norman nobility, who did
not want England and the duchy separated, to back him), and the
Red King had set an example in handling the situation which would
appeal mightily to Henry and which he would have followed if left
to make his own decision.

If further proof is needed, there is the elaborate system of pre-cautions which was adopted. One hundred copies of the Charter were made, and these were distributed throughout the kingdom, one being deposited in each of the cathedrals and the more important of the monasteries. Here they were open to inspection and scrutiny; here they lay as evidence of the King's promises, the surety of the rights of man. Again it must be pointed out that Henry himself would not have conceived this method of proclaiming the limitations of his own power, nor would he have carried it out of his own free will. Some force was at work, some influence strong enough to bring him to a decision so foreign to his arrogant nature. He would have rejected political pressure: that much is certain in the light thrown on his character in succeeding years. But a man in love (and by this time Henry was determined to have as consort and bedfellow the fair and hard-to-attain Saxon princess) will yield to gentle persuasion, particularly if he is sure that later he can rid himself of the inconvenience of compliance. The credit for winning Henry over to this method of registration of his promises must be awarded to Matilda if for no other reason than the absolute lack of any other acceptable explanation.

But it is too much to assume that the gentle lady saw the need for some such check and that she worked out the plan herself. Someone prompted her. Here is a mystery which can never be solved and which nags at the imagination. Was there in England at this time a man with the sagacity of a Dunstan or Godwine, some mute inglorious Simon de Montfort? Did such a man, a modest thane or courageous priest, perhaps, enjoy the opportunity of talking to the princess in the nunnery and of converting her to his own ideals? Did he also advise her on the answers she was to give before the Council at Lambeth so that the chance of seating her on the throne beside Henry would not be missed?

The records have no hint of such a man, but that does not mean he did not live. If he existed, he must be given credit for this first sublime vision of the way freedom could be won for mankind. His was the first effort to limit the power of kings by legal statute, openly arrived at and openly proclaimed.

This, however, is not the whole story. One hundred years later the barons of England rose against John, the extremely bad King who occupied the throne at the time, and forced him to sign Magna

Charta in which it was established that man enjoyed certain inviolable rights. When the need for this universal law was felt, it was pointed out by Stephen Langton, Archbishop of Canterbury, that the Charter of Henry I contained the basis for the new understanding. And now we come to the final phase of the mystery and, perhaps, to a confirmation of certain beliefs or theories. Of the hundred copies which had been distributed and displayed, one only could be found (later two more were discovered, at York and St. Albans), and this was produced by Stephen Langton himself. It served as the starting point in the drawing up of the Great Charter.

What had happened to the other copies? It is inconceivable that documents of such supreme importance could have been lost in a sudden wave of carelessness taking hold of all the clerical custodians. A few might have been stolen or mislaid, but not ninety-seven out of a hundred! Historians who have commented on this very strange fact have assumed that Henry himself was responsible. Once married to the lady of his choice, and with a secure hold on the throne, he is supposed to have gone to some pains to gather up and destroy the proofs of his earlier weakness. This is an entirely reasonable explanation. Henry from the start had ruled as he pleased and without any concern for these fair promises he had made his subjects, but it would be much more comfortable to be freed of the physical existence of the Charter. But if Henry took it on himself to make away with the evidence, it becomes clear indeed that the Charter was not his own idea and that he had not been responsible for its distribution.

This leads to another interesting speculation. The power was in the King's hands to hunt down and destroy each copy, and this he would have done if some special effort had not been made earlier to thwart him. Can it be that the same sagacious mind which gave birth to the Charter foresaw the likelihood of a change of heart on the part of its signer and made sure that at least *one copy would survive in spite of everything?* The fact that it was Stephen Langton who produced it suggests that it had been kept at Canterbury. Had the conscience of Anselm seen the need for precautions against any attempts later to do away with it? The pleasantest supposition of all, of course, is the possibility that it was the Queen herself who was responsible.

And why have the eyes of the world focused on Magna Charta

and overlooked the earlier Charter which prompted it? Was it because Magna Charta was wrung spectacularly from the perfect model of a wicked king by the awakened will of a people in arms, while nothing definite is known of the genesis of the earlier measure?

4

"Mold" being a popular contraction for Matilda, it did not take long for the public to apply it to their now beloved Queen. Good Queen Mold she became to them, and by that name she was affectionately remembered after her death.

The people of England had no doubt that it was their Queen who had influenced the King in the matter of the Charter. They took it for granted that a wifely voice in his ear brought about every piece of favorable lawmaking thereafter. The severe justice of Henry's rule was thoroughly approved by all law-abiding citizens, and again it was assumed that Good Queen Mold was pulling the strings.

Naturally she was given much more credit than she deserved, but at the same time there can be no doubt that all her influence was exerted on the side of fairness and justice. She was gentle and yet she was always ready to fight for any cause which had won her support. The proof of this is in the stream of writs which issued from the royal castles on her authority. In them she made grants out of her own funds to churches and schools, she provided for the improvement of the roads of the country and for bridges where needed. In some she righted individual wrongs or extended mercy to offenders. She released Bricstab of Chatteris, for instance, after he had lain for five months in prison on a charge of concealing treasure-trove. She acquitted the abbot and monks of Eynsham from driving the deer on occasions when the King hunted in that part. She addressed a writ to Robert Gernun to permit the tenant of lands at Colnbrook, which she herself had given to the monks of Abingdon, the right to enjoy his possessions in peace. In the last instance it is easy enough to assume that the gift had been made without considering what might happen to the poor tenant and that she came to his rescue quickly when the monks sought to make him vacate.

The presence of Matilda at the King's side made a great difference to the Anglo-Saxon people. They were sure that at last they

could count on fair treatment. A new sense of content took possession of the men of the land and the humble residents of the towns,
and at this stage, for the first time, the word "merrie" is used in
connection with England. It was a strange word applied to a country
still under a foreign yoke, where the villeins, the men of the soil,
were little better than slaves, and the poor men of the towns lived
meanly and precariously. But England was a rich land. The abun-
dance it produced amazed the Normans when they first came over
in the wake of Edward the Confessor. William Rufus once bought
an English horse and paid fifteen silver marks for it, an enormous
price for those days; which speaks well for the agricultural standards. The yeomen always had well-filled stomachs and, after their
day's work was done, they could take a turn at the archery butts
and down a flagon of something musty and cool at the nearest
tavern. They had no prospects and so were not disposed to worry
about the future. They sang a great deal, and a high clear note of
laughter began to seem like the voice of England.

But Good Queen Mold was not always able to look after the interests of the race from which she sprang, and a distressing story
must be told in that connection. Anselm had returned to England
with the determination to rid the Church of certain laxities. He was
particularly concerned about celibacy. Many English priests had
married and raised families, and the high officials had paid no attention to it. And now the venerable Anselm, an old man with a new
broom and a short time only in which to use it, began to make the
dust fly. Celibacy, he declared, must be the rule, and all wedded
priests must put their wives aside or leave the Church.

One day the King and Queen rode together into London. It was
a clear autumn day and the young Queen was in high spirits. She
had every reason to be, for she had already presented her royal
spouse with a son, a healthy youngster who had been named William and to whom the King was passionately attached. Although
motherhood had lent a slight touch of maturity to her figure, she
was conscious that the blue of her riding gown was becoming and
that her hair shimmered in the sunlight and, most important of all,
that Henry was entirely aware of her charms. She was very happy.

And then they turned down to the river, to the section of town
where the vintners lightered their stores ashore and the ships' chan-
dlers had their places of business, and a lamentable train stopped

them. One hundred priests or more, all married men as they made clear, knelt along both sides of the street, raising their hands in the air and weeping copiously. They did not want to abandon their wives and children, they declared passionately, and yet they were consecrated to God and must continue with their work. Only the noble King and the good Queen could help them.

Henry was in agreement with Anselm about the need for house-cleaning. He was convinced the Church in England must be purged. As he had already signified his concurrence, he became angered at the priests for their persistence. He touched a spur to the flank of his horse and rode on, forcing the suppliants to get back out of the way.

Matilda did not follow him immediately. The brightness had gone out of the day and the feeling of content from her heart. She looked down at the unhappy men and her eyes filled with tears. She knew there was nothing to be done for them. When they turned to her with their supplications she began to weep in earnest and slowly started to follow her impatient husband.

"God have mercy on you!" she cried. "I can't help you, I can't help you!"

Henry was much away in his French possessions, but no absence was long enough to create a rift in the mutual regard of the royal couple. He continued to have mistresses, of course, but on the many occasions when they sat together and received their subjects it was only too apparent to the Normans, who still called her "that Saxon woman," that the bond between them remained strong. They had four children: William, the heir, Alice (usually called Ethelric), a second son Richard, and a second daughter Euphemia. The last must have died early, for nothing is heard of her in later years. The first daughter was very much like her father, a dark-eyed child with a royal temper and a habit of stamping her small foot when she could not have her own way. At the age of seven little Princess Ethelric was sought in marriage by Henry V of Germany, who was forty-five and a widower. The child was married by proxy to the middle-aged Emperor and her name was changed, as her mother's had been, to Matilda. Five years later she was sent to Germany, where the wedding was properly solemnized between the girl not quite in her teens and the now somewhat decrepit ruler of the Germans. She was then crowned in the cathedral at Mainz.

Good Queen Mold and the Charter

There is not much more to tell about the Good Queen. The years rolled on and the King seemed to be continuously in France. At home there was peace and the land became prosperous. The Queen remained as much loved to the end, and when she died on May 1, 1118, in her forty-first year, the nation sorrowed deeply. Henry was away when her death occurred, and she was surrounded entirely by the Anglo-Saxon ladies of her household. Three of them, Christina, Gunhilda, and Emma, were so heartbroken that they took their vows at the priory of Kilburn. The Queen was buried at Westminster, beside the body of Edward the Confessor.

One portrait exists of Queen Matilda, a miniature in the Golden Book of St. Alban's. She is depicted as of fair complexion and with a figure rather tall and slender in her royal robes of scarlet trimmed with ermine. In her hand is a rolled charter. A statue of her is in Rochester Cathedral, and in this again she holds a scroll. It is not unreasonable to think that this tendency to show her with documents in her hands is an indication that in her own time she was given a full share of credit in the matter of the Charter.

England was to have many fine queens, but Matilda, the first and perhaps the best of them, has been largely forgotten. This is to be deplored, for it is certain that she concerned herself as none had done before and few after with the welfare of the people over whom her husband reigned. Good Queen Mold was deserving of longer and better remembrance!

CHAPTER V

A Bad Man Can Be a Good King

ENRY I was not a great man, but he was in many respects a great king. As a man he was selfish, unscrupulous, revengeful. He did not hesitate to break his word. He was a promiscuous lover. As a king he had some of the genius of his father; he was a careful planner, a keen judge, a capable general. But he fell short of the Conqueror's mark, lacking the violent ambition and the astonishing capacity for invention of that remarkable man. Henry's record as King shows that he possessed a quite extraordinary gift for administration, a will which could not be bent, and a determination to keep the peace. He fought when he had to, and fought well, but he was always happy to sheathe the sword. As a result the English people enjoyed a quarter century of peace. Bells tolled mournfully in London when news came from the Continent that he had died. In spite of his faults he was called the Lion of Justice.

He has carried a reputation as a scholar down the centuries, the nickname of Beauclerc being given him by all historians. In the chronicles of William of Malmesbury he is compared to Plato—and it is then naïvely stated that he could not read aloud! It is recorded that he was the author of a poem entitled *Le Dictie d'Urbain* which deals with polite behavior. He has been called the equal of great scholars such as Adelard of Bath, who was a visitor at his court, and William of the White Hands, the famous Archbishop of Reims, who came at a slightly later date.

A Bad Man Can Be a Good King

The truth of the matter was that, coming after the kind of kings the world was accustomed to, Henry looked like a veritable oracle, a prodigy of learning. He had no desire for bookish knowledge, but he had the common sense to believe a saying of the period that "an unlettered king is no better than a donkey with a crown." Not for him the boorish ignorance of his brother William Rufus. Having a quick and agile mind, he made himself master of the French language. He could read, but not write, Latin. He could even stumble through a little English. But that was all. He never read books, and his handsome dark face would have been wreathed with astonishment if a seer had told him that future ages would think of him as a scholar and writer.

Historians have used the term Beauclerc as though it had been applied to him during his lifetime. One would think it had been bandied about the courts of Europe and that his own courtiers had whispered it behind his back. As a matter of fact, it was coined by a writer two hundred years after Henry's death and was pounced upon avidly by historians who followed.

Henry ruled well, not because he believed it his duty, but because it was his nature to do so. He saw to it that the laws were obeyed and he punished offenders with a heavy hand. When he ascended the throne he found such legal machinery as existed insufficient and creaky. One of his first steps, therefore, was to set up a more suitable structure. He formed a royal council composed of barons of his household, with a justiciar or lieutenant general of the kingdom at its head. This body acted as a supreme court of appeals as well as a financial board. To handle detail and carry out the decisions of the Council, he organized the clerks of the royal chapel under a directing head who was called the chancellor. The Council held its deliberations around a table with a chequered top, and from this developed the word Exchequer.

Here was a solid and workable system, and soon order had been established out of the chaos into which the tyranny of the Red King had thrown the nation. Twice a year the sheriffs of the counties appeared before the Council, making their reports of what was due the Crown at one department, called Accounts, and then paying the amount at a second department, called Receipts. Sometimes the payments were made in produce—hogs, corn, honey, wax, wool, fowl. To settle disputes which could not be left to local authority, and to try cases, a selected number of the councilors made a yearly round of the shires to make decisions. This last feature was worthy of the inventive mind of the Conqueror. It proved so effective that it was continued thereafter and still exists in the system of judicial circuits. Henry's reputation might rest securely on this one contribution.

The taxes laid by Henry on the backs of his subjects were heavy. The people groaned, but they were willing to swallow these exactions in return for the restoration of national order. Once again there was a legal way of doing things, once again an effective machine for the netting and punishment of wrongdoers. It was a fair exchange.

Henry was ruthless and unbending in carrying out his laws. One incident will serve to give an idea of how hard he struck at offenders.

He knew that the coinage of the realm was being tampered with and debased, and on several occasions he gave warning to the moneyers to amend their ways. It must be explained that the minting of money was then an industry and that between seventy and one hundred men in different parts of the country were licensed to make and circulate coins. Many of them had fallen into the practice of making money which lacked the proper percentage of silver, despite the fact that they were compelled to put their names on all pieces which went out from their shops. Even after the stern King's sharp demands for reform, the situation grew worse and worse. Things finally reached the stage where a man might have twenty coins, which he had received for labor or for goods, and find that only one of them could be used as legal tender.

A report on these bad conditions was sent to Henry when he was in Normandy. Back came one of the most harsh orders ever issued by an English sovereign. Every moneyer who could not establish his innocence was to be subjected to the penalty fixed by law for this offense—the cutting off of the right hand! This was to be done immediately and without regard to rank, caste, or connection.

It was early in December when this royal order reached the chancellery. The horrified crown officers hesitated to obey, but finally, seeing no way of evading the responsibility, they summoned all the moneyers to appear at Winchester. It took twelve days to hear the cases. Comparatively few of the unfortunate men were able to prove that they had been innocent of fraud, and through all those twelve grim days the executioner was at work cutting off the right hands of the guilty, and through all those days the nauseating smell of burning flesh pervaded the royal buildings; for it was part of the penalty to have the severed member burned by the common hangman.

One chronicle declares that out of ninety-seven men tried only three failed to feel the sharp edge of King Henry's justice. This, however, is an exaggeration, for all of the London moneyers operating at this time were still coining money in the years which followed.

For as long as men could remember, the Yuletide season of this year was called Bloody Christmas.

On the military side of the slate, Henry's record was remarkably good. He quickly suppressed armed resistance on the part of Robert's supporters in England and exiled their arrogant leader, Robert de Bellême, who had built for himself a powerful feudatory in the west shires. In Normandy the King was invariably successful against his brother and the French King, and later against William Clito, Robert's illegitimate son. Poor Robert, whose shortness of stature had won him the nickname of Curthose (which might be translated literally as Low-Pockets), was one of those unfortunates who could never do anything right. In spite of a certain goodness of heart and more than a glimmer of honesty, he was a very bad ruler. He kept Normandy in a continual uproar, which subsided when he went to the Crusades but broke out again when he returned and took the reins into his own hands. He made efforts to take away the throne of England from Henry which were sorry failures; and when Henry turned the tables and decided to oust him from his duchy, the result was quick and complete defeat for thumb-fingered Robert. He and the French King were decisively beaten at the battle of Tenchebrai, where Henry's army was largely made up of English levies. Robert was taken prisoner and brought to England, where Henry had him lodged in a gloomy castle on the borders of Wales. It is said he was punished for attempting to escape by having his eyes burned out, but there is no positive evidence that this happened. The general tendency of historical writers to accept it may be an injustice to Henry's memory. This much is true: Henry took over Normandy and governed it sternly and well while ineffectual Robert lived out the rest of his days in his castle prison. Even allowing the story of the blinding to be untrue, Henry's conduct to his older brother is a black mark on his record.

[65]

The Conquerors

There was no sympathy for Robert among the common people. They had always feared his coming to power over them so much that he had symbolized the Norman menace. His defeat at Tenchebrai had been hailed with a deep sense of satisfaction. Tenchebrai, where four hundred knights and ten thousand French foot soldiers had been captured by English troops, was sweet revenge for the humiliation of Hastings.

Two years after the death of Matilda, Henry decided to go back to England for good. His law ran in Normandy, through the whole length and breadth of it, and there was peace at last in that much-fought-over country. His son William, variously called William Fitz-Roy (the term "prince" was not used by the Normans) or William Atheling, after the Saxon fashion, had been accepted as successor to Henry by the first real parliament summoned in England since the Conquest, which had met at Salisbury for the purpose. The young man had accompanied his father to the duchy and had remained there, taking as his wife Alice, daughter of Count Fulk of Anjou. When the old King made his decision to return, Normandy seems to have been full of members of the royal family. The second son, Richard, was there, several of the King's natural children who were grown up and married, the Earl of Chester and his bride. It was decided they would all go back together.

The King was in a hurry and went on the first ship, but he agreed to let the heir to the throne and the rest of the royal party travel on the finest galley in the navy, *La Blanche Nef*. It was captained by one Fitz-Stephen, whose father had commanded the *Mora* on which the Conqueror had sailed to England for the great adventure and who claimed on that account the right of taking the future King with him. *La Blanche Nef* sailed at night to overtake the King's ship, and this led to one of the greatest tragedies of English history. It was a fine evening and the young people decided to make a festive occasion of it. They congregated on deck and drank and danced and sang. William Atheling kept urging Fitz-Stephen to more speed, and the captain obliged by cracking on additional sail and sending orders for greater efforts to the men who strained at the double tier of oars below. All would still have been well if the prince had not instructed that three casks of wine be broached for the crew. The result of this ill-timed generosity was that the high spirits on deck were reflected soon among the *yonkers* in the rigging, while the sound of voices raised in song came up from the wooden benches where slaves labored at the oars.

The ship crashed headlong on a reef called *Le Ras de Catte* and began to sink at once. They were not far out, but there were one hundred and forty passengers of noble birth on board and not enough boats to take them all back to shore. Captain Fitz-Stephen saw to it that the heir was put into the largest of these and that it was sent off first. William Atheling would have reached safety without any difficulty if he had not heard the agonized plea of one of his natural sisters, Matilda, who had married the Count of Perche and who had been left behind. He was fond of her and could not bear to leave her to drown, so he ordered the boat back. When it reached the side of the sinking craft, so many frantic people jumped in that the boat turned over, spilling everyone into the sea. The heir to the throne went down with the rest. When the captain, swimming about vigorously and trying to bring some order out of the mad confusion, heard that William had drowned, he threw his arms into the air with a despairing cry and went down himself.

Of all on board, only one person survived to tell the story of the disaster, a butcher of Rouen who climbed to the head of the mast and clung there, just above water, until help came in the morning.

It was three days after the word reached England before anyone dared tell the King. A page was sent in to him finally, and Henry, gathering the truth from the distracted efforts of the boy to repeat what he had been instructed to say, fell from his chair in a swoon. It is said in all the chronicles that the bereaved monarch was never seen to smile again.

2

For three months after the loss of *La Blanche Nef*, Henry remained sunk in the deepest gloom. He had no appetite, he sat alone and stared at nothing, his temper was so fitful that the people of the court tried to keep out of his way, he did not pay any attention even to affairs of state, which was the surest indication of the mental condition into which this most painstaking of rulers had fallen. His chief minister, Roger of Salisbury, began to take it upon himself to govern and to issue writs "on the King's part and my own." This was too much for the rest of the royal entourage, who, of course, hated

Roger. A concerted effort was made to bring the sorrowing man back to an interest in life, and he was finally persuaded, much against his will, to marry again in the hope of having a male heir to take the place of his lost William.

The wife selected for him was Adelicia, daughter of the Count of Louvain, an eighteen-year-old girl of such beauty that she was called the Fair Maid of Brabant. Rhyming Robert of Gloucester said of her, "no woman so fair as she was seen on middle earth." Adelicia was gentle and understanding and she strove to be a good wife to the melancholy Henry, but she failed in the most important respect: she did not bear him children. The situation looked hopeless until the King's last remaining legitimate child, the Empress Matilda, was left a widow by her aged pantaloon of a husband and returned to England.

Henry's interest in affairs of state revived in earnest with the arrival of his daughter. He proceeded with the vigor of his younger days to insure her succession to the throne, calling another parliament and demanding that her right be acknowledged by all. He had one precedent to quote in support of his claims. Serburge, the wife of Cenwalch, King of the West Saxons, had been chosen to succeed that monarch. This had happened a long time before, and Queen Serburge had reigned for one year only, after which the nobility had expelled her, not being able to stand any longer the humiliation of taking orders from a woman. If he had wanted to go back to Celtic days he could, of course, have mentioned Boadicea of immortal memory, but it is doubtful if he had ever heard of that spirited ruler. Support of this kind was not needed, however, for the assembled nobility decided unanimously in favor of Matilda. The first to take the oath was Stephen of Blois, son of Adele, the Conqueror's fourth daughter.

Stephen was said to be the handsomest man in Europe. He was, at any rate, tall and striking-looking and debonair. There must have been tension in the air when he knelt before the young woman of twenty-four who had been an empress and pressed on her white hand the kiss of fealty.

The old Lion of Justice (this name for Henry came from some garbled nonsense of Merlin's) lived for fifteen years after he married the Fair Maid of Brabant. He became less active and developed a liking for the mild pleasure of processionals about his domain. His radiantly lovely wife was always by his side, but the royal countenance remained as unsmiling as in the days following the death of his son and the end of all his hopes. He won another, and final, campaign in France and allowed himself an act of retaliation which seems more in keeping with the character of his father. A bard named Luke de Barré, who had once been on friendly terms with the English King, fought on the French side and was indiscreet enough to sing some ballads which held Henry up to ridicule. The unfortunate bard was captured, and Henry ordered that his eyes be burned out. The victim, who had always been a gay fellow with a great zest for life, struggled with the executioner when he was led out at Rouen and sustained such bad internal burns that he died of them. Perhaps the monarch felt some remorse, for he began after that to complain of bad dreams. In his sleep angry peasants swarmed about him, and sometimes knights who threatened his life. These nightmares became so bad that he would spring out of bed, seize a sword, and slash about him in the darkness, shouting at the top of his voice.

Finally he accomplished his purpose of marrying Matilda to the man he had chosen for her, Count Geoffrey of Anjou. Geoffrey was a handsome youth who was called Plantagenet because he always wore in his helmet a sprig (*planta*) of genesta, the broom of his country. After six years of fruitless union a son was born to them who was named after his grandfather and grew into a fine, strapping boy. He was called, in England, Henry Fitz-Conqueror (the proud grandfather's choice) and, in France, Henry Fitz-Empress. It was generally believed at court that his belated arrival had settled all dynastic troubles.

When the King made his last journey to France he was getting a little unsteady in his legs and his temper was worse than crotchety, but the keen old mind was still functioning as well as ever. The first thing he did when he reached Rouen was to go hunting, and he came back to Lyons Castle with a ravenous appetite. He had always been temperate about food and drink, but he proceeded to eat heavily of a dish of lampreys, a favorite food although not one that agreed with him. The result was a general upset of his digestive organs, a high fever with increasing weakness, and, after seven days of illness, his death on December first at the hour of midnight. The body was embalmed with salt and wrapped in a bull hide in preparation for its return to England.

The Lion of Justice was buried at Reading, and his lovely widow transferred one of her grants, called the Queen hythe, for a lamp which was to be kept burning before his tomb for all time.

Ever since the passing of the Conqueror there had been two schools of thought about continuing the union between England and Normandy. The first, which included most of the Norman nobility, were against separation and had supported Robert's claim on that account. They estimated correctly that a separation would result ultimately in their absorption into the English nation. The other party, which contained all the Saxons, wanted separation for that very reason. As additional cause they knew that, if the King of England continued Duke of Normandy as well, they would be involved in the internal quarrels of the French.

Henry had always been conscious of this cleavage and he had striven to alleviate the anxieties of his native subjects, even while he was fighting successfully to bind England and Normandy together. In his last days, however, he made a mammoth error in marrying his sole remaining child and successor to the Count of Anjou. The Angevins had always been cruel and proud, with something demonic about them which showed itself in a disregard of religion. It must be said for them that their faults were never petty, that there was greatness even in their guile. The Normans, being neighbors of the Angevins, had an especially strong dislike for them, calling them *Guirribecs,* and the match found no favor with them. The English, naturally, did not want to see any of the Angevin breed on the throne. The birth of Henry Fitz-Empress had not caused any rejoicing on either side throughout the country. The news, in fact, had been received with angry mutterings. Seeds of discontent had been planted which would raise a bitter crop.

The Archbishop of Rouen was at the bedside of Henry when he died and he wrote, "God give him the peace he loved." It is to be hoped that Henry found it, but there was to be no peace for the unhappy land he had ruled so long. England was to know nearly twenty years of terror and suffering because of the old man's grievous error.

CHAPTER VI

A Royal Triangle and the Wars It Caused in the Sorry Reign of Stephen

O TELL the story of the next reign, it becomes necessary to recapitulate in greater detail the events preceding the death of Henry I.

Matilda brought back three things from Germany: the richly jeweled crown she had worn, the sword of Tristan, and the most imperious temper that ever plunged a nation into conflict. Picture the long White-Hall at Westminster crowded with the people of the court waiting to see her, the men in their most be-banded and embroidered tunics; the ladies, with their hair hanging down over each shoulder in front in tight silk cases, and their sleeves so long that the tips almost swept the floor; the old King in his short black tunic and tight-fitting black hose over legs which were showing a tendency to shrivel, a massive gold chain around his neck at the end of which dangled a ruby worth a king's ransom, sitting on his low throne chair and staring straight ahead of him with unseeing eyes and causing one of the long and intensely uncomfortable spells of complete silence which his courtiers had to suffer through. The first glimpse of her was most exciting: a fine-looking woman, truly regal, rather tall and graceful and with a way of carrying her head up which was an indication of her character, eyes dark and with a light in them, skin white.

She was displaying a garment which had come into an amazing popularity on the Continent but which was still new to English eyes, a silken sort of coat worn over her rich ceremonial gown. It had short sleeves and fell almost to the knees. Drawn in tightly at the waist, it flared out with such a gay effect that every woman there possessed one of them as soon as the nimble fingers of a lady's maid could cut and snip and sew it together. This new garment was a pelisse, and it was perhaps the first important style departure of those early days. Matilda's would be in one of the new colors she introduced to a country which had used only reds and blues and greens; violet, perhaps, or gold or rose madder; whichever it was, a shade to set off best her fine dark hair.

She met at White-Hall, of course, and for the first time, Stephen of Blois. How well he looked, this tall cousin, in his wine-colored cloak over tunic of silver cloth, his gray leather shoes fitting him tightly to the rounded portion of his handsome calves and then turning over to show lining of the same rich red of the cloak!

It did not matter at all to the Empress that the small fair woman beside Stephen was his wife and that she was showing her deep devotion in every move and every look she gave him. This was another Matilda, a daughter of the Princess Mary who had been at Rumsey with Good Queen Mold and who had later been married to Eustace of Boulogne. Eustace was a fine soldier and had come within a trace of being elected King of Jerusalem after his brothers Godfrey and Baldwin had occupied that perilous throne. The Empress (it will be necessary henceforth to use this title to prevent confusion with the other Matilda) knew also that her father had been so pleased with the marriage of Stephen to the heiress of rich Boulogne that he had built the Tower-Royal for them, a very strong castlelike structure which reared its battlemented peak almost as high above the roofs of London as the White Tower. Stephen, affable, easygoing, prodigal, had won the sincere affection of the Londoners since he and his fair Matilda had occupied Tower-Royal. Every man was his friend, and every woman kept somewhere in her mind or heart the image of the handsome earl. The children of the pair, an ailing son named Baldwin and a daughter who had been christened Matilda, were treated as though they were royal.

The Empress was a discerning woman in some matters. She realized at once that Stephen's wife was so deeply in love that she would never do or say anything to injure him. The home-comer does not seem to have made any effort as a result to prevent herself from falling in love with Stephen.

A Royal Triangle

It is abundantly clear that she would have married him, instantly and gladly, if he had not already led another woman to the altar; and it may be that as partners they would have ruled England as well as could be hoped for in those days. Matilda's severity, her Norman sense of possession, her instinct for order inherited from her father would most certainly have offset the free-and-easy tendencies of Stephen. On the other hand, his amiability and sense of moderation might have tempered the imperious instincts of the regal Matilda.

But standing beside the tall earl was his very attractive wife, and hovering around them all was the scheming King with a look in his eyes which told that he at least was taking account of certain realities. There was a glint in them which indicated that he had plans of his own for his new-found daughter.

In the weeks which followed, the Empress saw many things which pleased her, chiefly Stephen, and many things which did not please her at all. The first glimpses of her father's household had been disillusioning to the proud widow who had presided over the most brilliant court in the known world and in the Eternal City itself. She was puzzled to see groups of men standing about in the anterooms, common men who wore dull-colored tunics and some of whom had even allowed their yellow hair to grow so long that it hung down over their shoulders like an untidy woman's. These ill-bred clods surrounded the King whenever he appeared and actually seemed to dispute with him. Were these uncouth fellows Saxons? Could this be the race from which her own lovely mother had come?

She was puzzled also that no commotion was created when that silent man, her father, entered or strolled down one of the royal corridors. When she, the Empress Matilda, had walked into or out of a room there had been court functionaries to carry four high-arched iron candlesticks in front of her, the lights flaring and flickering with the motion and the drafts, and a seneschal in the lead intoning, "Her Supreme and Excellent Lady and Most Royal Highness!"

Particularly disconcerting was the fact that the aging but still impatient Henry wanted church services hurried so he would not have to spend much time in chapel. His daughter remembered how this had hurt her devout mother and what talk there had been when the King had made a certain Roger le Poer his own royal chaplain because that clever rogue knew enough to keep his exhortations short. Could it be that the aging and corpulent ecclesiastic who was now jumbling the Latin phrases and wheezing in his haste was the selfsame Roger? She was horrified to find that it was and that he now filled as well the high post of chancellor. She thought of the great cathedrals of Germany and Rome where the Gregorian chants, intoned by hidden choirs of trained singers, made her flesh tingle with delight, and of mighty chords crashing about her ears from the bronze pipes of the organs.

It was not long before London was dumfounded to learn that the Empress, after this triumphant return to her father's court, had retired from the public eye. She had withdrawn herself into the household of Queen Adelicia in the Cotton-Hall at Westminster and was not seeing anyone, not even the handsome earl, most particularly not Stephen. Tongues clacked furiously, and a score of reasons were advanced for this strange state of affairs. It is doubtful if anyone guessed the exact truth.

2

Two explanations for the sudden withdrawal of the Empress found most favor. The first was the obvious one, that she had been so taken with Stephen that the King had resolved on this step to prevent a scandal; and in this, of course, there was a large measure of truth. The second, and most widely favored, was an absurd story about Matilda's first husband, the deceased Emperor Henry V. It was based on the well-known fact that the Emperor had passed his last days in vain regrets for the sins of his youth, which had included the despoiling and deposing of his own father. One of the chronicles has this to say about it: "One night he rose up from the side of the Empress and, taking his staff in his hand, he wandered forth with naked feet into the blackness of the night, clad only in a woolen garment, and never again did mortal eyes rest on him." Another record went even further and had the repentant pilgrim wander as far as England, where he settled down as a hermit and was still, perhaps, alive. This was the worst nonsense, of course. There had been plenty of witnesses at the deathbed of the Emperor, and there could be no doubt that he had been well and deeply buried at Spires.

A Royal Triangle

If it was his ghost which was at large it would be brooding over the scenes of his unfilial crimes in Germany and not flitting about the unfamiliar walls and corridors of Westminster and driving his young widow into seclusion.

The real reason was that the Empress was refusing, emphatically and passionately, to concur in the marriage with Geoffrey of Anjou on which Henry had decided. She had many good reasons for objecting to this match. She had been an empress and for eleven years had outranked all the queens of Europe. Must she now marry a mere count, a descendant, moreover, of some wild creature of the woods called Tortulf? Geoffrey, apart from his comparatively humble station, was thoroughly unsuitable in her eyes. He was a youth of fifteen years, and it could be assumed that his interests had not yet risen much above the horse and dog and brawling stage. What kind of husband would this adolescent ignoramus make for an accomplished woman of twenty-five? Finally, and this reason was the real one and the hardest to combat, the passionate heart of the King's daughter had been bestowed elsewhere.

She remained in seclusion for several months, and during that time there were many violent discussions between father and daughter, and much raising of voices and protesting of vows and stamping of feet. The Empress seems to have continued, however, on the friendliest of terms with Adelicia, although it would have been hard to find two natures more diverse. The beautiful and gentle Queen entertained a real affection for her dark and willful stepdaughter, who was practically her own age. How the Empress occupied herself during the long days and interminable weeks is difficult to guess. Adelicia was given to fine needlework, and it was the custom of her ladies to gather about her each day in the sunniest apartment of Cotton-Hall and assist her in this work. This was an activity in which the restless Empress could not have played much part. One thing is certain, the Queen had enough realization of her responsibilities to refuse her brooding charge any opportunity of seeing Stephen. They heard of him and his exploits: of his prowess in the tilting yards, of his untiring addiction to the chase, of his curious habit of strolling about the streets of London, where all hats were doffed to him, and of dropping in at countinghouses and shops for friendly chats. But they did not see him.

How the artful King succeeded in winning her over is not known.

Behind the gloomy eye an agile and crafty mind was still at work. He was hard to resist long, this devious tactician who had found means of getting his own way all the years of his life. Somehow the daughter was persuaded to consent. Perhaps the fact that Stephen's wife was soon to bring another child into the world had something to do with it, as it would make her realize the hopelessness of *that* situation. Certainly her father employed the argument that she was to be Queen of England and that they were selecting nothing but a consort. At any rate, give in she did, emerging from her retirement with a smoldering air of resignation. Henry went to Normandy himself and saw to it that the nuptials were solemnized by the Archbishop of Rouen on August 26 in the year 1127.

That the marriage had been a mistake was apparent from the first. Even Henry, the matchmaker, must have realized it. Three times the Empress left her husband and her dark eyes flamed mutinously as she explained her reasons to her rapidly aging father, and three times the smooth tongue of the consummate diplomat encouraged her to go back to Geoffrey. Finally, after more than five years without issue, she raged back to England and declared that this time the separation was final. She was able to convince Henry of the iniquities of her still adolescent spouse, and he allowed her a long stay before exerting any pressure on her to return.

She made the most of her visit, seeing a great deal of Stephen and starting the old rumors to flying and tongues to clacking. Stephen had thickened a little about the waist and there were small rolls of flesh under his jowls, but his color was as fresh as ever and his spirit as buoyant. He had another son now to take the place of Baldwin, who had died, and the new heir, who had been named Eustace after his fine old grandfather, seemed perfectly strong and happy. Stephen was still, quite obviously, the most popular man in England.

When Henry finally told the Empress she must return to Anjou, she seems to have agreed without much protest. England was at peace after that, and there was little for the King to do but sign the writs which Roger the Treasurer laid before him. A disastrous fire swept London, cutting black swathes on both sides of the Thames. Henry thought of going to his new palace at Woodstock, where he had collected a menagerie and which he liked to visit, but the pleasure to be anticipated did not seem to justify the rigors of the journey. Time, of which he had never had enough, seemed at last to be standing still; waiting, perhaps, for younger and more active participants. And then one day he received news which sent him skurrying to the Cotton-Hall, his feet recapturing some of the spring of youth. His eyes had lighted up and the message they conveyed to Adelicia was easy to interpret: "At last, sweet child, it can be forgiven *you* that I have no son."

Matilda's son Henry had been born. Historians say that the nation rejoiced, but that statement has a spurious ring. The arrival of an heir made it certain that one day a scion of the much feared Angevin family would sit on the throne. Certainly there could not have been any rejoicing in London, where English opinion was cradled. It is impossible to conceive of these independent thinking burghers throwing their hats in the air because a man-child had come into the world who might someday try to trample on their hard-earned rights.

Events followed rapidly thereafter. The King went to Normandy to see his grandson, his cook put too much oil in a dish of lampreys, and the end came to a long and in some respects a memorable reign. And back in England all men paused in dire apprehension and wondered what would happen now.

3

Stephen was at the bedside of Henry, and he heard the dying King give instructions to Robert of Gloucester, who stood on the other side of the couch, for his burial. He heard also the low tones in which Henry asserted that he bequeathed all his dominions to his daughter.

Could any intimation of coming events, of the struggle they would wage between them, have communicated itself to these two men who saw the old King breathe his last? Stephen would have been more likely to sense what was ahead than the other. Robert of Gloucester was one of Henry's score of natural children, the best of the lot, his mother a Welsh princess named Nesta who had been made a prisoner during some fighting along the Marches. He was a man of lofty ideals, of great courage and compassion, a capable leader and soldier. It would not occur to one of his high honor that the wishes of the dead monarch might be set aside, and it is unlikely that he entertained any suspicions when Stephen disappeared abruptly.

Stephen made a night crossing from Wissant, and it was dawn when he landed near Dover. A sleet was falling which turned the roads into sheets of ice. The warders at Dover had been expecting arrivals of this kind, and they refused to allow Stephen and his small party of knights inside the gates. Stephen knew only too well his great need for haste, so he did not linger to dispute the matter. In addition to the Empress, who would have heavy support in view of all the oaths which had been sworn, there was his own older brother Theobald, who also had an eye on the diadem of Henry.

The repulse at Dover sent the first of the claimants galloping over the road to the north. The icy surface struck sparks from the hoofs of the horses, and some of the riders had falls. Reluctantly, then, the ambitious earl turned off the road and led his supporters over the fields to London.

Although his intentions had been known to some and he had even gone to the extent of forming a secret party pledged to his elevation, not one man joined the bedraggled group as they rode in dismal spirits from mark to mark and town to town. It was a disappointed lot who saw finally the smoke and the roofs of the great city on the horizon ahead of them.

How different it was here! London was for Stephen, and London did not fear to proclaim the fact to the whole world. No skulking behind high walls for these stout makers of cloaks and sellers of corn! They rushed out in excited droves to meet him, and Stephen found himself surrounded by vehement friends who tossed a dry cloak over his shoulders and placed a flagon of hot wine in his hand and who fairly hung to his stirrups as he slowly finished the last stage of his dangerous ride. "Stephen is King!" was the cry he heard on every side.

Stephen was King. The stouthearted citizens had settled the issue. They called together their folkmote and agreed on him unanimously as the new ruler. There was not a nobleman present, but the mere fact of his selection seems to have carried the necessary weight. Members of the nobility began then to come in and give their submissions. This was not due to any feeling against the Empress but rather to the fact that every man realized the need for a strong hand at the helm. No stage of history was less propitious for an experiment in female rule. In addition, Matilda was in Anjou with her well-hated husband, and Stephen was on hand, ruddy and smiling, his arms stretched out in friendship for all men. In a very short time the popular earl was able to ride to Winchester with a substantial train of backers, including some of the best known of the Norman aristocracy. Here he made his formal demand for the crown.

He was reluctantly received by the archbishop, but the ministers of the late King went over in a body to the winning side. The seneschal went still further by swearing that Henry, with his last breath, had passed over his daughter and selected Stephen as his successor. This was a palpable falsehood but the kind of thing, nevertheless, which carries weight. The upshot of it all was that Stephen was allowed to break the seals on the stores at Winchester, finding that the old King had accumulated savings of more than one hundred thousand pounds as well as a great collection of plate and jewelry. With this in his possession he was free of all competition.

The reign of Stephen is important for this one thing only, that a truly revolutionary precedent had been set. Common men had chosen a king!

Stephen was crowned on Christmas Eve. Queen Matilda was on hand, of course, hardly daring to look at her beloved husband in his new glory, and their young son Eustace, who would become King of England himself in God's good time, or so it seemed. The new ruler made fair promises (and meant to keep them), confirming the laws of Henry and agreeing in addition to relax the royal control of the forests.

The Empress had made no move. What she thought of Stephen's treachery (not too strong a term in view of his public pledges and the personal avowals which most certainly had been made between them) can be imagined. She was shackled at the moment by the incompetence of her unsatisfactory husband, whose misrule of his own dominions had caused an uprising. When Geoffrey found himself in a position to do something for his wife's cause, he led some troops into Normandy, expecting that the people of the duchy would rise to accept their rightful ruler. What the Normans did was to shove him back into his own territory with such angry vigor that he lost his appetite for further efforts along that line. All the Empress could do, therefore, was wait.

She did not have to wait long. Stephen proved a very poor administrator. Fully conscious that his personal popularity had won him his crown, he felt he could hold it on the same basis. He was prone to smile and say "Yes" to suggestions which should have been met with a frown and an emphatic "No." Having thrown the kingdom into serious disorder with his ill-advised leniency, he then reversed himself, as weak men always do, and became unduly harsh. He proceeded to throw his nobles and his bishops, including Henry's old ministers, into prison on the most insufficient of pretexts. The country, accustomed to the even and just, though stern, rule of Henry, became uneasy. What kind of king was this?

Robert of Gloucester, that wise and honest man, had been waiting and watching. Convinced that the hour had struck, he raised his sister's standard in Normandy and soon had a full half of the duchy in his possession. At the same time King David of Scotland came swooping down on the northern counties with an army of Highland clansmen and imported Galway levies. The result here was favorable to Stephen. The savagery of the invaders, who wasted the country as they advanced, rallied the people against them, and the English won a most bloody encounter at Northallerton. It has come down in history as the Battle of the Standards because the northern bishops combined their banners on a single pole which was elevated above the ranks. This setback, however, did not alter the plans of the Empress and her half brother. They landed the following year at Portsmouth with a party of only one hundred and forty men, firm in the conviction that the nation would rise against the inept usurper. They had in their pockets, in fact, the promises of many of the nobles to join them.

The Dowager Queen Adelicia had remarried in the meantime, her second husband being William d'Aubigny, son of William the Conqueror's cupbearer. This new husband was a handsome, brave, and honorable knight, and it had been in every sense a love match. They were living at Arundel Castle, which Henry had bestowed on his wife, and so the saying,

> *Since William rose and Harold fell,*
> *There have been earls of Arundel,*

did not apply to this particular juncture, Adelicia's husband not being awarded the title until the next reign. The great castle stood close to the coast of Sussex, and the Empress and her party stopped there, asking shelter of the ex-Queen. The dowager very wisely had taken no part in national affairs and had held aloof from support of, or opposition to, the incumbent. Now, however, she threw open the gates of the castle and received her weary stepdaughter with warmth and affection. Realizing the 'need for quick action in raising the country, Robert of Gloucester rode away to Bristol, leaving his sister at Arundel.

The chatelaine of Arundel had grown still lovelier with the passing of time, although she was probably a shade more matronly in figure. By her side when she welcomed the Empress was a young son, William, who showed signs of inheriting from his father the fine physique which had won the latter the name of Strong Arm. In a cradle close at hand was a second son, Reyner. Adelicia had borne Henry no children, but she was to go on bringing sons and daughters into the world for her second husband: Henry, Godfrey, Alice, Olivia, and Agatha.

To this late blooming of the fair dowager, the Empress presented a rather sad contrast. The frustrations and disappointments to which she had been subjected had taken an inevitable toll. Her dark eyes had lost all trace of softness. As she had not had any opportunity since setting out to make use of the contents of the dye-beck she carried in her saddlebags, there were streaks of gray in her once lustrous black hair. She was thin and showing every indication of nervous strain, and her voice would sometimes rise to a shrill note.

Stephen acted in this crisis with dispatch. He appeared before Arundel Castle and demanded that the Empress be delivered into his hands. This put Adelicia and her husband in a most difficult position. The castle was strong, but at this juncture they had only the peacetime complement of men there, a few squires and a handful of men-at-arms, and a drove of servants who would not be of much use. Stephen, on the other hand, had with him a sufficient force to carry the castle by storm. While the owners conferred, the Empress showed herself boldly on the battlements in full sight of the King and his troops. This was intended as an act of contempt and defiance, but it may have been also that she wanted one more look at this man Stephen who was playing such varied roles in her life.

The situation which had arisen in England was of a nature to bring out in the main participants their real characteristics. Stephen was showing himself brave and chivalrous but also as an insufficient opportunist. The Empress was to throw away a kingdom through sheer arrogance and an uncontrollable desire for revenge. Queen Matilda was to become later a national heroine and to perform prodigies of daring and faith for her unfaithful husband. Adelicia, more than the rest, was to come out in a new light.

This gentle lady, who had sat so unobtrusively and so decoratively by Henry's side, sent out word to Stephen that she would protect her stepdaughter and friend to the last extremity!

And now Stephen proceeded to do one of the most generous but decidedly one of the most stupid acts of his life. He sent in a safe-conduct for the Empress to join Robert of Gloucester at Bristol, appointing his brother, the Bishop of Winchester, and the Earl of Mellent to escort her. Then he waved jauntily up at the battlements and rode away with his troops! By this he proved that he had an honorable side to him and that he could respect a memory. But by the same act he unleashed the forces of civil war and condemned the English people to fourteen years of the most abject misery. Chivalrous gestures often produced results such as this.

4

The presence of the Empress in England roused to armed action the enmities Stephen had created. The barons, pretending a sudden uneasiness of conscience on the score of their vows, came out in large numbers for the daughter of Henry—Talbot, Fitz-Alan, Randulph of Chester, Mohun, Roumara, Lovell, Fitz-John. "They *chose* me King!" cried Stephen, unable to understand these defections. "Why are they deserting me?" Like all weak men, he did not see that the fault was in himself. He tried to prepare for what was coming by bringing in mercenaries from Flanders under the command of a very capable soldier named William of Ypres. This was a serious mistake because the people of England resented these hired troops bitterly and tended more and more to favor the cause of the Empress. In the meantime Queen Matilda took her youthful son Eustace to France and negotiated a marriage between the boy and the Princess Constance, sister of Louis VII, in the hope of cementing an alliance.

The war which now broke over England with full fury fell into a certain pattern. The west was for the Empress; London and the eastern counties remained loyal to Stephen. In some parts of the country the barons found themselves divided in their allegiance and so under the necessity of making war on each other. Everywhere was heard the clash of arms, the tumult of armed forays, the grim echo of sieges. All attempt at national maintenance of law and order, the goal which Henry had achieved with such effort, had ceased. What remained was the justice of the overlords and the sheriffs, or viscounts as they were called then; and judgment of this kind was cruel, sharp, and summary.

The first important victory was won by the forces of the Empress. Stephen had taken a small army of his Brabançon mercenaries to oust the other faction from the city of Lincoln. While he was about the tedious and bloody business of ferreting them out of reinforced corners, Robert of Gloucester appeared suddenly on the scene with a much larger army. It was Candlemas Day and very cold, and Stephen was taken completely by surprise when they swam the icy waters of the River Trent and came in behind him on the other side. The wisest course for the King would have been to get away as fast as he could and with as little loss as possible. Stephen, however, elected to fight it out, a decision in which his followers did not concur, a small part of them only remaining to stand behind him. It is a favorite device of the chronicles, in fact, to depict the handsome King as holding the hostile forces at bay singlehanded. Matthew Paris, who has been responsible for introducing much high-flown fiction into English annals, describes Stephen as "grinding his teeth and foaming like a furious wild boar" as he fought on alone. There can be no doubt that the King gave a good account of himself, laying about him with his battle-ax. When this was broken he resorted to his heavy two-handed sword with which he did great execution also. In the end he went down, and a common soldier, coming across him as he lay unconscious among the dead, cried, "I have found the King!"

He was taken to Gloucester, where the Empress was in residence, and shoved into one of the tiny and almost airless rooms scooped out from the thick walls of the castle. The records make no mention of a meeting between the two rivals, but it is certain that Matilda had Stephen summoned to her presence. Not sufficient for her that he was now her prisoner and that the crown was within her grasp;

the proofs she gave later of a hunger to taste to the fullest the sweets of triumph and retaliation make it clear she would not send him off to the imprisonment she had arranged for him at Bristol without a single chance to vent her feelings. There was at least one meeting, of that we may be sure, and it is equally certain that Matilda heaped him with reproaches, her words lashing him as though she used a whip.

Despite the briefness of the time he was kept at Gloucester, however, Stephen succeeded in aggravating the temper of the Empress to an even more bitter ferment. One of the chronicles thinks this was due to an attempt at escape. Whatever the cause, he was heavily loaded with chains and taken to Bristol. No safe-conducts to Bristol this time! People crowded the roads and filled trees and church steeples when he passed, as indeed they might, for this was an unusual spectacle, the King of England shackled to his saddle, much like a bear on its way to a baiting.

At Bristol he found himself in the care of a very shrewd lady. She had been the heiress of Fitz-Aymon of Glamorgan and, as such, a ward of King Henry. When that monarch decided to give her in marriage to his illegitimate son Robert, Mistress Amabel had objected with great spirit. She told Henry flatly she would not take a bastard as husband. The ladies of her house were not in the habit of marrying nameless persons.

Henry had replied that this objection, which he conceded to be a fair one, could be overcome. Henceforth his son was Robert Fitz-Roy.

The heiress was still unreconciled. "A name is not everything," she demurred. "What lands go with this name? And what lordship?"

Henry was not accustomed to parting with lands or honors easily. He regarded her sternly for several moments. Then he gave in. "I will endow my son Robert," he said, "with the lands and honor of Gloucester, and by that name shall he be called."

It seems highly probable that this spirited girl of sixteen had been well disposed toward Robert from the beginning. At any rate, having won both points, she gave in quickly and gracefully. She had made Robert of Gloucester a good wife.

It was into her hands that Stephen was now committed, a wise choice. The Lady Amabel knew that her husband's chance for high honors and responsibilities in the state depended on the success of his sister's cause. She could be relied on to see that Stephen did not escape.

In the meantime the Empress made a triumphal entry into Winchester and was met at the gate by the bishop, who was Stephen's brother but who knew when a change of coat was advisable. She followed the usual procedure of scooping in whatever was there in the way of royal treasure. A court of nobles and bishops was invoked and a quick decision reached. Robert of Winchester announced it. "Having first, as is fit, invoked the aid of Almighty God, we elect as Lady of England and Normandy the daughter of the glorious, the rich, the good, the peaceful King Henry; and to her we promise fealty and support."

The new Lady of England might well have thought that a somewhat unnecessary emphasis was thus laid on the merits of the deceased King and that too little was said about her. If she felt that way, she undoubtedly let them know it. Victory was not sitting well on her shoulders. She was becoming more arrogant by the hour, more determined on retaliation, less prone to listen to reason, even when reason spoke to her in the tones of her sagacious brother, to whom she owed her elevation.

5

The third member of the triangle must now be accorded the center of the stage, Stephen's Queen Matilda. This gentle lady had returned from France to find her husband's cause in complete eclipse and his person in the hands of his unrelenting adversary. It is clear that Matilda's regrets were for the plight of her lord and not at all for the honors he had lost. This is made evident by the appeals she addressed to the Empress, all with one purpose, his release. She had dreadful visions, this faithful wife, of her husband immured deep under the earth like Robert de Mowbray and left there to rot in misery and rags. Perhaps she feared even more violent measures, the barbarous tortures to which prisoners were too often subjected.

At any rate, she took it upon herself to make promises. Stephen would relinquish all claim to the throne and leave England, she declared. This having no effect, Matilda went much further and made an offer which proves she had been aware all along of the attachment of the Empress for Stephen and of his response. She promised in his name that he would not only renounce all pretensions to royalty but would leave England and devote himself to religious observance and that she herself would engage *never to see him again*, the only stipulation being that their son Eustace was to retain the earlship of Boulogne, which had been hers, and of Mortagne, a special grant from Henry to his favorite nephew.

Perhaps never before had a woman so humbled herself to a triumphant rival. Matilda was stating her readiness to spend the balance of her life in loneliness if there would be enough satisfaction in that for the Empress to strike the shackles from Stephen's wrists. In that savage era the figure of Stephen's Queen stands out in sharp and grateful contrast, a bright gleam of light in the prevailing dark.

The Empress rejected this last appeal with scorn. It was assumed that she objected to allowing them Boulogne and Mortagne and wanted to reduce the whole family to penury. This had nothing to do with it. The Empress had no intention of releasing Stephen on any conditions which might be conceived. Nothing she had ever experienced in life had given her as much satisfaction as the knowledge that he was chained in a dungeon, that he was in her power, that she could turn him over to the rack or the boot or bring about his death with a movement of her hand. No, the Empress did not intend to give up Stephen so long as there was breath in either of their bodies.

Failing in her efforts to secure Stephen's release, Matilda decided to fight. With the assistance of William of Ypres, she roused the men of Kent and Suffolk, who had always been for Stephen, and created the nucleus of another army to contest the kingdom. Some historians say she rode in armor at the head of these eager volunteers, but there is no mention of it in the records. Certainly it would have required the most careful use of the armorer's hammer and chisel to create casque and hauberk to the delicate proportions of the Queen. It was not unusual at that time, however, for ladies to take the field and to ride and fight, and even swear the oaths of their husbands and fathers. A troubadour named Rambaud de Vaqueiras has written of seeing through a half-opened door a lady of great beauty and apparent delicacy drop her skirts to the floor, take a sword from the wall, toss it in the air like Taillefer at Hastings, and then go through a series of sword exercises which left him dizzy.

In the meantime, while Matilda organized forces to go on with the struggle, the victorious Empress, fresh from her election as Lady of England, came to London; for not until London acquiesced could the crown and ermine be properly bestowed.

Unfortunately for the prosperity of her cause, the Empress arrived in the full glow of victory and with the intention of imposing her will. The citizens of the great town, believing the struggle over and conscious of the fact, as one of the chronicles says, "that the daughter of Mold, their good Queen, claimed their allegiance," were prepared to accept her. When a deputation appeared before her at Westminster, it was at once clear, however, that the lady who received them with haughty reserve and frown was no true daughter of their gentle Queen Mold. Norman to her fingertips, to the inmost recesses of heart and mind, the Empress was not ready to reason with them.

Nevertheless, these men of London, who still called themselves by such Saxon titles as chapman and burgess and butsecarl, spoke up stoutly for a renewal of their charter. The answer of the Empress was a sharp demand for the immediate imposition of a heavy tax called a taillage.

"The King has left us nothing," declared the chief spokesman.

The Empress looked at these men who had put Stephen on the throne in the first place and who now stood before her, with caps in hands, it is true, but with no bending of knees, no cringing for her forgiveness and favor. She could hardly contain the rage created in her by the sight of them.

"You have given all to my enemy!" she cried. "You have made him strong against me. You have conspired for my ruin, and yet you expect me to spare you!"

The Londoners now understood the situation they faced, but they showed no signs of giving in. They demanded instead an assurance that she would rule by the laws of Edward the Confessor and not by the exacting methods of her father, who had been oppressive as well as just.

Robert of Gloucester stood at his sister's shoulder and it is certain that he whispered to her to be calm, to weigh her words, to dissemble if she could not agree. If she heard him, she ignored his wise counsel. Instead she raged at the deputation, calling them rebels and base dogs of low degree, finally driving them from her presence with threats of what she meant to do.

When the Londoners left it was plain to Robert of Gloucester and the rest of the group about the Lady of England that a serious mistake had been made. They had been disturbed by the unbending attitude of the merchants, the independence shown as they withdrew in a silent body.

That same evening their fears were confirmed. The Empress was entering the White-Hall where supper was to be served, preceded perhaps by four tall iron candlesticks in the hands of court servants, when the bells of London began to ring. London had many churches, and when the bells joined in together, the clamor could either heat or chill the blood. It meant news of disaster, a summons to arms, or a wild paean of triumph. This time it was a summons to arms, the leaders having taken counsel among themselves and deciding to resist the exactions of the Norman woman. In a trice the streets were filled with armed men shouting defiance and converging by preconceived plan on the precincts of Westminster.

Robert now gave a piece of advice which was heeded, "To horse!" Without waiting to change her clothes, the Lady of England mounted and rode at top speed from the city with her brother and a party of her closest adherents. They did not realize it then, but as soon as those bells started to toll she had ceased to be Lady of England.

The fleeing party rode hard and fast, allowing themselves few stops for rest, until they reached Oxford, where they finally came to a halt. It is said that after each stop several faces were missed from the ranks. Doubts had entered the minds of the barons. They were no longer sure they wanted as ruler a lady of such haughty temper.

6

Now the struggle was on again. The Londoners swelled the ranks of the men from Kent and Suffolk, and under the lead of Matilda and William of Ypres they advanced to the siege of Winchester. The forces of the Empress, led by Robert of Gloucester and her uncle, King David of Scotland, decided to make this a test of strength by marching to the relief of the city. Stephen's bishop brother had changed back and had ensconced himself in his strong episcopal palace which lay outside the walls and from which he rained fireballs into that storied city of high church spires. In the course of the struggle, which lasted nine weeks, a score of the fine churches were destroyed and whole sections were laid waste. The army of the Empress was finally compelled to retreat. Robert of Gloucester, fighting a rear-guard action to cover the escape of his sister, was made a prisoner.

Now the situation was much improved from that desperate phase when Matilda had made her pathetic proffer to her stern rival. Being scrupulously careful to have the new captive comfortably housed and kindly treated, the Queen offered to trade the brother of the Empress for Stephen, who was still, from all reports, shackled to the wall of his Bristol cell. The refusal of the Empress was as short and sharp and peremptory as ever. Her brother was so completely the soul and brain of her cause that his absence might very well bring her to disaster; knowing this, she still held out. Twelve captive earls she would give and even throw in a sum of gold, which was getting scarce in both camps, but not Stephen.

Then the Queen went direct to the Lady Amabel, who acted as keeper of the person of the King. The Lady Amabel did not stand on ceremony, nor did she consult the Empress in the matter. She had heard that Robert was to be sent to one of the massive Norman keeps in Boulogne where, presumably, he would find captivity as hard as Stephen. Before the Empress knew what was in the wind, the two wives had agreed to trade even. Stephen, a free man, rode in to Winchester to be greeted by his victorious Matilda, a sadder, certainly, but not much wiser man.

The war dragged on for several years, the one dramatic occurrence being the siege of Oxford Castle into which the Empress had withdrawn while her brother went to Anjou for her young son Henry, it being thought that the presence of the princeling would inject new enthusiasm into a waning cause. The attack was pressed by Stephen with such vigor that it soon became apparent the defenders could not long hold out. When things reached this desperate pass, the Empress and four of her supporters garbed themselves in white robes and ventured out from a postern which opened on the river. It was in the dead of winter, the ground was covered with deep snow, and a blinding storm was sweeping down from the north. The sentries posted along the river did not see the five ghostly figures fighting their way through the lines. After as grueling a struggle with the elements as any woman ever endured, the party reached a village to the west where horses were obtained.

While the rival claimants continued the contest with siege and countersiege and foray and skirmish, merrie England became the least merrie country in the known world. As no attempt at administration was made in a land given over to factional strife, the barons became the rulers. Each was now a petty king. They did as they pleased, seized everything they wanted, from the lands of a freeman to the pretty daughter of a villein, turned their tall castles into headquarters for an iron oppression, and built new ones at points which made possible the extension of their operations. In the dungeons of these castles the instruments of torture were installed: the rack, the thumbscrew, the boot, the *chambre à crucit* (a chest lined with sharp stones into which bodies were forced until muscles were torn and bones broken), and iron chains on which men were suspended by heels or thumbs over slow fires. A favorite device seems to have been a knotted rope which was bound over the temples and tightened by degrees until the knots cut into the brain. If a baron needed labor for the building of a castle or a dam or the laying of new roads, he rounded up everyone he could find, women as well as men, and set them to work with guards over them, like the chain gangs of later years. A special tax, which all the baronage seems to have adopted and which was completely illegal, was imposed on towns and villages and called *tanserie*.

Thus, while the matter of the succession was disputed, England suffered and starved. Few crops were put in because the barons were likely to take the harvest for themselves or destroy it in sheer wantonness. One chronicle says the people became afraid that God and all His saints were asleep.

As an added stimulus to confusion and struggle and hate, the two rivals were bidding contentiously for the support of such of the nobility as remained neutral or undecided. Lands were granted lavishly, titles were distributed wholesale, every kind of inducement was offered to bring the laggards into camp. The result of this bribery was that many properties and honors had two claimants, so that private wars were fought at the same time that the armies of Stephen and the Empress advanced and retreated and struck here and struck there in the strategic conception of the day, which was to avoid battle and concentrate on siege. Stephen went so far as to create batches of titular earls to please the vanity of his lieutenants. An earl had been an officer of the Crown with the supervision of a county. As Stephen's course was followed by later kings, the title ceased in time to have any official significance and became instead a badge of aristocracy.

Robert of Gloucester died on October 31, 1147, and, realizing that it would be useless to fight on without the aid of that strongest prop of her cause, the Empress followed her son to Anjou, and the struggle ceased for a time. Certain that the threat to his royal tenure had now been removed, Stephen tried to have his son Eustace accepted as his successor. A few of the nobility took the oath of fealty, but the majority held aloof, a sign that the peace was on the surface only.

Four years later Stephen suffered his greatest loss in the death of his Queen. This admirable lady had been so worn out by anxiety and the stress of war that she had little strength left to enjoy the peace she had done so much to bring about. She passed away at Heningham Castle in Kent on May 3, 1151, and was buried in the abbey of Feversham, which she and Stephen had founded in their gratitude for victory.

But the war was not over. Henry Fitz-Empress was growing up and showing already the decision of character and sagacity of mind which later were to make him an able king. Geoffrey, his father, the handsome youth who had become such a futile man, was now dead and Henry had assumed the government of Normandy. When Eustace appeared at the French court and was invested with the duchy by Louis, the young Henry realized that the time had come to settle the issue once and for all. He organized a small force and landed in England in January 1153, setting up his mother's standard and summoning her supporters to take up arms again in her behalf. Enough of them responded to swell his ranks to formidable size, and he marched toward Wallingford in readiness to do battle. Stephen's men held the northern bank of the Thames in equal readiness.

The stage was now set for the first pitched battle of the war, which would also be, without a doubt, the decisive one. Most of the dramatic moments of this internecine strife had come in the dead of winter, and this was no exception. The banks of the river were heaped high with snow, and there was ice on the surface of the water. A fierce wind tossed and tore Stephen's banner, with its leopards, and did the same for the Angevin banners on the other shore.

And then, as the knights tested the edges of their swords and the squires greased harness with avid fingers, a gleam of great good sense came to one of the combatants. This was William d'Aubigny, a widower two years and still disconsolate over the loss of his fair Adelicia. He seems to have been on the King's side of the river. At any rate, he went to Stephen and protested that the peace of the country should not be disturbed further when an amicable arrangement should be possible to arrive at. Some historians credit Archbishop Theobald with being the agent of peace, but it is not important who was responsible for the urgent suggestion that the stage of the olive branch had arrived. The important thing is that Stephen rode down to the river on his side and young Henry Fitz-Empress came up on the south and a conference was held from bank to bank. The result was peace at last, a solution of the differences which had reduced England to such desolation.

Stephen was to be King for the balance of his life and Henry was to succeed him. The Treaty of Wallingford, as it was called, provided, moreover, that Stephen was to disband his mercenaries and send them out of the country, the new castles were to be razed, and new sheriffs were to be appointed to proceed with the restoration of law and order.

At this point Matthew Paris peers once more around the backdrop of history and prompts the chief actors with words of his own. The Empress, he declares, was at Wallingford and the settlement was due to her efforts. "The Empress," he writes, "who would rather have been Stephen's paramour than his foe, they say, caused King Stephen to be called aside, and coming boldly up to him, said, 'What mischievous and unnatural thing go ye about to do? Is it meet the father should destroy the son, or the son kill the sire? etc., etc.'"

This, of course, has no roots in truth. The Empress was not in England when these events occurred, and had she been there, her last thought would have been to counsel peace. Not that resolute lady whose whole life had been dedicated to the winning of the crown! There are certain pieces of evidence on this point, however, which make the possibility of Henry being the son of Stephen a little more than mere surmise. The Empress was in England the year before the birth of the prince and swore at first furiously and definitely that she would not go back to Geoffrey, then changed her mind hurriedly. In some sources it is said that Henry called Stephen his father during the cross-water negotiations, a statement which seems to carry the hallmark of invention on the face of it.

There is still, however, another bit of evidence, and this time it is both more important and credible, being based at least on fact. When Geoffrey of Anjou died, he left instructions that he was not to be buried until his son Henry had agreed to accept the terms of his will. Now the will had not been opened and could not be immediately, and Henry found himself in a most uncomfortable dilemma. What unacceptable terms might the will contain? What sacrifices might it demand of him? Henry was not the kind of man to enter into blind compacts. And yet there was the body of his father awaiting burial and, it may be assumed, losing something in preservation with each hour. Finally, and most ungraciously, Henry gave in. He would accept the conditions. Without a doubt the body of the dead earl was then lowered at once into the grave.

When the will was read, it was found that the earldoms of Anjou, Touraine, and Maine, which Geoffrey had held in his own right, were left as a matter of course to the eldest son. Geoffrey, the second son, received three castles, Mirabeau, Chinon, and Loudon. It was added, however, that should Henry become King of England the three earldoms were then to go to Geoffrey. Such wily precautions to trap Henry into acceptance would not have been resorted to if the father had not felt strongly that his own possessions should go to the second son.

There is still one more point. When Henry became King of England and did *not* give up the earldoms, being a highly possessive man, the brother loudly proclaimed that the will had been drawn to favor him, whose legitimacy could not be doubted.

It is still barely beyond the limits of surmise, but it cannot be passed over. There has always been a pride displayed in certain qualities of the English kings who are grouped under the heading of Plantagenet. They were tall, golden men, with piercing blue eyes and immense physical strength; cruel and possessive and revengeful, but nonetheless rulers of ability and of considerable character. How ironic it would be if not a drop of Plantagenet blood had ever flowed in the veins of an English king!

7

Stephen survived the Treaty of Wallingford by little more than a year. His strength was depleted and he had become slow and lethargic. It does not appear that he stirred himself to restore order out of the general chaos. The tyranny of the barons continued unchecked. The despairing cries of the people do not seem to have reached his ears. No castles were torn down for their relief. The coinage had become so debased by clipping and filing that trade agreements read *in weight,* which meant that payment was to be made according to the weight of silver in the coin and not at its face value. Nothing was done about this.

Stephen had twice been close to death in a condition verging on coma. Now for a third time he lost the power of movement and lay as one dead in the citadel at Dover where he had been when the seizure came. There was no devoted wife to nurse him back to health as had been the case on both other occasions. In any event, it is very doubtful if even the loving care of Matilda could have helped him. His hour had come. He died on October 25, 1154, and the physicians said death had been due to piles and an iliac passion. The symptoms seem to point rather to apoplexy.

This handsome man, who had wanted everyone to like him, was probably the worst king England ever had because of the suffering he brought the people. During the nineteen years of his reign 1,115 unlicensed castles were built by the lawless barons. In some chronicles it is said that one third of the population died during that short space of time.

CHAPTER VII

The Epic Reign of a Great King

THE reign of Henry II, called the first of the Plantagenets or Angevins, has all the elements of an epic novel, all the romance, color, conflict, and guile of the Arthurian legends which men began to write at this time. It is the record of a king who had all the qualities of a great monarch together with many of the faults of a bad one, who corrected Stephen's anarchy with a sure, iron hand, and who governed, part of the time at least, like a medieval Solomon. He dreamed, this great Henry, of making England the center of an empire more powerful than Charlemagne's and nearly succeeded in making it so. He married the most glamorous woman in Europe after antlering her husband, Louis of France, so that men called the latter cuckold. He was blessed, or cursed, with many sons, including Richard of the Lionheart and the base John. He loved many women and stole the intended bride of one of his own sons. He put his beautiful wife in a prison for sixteen years. His whelps rose up in rebellion against him and made his last years a nightmare of hate and treachery.

In this amazing reign of more than a third of a century, chivalry came to its fullest flowering and the voice of the troubadour was heard as often in the land as the clash of arms. Much more important by far, the first whispers rose of a religious unrest which led to John Wyclif and Lollardism and, eventually, to the Reformation. It was then that men began to dress like men, shortening the long womanly tunic in which they had looked like biblical prophets and encasing their legs in close-fitting hose. The first and only English pope was selected by the conclave at Rome at almost the same time that the *Veni, Creator Spiritus* was sung over Henry at Westminster. It was the period of the dark story of Irish conquest.

It was, above everything else, the time in which two strong men, Henry himself and that unsolved enigma, Thomas à Becket, split the nation into camps in a contest of wills, giving to history one of its strangest stories.

Henry II was twenty-one years old when he ascended the throne with the staggering responsibility of redeeming the land from the anarchy. He was already married to the beautiful Eleanor of Aquitaine, divorced wife of Louis VII of France. He had won two highly creditable campaigns: the invasion which had led to the Treaty of Wallingford, and a whirlwind of march and countermarch in which he had driven out of Normandy a hostile confederacy headed by Louis and his own brother Geoffrey. He had done very well, it would seem, for a man of his years. His chaplain, Peter of Blois, says of him: "He was ruddy but you must understand that my lord the king is sub-rufus, a pale red . . . His head is round as in token of great wit . . . His een pykeled and clear as to color, while he is of pleased will, but through disturbance of heart, like sparkling fire or lightning with hastiness. His head of curly hair when clipped square in the forehead, showeth a lyonous visage . . ."

So much for Peter of Blois, who is quoted only to prove that a true picture of the young King may be gained from direct sources. He was a thickset youth, with the chest of a distance runner, a bull neck, and a leonine head. His color was high and his eyes, which were gray, protruded slightly and were said to show fire beneath the surface. He was a man of furious energy. Partly because of this, partly to fight corpulence to which even then he was prone, he seldom sat down. It was his custom to ramble about at meals, getting up from his gold-backed chair on the dais, to take a chop in his hand and eat as he wandered along the length of the table and tossed remarks here and there; coming back, perhaps, for a slice of beef or the leg of a capon before another saunter. He was sparing of food and drink, and this was a great hardship, for he was a man of enormous appetites, for lands and power and gold and, yes, for women, as well as for the beef of England and the wines of Normandy.

The Epic Reign of a Great King

This is the first and most enduring impression one gets of Matilda's great son, his tremendous and never-ending energy. It shows in everything known of him. It enabled him to carry a burden of administrative detail impossible to any other single individual. Daily he would be seen in the office of the clerks of the chancellery, preparing writs for distribution, a score of them, perhaps, in a single day. Not one escaped the scrutiny of the royal eye. If he found one which was not phrased to his liking, he took it in hand and redrafted it himself, quickly, accurately, his pen traveling at furious speed. He was much more of a scholar than Henry I, although he laid no claims to such laurels, nor have such claims been made for him. He read a great deal and liked to discuss what he learned with scholars and wise men. They were about him all the time—all the time, that is, that he spent in England—John of Salisbury, Hugh of Lincoln, Foliot of London, perhaps the most widely read scholar of the day, and John of Oxford. This was one of the bonds which at first bound him to Becket.

Another proof of Henry's desire to rule well was his practice of visiting the outlying parts of the kingdom. This habit was a cross which chafed the shoulders and shortened the tempers of the royal entourage. It was no particular hardship on his knights, who spent their days in the saddle anyway, but the priestly clerks and scriveners were a different case. They were not trained to riding, and so it was unfortunate that Henry, that difficult and tumultuous man, did not believe in carriages, holding that their use tended to rob men of strength in their legs. When therefore the word flew through the offices of the *Curia Regis* and the humbler quarters of the chancellery that another terrible pilgrimage had been ordained, there would be a furious scramble for the gentlest palfreys and the least obstinate mules, and the disconsolate men of the court would pad themselves against the bruises and saddle burns of the canter.

This mad young King! In addition to his accursed belief (to quote his staff) that a ruler should know his country and his people, he was completely unpredictable. The happy word would be circulated at Gloucester, say, that they would be staying all of the next day and night. The grateful servants and scriveners, and the hangers-on who always follow a king in progress—the dancers, the gamesters, the mountebanks, the jugglers, the prostitutes and pimps, all the parasites, in fact—would open their saddlebags in

great content and settle themselves down for a rest on their straw
pallets in corners of the packed inns. And then suddenly there
would be a buzz of voices, a shouting of orders, the snapping of
whips and the creaking of leather, and they would learn that their
royal master (that rampaging bull of an Angevin!) had changed his
mind. They were starting at once for Hereford!

Henry might set ten o'clock of a morning for his departure and
be up at dawn, roaring orders and bundling up state papers himself to facilitate an immediate start. He was a hard master, but
hardest always on himself.

He had an infallible memory, an inheritance from his otherwise
insignificant father. He never forgot a good turn or an ill one, he
never entirely lost an affection, and certainly he never relaxed a
hatred; more, he carried this prodigious capacity into the smallest
details, seeing the mean face of a lawyer and recalling every item
of a squabble twenty years before over a hide of land, or hearing
the whine of a beggar at Bishopsgate and recognizing him as a
man-at-arms who had followed him to Wallingford.

There are conflicting reports on his religious views. In some
chronicles he is said to have been pious. It is written of him that
he regularly watched with the monks of Merton for three full nights
before Easter and that one of his favorite habits was to visit in disguise the churches of the poor. Others say he had no reverence in
him, that he talked in church and scribbled on the back of the royal
pew, that he seldom if ever confessed. One thing can be set down
as true, that when his great temper was roused he blasphemed with
all the ingenuity and color of an Arab street beggar. The truth lies
somewhere between the extremes of opinion. An impression grows
as one reads farther and farther into the fantastic annals of this
reign that he had deep down within him the normal religious belief
but that he lacked the patience for the observance of its outward
forms.

He was rough and ready in everything. It is a fact that he appeared at his coronation in a doublet and short Angevin cloak
(which earned him in some chronicles the name of Curtmantle)
made of rich brocade and that he fairly blazed with jewels. This
was one occasion when a man had to appear at his best. Ordinarily
he wore garments of costly material which did not fit him because
he refused to waste time with his tailors. He invariably looked like

a king of the vagabonds or a squire who had been handed the used clothes of his master and who found them tight in the waist and cramping in shoulder. He considered it enough tribute to his high station if he wore on his person some insignia of royalty. When he desisted from his sauntering at meals to help himself to wine, his nails might show need of attention, but there would be rings of great value on his fingers, and the flagon from which he drank would be rimmed with rubies and emeralds.

In an age of mad passions and deep superstitions, Henry was as full of common sense as a modern titan of industry. A story may be told to show how level was the head he carried on his great, muscular shoulders. When he returned from his one journey to Ireland, he stopped at St. David's in Wales. An old woman approached him to beg for some favor. He did not grant it, and the beldame burst into a loud denunciation of him.

"Avenge us, Lech-laver!" she screeched, waving her skinny arms above her head. "Avenge us this day!"

The knights in Henry's train turned pale in superstitious dread. Lech-laver had figured in a prophecy by Merlin. A king of England, returning from the conquest of Ireland, would meet his death on a rock of that name. A small stream ran by close at hand, and stretching across it was a rock of the most curious conformation. Clearly it did not owe its position to nature and it probably had been placed there by the Druids. A native, questioned by the uneasy knights, mumbled that this rock was called Lech-laver.

In this day men were so full of superstition that they stared in dread if a shadow fell unexpectedly across the sky, fearing it might mean the end of the world. If a monk in some isolated monastery had a dream involving a king, any king, the abbot would send out mounted messengers to carry the story so that the ruler in question would be in a position to guard against what it portended. There were words which meant death if uttered by human lips, and men would die on the rack rather than speak them. Everyone had heard of Merlin's prophecy and believed in it implicitly, and so it was no wonder that Henry's followers looked at the curiously shaped rock and begged him to ride away as fast as his horse could gallop.

Henry laughed. He walked to the end of Lech-laver, mounted it, and crossed the stream to the other side. Then he retraced his steps without any haste. He was cool, amused, a little contemptuous. With an eye on the old woman, who had ceased her screeching and had watched him with fascinated fear, he said to his men:

"Who will now have any faith in that liar Merlin?"

Here, truly, was a man. How fortunate for England that the power fell into his hands at this time when the need was so great for the restoration of order after the anarchy. How much more fortunate it would have been if he had been content to rule the country, if he had not been consumed by an ambition which kept him away from the island for so much of his time. It has been estimated that of the thirty-five years of his reign only thirteen of them were spent in England. For the rest he was following a star which blazed directly above him and so blinded him that he found it hard to see anything else.

A final word about his character: one writer of the day says, "When at peace, there was a great sweetness in his eyes."

2

The first thing the young King did was to summon back the ministers of his grandfather, Henry I, who had been so recklessly discarded by the simple Stephen. Roger of Salisbury was dead, but his nephew Nigel, now Bishop of Ely, was appointed to the post of treasurer, which he had formerly filled. Robert de Lacey was made justiciar. They were old men but wise in the ways of the wise old King, and Henry showed good judgment in bringing them out of obscurity. At the head of his Council was the Archbishop of Canterbury, gentle and pious old Theobald.

They held their first meeting on Christmas Day, 1154, in a small room of the chancellery. Eleanor's eyes had been red that morning, and the ladies she had brought with her from the south sat around her in another small room in a dismal circle, extending their feet toward a tub of steaming water. To them Christmas was a day of sunshine and gentle winds softening the peal of the bells; and to see the snow piled up on the sills and to hear a blustering wind about the roofs was just cause for melancholy. The yule log had been dragged into the White-Hall and was blazing there, and the royal officers of minor degree were already gathered about it and in a sufficiently convivial mood to fill the palace with a hint of revelry.

The Epic Reign of a Great King

Henry, one thumb tucked in his belt of blue leather and gold plate, his other hand tossing a walnut in the air, stalked about the room in complete unawareness of the season. It was not a large apartment and it was not comfortable, for the only heat was supplied by a charcoal brazier in the center. The old men clustered around this while their sovereign paced vigorously about. Already he had seen to it that his own armorial bearings were cut into the gray stone of the wall. He had changed the leopards to lions in the insignia of the kings of England and had added a third, some say in honor of Eleanor.

As he strutted, he talked briskly, making it clear to his newly appointed ministers that in dealing with conditions he would not be swayed by weak scruples. The only thing to come out of this Christmas Day conference, however, was another appointment. Theobald sang the praises of the Archdeacon of Canterbury, whose name was Thomas and who was the son of a prosperous merchant of London of Norman descent named Gilbert Becket. Theobald had come to lean on this man in everything and was so insistent on his worth that Henry finally gave in. By the body of God, let him see this prodigy!

The man who entered the room shortly thereafter was verging on his middle years and the most compelling personality Henry had ever encountered. He was very tall, some say over six feet, and of slender build. His nose was long and beautifully modeled, and his eyes were so dark and so intense that the young King fell under their fascination at once.

Henry, it is clear, took an instant liking to Thomas à Becket, realizing that here was a man of unusual parts who would perhaps prove to be the blade of fine steel he had been seeking. The King stood in front of the newcomer, both hands tucked in his belt now, his protuberant gray eyes sparkling excitedly, the jeweled tuft of his hat bobbing as he nodded his head. Then he smiled. After the interval enjoined by deference, Thomas à Becket smiled back. One of the great friendships of history had been born.

Henry had full faith in his own judgment, no matter how quickly it might have been formed and on what slight evidence. He was certain he had found the man he wanted for chancellor. He even considered sending for the Great Seal of England, which was always placed in the possession of the chancellor, and thus settling the matter there and then. But his native caution asserted itself and he went no further, even though his mind was made up. He would take this archdeacon into the offices which clustered around the *Curia Regis* in a lesser capacity. Later, he was confident, the higher appointment could be made. This was the way it was done.

The post did not have then the importance it was later to carry. It came sixth, in fact, in the list of royal offices. The chief justiciar was ranked at the top, followed by the constable, the marshal, the steward, the chamberlain, and then the chancellor. Becket's great ability was to raise the post to something approaching the stature of later centuries when it combined home ministership with control of foreign affairs. He was to prove himself the first of the clerical statesmen who played such important roles in history: Wolsey, Richelieu, Mazarin, to name the most obvious.

The young King walked to one of the windows. From here he could look into the main courtyard, where the snow had already been trodden down to the hardness of masonry by all the feet bringing people to see the King, even on Christmas Day. It was filled with men of all stations, skipping and jigging and threshing their arms about and blowing on their fingers. He recognized Godobert the white-tawyer and frowned; the fellow would be here about some costly leather articles for the Queen and, although he was not parsimonious, such trivialities annoyed him. Then he saw the stolid and well-muffled figure of William Cade standing behind the fashioner of fine leather. So Cade had come to see him, after all, about the loan he wanted!

Across the road a sound of chanting rose from the great minster. Henry could see a stretch of the road which ran north and east through the village of Charing to Ludgate. It was black with people coming from and going to London, on foot, on horseback, on runners behind horses. He began to envision many such roads, leading to Rouen, Rennes, Bordeaux, Dublin on the Liffey, all of them black with people coming to see him.

3

The first task facing Henry and his small circle of advisers, now increased by one, was to take from the barons the dictatorial powers they had assumed during the lawless years. This was done in four steps.

The Epic Reign of a Great King

The first, and most urgent, was getting rid of the mercenaries. This was accomplished with such dispatch and thoroughness that even William of Ypres, who had been made Earl of Kent by Stephen and believed himself comfortably settled, was bundled out with the rest. He was reported to have wept bitterly when he had himself admitted to a Norman monastery.

Second, new sheriffs were appointed to control the administration of justice and collect taxes.

Third, the clause in the Treaty of Wallingford which provided for the demolition of unlicensed castles was carried out, quickly and relentlessly. Practically all of the eleven hundred were torn down during the early years of the reign.

Fourth, all grants and concessions made during the previous reign were revoked. His handling of this situation showed the real mettle of the young Henry. A good share of the grants had been made by his mother during the period when she was competing with Stephen for the support of the baronage. They had been to men who had fought for her, whose aid had been given, moreover, in placing him on the throne. To take away from them the rewards of their loyalty would seem to be a rank injustice. But Henry, young though he was both in years and experience, knew there was a broader view than this. If he revoked Stephen's grants and left those of his mother in force, he would be keeping the schism alive and laying up cause for further strife. He knew, moreover, that Matilda's largesse had been lavish and that the holders of her bounty had no reasonable claims to the lands and honors she had showered about her. It required the sternest of resolution for Matilda's son to tell his friends they must disgorge; but he did, and so saved the country from trouble later on.

Despite the sharp medicine of Bloody Christmas, the moneyers had been up to their tricks again and, in addition, the holders of money had fallen more than ever into filing and debasing coins. The anarchy had added to the monetary confusion, and there were many coinages in the country when Henry ascended the throne: Stephen's own, which had been rudely made with his name spelled wrong, Stiefne or Stefne; Matilda's, which had been of better design; the coins he had issued himself during his campaigns in England and which were called Duke's Money; and various others by Eustace, Robert of Gloucester, and a mysterious unknown who had put out an issue in the name of Pereric.

One of Henry's first acts was to call in all old money and replace it with a new penny issue. According to one historian, he assumed the loss himself, but this seems highly unlikely in view of the great amount involved and the far from healthy condition of the royal finances, as well as the obvious fact that it would have been a stimulant to future clipping and sawing and filing. Although the financial transactions of the day bristle with references to pounds, marks, and shillings, they did not exist. They were "coins of account," having established values and being used as terms in settling the price of goods and in making calculations. The only money in existence in England was the penny. Soon after this period the need for coins of larger value was felt, and several were turned out at the mint in the Tower of London. The first was a gold penny with a value equaling that of twenty of the established pennies, but it was such a thin and inconvenient coin that the London merchants complained, and it was soon thereafter withdrawn. Next in order came groats, florins, nobles, and rose nobles, all of which continued in circulation through several reigns. The first pound was made in 1487 and was called a sovereign because the King who ordered the minting, Henry VII, one of the least kingly of rulers (Francis Hackett calls him "one of those elderly potentates who bring with him a whiff of the backstairs"), elected to have himself shown on the obverse side seated in state and holding his scepter, orb, and cross. No attempt was made to produce an English mark, but it continued in use for centuries as a term for one hundred pennies. It was Henry VII also who decided to give the shilling, the *scilling* of Saxon days, an existence of its own after nearly a thousand years of use. The first shilling was minted in 1504.

All coin issues during the days under consideration, therefore, were pennies. The issue which Henry put out to replace the dross of the anarchy was hastily conceived and rudely executed (he did not care about such matters), but it was an honest penny. Most issues had been good for several years only, but this first one to carry the name and the bust of Matilda's son remained in exclusive use for twenty-three years. The young King saw to it that it continued honest. He cut down the number of licensed mints to fifty and had a continuous inspection made of their output. In 1180 he put out a second issue, a much more artistic one this time. This minting was so sound that no more coins were struck for sixty years. It was so strictly backed up during his lifetime, and his likeness continued even after his death to strike such terror to wrongdoers, that Richard and John, who followed him, both of whom were vain and jealous men, were content with it and issued no money of their own.

Money hoarding was a general tendency in these unsettled years. At the time of the Conquest, when it seemed to the poor Saxons that all security had been lost, and subsequently when civil wars threatened, men would hide their negotiable wealth against the dire needs they anticipated later. Often they died without a chance to divulge the location of the buried money. From time to time these deposits come to light. In London in the year 1872 one supply of more than six thousand pennies was found, all of them newly minted coins of William I. The largest find has been the Eccles Hoard, which was dug up in Lancaster in 1864 and consisted of more than eleven thousand pennies. Nothing could be more indicative than this of the state of mind of the unhappy Saxons in the early days of Norman rule.

All through his reign, when not concerned with war and conquest, Henry continued to improve the laws with *dome* and *ban,* by either of which terms royal proclamations were called. He stopped the hideous Norman custom of deciding criminal charges by having the contestants fight it out in full armor, in the belief that God would grant the decision to the one whose cause was right, and of testing the guilt of prisoners by making them lift white-hot irons or walk barefooted over heated plowshares. In the place of these cruel absurdities from the dark ages, he went back to trial by jury. It had been tried by the Saxons, sometimes with panels made up of witnesses in the case, sometimes with jurors who had not participated in any way, sometimes a combination. Henry now gave more definite substance to the institution by having jury lists maintained in all counties. This was an important milestone in the growth to present-day conceptions of law enforcement.

That it was difficult to escape entirely from the cruel Norman customs, which had prevailed for two generations, was felt in many ways. One incident may be told in this connection. Eight men were charged with breaking at night into a house in London and killing the owner. The jury decided that their guilt had been established sufficiently *to warrant their taking the water test!* The water test, ordinarily, consisted of throwing the prisoner into a pool with arms tied. If he floated, he was considered guilty and was taken out and hanged. If he sank, he was judged guiltless but, unfortunately for him, he drowned in the demonstration of his innocence. In the case of the eight prisoners, however, a different form of the test was used. They were required to dip their arms into a vat of boiling water and lift out a bar of iron from the bottom, and moreover they had to show no signs of burn or scald two days later.

Two of the eight had the extreme fortitude, or the lack of nervous sensibility, to lift out the bar. As both failed to show later any serious injuries, they were declared innocent and set free. The other six, none of whom was more guilty than the pair who escaped, if guilty at all, could not stand the excruciating pain of the boiling water and so failed to pass the test. They were taken to the place of execution and hanged in a row.

Much later in the reign, as late as 1176, Henry divided the country into six districts, each with three itinerant judges, a further development of his grandfather's plan. These judges were responsible for the holding of courts and were expected as well to collect the taxes.

Almost as important was his decision to establish again the militia of the country. This pared the claws of the barons still closer to the quick, because the Crown was no longer dependent on them for levies of troops in time of war and so was not under the necessity of giving great grants of land. When Henry needed troops he issued a general call, and the townsman and the freeman on the land were supposed to respond as well as the baron. It was, therefore, not an unmixed blessing. At that juncture, however, the only important thing was to find ways and means of reducing the barons from lords of their small creations to mere holders of land and privilege, and anything which contributed to that end was acceptable.

From the standpoint of legislative advance the reign of Henry II was quite monumental. If the sturdy, sub-rufus, energetic King had been able to curb his ambition for power and keep out of wars in France and not clutter up his life with shoddy love affairs, the thirty-five years he ruled might well have become the most notable period in all history.

4

It was amazing how quickly the country recovered from the carnage of the last reign under a ruler like this to plot the course of revival and keep a steady hand on the tiller. None of the hundreds of thousands of sad, starved people who had died under the oppressions of the baronage could be brought back to life. But the country responded with alacrity as soon as evidences of stable government were felt.

Most particularly was this true of London. That city, always of a cosmopolitan aspect, had recovered from the great fire of 1132 and was built up again to a swarming tightness from end to end. The houses were still of frame for the most part (for reasons of economy, not because there was no realization of the danger) and most often also of one story. Where a second story was added—and this was an evidence of the prominence of the owner and perhaps of ostentation —it was called the solar and extended out over the street. The solar had to be a certain height from the ground, prescribed by law, and officials were always going around and measuring and raising great difficulties when a man had transgressed by inches. The idea of numbering the houses had not yet been thought of, and so each residence had a sign of its own suspended over the front door. Gilbert Becket, a citizen of some prominence, had a snipe painted on a board which swung in the wind and creaked in winter; and because of this his young son had been called by playmates Thomas of the Snipe. These signs lent a picturesque note to the old Roman town. Painters must have been kept busy designing them for well-to-do burghers. There was great variety, of course, running from plain household articles like baskets and spades, through such rather costly types as horses' heads and cows and swine, and ladders and merrytotters, to the very expensive kinds which showed dragons and griffins and ships under full head of sail.

It was on these signs that the King's officers would mark two lines with chalk when it had been decided to use the house for the billeting of troops or the servants of prominent visitors; and a very effective method it was, for the signs were easy to remember and so rubbing the marks off did no good.

The city was so closely packed inside its two-mile bow of wall that some of the parishes covered no more than three or four acres of land. Each parish, however, had its own church and generally it was built of stone, with an imposing gateway and great crossbeams painted red and gold, and with figures of angels suspended from the roofs. There were more than one hundred parishes in all, and the spires of the churches showing above the top of the stout walls gave the city a magical atmosphere.

The badge of budge (lambskin) on which the clothworkers had their insignia of the ram and teasel might very well have carried the arms of London, for the great city on the Thames was founded on wool. The ships which came into the estuary from all the ports of Europe and reached their moorings to the sound of *Praise to the Good Christ and Kind Virgin* sung by the whole crew (a hymn heard in every language and in every port on the Continent at the end of each safe journey) brought all manner of goods to England —fine fabrics, spices, wines, armor—and what they took back in exchange was wool. There was always more than enough wool for export to balance all the fancier imports which came to England.

It must not be assumed because so much wool was sold abroad that the English had failed to become makers of cloth themselves. The Drapers' Company in London was the oldest of the guilds and one of the strongest and richest. A draper in those days was a maker of cloth and not a dealer in the finished article. The London drapers not only used much of the best English wool, but they also imported a special variety from Spain. The rich purple cloths for supertunics, the wine-colored varieties, the deep blues, and the tawny yellows so much favored in those days were made right in London. The company had a fine hall in St. Swithin's Lane, and their annual feasts were of such note that men of high title were glad to be invited as guests.

Henry I granted them a charter for which they paid an annual fee of sixteen pounds. Henry II renewed this and established a yearly cloth fair to be held in the churchyard of the priory of St. Bartholomew, Smithfield.

There was much activity, therefore, in the houses where the drapers lived and carried on their trade. The front of the house was always used as a shop for the display and sale of the cloth. Behind this, and sometimes in full view, the apprentices worked at heddle and shuttle, and reed and treadle, weaving the enduring cloth into handsome patterns.

The drapers had another great distinction. It was from their ranks that the first Lord Mayor of London came. His name was Henry FitzAlwyn, and he was of very considerable wealth. He had a large house near London Stone and he was a sagacious and resolute man, and a popular one, with his ruddy face and waxed beard, his hearty laugh, strutting in clothes as rich as any great nobleman. He was a perfect choice for the new post which was created about the middle of Henry's reign. That he continued to hold it for twenty-four years was proof that the first of the lord mayors was also one of the best.

FitzAlwyn's selection was an indication that the fusing of the two races was becoming an accomplished fact in London. The trade of the city had continued largely in Anglo-Saxon hands. All the money-ers of the city seem to have been Saxon, and the heads of the guilds were known by such names as Leofwine and Athelstan and Bricstab. FitzAlwyn, clearly, was of Norman extraction, and it was highly indicative that he had the undivided support of the stout burghers of London Town.

London, of course, was dedicated to trade, and most highly and intricately organized it was. Each trade had its guild, and each guild had its own part of the town, its patron saint, its livery, its insignia. Wherever men gathered would be seen the crescent moon of the mercers, the camel of the grocers, the dolphin of the fish-mongers. Most of the proud wearers carried their tallysticks along with them to be used in keeping track of sales and purchases, none being able to read or write. They were not *burel* men and humble; they were prosperous and a little arrogant. Never before nor perhaps since had the trades been so minutely specialized. If a man was a wimpler, he made wimples, a scarf for women's heads, and he made nothing else. If he had chosen to be a gorgoaricer, he made gorgets and was not allowed to try his hand at any other part of a knight's armor. Each section of London, the London of St. Nicholas Shambles, Blowbladder Street, Labor-in-Vain Street, Candlewick, Cordwainer, had special trade associations. The moneylenders lived in Old Jewry, but not all of them, for the William Cade who loaned money to baron and bishop and the King himself, under the very modern-sounding business name of Cade, Cade and Co., was on

West Chepe; and the very king of moneylenders he was, charging as high, when he dared, as twopence on the pound *per day!*

There was a growing foreign note in the busy, brawling, bellicose Citadel of Wool. Tradesmen had been pouring in since the Conquest, largely from Flanders and the north of France. This was a good thing, for it introduced new ideas and methods and it provided competition. The old Londoners, of course, did not like it. Henry's marriage to Eleanor had wedded at the same time the island kingdom to the rich lands of western France. Already trade was booming with the merchants of Bordeaux and Bayonne and La Rochelle. Ships from Aquitaine were bringing in goods from the Orient and their own abundant crops of figs. Mostly, however, they brought in the wines of Bordeaux, and some of the shrewd vintners from Gascony were settling down in London. St. Martin being the patron saint of all rubicund fellows who dealt in pipe and tun and cask the world over, the newcomers built St. Martin's Vintry as their place of worship. They introduced a new wine to English palates, an early form of claret. But it was not their best. It was, in fact, a thin and sourish variety. The best they kept for their own consumption.

Queen Eleanor had been given Stephen's former home, Tower-Royal, as well as a palace at Bermondsey across the river. She liked the busy life of London, and the presence of the court did much to keep trade in a bouncing condition. Construction was going on all the time, particularly at the Tower of London, where now the walls bristled with the turrets and peaks of smaller towers, the Beauchamp, the Bloody, the Lantern, the Belfry, the Broad Arrow, the Develin. The Cathedral of St. Paul loomed high over the city with its mighty roofs and great bays and its impressive Gothic arches. There was talk of replacing London Bridge with one of stone.

A great city was London by day, a grim and forbidding city by night. The curfew bell rang at eight o'clock from two churches, St. Martin's le Grand and All Hallows Barking. Trade ceased, the cries of the last regatess with her beer and ale died down, and all citizens of good sense locked their doors and bolted their shutters for the night. After that the only sounds heard were the droning chants of the watch; the occasional jingle of a galilee bell on the porch of a church, which meant someone seeking lodging for the night or sanctuary; the strident "Through!" of wool barges, with lanterns in

LONDON
in the XII Century

Scale
0 500 Feet 1000 1500 2000

THE THAMES RIVER

The Tower

Postern Gate

London Bridge

Aldgate

The Priory of the
Holy Trinity or
Christ Church

Bishopsgate

THE MOOR

Cripplegate

THE WALBROOK

EAST CHEAP

The Vintry

Queenhithe

The Guild Hall

The Jewry

WEST CHEAP

Watling St.

The Site of
the Folkmote

St. Martin
le Grand

The College of

St. Paul's

Baynard's Castle

Aldersgate

The Priory of
St. Bartholomew

Newgate

Ludgate

Fleet St.

To Westminster
Abbey

The Fleet

THE HOLBORN

E
N
W
S

the rigging, rowing down to unload their great bales at dawn; the more occasional and less assured " 'Cross! 'Cross!" of river boatmen defying the law by taking some belated noble or churchman over the river. If men had to traverse London at night, they traveled in groups and kept in the wake of the watch, when possible.

In the warm months gardens were full of color along the water front and trees supplied touches of green, even in the densest parts. London kept an almost gay look from spring to autumn. In winter it looked dirty and depressing, and it was cold and raw. But the citizens, even to the poor fripperers who dealt in rags and old clothes and the rakerers who cleaned the streets, had warm cloaks. Wool was king and took that much care of its subjects!

5

And now we must have something to say about Eleanor, the loveliest, the richest, the most fascinating, the most notorious, and most talked-about woman of the age.

Extending along the western coast of France from Brittany to the wild barrier of the Pyrenees, taking in the fat meadows and the rich vineyards of Poitou, Lusignan, Angoumois, Saintonge, and Perigord, terminating in the south with that country of shrewd men and valiant fighters called Gascony, and then jutting far over into the midriff of France to include Limousin and Auvergne, was a land of fabulous richness which was then called Aquitaine. The kings of France, hunched over charcoal braziers in their drafty Paris palaces or smarting from the smoke of the *reredos* (fire pots without chimneys) in their gaunt castles thereabouts, had accepted the homage of the Duke of Aquitaine but would have changed places with their fortunate vassals who lived in this land where the cattle were fat and the trees were laden with figs and the evenings were warm and scented. Aquitaine had become the world center of Courts of Love.

Duke William ruled Aquitaine and he was very old. He had one son who had gone to the Crusades and who was so good that the people called him St. William. The old man had not been a saint by any means but had spent a large part of his life wandering up and down his broad domain looking for romance, and always finding it. He now wanted to abdicate and spend his last years as a pilgrim and penitent, having in full degree that fear of the hereafter and the torments of hell which motivated so much of what happened in those days. His saintly son had two daughters only, Eleanor and Petronille, both of whom took after their grandfather.

When Eleanor was fifteen and already recognized as Queen of the Courts of Love, her father died and the unsaintly grandfather would no longer delay his plan to balance a lifetime of lechery with a year or two of penitence. The question of a husband for the luscious little beauty became, therefore, an issue of international importance. The husband selected for her would assume the title of duke and rule the country in her right. Louis the Fat was King of France at this juncture, and his avoirdupois made it impossible for him to be lifted out of bed. The mind functioning in this mass of fatty degeneration was keen, nonetheless, and fully conscious of the necessity of finding a French husband for the vivacious Eleanor. He finally decided to marry her to his own son, who was to rule after him as Louis VII.

This Louis was a nice young prince with a great reputation for saintliness, although in reality his piety was more a love of ordered ritual. He had enough of worldly appetites to become enamoured of the dark-eyed, long-lashed Eleanor. It would have been hard for him not to fall in love with her, for the Lady of Aquitaine was lively and amusing as well. She dressed herself well, and the first time Prince Louis saw her she swept into the room in a skirt which was fifteen yards around at the hem, one for each year of her age, and which swayed and rustled voluptuously as she walked. For her part, she liked the idea of being Queen of France, and so on August 1, 1137, the marriage took place.

It was not a success, not even at the start. A saint in the nuptial couch was not Eleanor's idea of a marriage. To make matters worse, her sister Petronille, who took after that philandering old grand-father even more than Eleanor, fell in love with a married man, the Count of Vermandois. He secured a divorce and married Petronille, and this led to a war in the course of which Louis led some troops against the family of the set-aside wife, on Eleanor's urging, and it happened that more than a thousand innocent people were burned to death in a church. Louis, who was a man of much fine feeling, never did escape the sense of guilt which possessed him because of this. His persistent melancholy made him less and less a suitable match for Eleanor. She had borne him two daughters, however, when the saintly firebrand, Bernard of Clairvaux, began to preach the need for another crusade. Louis, now King, decided to go, and he was so imbued with fervor that he gave in to Eleanor when she decided she would accompany him and take a troop of lady crusaders with her.

There was a scramble to join the Queen's detachment. She wanted young ladies only, and it was necessary, of course, for them to be noble and married. The Countess of Toulouse joined and Sibyelle of Flanders and the Duchess of Boulogne. They were to be a mounted division and they drilled in public and created a great deal of admiring comment. There was much consultation and secret discussion over the question of uniforms. When the King and his military advisers came to inspect them finally, it was found they had adopted something so distinctly masculine that the advisers gasped. They were wearing over-all white tunics, slit up the sides to permit freedom in walking and riding, and with a red cross stamped in front and back. Over their tight-fitting hose they had red leather shoes which came to the knee and turned over to show the orange shade of the lining. Eleanor, as their leader, had some special touches of her own, the royal crest on her arm and a plume in her hat.

The dismay of the King and his officers must have been hard to conceal. There was nothing to be done about it, however. The King's word had been given; they were all ladies of high degree and not to be offended; they had to be allowed to go with the army, in their amazonish hose and their gay red shoes. There was, to be sure, much shaking of heads and muttering, all of which was fully justified in the light of subsequent events.

Queen Eleanor's Guard, as they called themselves, proved a drawback from the start. They had so much luggage that they slowed up the marches, and the younger knights were always so conscious of their presence that they paid too little attention to duty. They were directly responsible for one great military disaster. Finding a cool, green valley much to their liking, they insisted on camping there. The King and his generals were weak enough to give in, even though they knew the place might be a deathtrap. The valley was surrounded by high wooded slopes on which a hostile army could lurk unseen. The wooded slopes *were* filled with Saracen forces, who waited until the French were engaged in pitching tents, setting up the horse lines, and drawing water. Then they struck, coming down on the startled Crusaders like an avalanche and shouting their battle cry of "Allah! Allah!" The French were caught off guard so completely that it seemed they might be wiped out, Queen Eleanor's ladies with the rest. However, they managed to pull themselves together, and Louis fought with considerable courage in his fervid desire to atone for the great error he had been cajoled into making, and finally the screeching white-turbaned hordes were beaten off. Seven thousand Frenchmen had been killed.

Eleanor seldom saw the King, who was kept busy in futile efforts to drive the Saracens back far enough from the coast to relieve the strain on Christian-held Jerusalem. It was inevitable that she would get into trouble. She discovered that her uncle Robert, who ruled in Antioch, was a handsome man of impeccable manners and in-gratiating address, and very little older than herself. Robert, in fact, had inherited all the bad qualities of his father, the wicked old rogue of a duke. He and his beautiful niece were in each other's company a great deal. Robert had grandiose ideas and had been hatching a scheme to weld all of the Near East into one strong confederation (with himself at the head, of course), and to aid in working this out he wanted to get his niece free of the good Louis and marry her to the Sultan of Iconium, as the price of that poten-tate's support. From the reports which were current, Eleanor would have preferred to remain in close relationship with the handsome Robert to being head wife in the harem of a heathen ruler. At any rate, the gossip about them became so great that it even reached the ears of the fatuous Louis. There was also a Saracen sheik who saw her and was so ensnared that he came to the French camp many times in various disguises and was always admitted to see her. Some historians say this was the great Saladin himself. Inasmuch as the future opponent of her still unborn son Richard was then barely out of swaddling clothes, it must be assumed that the mysterious visitor was someone else.

Through one cause and another the Crusade was an unqualified failure. When Louis and his disgruntled army and Eleanor and her complaining guard (their cheeks tanned to leather, their hands rough and broken, their tempers short) turned about to slink back to France, it was thoroughly understood from Louis down to the lowliest scullion scraping grease in the kitchen tents that there would be a divorce.

In such an exalted place, however, there were grave difficulties attached to getting a divorce. If it were granted for adultery, neither of them would be allowed to remarry. Eleanor would not have wanted it on those terms, nor would Louis, who had not yet been blessed with an heir. Under the circumstances they decided to patch things up, and if the next child she bore him had been a boy, the whole face of history would have been changed. She would have remained Queen of France, and the Hundred Years' War might not have been fought. But the child was a girl.

It was during this period of indecision that Henry came to the court of France with his father Geoffrey, who was renewing his oath of fealty to the French monarch. Geoffrey was still a handsome man, and the Queen coquetted with him openly. She even looked under her long lashes at the son, who was only seventeen but a well-set-up fellow with an eye bold enough to look back at a queen. Two years later Henry returned alone. His father was dead and, although Louis was giving Stephen's son Eustace a somewhat halfhearted advocacy, it was generally expected that the next King of England would be Matilda's son. Eleanor now saw him with new eyes and with a sudden intentness. Young men find beautiful wives of other men attractive, especially when they are older than themselves, and Henry's interest in Eleanor was at least the equal of hers. An agreement was made between them that as soon as she could achieve her freedom they would be married.

It may seem hard to believe that a woman would thus arrange to take as her second husband a man nearly twelve years younger than herself, but the explanation is clear enough. Eleanor did not want to relinquish her crown as Queen of France unless something equally good was obtainable. She would not have married Henry unless she had been sure he would be the next King of England.

Henry had seen in Eleanor more than a beautiful and willing woman. She represented to him the chance for an empire. All of Aquitaine and its allied provinces, added to England and Normandy and Anjou, would make him ruler over lands twice as extensive as those of Louis of France. Her tarnished reputation meant little to him under these circumstances, her greater years even less.

The marriage between Louis and Eleanor was finally dissolved on March 18, 1152, at Beaugency, the grounds being consanguinity. Her patrimony was returned to Eleanor without any restrictions.

This was a surprise, for she now became again Duchess of Aquitaine in her own right and the greatest catch in Europe. If Louis had entertained any suspicion of what was coming, he would not have acted with such generosity, for France could not tolerate willingly the union of this great territory with the kingdom of the north. The news when it came was like a thunderbolt.

Disguised as a private gentleman and with a small train of attendants, Henry crossed French territory into the domain of his lady and arrived at Bordeaux in time to marry her on the first day of May. A stunned world heard that the ceremony had been solemnized with great pomp and a lavish display of ducal wealth. The news caused alarm, chagrin, and fear in French high circles. The councilors of the King wanted Louis to invade Aquitaine immediately and dislodge the errant duchess and her youthful bridegroom before any trouble for France could be planned. Louis, however, shared the unreadiness which had made Ethelred of England such a failure as a king. He fumed and raged and did nothing. The next disturbing piece of news to reach his ears was that the bridal couple were in Normandy and that Eleanor had assembled a fleet of thirty-six ships with which Henry would invade England. The invasion was successful, as has been told, resulting in the Treaty of Wallingford.

At Rouen on August 17, Eleanor gave birth to a son who was named William, after the Conqueror, it is to be hoped, and not the old gander of Aquitaine.

6

The Eleanor who came to England was not the vivacious girl who presided over the Courts of Love in her own warm southland, nor was she the vain and passionate woman who had kept the household of Louis in such turmoil. She had not changed entirely. Her temper was still high, she was as vain as ever, she thought more of the adornment of her person than of the state of her immortal soul. But she had steadied in purpose and she meant to comport herself as a queen should. Like the astringent persimmon which becomes sweet after the ripening period or a touch of frost, Eleanor of Aquitaine was showing signs of mellowing. In addition to her more obvious and material reasons for marrying Henry, there was certainly another one: that she hoped to recapture her youth and live over the years she had wasted with a man for whom she had nothing but contempt. She was in most respects a good wife to her youthful spouse, presenting him with eight children. The infidelities were all on his side, and he was at least equally to blame with her for the differences which led to her confinement at Woodstock. When he left her in the role of regent while he went to the Continent, she acquitted herself well. At any rate, she did not interfere with the Norman officials he placed beside her to make sure she did nothing wrong, such being Henry's way.

But the people of England did not know of this change in the character of the notorious Queen Eleanor, nor were they able to look into the future and see her as a wise and tolerant old woman trying to keep her sons in the path of good kingship. They had been shocked by the circumstances of the marriage and they watched for her arrival with not a little dread, as well as the most intense curiosity.

The royal couple landed at a small fishing village on the Sussex coast early in December, having waited a month for favorable winds. A dismal rain was falling and they took to horse at once to reach more comfortable quarters for the night. There was, of course, a large crowd in the village to see the young King and his wicked wife as they cantered through. Henry looked rather savage, setting the pace in the van of the party, his head in a hood, his silver spurs jingling as he urged his mount forward. All they could see of Eleanor was a pair of dark eyes in a face of ivory pallor. She was wearing a barbette, a close-fitting cover for the head with a strap under the chin; the first seen in England, without a doubt. Despite the very bad opinion they had of her, they cheered her as she rode past them. If the smile with which she acknowledged this welcome was somewhat casual and wintry, it must be borne in mind that her first sight of England was proving a most depressing one and that she undoubtedly was thinking of the blue waters of Biscay rolling in to smooth white shingle and above this a palace wide open to the sun.

The first real look that England had of her was at the coronation. Henry rushed it along, being in a furious impatience to get at the neglected tasks of government, and it was held a fortnight after their arrival at Westminster, on a Sunday, in fact, December 19.

The Epic Reign of a Great King

The sun had sulked since the advent of the royal party, but on this most important of days it came out and shone in splendid vigor. If Henry had entertained any fears of opposition, they were quickly dispelled, for all the nobility came to the Court of Claims held by the steward with their petitions of right to perform certain parts in the ceremony. The Earl of Chester was on hand to carry the sword *Curtana*. The head of the house of Bohun arrived to officiate as constable. The current incumbent of the manor of Addington, Bartholomew de Chesney, was seeing to it that a fine dish of dilligrout was being prepared for the coronation feast. Of ill will or signs of a preference for the surviving son of Stephen, not a trace.

All medieval coronations were intensely colorful, and this one, in spite of the haste with which it had been arranged, was one of the most spectacular. The sanctuary seekers who at all times infested the grounds and the chapels of Westminster (sometimes there were as many as a hundred assorted thieves and murderers defying the law within the abbey) had been forcibly rounded up and locked into a single chapel on the east side, where they sat in a glum silence, some bristling with insolence, some sunk in hangdog despair. This gave more room in the limited space between the White-Hall and the great church, and it seemed as though all London was packed therein, pushing and shouldering and standing on tiptoe.

The nobles headed the procession, carrying the regalia: the cross of Alfred, the scepter, the orb, the four swords, St. Edward's staff, the ring of the Confessor, and the crown. There was a story about the ring which everyone believed and which made the spectators crane their necks to get a glimpse of it. The Confessor had given it to an old man who asked him for alms, and more than a century afterward two weary and hungry English pilgrims in the Holy Land had it returned to them by a strange patriarch who said to them, "I am Johan Theuangelyst." The crown was a new one, a circlet of gold with four strawberry leaves between which were pearls and precious stones.

Next in line were the churchmen, the bishops and abbots and priors, all in full vestment and lending a note of solemnity. The lesser nobility followed, walking slowly along the blue cloth which had been stretched from the White-Hall to the western entrance of the abbey, wearing richly colored garments, brocaded and furred and jeweled, their coronets sparkling in the welcome sun.

The Conquerors

There followed lesser men: plain knights, aldermen, portreeves, wealthy merchants. There was little interest in this part of the procession, for all eyes were fixed on the White-Hall entrance where the coronation canopy had appeared, held by knights in armor at each corner, under which the King and his Queen would walk to the crowning. The resonant chords of the organ and the chant of monkish voices coming from the interior of the abbey seemed to swell to higher volume when the royal couple appeared and came slowly up the blue walk under the golden tasseling and jeweled bands of the canopy.

The young King wore his short Angevin cloak, the novelty of which might have caused amusement if first seen on a lesser man. He looked kingly enough, tall and strong and hard, and, as he was not at peace at such moments, with no hint of sweetness in his eyes. They liked him, the pushing and struggling Londoners, having no desire left for amiability and easy charm in their rulers.

The Queen was in white and gold, her head uncovered and her hair in four plaits, as the fashion of the moment demanded. She looked radiant and as beautiful as the first time she had been crowned, which was nearly seventeen years before. English eyes were well accustomed to feminine beauty but mostly of the fair and rose-cheeked variety. They were not accustomed to the soft duskiness of hair, the ivory luster of brow and cheek, the sparkling brown of eye of this Queen from the south. They paid tribute to her loveliness at once, glad she was not what they had expected, cold and brilliant and disdainful. Perhaps the jostling crowds, stretching their necks for a closer look at her, were a little proud that their burly young King had taken her away from her foreign suitors.

Her coronation robes must be described: a kirtle of white, closely form-fitting to the waist and with tight sleeves, over this a pelisse of gold bordered with fur, the sleeves lined with ermine and so gracefully bell-shaped that they allowed the white of the kirtle to show beneath. The wide rustling skirt of white had a train (another innovation she had brought with her), carried by two pages fairly strutting with importance. There was none of the almost barbaric splendor about it which was a part of the times, but it was a courageous costume for a woman of thirty-three who wanted to take ten years off her age in order to look as young as her husband. Her maids, needless to state, had worked long and earnestly over her face before she donned the gold and white, kneading the first pucker of fine lines around her eyes, removing as far as possible the traces of encroachment by lovely woman's worst enemy, time. They seem to have succeeded.

What thoughts fill the heads of monarchs when they stand up for the ceremony which seals the relationship between themselves and their subjects is a matter, naturally, of temperament and mentality. As Henry sat on the faldstool for the sermon and litany and then later, when he had taken possession of the coronation chair on the high platform raised for the purpose in the upper part of the chancel and heard Theobald proclaim *Si ipsi consentire vellent,* he was not thinking of the meaning of this, that he was assuming the crown with the consent of the people. More likely his thoughts had leaped far ahead to a more important crowning, perhaps, and the conferring of a much greater title than King of England. Eleanor's thoughts may have been keeping him company in this glimpse of future greatness. More certainly, however, she kept in *her* mind some realization of the glaring errors of the past, of the need to make this a lasting marriage.

Immediately after the coronation Henry set about crushing all traces of disaffection which existed in the country. He settled the pretensions of the Count of Aumale, who had been ruling the north with a high hand, and of the lords of Hereford and Wigmore in the west. The youthful King of Scotland, another Malcolm, paid homage to him and restored Northumberland and Cumberland, which had been appropriated during the civil war. He invaded Wales and forced Rhys-ap-Grythyff to give hostages for peaceful behavior. In a short space of time all England was brought to acceptance of his rule. In gratitude for his uninterrupted successes, Henry took Eleanor to Worcester Cathedral, and on the shrine of St. Wulfstan they laid down their crowns, swearing never to wear them again.

This act was one of considerable significance. Renunciation of the showiest aspect of kingship was not in keeping with the spirit of the times, but it was a first step to something which occurred later, the crowning of their eldest son while Henry himself was alive. Henry, who gave up nothing willingly, was already thinking of the English throne as a steppingstone. Of still greater significance, however, was the fact that the crowns had been laid on the shrine of the only

English prelate retained by the Conqueror, saintly old Wulfstan. The best of the many stories told of him was that, when William's Norman archbishop Lanfranc had demanded of him his pastoral staff in token of resignation, the old man said he had received the staff from his master Edward and would gladly give it back to him. Advancing to the Confessor's tomb, he said, "Take this, my master, and deliver it to whom thou wilt." He placed the staff on the tomb, bowed, and began to rid himself of his episcopal robes. The staff, however, was firmly embedded in the stone when Lanfranc tried to pick it up. It remained there until Wulfstan himself stretched out a hand, when it yielded itself into his grasp. They did not interfere with such a doer of miracles after that.

That Henry and his bride, who was already beginning to have a little popularity, went to this shrine for the purpose was the surest indication of what was happening in England. The two races were beginning to merge; Norman was wedding Saxon, and Saxon Norman; both were inclined to think of themselves as Englishmen and to use the term. So far it was no more than a beginning, but the evidences were unmistakable.

7

It has been said already that Eleanor gave her husband eight children. The second was a boy, born soon after the death of the sickly little William, who had escaped the stigma of illegitimacy by such a narrow margin. The new son was called Henry, and he was healthy and strong. His father conceived for him a love which nothing could break, not even the boy's early assumption of the role of Absalom. The sweetness in the King's eyes was apparent to everyone when little Henry was about. The King was an indulgent and affectionate father to all his children, but his own namesake remained the favorite through all the stresses of the bitter years ahead.

A daughter was born next. She was named Matilda, inevitably, and in course of time she was married to Henry the Lion, Duke of Saxony. This fine knight had been given his nickname because of his amazing personal bravery and strength, but he seemed to lack political sense. At any rate, he set himself up against his cousin Frederick Barbarossa, the Holy Roman Emperor, and twice that great juggernaut rolled him right out of his dominions. This made it necessary for him to seek refuge in England with his young consort and their growing brood of children. Finally, after Matilda had shared many vicissitudes, the Lion agreed to settle down in Brunswick and give up any attempts at ruling. Matilda was a second wife, but she seems to have been happy with her unruly spouse and brought five sons and a daughter into the world.

Then came a great, handsome boy who was named Richard. If the gods and the heroes of legend still inhabited Valhalla, there must have been much stamping of feet and boisterous drinking of toasts when this infant found his breath and uttered his first cry. Little Richard was his mother's favorite, and her love deepened as he grew into big Richard and finally became a tall and inordinately strong man with yellow curly hair and flashing blue eyes: the famous Coeur de Lion, who soon put Henry the Lion in the shade; Richard Yea and Nay, most fabulous of Crusaders, whose memory by the name of Melech-Ric was used to frighten Saracen babies into obedience for centuries after. "My Richard!" his mother called him proudly when he lorded it over other boys and when he grew up and crashed all opposition down in the tilting grounds. All the passion of her nature went into her worship of this golden son. It was to become one of the causes of bitter family troubles later.

Next was a daughter named Joanna, who became the Queen of William II of Sicily and went with Richard and his bride Berengaria to the Crusades. A son followed, who was given the name of Geoffrey and who married the heiress of Brittany. The seventh child was a daughter named Eleanor, who married the King of Castile, reputedly the wealthiest man in the world. The importance England had assumed in the eyes of the world may be judged by the fine matches each of Henry's daughters made. Every monarch in Europe wanted an English bride and the share she might bring him in the fast-rising power of the three lions.

The last child was a son, who differed from the other boys in having a dark cast of countenance and rather fine features, and who tended to a slight degree of fattishness. He was christened John, and of all men born of woman he least deserved the name of the gentle and holy companion of Christ.

With the exception of the unfortunate infant William, sleeping now at the feet of his great-grandfather, Henry I, they were all healthy and handsome children, full of their father's strength and will, blessed with something of their mother's beauty and charm.

It had been an axiom that a wife who gave her husband sons was a good wife. Eleanor, the notorious beauty, the woman put away by Louis of France, was, then, a good wife to Henry.

8

The boy born to the Brakespeare family in the village of Abbots Langley, which lies close to St. Albans in Hertfordshire, was named Nicholas and he was a fine child from all accounts. A later description makes him "elegant in person, pleasant in countenance, prudent in conversation." Any young man answering to that description in those days had his feet set in the direction of prosperity and even greatness. At first, however, there seemed some doubt of it in the case of young Nicholas Brakespeare. He was rejected when he applied for admission to the Benedictine monastery at St. Albans, one of the largest and richest and most influential in the country. This circumstance, which seemed most unfortunate to his parents and relatives, proved to be the most favorable thing which could have happened to him. He went to France and studied at Paris before taking holy orders at St. Rufus. Advancing to abbot there, he came under the notice of Pope Eugenius III and was summoned to Rome, where he filled various important posts. He became the second English cardinal, the first to receive that honor being Robert Pulleyn, who is sometimes called the father of Oxford University.

Brakespeare's great opportunity came when a most delicate situation developed in the Scandinavian countries. No longer content to be governed from the see of Hamburg-Bremen, the people of the north were clamoring for archbishops of their own. As their conversion had been accomplished for the most part by English missionaries, it was deemed wise to send an Englishman as papal legate. Brakespeare, accordingly, was selected.

The Scandinavian countries included Norway, Sweden, Denmark, Iceland, the Faroe Islands, the Orkneys, and Sodor, and the legate had to please all of them if possible. He had, in the first place, to make a choice among three embattled antagonists in Norway: Sigurd of the Mouth, Inge the Hunchback, and Eyestein. His choice fell on Inge, but he found means somehow of placating the unsuccessful candidates. In Sweden he could not set up a parent see because of the racial enmity between the Sviars of the north and the Gautors of the south. This difficulty he solved by placing Sweden temporarily under the Danish see he established at Lund. Brakespeare acted with such vision and discretion, in fact, and with such supreme tact that the northern countries, when he left, were satisfied with everything and so well disposed to him personally that a friendly recollection of him seems to have been retained for a long period of time after.

His success on this trying mission led to his selection as Pope in succession to Anastasius, when he assumed the name of Adrian IV. This was in 1154, and it thus happened that he and Henry came into power in the same year.

If the new Pope had been no more than a suave diplomat, he would have failed miserably in his exalted post. His elevation came at a juncture when a firm hand and a cool and resolute head were needed at the Vatican. Under the leadership of Arnold of Brescia, a devout and fanatical reformer, Rome was in revolt against the temporal power of the Church. A republic had been declared and it had been found advisable, and perhaps necessary, to withdraw the papal offices from the Leonine City. There were dynastic difficulties as well. William of Sicily had been crowned without any attempt being made to obtain apostolic sanction. In Germany the young Holy Roman Emperor, Frederick I, called Barbarossa because of his flaring red beard, was showing the early symptoms of a boundless ambition and a willingness to swallow all Italy.

The rather frail cardinal, who had been such a success in the field of diplomacy, brought to these trying problems a strength of will and determination which could hardly have been anticipated. When he first met Barbarossa, that haughty monarch refused to hold the papal stirrup while he dismounted. Adrian remained sternly in his saddle, withholding the kiss of peace. The anger of the Emperor was so violently expressed that all the papal officials, who had ridden out with the Pope, turned and fled for their lives. Adrian was not disturbed, and wiser second thoughts replaced the rage of the red Frederick. He asked Adrian to meet him the following day and he then performed the ceremony of the stirrup. After that, Pope and Emperor seemed to work in concert and even amity. The English-born Adrian went to the length of crowning Frederick Emperor at

St. Peter's in spite of the violent protests of the people of Rome. Earlier he had dared to lay an interdict on the Eternal City. Now, with Barbarossa, he succeeded in driving Arnold of Brescia out of Rome and later in having him captured. Arnold, who had called the *Curia* "a house of merchandise and a den of thieves," was brought back to Rome a prisoner and was hanged by the prefect, if not on instructions of Adrian, at least with his full consent.

Certain parallels can be drawn between the ruler at Rome and the young ruler at London. They possessed in common the gift of decision; they believed equally in vigorous action when their judgment said it was necessary; they were not held back by scruples, nor did they balk at risks. There were dealings between them, of course. Adrian's decisions on English problems seem to have been entirely those of the Pope of Rome without any prompting from Nicholas Brakespeare of Abbots Langley. In the matter of Henry's ambition to invade and conquer Ireland, however, he may have been less completely detached. Henry's ambassador in this matter was John of Salisbury, with whom the Pope had always enjoyed the most cordial relations. John of Salisbury based his plea on the desire of the English King to enlarge the bounds of the Church and to bring a higher degree of civilization to the savage Irish tribes. Adrian listened, was convinced, and was supposed to have issued his bull *Laudabiliter*, putting the papal sanction on the project. The authenticity of the document is now doubted. A paper was in existence, however, which reads as follows:

Adrian, bishop, servant of the servants of God, to his very dear son in Jesus Christ, the illustrious king of England, apostolical greeting and benediction.

Thou hast communicated unto us, our very dear son in Jesus Christ, that thou wouldst enter the island of Hibernia, to subdue that people to the yoke of the laws, to root out from among them the seeds of vice, and also to procure to payment there to the blessed apostle Peter of the annual pension of a penny for each house. Granting to this thy laudable and pious desire the favor which it merits, we hold it acceptable that, for the extension of the limits of the holy church, the propagation of the Christian religion, the correction of morals, and the sowing of the seeds of virtue, thou make thy entrance into that island, and there execute, at thy discretion, whatever thou think proper for the honor of God and the salvation of the country. And that the people of that country receive and honor thee as their sovereign lord and master, saving the rights of the churches which must remain untouched, and the annual pension of one penny per house due to the blessed Peter; for it is beyond a doubt, and has been acknowledged, that all the islands upon which Christ the sun of justice hath shone, and which have been taught the faith, belong of lawful right to St. Peter and the most holy and sacred church of Rome.

If then thou think it fit to put in execution what thou hast conceived in thy thoughts, use thy endeavors to form that people in good morals, and let the church in that country, as well by thy own efforts as by those men of acknowledged sufficiency in faith and words and life, be adorned with new lustre. Let the true religion of Christ be planted there and increase. In a word, let everything which concerns the honor of God and the salvation of souls be, by thy prudence, so ordered that thou shalt become worthy of obtaining in Heaven a reward everlasting, and upon earth a name illustrious and glorious in all ages.

The morality of the King's plea and the Pope's compliance will be discussed later. Henry, as it happened, found himself too concerned with other matters to proceed with his designs on the sister island. The project languished for many years, and the Pope had been at rest for a decade in his red sarcophagus of Egyptian granite when Henry finally made a move.

Adrian's early death may have been due to the extraordinary difficulties which confronted him at every stage of his brief incumbency. It was a tired and unhappy man who closed his eyes on September 1, 1159, at Anagni.

The only Englishman to wear the rochet and the red mozetta and to hold spiritual sway over the Christian world was a strong pope, but he could not be listed among the great men of the papacy. He was too much a product of his times for that. Adrian's policy was that of Thomas à Becket, who died to elevate the Church above the authority of kings. Because of the Pope's determination on that score, Arnold of Brescia's body was burned and his ashes, the ashes of a great man, were consigned to the waters of the Tiber. This can be said for English Adrian, he was pure to the point of austerity and as free of personal corruption as any man who ever held the vast resources of the papacy in his hands. One of the charges hurled at Becket when he was Archbishop of Canterbury was that he had failed to do anything for the old mother of Adrian, who lived, long after her great son's death, in unrelieved poverty in the small house in Abbots Langley where he had been born.

An interesting speculation is raised by the early death of Adrian. If he had lived longer and had seen Henry's ambitions mature, would he have been disposed to grant what was so clearly in the English King's mind, though never expressed in word or the scratch of a paper, the creation of an empire of the west? *Hail, Caesar!* And if it had so come about, where would the new emperor have established himself in a capital city? London, Rouen, Bordeaux? It would almost certainly have been London, for that city always had capacity for greatness.

CHAPTER VIII

The King and the Archbishop

GILBERT BECKET was not a Norman soldier who went on the First Crusade and married a Saracen princess, as many early historians asserted, nor was he a dull Saxon merchant who sent his son Thomas to France to acquire the education and manners of a Norman, as others have contended. The truth lies between. Gilbert Becket was a London merchant of Norman birth who married a Caen woman named Rohaise and became quite wealthy. He was rich enough, in fact, to have a fine solar apartment in his house in West Chepe, containing a bed of the very new tester type, with a most convenient canopy, on top of which blankets and sheets and pillows could be stored. He owned other property within the walls and he founded a chapel in the churchyard at St. Paul's, originally, perhaps, a chantry.

They were devout people, the Beckets, and on each birthday of her only son, Madame Rohaise made a ceremony of weighing him and then sending to the poor the equivalent of his weight in food, clothing, and money. This quickly became a costly charity, for Thomas of the Snipe grew rapidly. He kept growing until he had reached his reputed six feet, which would make him one of the tallest men in England. The handsome youth was sent to the fashionable priory of Merton and then to Oxford. Then he returned to London, where he was occupied for a few years in business, and it was during this London phase that the Archbishop of Canterbury, good old Theobald, a friend of the family, took serious notice of him. The

primate had made a practice of keeping about him a circle of promising young men for service in the Church, and Thomas Becket became immediately the one for whom the highest hopes were entertained. Believing that his prodigy needed the advantages of a legal
education, Theobald sent him to Paris and Bologna, where he gained
a thorough grounding in both canon and secular law. He came back
a polished man of the world, a convincing talker, a diplomat of
great charm, and the possessor of a keen and active mind. The
archbishop now took him into his own organization, making him
Archdeacon of Canterbury and provost of Beverley. A deacon's degree sufficed for these posts, but it was understood that later he
would take holy orders. Certain other benefices were given him, and
he began to enjoy a quite considerable income.

His first chance to show his full capacity came when Theobald
sent him to Rome on a secret mission to Pope Eugenius. Stephen
was King and trying every means to have his son Eustace declared
his successor. Becket's instructions were to convince the Pope that
to do this would be to perpetuate the division in England and that,
apart from the political issues involved, Matilda's son Henry gave
great promise of developing into a wise ruler while Eustace gave
very little. It appears that the tall young Becket handled this delicate mission with much discretion and address and succeeded in
persuading Eugenius that papal influence should be thrown quietly
to the Angevin succession. Young Henry did not know at the time
that such skilled advocacy was being exerted in his behalf, but he
heard of it later. The success of Becket's diplomacy had something
to do, of course, with the favorable impression he made on Henry
at their first meeting, and it certainly was a factor in his selection
for the post of chancellor.

The chancellors in the past had been members of the *Curia Regis,*
acting in the capacity of legal advisers. They had superintended the
work of the clerical staff around the King; they presided at "the trial
of the pyx," when the accuracy of new mintings was decided by a
panel of London silversmiths; they were custodians of the Great
Seal. The post took on a fresh importance and significance, however, from the moment that Thomas Becket stepped into it. The era
he inaugurated amazed the men about the King, accustomed to the
old ways. The chancellery had been quiet enough: two guards with
bared pikes at the entrance; a long and drafty hall in which church-

men were certain to be encountered, walking sedately and talking in low tones; a few open doors into small stone apartments where clerks could be seen at work; an anteroom filled with the usual sour-faced petitioners.

Becket's staff grew so quickly that he soon had fifty-two clerks. How they were disposed of is a mystery. There had been no enlargement of the Westminster facilities when Henry I put government on a businesslike basis, nor had there been any since. It can only be assumed that in the Becket period the small stone apartments had three or four occupants instead of the customary one and that the anteroom was taken over for clerical work, driving the sour-faced petitioners to waiting in the long hall. The chancellery, as all records agree, became a hive of industry, and the chancellor himself was the busiest man there. He saw visitors without delay, sometimes walking along the line and pausing for a few words with each, disposing of their concerns fairly as well as quickly. He wrote scores of letters each day; he was always in attendance at the *Curia Regis;* he always had time for long consultations with the King.

Henry was delighted with the change which had come about. This hum of activity, this furious driving of quills in the hands of competent scriveners meant that the work of all the earls and sheriffs throughout the kingdom was being supervised and corrected. No corner of the country, he knew, was now unwatched. This was government as he understood it, as he wanted it.

That a new star on the political horizon had arisen was soon recognized by everyone with the results that might be expected. People went to great pains to make the acquaintance of the new chancellor. His table was frequented by the great nobles and courtiers. More and more the young men of his staff were driven to the extreme ends of the table. Thomas Becket never sat down to meat without a large company, and he saw to it that his guests were well fed. The fancy era in cooking had begun which was to reach its peak a century later in the fantastic embellishments of the great French royal cook, Taillevent. There were carvers at the chancellor's side tables to baste the joints with the rare spices now coming from the East and with rose water and sauces of onion and young leeks before they were carried along the tables. One writer of the day asserts that a hundred shillings was paid on one occasion by the chancellor for a dish of eels from across the Channel, but this is one of the absurd exaggerations which are often copied and believed. One hundred shillings was a very considerable amount, enough to set a man up in the fishmongering trade with warehouse and kiddles to catch fish in the Thames.

The new power in the kingdom generally appeared at table in a supertunic of a deep wine shade which had no suggestion of the clerical about it. He wore a long gold chain around his neck and a girdle of gold links with a sapphire in the clasp. He was abstemious about food and so had plenty of opportunity to talk. His conversation was lively and diverting, and it is said that he never had a guest who failed to fall under his spell.

Henry had become so fond of his new minister that he would often drop in for supper after an afternoon's hunting. He would ride his horse right into the hall, bring it up sharply with jingling of accouterments and stamping of hoofs, spring from the saddle, and then vault across the table, to take the seat always reserved for him beside the chancellor. He was hungry, he would boom in his deep voice, hungry for food and good talk. He would get both in as much quantity as he desired. The young King never tired of the talk of Becket, which was sometimes witty and entertaining, sometimes contentious, always wise and discerning. The supper would last well into the evening, neither the King nor the chancellor drinking much but monopolizing the conversation between them with a cross fire of question and answer, a verbal jousting with some of the impact of tipped lances; while the other guests, often men of the highest degree and the deepest pride, listened and had nothing to say but drank a great deal.

The minds of Henry and his new minister met on common ground so far as the problems of administration were concerned. But Becket had mental resources which the young King lacked and willingly conceded: a subtlety in reasoning, an ingenuity which led to unusual improvisation in ways and means. He could think of new methods of arriving at a desired result which surprised and delighted the King.

There seemed no limit to the qualifications of the merchant's son who was now recognized as a power behind the once all-sufficient throne. When Henry took an army into the south of France to substantiate his claim as overlord of Toulouse, a most imposing army with the King of Scotland and a prince of Wales in his train, Becket led a company of seven hundred knights, organized and equipped at his own expense. There were four thousand foot soldiers in the troop, the best-trained body of men in the whole army. The semi-clerical chancellor showed himself an amazingly fine soldier, surprising everyone without a doubt. He was supreme in the tilting grounds; he led his men through the first breach in the walls; he displayed the strategic sense of a great captain. It should be added that among the seven hundred knights in his train was a certain Reginald Fitzurse, who was as Norman in appearance and temperament as his name—dark of eye and long of nose, almost passionately resolute, and with a furious temper. There is no reason to suppose that the chancellor paid any more attention to the touchy, black-a-vised Fitzurse (of whom there will be much to tell later) than to any of the rest. It is quite probable that the young knight would have remained in his service if he had not given up the chancellery for a higher post.

When it was found that Louis of France, caught off guard by the English move on Toulouse, had thrown himself into that city with a few knights only, Henry hesitated to make an attack, because on French soil the King of France was his suzerain. Becket, more realistic about it than the usually hardheaded King, contended that Louis had entered Toulouse in an obvious effort to thwart English plans. He believed the city should be stormed as first intended. For once Henry did not follow his minister's advice and he regretted it later, for he did not accomplish what he had set out to do in this expensive southern foray.

The chancellor's household became even more splendid after the return to England. He had kept all his clerical posts and the stipends thereof, and the funds of empty bishoprics passed through his hands. Henry, as plain and unpretentious as the shabby shoes he wore, wanted no such pomp himself, but he did not object to the way Becket displayed his wealth and importance. Sometimes he made a jest of it. One winter night they were riding together through London and passed a beggar who whined for help. Henry looked at Thomas Becket riding a few feet behind him and most handsomely wrapped up in a cloak with ermine lining. He grinned delightedly. The poor man was in bad stead, he declared, lacking a cloak on such a night. Should not his gossip Thomas, who had many cloaks, give the beggar the one he happened to be wearing?

The chancellor made a facetious reply, something to the effect that to give such a cloak to this lousy scamp would be as unfitting as to transfer the doors of Canterbury to a London spitalhouse. Henry then reached out and tried to take the cloak from his shoulders. Becket resisted. The pair of them wrestled and tussled in their saddles, roaring with delight the while. The King won, of course, and the fine cloak was handed over to the shivering and probably frightened beggar. Later Henry saw to it that a new cloak, quite as grand and sumptuous, was sent to the chancellery. How the beggar disposed of this embarrassing largesse was never discovered.

Becket's magnificence and his sense of showmanship reached a peak when he was sent to France to negotiate a marriage between Prince Henry and Marguerite, daughter of Louis of France by his second marriage. The princess was seven at the time and the English heir a little older. The chancellor had two hundred horsemen in his train and eight wagons drawn by double teams of gaily caparisoned horses. One of the wagons was fitted up as a traveling kitchen, one as a chapel; two contained ale to be distributed wherever they went; the rest were used for the plate and the costumes of the party. There were singing boys to lead the procession, and pack horses with monkeys in the saddles, and all manner of devices to attract attention. In town and village the same question was always asked: Who was this great man making a journey in such state? They were told it was a very great and wealthy and powerful man who, nevertheless, was servant to the King of England.

Henry was delighted. He knew that such display gave Europe an appreciation of his importance. Unwilling to indulge in such capers himself, he was happy there was someone to do it so well for him.

Becket was soon on the best of terms with Louis of France, and the negotiations for the marriage were concluded without difficulty. The princess, according to the custom of the day, was to be educated in England. When she arrrived in London shortly thereafter, she and the prince were placed in the chancellery so that Thomas à Becket could act as tutor to them. The heir to the throne and the stranger from France developed an affection for him which nothing could change, not even the tragic differences which developed later. The princess in particular was so attached to him that when her young husband was crowned King of England by his father while Becket was in France after his breach with Henry, she refused to be crowned at the same time because her beloved master could not officiate. She spoke continually of how understanding he had been when she first arrived, a small and very frightened girl in a strange land, and how patiently he guided her somewhat unwilling feet in the path of knowledge. His life was a continuous mystery to her, for he never seemed to have time for sleep. When he did slumber, it was not in his imposing bed but on the hard boards of the floor beside it. Here is evidence that even in his most ostentatious stage the ascetic in him was beginning to assert itself.

In the year 1162 an event occurred which was to end the amity and the perfect teaming of Henry the King and his most useful and versatile servant. Theobald died and, without a doubt, was translated to the very special share of heaven reserved for the rare men who succeed in living saintly lives in high office. A successor now had to be found.

Henry had made up his mind in this matter long before. He had followed an aggressive policy in any clash between Church and State, and Becket had never failed to range himself on the side of kingly authority. To make his chancellor archbishop as well seemed to him a shrewd stroke, assuring himself of leadership in the Church in sympathy with his own desires and designs. He lost no time in letting the merchant's son know what was in his mind.

The King was in Normandy, and Becket had made one of his periodic visits, probably to discuss the situation created by the death of Theobald. Henry drew the chancellor aside and told him what he desired. Becket was wearing a crimson dalmatic over his shoulders, an unusually handsome garment. He laughed and extended his arm to show the pearls embroidered in the cuff.

"You would be choosing a gay dress," he said, bending down from his great height to speak in a low tone in the King's ear, "to figure at the head of your sober monks of Canterbury."

When Henry pressed the matter, saying that no other appointment would suit him, the chancellor became equally serious. He shook his head doubtfully. "If you do as you say," he declared, "you will soon hate me, my lord King, as much as you love me now."

Henry was not to be denied. He did not seem willing to put any belief in his minister's objections, not even when the latter said that as archbishop he would not be able to agree with the royal policy. It was firmly in the King's mind that it would be a perfect arrangement to have Becket at the head of the Church as well as State so that he, Henry, could devote himself more to his continental possessions, where the imperial dream was taking on firmer substance all the time. If Becket had stated categorically that he would relinquish the chancellorship if made primate, the shrewd King would have declared that retention of the secular post was an indispensable consideration and that the appointment to Canterbury could not be made otherwise. That the discussion did not reach this point is proof that Becket did not so declare himself.

In any careful sifting of the little evidence which exists, in the light shed upon the character of Becket by later events, the conclusion cannot be avoided that his objections were not deep-seated. He was fascinated by the greatness offered him, for the Archbishop of Canterbury was second in the kingdom only to the King himself. Knowing the attitude he would adopt, conscious of the inflexibility of which he was capable, he found this great role not one to be rejected. Even aware that there could be one ending only to the part he intended to play, he was prepared in his heart to accept the tragic consequences. Whether from deep convictions which he had kept suppressed or a less praiseworthy desire to strut importantly on the pages of history, he raised no positive objections to the King's will. A clear-cut statement would have ended the matter. But he did not make it.

A year passed and Henry was still in France when the matter of the appointment came up. The King sent Richard de Lucy to inform the chapter of his desire and resolve to see the chancellor chosen as successor to Theobald. The members of the chapter were stunned. It seems that the possibility of this nomination had not occurred to any of them. Becket had been a capable administrator and he was popular, although the lordliness of his ways had aroused some criticism and jealousy. But he was not in holy orders, and on all clashes of authority and policy he had stood against the Church. The leading men of the Church knew what was in the King's mind and they were unanimously and bitterly opposed to such a selection.

The matter was debated for some days. It was whispered around that the King's mother, the old Empress, now living quietly in Rouen and refusing fiercely to visit the land of her birth, which had rejected her, had warned her son against Becket. The meetings were held in London, and it was apparent that even the citizens were puzzled and to some degree adverse, despite the fact that the great honor was designed for one of themselves. The offices of the chancellery were being crowded to the point of suffocation by place-seekers, priests and laymen alike, who could not wait to curry favor. Becket was going methodically about his duties, seeing the visitors, of course, and smiling pleasantly—and saying nothing whatever.

It seems quite possible that the opposition of the chapter would have hardened to the point of refusal if the chancellor had expressed any objections on his part. Becket, however, continued throughout to say nothing.

Finally, therefore, "the whole Church sighing and groaning," the will of the King prevailed. Thomas à Becket was chosen. He accepted and was quickly ordained priest. On the third day of June he was consecrated Archbishop of Canterbury by Henry of Winchester.

He thus became the first man born on English soil to fill that great post since the Conquest.

2

The Church in England, to the overlordship of which Thomas à Becket had thus been called, was at a high peak of its power and influence. It is impossible to exaggerate or overemphasize the faith which men had in the early Middle Ages. They worshiped God and His Son and the Virgin and all the saints openly and humbly. They might be guilty of violent crimes, but in the end they came back to be forgiven and eased of their burdens of sin. At no other period could the fanaticism of the Crusades have been aroused.

It is not surprising, therefore, that the tendency to monasticism became so widespread and that the bell towers of holy buildings began to dot the landscape. It is recorded that one hundred and thirteen new monasteries were built in England during the reign of Henry II, three to a year. These, unhappily, were established by foreign orders, and they were not only under the control of Norman abbots but the first quota in every instance was of Norman monks.

The Gilbertines, the only order of English origin, never became either powerful or large, twenty-six houses being the total number of branches. St. Benedict, whose rule had so sensibly avoided the extremes of austerity, was responsible for most of the monasteries in England, including that of St. Martin at Battle with its high altar above the spot where Harold fell. But that very lack of severe discipline was now beginning to show the inevitable consequences in a certain sloth in field work, in gluttony, and a slackening of fervor. When the brothers sat in the chapter house, the proceedings did not always take the form of readings from the lectern or open confession, but there could be general discussion which might turn on whether the head cook would provide a *pittance*, an unexpected extra at a meal, such as one of his round steamed puddings, rich with suet and filled with raisins like the beady eyes of homemade dolls. When the sound of the *skilla* summoned them to meals it was not to partake of *mixtum*, bread and wine. Giraldus Cambrensis, the Welshman who was twice nominated Archbishop of St. David's and twice was ousted in favor of royal choices, visited Canterbury on one occasion and saw sixteen courses served. The cheerful Benedictines did not wait to talk until their feet carried them out of the cloisters and into the *stype*, the passage leading to the cemetery, where conversation was in order; they were disposed to chat on all occasions, unlike the grim Carthusians, on whom was imposed rigorous silence.

And the Black Benedictines were very rich. They had been so well endowed and had been made the recipients of so many rich bequests in wills that they owned great tracts of lands and they collected tithes and rents and exercised feudal power over the bodies of men and women of mark and moor. An abbot's household read like a royal establishment with chamberlain, seneschal, marshal, pantler, master of horse, valet, cook, palfrey men, and porters.

Out of the Benedictines, however, there had now arisen a much more vigorous order, the Cistercians or Gray Monks, who wore habits of that color with no more than a black scapular to remind them of their derivation. As the second abbot of the parent Cistercian house at Cîteaux in France had been an Englishman, St. Stephen Harding, it was natural that the first step in expansion should be across the Channel. They initially came over in 1127 and founded an abbey at Furness. This was to prove a wonderfully fine thing for the country. The Gray Monks, who had gone back to the sterner provisions of St. Benedict's rule, were refusing donations. They were raising simple buildings, not allowing bells to weigh more than five hundred pounds and refusing to display gold and silver in their chapels. They established the rule that a monk must be bled four times a year to keep him in bodily docility as well as spiritual humbleness. And they were great farmers, depending on what they raised from the land for their subsistence. As it fell out, they were particularly successful in the raising of sheep and the proper preparing of wool. Many of the new monasteries established in Henry's time were Cistercian, and it was partly due to them that the barges on the Thames were so well filled with wool of the very finest quality.

A great man indeed was this Englishman, St. Stephen Harding. He was directly responsible for the sternness of the Cistercian concept and for the great growth of the order. He it was who trained a young novice of great physical beauty and purity of mind and set his feet so firmly in the path of piety that the youth became the famed St. Bernard of Clairvaux, the passionate advocate of the Third Crusade. On one early occasion when the members of the new order had nothing to eat, Stephen and one lay member went out to beg alms. The lay brother collected more than was needed, but when Stephen found that the bread had been given by a priest who had obtained his benefice by simony, he gave the food to some nearby shepherds. "God forbid that we should eat of his sin," he declared, "and that it should be turned into the substance of our bodies." He was the first of that long line of truly holy men who carried the title of the abbot of abbots.

The Cistercians were injecting new life into the monasterial body, but practices had grown up in the Church itself which played no small part in the growth later of Lollardism. There was, for instance, the great absurdity of sanctuary. The Church, out of a deep compassion for the unfortunate and a desire to check violence, had in the earliest days followed the Hebrew practice of setting aside certain edifices as places where fugitives could go and receive a hearing. This had become so blown up into excess by this time that no one could be taken by the law from the bounds of a church. Every innocent man had, therefore, a chance to get himself free of persecution; but also every scamp, every thief, every assassin with blood on his hands could throw off pursuit by prostrating himself before a shrine or even by the act of ringing the galilee bell. Sometimes the sanctuary seekers would "abjure the realm," which meant their consent to exile, but this was unlikely unless their crimes were heinous enough to involve the strictest punishment. The self-made exile would be stripped by the monks and given a cloak with a cross on the shoulder, and in this garb he would be sent by the nearest route to the coast. With a few pence only in his pocket he would be shipped abroad on the first boat and dumped ashore. Mostly, however, the hunted men preferred to wait in the kind shelter of the churchly wing.

Such popular sanctuaries as St. Martin's-in-the-Lane and Westminster Abbey itself were as much infested with refugees as the head of a beggar with lice. It was disconcerting to find men with hangdog faces sitting in the grounds, peering out from the entrances and slinking through the gloom of the chapels; most particularly startling to find in the frith-stool, which had once constituted the whole of sanctuary, some shifty-eyed rogue whose crimes had stirred the countryside, knowing that as long as he sat there the law could not touch him. Sometimes these furtive guests would be supported by relatives and food would be sent in to them. Sometimes, if they had learning, they supported themselves by copying. Frequently they would venture out at night and rob passers-by and then rush back into the zone of safety.

Although this was like a hair shirt on the back of the Church and a condition which the priests hated and deplored, they were committed to it by the tradition of compassion. They refused resolutely to surrender as much as an inch to the state, and they followed up with outraged vigor any desecration of sanctuary. It is even recorded of Hugh of Lincoln, most saintly of bishops, that he once stopped a procession taking a young thief to the gallows and, out of pity for the terror on the youth's face, conveyed him to safety. One may sympathize with the kindly bishop, realizing that one of the foulest of earlier cruelties was to hang men for the theft of a horse or a purse or a loaf of bread, and yet concede that this was stretching priestly privilege to a dangerous point.

Sanctuary was particularly galling to Henry, who was striving to set the administration of justice in order. He had gone to the extreme of putting the nobility on a level with common men in the matter of the "frank-pledge," by which groups of ten were formed to act in the interests of justice and to serve as pledges for each other. A system of co-operation had been established among the various counties so that the hue and cry could carry from one end of the country to the other. No man might take a stranger into his home for more than one night without becoming responsible for him. Above everything, the King was struggling to turn trial by jury into a workable system. Sanctuary, that worn-out and fantastic survival from biblical days, was a continuous thorn in the flesh of legal process.

The chantry, and the cantarists who lived on its bounty, was also reaching the proportions of a scandal. It was growing, nevertheless, out of the great depth of men's faith which created a desire for remission of sin by every means possible. When a rich man came to die he was haunted by his sins and left money for prayers to be said for the good of his soul. If he were rich enough, he would provide a fund to pay for masses and prayers over a period of years, even sometimes in perpetuity. If the funds sufficed, a chantry would be set up for the purpose. A chapel might be added to the exterior of a church or even erected by itself, and a priest would be selected to perform the duties. Early wills left such sums as six pounds, thirteen shillings, and fourpence a year for the living of the priest, with a house and a "proper garden" for his shelter. Lesser bequests kept cantarists at work at stated intervals, and they were then called *annuallers*, praying before shrines in stated churches or cathedrals. As many as thirty shrines might be found in a single edifice, with priests kneeling before them at all hours, begging mercy for dead donors. It has even been asserted that the larger churches had to keep a close schedule for the use of the various shrines and to maintain daily notice boards so that chantry arrangements might not become tangled.

A chantry post was a desirable thing to a priest who had entered the Church without a sense of dedication, and great was the competition for them. There is no way of computing the number which existed at this time, but there were literally thousands of them. It became a marked evil later on, particularly during the Black Death, when the ranks of the clergy were decimated. Not even the necessities of those dreadful days could persuade some selfish cantarists to give up their well-cushioned existences.

An intellectual awakening was under way in Europe, but this early renaissance does not seem to have touched England to any extent. Such learning as existed was in the Church, and it must be said that the standard of scholarship was not high in English cloisters. There were only one hundred and fifty books in the library at Canterbury. A small theological school existed at Oxford and would grow into the great university, but English youths who desired learning were sent to France or Italy.

The indomitable pride in the power of the Church which Thomas à Becket was to display in his struggle with the King was a reflection of church policy, although he alone had the audacity to proclaim it in unqualified terms. As the bishops had been military leaders in the early days of the Norman occupation, under obligation to maintain certain armed forces, it was not surprising that a militant note was still reflected. Churchmen were as arrogant as the barons and did not hesitate to fight for what they conceived to be their rights. There was the episode in 1176 when Cardinal Hugezin arrived as papal legate. A bitter dispute arose between the two English archbishops, Richard of Canterbury and Roger of York, as to which should sit on the right hand of the man from Rome. The Yorkist pretensions so enraged the officials in Richard's train that they knocked Roger down and jumped on his prostrate body. This, needless to state, created a great scandal, with appeals to the King and then to the Pope, and it ended in Canterbury's paying a heavy fine.

The disregard for the Saxon people which had actuated all Normans, priest and nobleman alike, was still not entirely eradicated from church leadership. High churchmen had too small regard for the lowliest of their charges and were prone to insist on everything allowed them under canon law. They still exercised a curious privilege known as *deodand,* which gave to the Church the instrument of a man's death, even if it happened to be a horse on which the continued existence of the bereaved family depended.

One cure for conditions such as these was soon to make itself felt on the Continent; but Thomas à Becket, most militant of English primates, was not to see the first glimmerings of a great reform in the Church for whose unstinted prerogatives he was to die. St. Dominic would be born in 1170 at Calaroga in Castile, and from him would come the inspiration of the Dominicans, the order of Preaching Friars. St. Francis would be born twelve years later at

Assisi and would give to the world his conception of religious asceticism in the order of Black Franciscans, dedicated to the help of the poor and the sick, and to service in poverty.

But the First Franciscans were not to arrive in England until years after Becket's death, when they would begin their magnificent ministrations in London, existing on charity and living in an unheated house in the most squalid part of London called Stinking Lane. The feminine branch of the order, known as the Poor Clares, would come still later to lend their gentle hands to nursing the poor and doing much to adjust the balance.

3

Something that was to puzzle all England and to set tongues wagging in every part of Europe was happening at Canterbury. The first intimation that the court had of it was when the new archbishop stalked into the White-Hall where Prince Henry had installed himself. The prince was now twelve years of age and as much devoted to his old tutor as ever. There also were the chief justiciar and several members of the *Curia Regis*. Their jaws must have dropped open in surprise at what they saw.

The once magnificent Becket, the lover of fine fabrics and silken shirts and costly jewels, was dressed in the coarsest of priestly garb. His compelling eyes looked out from under a heavy cowl, one hand clasped his breviary, his feet were in thonged sandals. The forty-four-year-old primate seemed to have aged. His face was pale, presumably from fasting.

He placed in the hands of the prince, as deputy for the King, his father, the Great Seal of England, saying briefly that his new duties made it impossible for him to continue in the office of chancellor. He asked that, with the surrender of the Seal, he be absolved at once of his former responsibilities. Having said this, he fell silent and waited, burying both of his long sensitive hands in the sleeves of his brown habit and keeping his gaze straight ahead.

All men knew that Henry's nomination of Becket had been for the purpose of combining the offices of archbishop and chancellor. The chief justiciar frowned in perplexity. What did this hasty relinquishment of the state office mean? What curious quirk had induced this unpredictable man to garb himself thus?

A question was asked. Did his lordship of Canterbury know the King's mind in the matter?

His lordship of Canterbury did not know the King's mind. But he knew his own. There was finality in the clipped tones he employed, the sparse sentence in which he reaffirmed his decision. He was no longer chancellor of England.

There was nothing for the openly worried group to do but accept the Seal, give him the written quittance he demanded, and then hurry off a report to the King of this amazing development.

The old Thomas à Becket no longer existed. In his place there was a zealot, a man who fasted so often that his cheekbones had sharpened and his long nose had come to dominate his face like the beak of an eagle. He prayed continuously and with the utmost humility, tears streaming down his face as his supplicating voice went on and on. He had removed himself from the archiepiscopal regality of stained glass and rich brocaded hangings to a cold room with thirl cloth at the window and no furniture save a bare pallet. He applied the knotted cord to his own back with less sparing hand than any flagellant of guilty conscience. When he went abroad he rode a poor cob or even a Cornish pony which allowed his feet to come close to the ground. He was giving to charity twice as much as the previous incumbent, who had been a compassionate man (and remembering poor Dame Brakespeare, it is hoped!); he had established the daily habit of inviting thirteen beggars into the cathedral and washing the feet of each of them himself, then feeding them well and sending them on their way with a penny. He had given up all recreations. The best chess player in England, he no longer touched the handsome pieces which had been carved for him out of walrus tusks. He donned the imposing vestments of his office only when occasion demanded.

His table was open to visitors, and the service was still on gold and silver as the dignity of the primacy demanded. The sybaritic instinct, which had once governed his way of living, continued to manifest itself in the food he served his guests. The roast capons were well peppered and seasoned with cummin; the fish was cooked in wine and water and covered with sauces made of sage, parsley, dittany, wild thyme, and garlic. But the gaunt man at the head of the table never partook of such dishes. *Mixtum* was now his daily food. His conversation was no longer witty; it turned on matters of the soul. He talked with a power and sincerity which convinced all who heard him.

He fell into the habit of visiting the cloisters and conversing with the Canterbury monks. Invariably he reached the thought which filled his mind, the power and the glory of the Church. His face would take on a rapt look as he spoke of it as the manifestation of God's rule on earth which could not be second to the sway of a king or subject to his laws. Later the monks were not surprised at the turn events took. They had read his purpose in his words and had seen in his eyes the willingness to die for what he believed. He still had the power to draw men to him and he was well loved at Canterbury.

Soon the militant archbishop bared his purpose to the world. He made a list of properties which had once belonged to the episcopal see but had been diverted to lay ownership, mostly at the time of the Conquest. The return of these lands was demanded. All the indignation that men can feel over a loss of property was in the protests of the owners, but Thomas à Becket tried the cases in his own courts and gave judgment for the return of the lands. He excommunicated Sir William Eynesford of Kent when the latter ejected a priest sent by the archbishop to a benefice controlled by the knight. The excommunication of a man was like the launching of a thunderbolt from heaven, and it seemed to everyone that the punishment in this case was much too severe for the offense; if indeed, cried the barons, it could be judged an offense at all. The news of this episode reached Henry's court at Rouen and caused a sensation there.

Henry, amazed, shocked, enraged, came back to England to discover the reason for the sudden madness of his one-time friend. Becket met him at the boat and was coldly received. Henry refused to look at him after a glance, and the words they exchanged were few. The King was aware that he need not demand an explanation of the strange conduct of the archbishop. The reason had been apparent at once in the proudly stiff carriage and the stern eye of the former chancellor. It was to be war between them.

The King struck first. He raised the point of plural appointments and insisted that the archbishop give up everything else, including the archdeaconry of Canterbury, which was a rich plum. He was on sound ground here, and Thomas had the good sense to accept his deprivations. Then the King appointed a Norman monk named Clerambault as abbot of St. Augustine's Monastery near Canterbury. He made the selection without a doubt because he knew it would be obnoxious to the archbishop. Clerambault was an odious scoundrel who began a campaign of annoyance by refusing to perform the act of canonical obedience by placing his hands in those of the archbishop, excusing himself on the ground that St. Augustine's had been independent of Canterbury before the Conquest. The case was laid before Pope Alexander, who found in favor of Clerambault. Becket, bitterly enraged, had to accept the papal rebuff. This same Clerambault will be heard of later in connection with the tragic ending of the struggle between Church and State. In 1173 also some visitors from the Vatican were at St. Augustine's and reported the abbot to be corrupt and tyrannical and the father, moreover, of twelve illegitimate children in the surrounding countryside.

Henry had not initiated the quarrel with his archbishop, but he seemed determined to fight it to a finish. He found an opportunity immediately to his hand. The Church had a vulnerable point, its refusal to allow anyone in holy or clerkly orders to be tried in state courts. The Church had its own courts, and there its servants appeared when they offended. The canonical courts were notoriously lenient. Murderers escaped with fines, thieves could count on light sentences. Only if the Church unfrocked one of its children for a misdemeanor could the King's law step in; and never under any circumstances now did the Church allow that to happen. There was a young man named Philip de Brois, of Norman descent and of reasonably high rank, who held a canonry. He killed a man whose daughter he had debauched. It was a glaring case, and the sheriff of the county moved to take Master Philip de Brois into custody for trial. Becket whisked the man out of the clutches of the common law and lodged him in safe clerical custody. The sheriff went to the King and demanded that something be done. Henry summoned the archbishop, who declared bluntly that the culprit had made settlement with the relatives of the murdered man, who were now satisfied, and that the case would be heard in the church courts in due course. Henry, striving to be moderate, proposed that the murderer be tried by a jury composed in equal parts of churchmen and lay members. Thomas gave a reluctant consent. He need not have felt concern. The jury, swayed by the superior learning of the clerical half, brought in a verdict that the revenue from his benefices should be denied the prisoner for two years and that he should stand naked before the sheriff to be flogged at the latter's discretion!

The verdict sent Henry into one of his rare rages. He foamed at the mouth, he rolled on the floor, he shouted and tore his hair. When he recovered his composure, he said to those around him in an ominously quiet tone, "Henceforth all is over between this man and me."

The conduct of Becket had been creating mixed feelings throughout the country. The nobility were against him because they saw that the flouting of royal power, even in favor of divine authority, went against feudal and hereditary privilege also. The bishops at first held aloof. Roger of Pont l'Evêque, who was now Archbishop of York, had been one of Theobald's promising young men at the same time as Becket and had never lost his feeling of jealousy over the rapid rise of his rival. Gilbert Foliot, Bishop of London, had been the choice of the chapter for the primacy before the King enforced his will, and he still smarted under the disappointment. These two dissenters, however, could not stand out against the rest of the bishops who had been caught up in the excitement and were resolved to stand by Becket's side. There was never any doubt about the rank and file of the clergy. Humble priests gave rapturous ear to their chief's talk of the power of the Church which elevated them above the servants of kings. The common people were for Becket. There will always be sympathy for anyone who stands out against authority, and in this case the mind of the populace had been dazzled and fascinated by the tales told of this strange man. Whenever he appeared in public, people ran at Becket's stirrups and fought to touch the skirt of his rusty habit.

Henry now realized that he could temporize no longer. The issue must be resolved. He summoned the bishops to a council at Westminster. They met him there on the first day of October, Becket cool and unperturbed, the others openly apprehensive. The King stalked in and, without any beating around verbal bushes, demanded brusquely that in future, for the safety of the realm, the common law should be upheld, and that when clerks and priests broke the law they should pay the full penalty, even when it sent them into the hands of the executioner.

The archbishop took a firm stand also. With a bluntness equal to the King's, he stated that the courts as well as the customs of the Church were above criticism and interference. He went on to picture the consequences if the barriers were let down which hedged the clergy in like the priestly tribe of the Levites. His final word was that churchmen in England would obey the King in all things *"saving our order."*

Henry, red of face and puffing with anger, called on each bishop in turn for his answer. All but one gave the same response, even Roger of York and Foliot of London. They would obey the King *saving our order.* This made it clear that they had reached a concerted stand in advance. The indignation of the King mounted to such a height that the bishops left the room in a panic and set out for their respective bishoprics as fast as palfrey and mule could carry them. Characteristically enough, the King reserved the most explosive of his verbal blasts for the one weak member who had lost his courage at the last moment and had not dared parrot the response *saving our order.*

It is not easy to defend Becket's refusal to clean house by seeing that priests guilty of crimes were properly punished. One point in his favor, however, has been rather generally overlooked. The function of the church courts did not stop with control of their own internal affairs. They shared with the secular branch the judicial control of the whole nation. They handled exclusively all questions of inheritance, wills, and marriage, and this constituted, apart from criminal matters, the most important arm of jurisprudence. In addition they decided all points which had to do with oaths, promises, verbal disputes. The church courts, in fact, took in more money in fees and penalties than the total revenues of the Crown. Inasmuch as learning was confined so exclusively to the clerkly orders, there was no dissatisfaction over this division, not even in the mind of the King. Becket argued that the machinery of church courts could not be disrupted as occasion demanded to pluck offenders out of the hands of the duly authorized church officers.

What was needed clearly was a thorough overhauling of the problems of divided authority. Henry saw this and proceeded at once to find a solution. Early in the following year, 1164, a conference was held at Clarendon to get these matters straightened out, attended by the peers of the realm as well as the bishops. The result was the Constitutions of Clarendon, containing sixteen articles. The most important changes made were as follows: that during the vacancy of any archbishopric, abbey, or priory of royal foundation, the revenues were to revert to the Crown; that the King's justices were to decide which court a criminal case was to be sent to and that, when it went to the clerical half, an officer of the Crown was to attend, and further, that a clerk or priest judged guilty of a felony was *no longer to enjoy the immunity of the clerkly orders;* that no tenant or officer of the King was to be excommunicated without application first to the King; that high churchmen were forbidden to leave the country without royal assent; that appeals on all points should end with the King and not be sent to Rome.

These terms spelt complete defeat for Thomas à Becket. Although he had received secret instructions from Pope Alexander, who disliked him and did not want to give him support, that he must be compliant and obey the laws of the land, the primate could not stomach this sweeping aside of everything for which he had fought. Now, however, he stood alone. The bishops had repented of their boldness at Westminster. No other course being open to him, he allowed himself to be forced into a verbal promise of acceptance. Knowing the conflicting interpretations which can later be given to a verbal statement, Henry placed the document in front of the primate and demanded that he sign it there and then. This was too much.

"Never!" cried Thomas à Becket, throwing aside the pen which had been forced into his hand. "I will never do this as long as breath is in my body!"

A last effort was made to commit him to the Constitutions. A copy of the document was torn in half, one to be kept in the royal archives, one for the archbishop himself. "I take this," he declared, "but without giving my consent or my approval." He thereupon withdrew from the conference and shut himself up in Winchester. As punishment for his weakness in making a verbal submission, he suspended himself from his office until absolution of his sin might be received from the Pope. But Alexander, who was making his headquarters at Sens in France, was not willing to support his own servant in such an open breach with the Crown. He sent legatine powers to Henry instead! To Becket he wrote in a reproving vein, absolving him from sin and advising that he resume his duties at once.

The Conquerors

Henry had won a complete victory. The Constitutions were put into effect at once, and the immunity of priestly lawbreakers was at an end. Assuming the new regulations to be retroactive, the officers of the Crown ferreted old offenders out of their clerical prisons and hiding places and brought them to trial before state courts. Those who had been guilty of crimes of violence were mutilated or hanged.

Thomas à Becket, betrayed by his own spiritual superior as he believed, had not given in. He would not do so until the Pope issued the customary bull confirming the Constitutions. And this was a step Alexander seemed singularly reluctant to take.

The bull was not forthcoming. Henry sent messenger after messenger to Sens to urge that it be issued. The Pope paid no attention.

Eight months passed, and in September Thomas à Becket was summoned to stand trial at Northampton Castle for contempt in having failed to appear in a case which had been withdrawn from his own court to that of the King. When he arrived at the castle he found there were no lodgings for himself and his train. They stayed that night in any unoccupied corners they could find, this being no hardship for the primate, who always slept on the floor. The next morning, emerging from mass, he encountered Henry, but there were no greetings between them. The King paused, frowned ominously, and walked on. It was then intimated to the primate that he must find quarters elsewhere, and he moved with his train to the monastery of St. Andrew on the edge of the town.

The records of the trial provide some interesting lights on legal procedure of the day. The castle of Northampton was one of the few in the kingdom large enough to accommodate the whole court or to house a meeting of Parliament. There were spacious chambers on each side of the Great Hall. In the room on the right the King assembled the members of the *Curia Regis,* a few important members of the baronage, and the bishops. This body proceeded to try the case without summoning the primate to appear before them. In the meantime the less important barons, the knights, and the officers from the counties were waiting in a chamber across the hall, to be summoned if the need arose. The defendant, as carefully avoided by everyone as though he had on his body the brown blotches of leprosy, stayed at the monastery, seldom stirring out from his small dark cell.

The King and the Archbishop

The hearing lasted for seven days. The results of the deliberations then began to show in the form of demands which were conveyed to the monastery and served on its grim, silent guest. First he was told he must pay for his contempt a fine of three hundred pounds. This was a colossal assessment, but the primate raised no objections. The next day a demand was made for the payment of sums he had expended in France during his term as chancellor. On the third day the heaviest blow of all fell, a demand that he make an accounting for all money received at the chancellery from vacant clerical posts while he was chancellor and to pay to the Crown the full amount. No man in the world, no king even, was rich enough to meet such an exaction. It was clear that an impasse had been reached and that the proceedings could lead to only one conclusion.

The King could not keep still while all this was going on. He strode up and down the Council Room, roaring at his officers when they advised caution or leniency, slapping at his heavy thigh with a riding whip. When one of the go-betweens returned, he would ask eager questions. What had the fellow said? How did he look? Did he bear on his countenance the signs of worry? "There can no longer be both of us in England!" he declared, again and again. "I as King, he as archbishop!" It was clear he was pressing his demands to force a resignation from Thomas à Becket. If these exactions were met by some miracle, he would think of others.

The primate continued to sit in his small cell. He was under as much strain as the King, but it showed only in the hollowness of his eyes. The bishops came to him, one at a time, suggesting this course, advocating that form of compromise. They were veering back to him spiritually but still lacked the courage to stand behind him. He had curt negatives for everything. To the arguments of Foliot, for whom he had contempt, he said scornfully, "Cease. . . . It is well known how *you*, being consulted, would reply!"

On the last day of the trial he went to St. Stephen's to celebrate mass, using the psalm *Princes sat and spake against me.* Then, arrayed in his full vestments and carrying the heavy archiepiscopal cross in his own hands, he rode to the castle, only two of his forty attendants daring to accompany him. A great crowd of the common people gathered and followed him to the gates of the castle, shouting to him to be of good cheer and praying loudly. The noise reached the chamber where the Council sat, and Henry cried out to those

[151]

about him to draw up a charge of treason against this man who was denying royal authority. The bishops, regaining a measure of their courage, refused to participate and were ordered truculently to withdraw. They changed sides of the hall, taking the chamber where the lesser nobility had stayed all these days, dicing, telling stories, cursing the obstinacy of this scurvy priest who thus kept them kicking their heels in pestilential idleness. The lesser nobles took possession of the Great Hall itself. Some stretched themselves out on the trestle tables and went to sleep.

Thomas à Becket dismounted in the courtyard and, holding the cross high in front of him, walked over the rough clay surface. There was a mist, and the tops of the towers could not be seen. A servant, more courageous than the bishops inside, dropped on a knee and begged the primate's blessing.

Inside the screens, the archbishop stopped and looked about him. Then, with an ironic sense of the fitness of it, he crossed to the chamber where his bishops were sitting. He stood in the door and looked at each one in turn with a brooding air. The Bishop of Hereford got to his feet and offered to carry the cross which the head of the Church still held out stiffly in front of him like a standard-bearer in the van of an army. The accused man shook his head. Foliot cried out at him angrily, "If you come thus armed into court, the King will draw a still sharper sword!"

Thomas motioned him to be silent and was met with another acrimonious outburst. "Fool!" cried the Bishop of London. "Fool thou hast ever been, and from thy folly, I now see, thou wilt never depart!"

The archbishop walked to the head of the chamber and seated himself, so that he seemed to be presiding at a meeting of the prelates of England. A few of the company became uncomfortable and left. The rest pressed him to give in, earnestly and vehemently. To all of them he had one reply only, "I hear you!"

Hours passed. Supper was served in the Great Hall and the sound of rattling dishes reached them and the chamber was filled with the odor of warm food. Darkness had fallen and servants brought in tall candleholders and placed them in the corners. The Bishop of Worcester, a bastard brother of the King, begged with increased heat that the primate give in and so put an end to all this. The answer was the same, "I hear you!"

The King and the Archbishop

Finally the earls of Cornwall and Leicester entered the chamber. The first named was a good friend of Becket and would remain so to the end, but when he opened his mouth to speak the archbishop cut him off impatiently.

"You come to speak of a sentence," he said. He rose from his chair, still holding the massive cross in front of him. "Do thou first listen to me. The child may not judge his father. The King may not judge me. I will be judged only by the Pope under God and, in your presence, I make my appeal to him." His voice rose to a higher pitch. "I forbid you, my lord, under threat of anathema, to pronounce your sentence."

He left the chamber and crossed the Great Hall. Supper was over and the servants were moving the dismantled trestle tables back to their positions along the wall. The place was filled with well-fed men looking for something to amuse them. They were all a little drunk from their potations, and the spectacle of the erect figure crossing the space with set face roused them to action. They began to jeer, to shout insults at him, calling him "Traitor!"

The floor was covered with rushes, on top of which lay the broken evidences of the meal, bones and the heads of fish and pieces of bread. The company began to pick up handfuls from the floor and to pelt the archbishop with this refuse.

Outside the castle walls great crowds were waiting for him. They had waited all day, being deeply concerned as to what might happen to him. "See what a glorious train escorts me!" said the archbishop. "These are the poor to whom Christ so often turned!" The people followed him to the monastery, where he had the doors thrown open and food served to them.

A small party of men, English from their faces and the special intonations in their use of the Norman tongue, entered an inn at Gravelines, a port on the Norman coast. Night was falling and so the moat around the town was deep with tidal water, locking everyone in as securely as by bar and chain within its tall stone ramparts. It was a bad time for trouble of any kind, escape being out of the question, and it was clear from the manner of some of the party that they were acutely aware of this. One of them was a very tall man with deeply lined face and a commanding eye. The landlord looked at him closely, noticing that the long and sensitive hands did not busy themselves with the good food on the table. Dropping on one knee beside the tall stranger, he begged his blessing.

One of the other men demanded in an angry whisper that the landlord get to his feet at once. Did he want to attract the attention of the other guests? The man rose slowly.

"You are the good Bishop of England, my lord," he said in a low tone. "We all know about you, my lord, and are happy you are here."

He had guessed correctly. Thomas à Becket had ridden out of Northampton in a pelting rain after leaving the castle and had made for the coast. With no attempt at disguise except that he assumed the name of Dearman, he had crossed the Channel and was now on his way to lay his case before the Pope. All over England letters had been received by the officers of the Crown, by the wardens of ports, by the captains of ships. This notice read: *Thomas, heretofore archbishop, a traitor to the King of England and a fugitive of evil intent, is to be seized and held.*

The letters had been issued too late.

4

For more than seven years the Archbishop of Canterbury remained in exile. At one time the King of France would shower him with favors and promise war in his behalf, at others he would close his doors to the uncompromising primate. Pope Alexander blew hot and cold. When Becket placed the Constitutions of Clarendon in his hands, he claimed never to have seen them and flew into a rage over the rigorous clauses. Having once commanded Becket to accept them, he now censured him for having made his first verbal submission. Henry was in Normandy, where he received the cardinals the Pope sent to him in efforts to arrive at a solution of the difficulties. The King was lavishing gold in all directions in bids for support. One meeting was arranged between King and archbishop at Montmirail which came to nothing. Through it all the primate kept suspended over the head of Henry the threat of excommunication and the laying of England under an interdict.

At first Thomas lived in the Cistercian monastery at Pontigny and about him, as always, legends began to grow. It was said that in dining with the Pope he had turned water into wine twice, not intending to do so (performing miracles before the Pope would smack of insolence) but not being able to control the divine power in his hands. Two of the stories told of him became widespread.

The first was that he wore hair drawers as well as shirts and was particular to keep them in neat repair. One night he was sewing patiently and with small success in his cell. Sensing a presence in the room, he looked up and found a lady of gentle face bending over him. She took the needle and thread into her own hands, completed the task, smiled at him with compassion, and vanished. He had recognized her at the first glance as Mary, Mother of Christ.

The other story was that on an occasion when he supped at the table of the King of France, the Queen noticed that the cuffs of his tunic were tight around his wrists and that something seemed to be moving under them. She asked him about it and he became evasive, not wanting to acknowledge that the movement was made by maggots. She insisted that he open his sleeves, and when he did the maggots were transformed into pearls which rolled onto the surface of the table and glistened in the light of the candles. The Queen would have liked one as a gift from this strange holy man, but something held her back from asking. And when the pearls had been replaced in the sleeves and the cuffs had been tied as securely as before, they turned back to maggots again.

It will be noticed at once that discrepancies exist between these stories. If the exile were as particular as the first anecdote indicates, he would not allow himself to fall into the condition involved in the second; but both seem to have been accepted generally.

At one stage of this long and bitter tug of war Henry became so incensed that he told the Cistercians in England he would confiscate their lands if their order continued to harbor Thomas à Becket at Pontigny. Accordingly Becket was under the necessity of moving and he elected to live at Sens, much to the discomfiture of Alexander.

It seemed that nothing could be done to settle the differences between these two strong and violent men who had been once on such close terms. Henry would be enraged over some episode and would unbuckle his baldric, roll himself up in the coverings of his bed, screaming with anger and biting the edges of the mattress. Becket wrote letters to his enemies in England which scorched them, and he seemed ever on the point of excommunicating the King. Persons who were thus thrust outside the Church were supposed to be damned for eternity; no one was to come near them or speak to them. A curse was on their food, on the glass from which they drank, on their clothes, on their couches, on the air they expelled from their lungs. The Pope was continually restraining Becket. The King, he would say, must not be put under the ban, not at least until after the next Easter. Then it would become the Easter after that.

At the end of five years Henry reached a momentous decision in another matter. He would have his eldest son crowned King of England. For a moment the contest with Becket must be set aside to consider what this meant. On the surface it indicated this much and no more, that Henry was removing all possible doubts of the succession and so insuring the country from any of the trouble which followed the death of Henry I. Such, however, was the smallest part of what was in the King's mind. There was no reason to anticipate opposition to his son after his own death. His position was so strong that no other claims existed. He had four healthy sons, and it was not within the range of possibility that all would die. In addition, Henry had the engrained Norman sense of possession and he would not give up willingly the brightest gem in his diadem, the kingship of England. No, his decision had a much more far-reaching implication. He wished to show that his dominions had outgrown the appellation of kingdom, that with such broad frontiers he must set up rulers under himself, his own sons: Henry in England, Normandy, and Anjou, Richard in Aquitaine, Geoffrey in Brittany, John in Ireland (alas, poor Ireland!), with himself the overlord of all; in other words, the empire of the west, with himself seated on a throne as important as that of Charlemagne. The crowning of the eldest son may be accepted as the final indication, after so many others, of the nature of the dream in Henry's mind.

At the time that he announced the imminence of his son's coronation, someone in his presence spoke of the King of Germany. Henry flew into a temper and cried, "Why do you diminish his dignity by calling him King instead of Emperor of the Germans?"

The decision to elevate the prince to royal rank raised a serious difficulty, for only the Archbishop of Canterbury possessed the right to crown a king of England. Henry had no intention of giving in to Becket in order to have him in England for the ceremony, and he wrote to Alexander asking papal dispensation by which the Archbishop of York might preside. The Pope obliged with the necessary authorization but, on receiving a vehement protest from Becket, changed his mind and wrote direct to Roger of York, withdrawing his consent. It was said that the second letter was not received. At any rate, the ceremony was performed and young Henry began to assume some of the responsibilities of kingship. This rather complicated affair was to prove the fuse which finally set everything ablaze.

In spite of the exile's bitterness over what had happened, a meeting was arranged between the two enemies at a place called Fréteval. Henry surprised the archbishop by agreeing that he was to return to England to crown the young King a second time and that the differences between them would be settled. After this had been arranged the two old friends rode to one side and talked together with no one in earshot. The churchman claimed later that the essence of their secret talk was this, that Henry agreed there must be punishment for the bishops who had officiated at the first coronation. Certain it is that Thomas suddenly sprang from his saddle with a return of his old agility and knelt beside the King. Henry dismounted in turn and held the clerical stirrup while Thomas à Becket climbed back into the saddle. Many saw what had occurred, and the incident caused much excited speculation. Had a full reconciliation been brought about?

When the time came for the two men to part there was a long silence between them. Then Thomas said in a low tone, "My lord, my heart tells me that I part from you as one whom you shall see no more in this world."

The archbishop encountered difficulties in arranging his return to England. He had been promised the restitution of his archiepiscopal estates and benefices and the immediate payment of some of the money due him. Nothing reached him, and the requests he sent to the King met with no response. Finally, after borrowing three hundred pounds to defray his expenses, he set sail from France and landed in due course on the coast of Kent.

It was the resourceful man of the chancellery days and not the uncompromising archbishop who took charge of the landing. He knew that the sheriff of Kent, Sir Randulf de Broc, had been taking the crops from Canterbury lands and had burned the stables and possessed himself of all the livestock. The sheriff was now riding up and down the coast like a raging lion, declaring that the exile would not be permitted to land alive. Becket heard also that the three bishops he planned to punish for taking part in the coronation had gathered at Dover and would try to prevent him from delivering his writs. The clever mind behind the austere brow, that resourceful mind which had once functioned so well in the King's behest, saw a way to outwit all of them.

He sent a small sailing ship ahead of him, and a boy was put ashore. It was later said that the boy was a woman in disguise. At any rate, this innocent-appearing arrival went at once to St. Peter's Priory, where the Archbishop of York was staying. He succeeded in placing in the hands of York the notice of his suspension and had vanished before the recipient realized what had happened. The same thing happened to the bishops of London and Salisbury, who had the notices of their excommunication pressed into their hands. The affair threw all of the King's party into a panic. The blustering Randulf de Broc rode about Dover but did not succeed in finding any trace of the clever messenger.

The whole coast was now ablaze. When Thomas à Becket sailed up the river to Sandwich instead of landing at Dover, he found the townspeople out in force and ready to defend him against the armed troops of De Broc. That far from subtle servant of the King arrived in time to witness the landing of the archbishop but found his hands tied by the royal safe-conduct which the primate carried. He sat his horse and glowered at the demonstration of the citizens, marking victims for future reprisals.

Becket rode at once to Canterbury. At each foot of the way, it seemed, he was passing through kneeling throngs. Processions of chanting priests met him, showing their joy at his return. It was a triumph for the man who would not bend his back to the storm, who dared the lightning.

At Canterbury a sad disillusionment awaited him. Seven years of neglect and poverty had turned his palace into a shambles. It was partly dismantled, with the windows devoid of glass, cobwebs everywhere, the beautiful brass on the doors defaced and broken. There were no supplies in the place, and the servants were cowed by long adversity.

But he did what he could to restore order and then set out for Winchester to see his old pupil and admirer who had now been crowned Henry of England. Many men had rallied to him, a few even of the nobility, and he rode through Rochester and up to London with an escort of armed attendants, as in the old days when he had been chancellor and proud of all the display he could mount. As he approached the great city a company of three thousand priests and soldiers joined him and marched ahead to London Bridge, chanting a *Te Deum*. All London, it seemed, had turned out to greet him. It was a truly royal welcome such as a primate had never before been accorded. Disregarding a command which reached him to return at once to Canterbury and stop stirring up dissension, Thomas à Becket rode as far as Harrow. Here he received word that the young Henry would not see him. His first thought was to remain where he was until his demand for an audience had been met. Finally, however, he decided he should spend Christmas, which was fast approaching, at Canterbury. His return journey was less triumphant, but nevertheless great throngs met him at every turn, and it was clear that his popularity with the common people was at its height.

In the meantime Henry had been informed of everything. He was in Bayeux at the castle of Bur, where William of Normandy had made Harold swear his oath of allegiance. The news of the excommunication of the bishops had been followed by the arrival at Bur of the three prelates. Henry saw York but was compelled to refuse audience to the others because they were under the ban. This chagrined him beyond words, being an acknowledgment of the validity of the writs, but as King he did not feel free to break the law of the Church. When the reports came of the welcome which had been extended to the exile, he fell into a long silence. Roger of York was with him at the time and is reported to have said, "As long as Thomas lives, you will have neither good days nor peaceful kingdom nor a good life."

The words of the prelate drove him into one of his furies. He raved and fumed and then was guilty of the greatest error of a lifetime. Raising a fist above his head, he fell into a tirade, concluding with, "What cowards have I about me that no one will deliver me from this lowborn priest!"

The fateful sentence, spoken in a moment of uncontrollable passion, had not been uttered for a purpose. Henry did not want Becket killed. Death would be a triumph for the recalcitrant archbishop; it would make him a martyr in the eyes of the world for all time.

There were other ways of dealing with him. The King must have repented the words as soon as they left his tongue. He was alert enough certainly to discover that four of his train had disappeared and to demand that they be found and halted. He sent mounted riders to all the ports of Normandy with orders that none of them was to be allowed to embark for England.

The precautions taken were of no avail. The four knights had been wary and had separated. Each had succeeded in getting away on small ships. Henry threw his arms above his head in despair when he learned this. He knew that he had lost. In a fit of temper he had thrown away everything for which he had striven so long.

The first of the four knights who thus set out to remove from the King's path the haughty primate was the same Reginald Fitzurse who had once ridden in Becket's train, grown heavier and darker and a little more passionate with the years and wearing on his shield *three bears passant*. The others were Hugh de Moreville, forester of Cumberland and owner of the castle of Knaresborough, who was reported to have had a young Saxon boiled to death on a false accusation; William de Tracey, who had a great reputation for bravery but was said to be base and ferocious; and Richard le Breton.

5

It was Christmas Day. A cold day, with frost in the ground and a leaden sky. But the cold outside seemed easier to bear than the frigid atmosphere in the untended and dilapidated palace of the archbishop. There was little to eat. A shipload of supplies from France had been seized by Randulf de Broc and the crew imprisoned. A brother of his, Robert de Broc, had stopped a train with food and had mutilated a horse and a mule belonging to the see. The members of the staff were an unhappy lot. It is hard enough at any time to face danger; it is doubly taxing to face it with empty stomachs.

Before the performance of high mass Thomas à Becket preached in the chapter house, taking as his text "On earth, peace to men of good will." So many came to hear him that they stood in the aisles and filled every inch of space from which the tall, spare figure could be seen and the passionate voice heard. But the tone of the inexorable man returned from exile had no passion in it at first. There was love and compassion only as he expounded his message. He made it clear that he knew the fate in store for him. With great emotion he referred to the death of Alfege, the primate who had been killed by the Danes, and when he said, "There will soon be another," people laid their heads in their hands and sobbed. The backs of the monks in the choir shook with the grief which filled them.

Perhaps, as he spoke, the archbishop's mind went back to the Christmas Day when he had first seen the King, when Henry had faced him with thumbs tucked in his belt and had smiled instant approval. Their relationship had started with mutual liking and confidence. Why had it become distorted into opposition and hate?

But if his thoughts turned back it was for a moment only. The voice of the passionate man changed. It was now raised in denunciation. For those who were not men of good will there could be no peace, there must be punishment. For the first time his listeners realized the significance of the candles burning beside the preacher. Excommunication was delivered by candle and book. A tremor of excitement and fear swept through the chapter house. What did the archbishop intend to do? Would he take the last desperate step, the final audacity, of placing the King outside the law of God? Or— and they shuddered at this possibility—would he ban by interdict all religious observances in the country and leave them to the machinations of the devil?

In a voice shaken with anger, Thomas à Becket cursed the men who had despoiled the precincts of Canterbury in his absence. He named Randulf de Broc and, raising one of the candles, he extinguished it and threw it behind him as though it were now contaminated. Next he named the other De Broc, the mutilator of animals, and a second candle was raised, blotted out, and cast aside. Finally he dealt with two church officials who were occupying incumbencies without his approval, and again candles were tossed away. "May they all be cursed," he cried in a loud voice, "by Jesus Christ, and may their memory be lost!"

As he descended from the pulpit and walked to the high altar, he said to his cross-bearer, "One martyr, St. Alfege, you already have; another, if God will, you will have soon."

Three days passed. On Monday, the twenty-eighth of December, the four knights arrived at Saltwood Castle, which belonged to the see of Canterbury but had been taken by Randulf de Broc. There they remained overnight, and early the next morning they rode the fifteen miles of Roman road from Lympne to Canterbury, where they stopped outside the walls at the priory of St. Augustine's and were received by that man of bad repute, the Abbot Clerambault. From there they rode, as the twilight shadows began to fall, into the city, Randulf de Broc accompanying them, grim-faced over the action taken against him, a troop of mounted men at his back. The black looks of the party froze the people with fear. Commands were given in sharp tones: Stand back, no interference, no noise! Then Reginald Fitzurse, taking upon himself leadership, issued a definite order. All the people of Canterbury must return to their homes and stay there behind closed doors and without lights.

A meal had been served at three o'clock in the palace, not a good meal, for the household was still badly disorganized. There was no rich sauce on the fish to please the once cultivated palate of the archbishop. It did not matter. He finished his food and drank a glass or two of wine. It was a silent repast, the servants moving on tiptoe and with lowered heads. The primate as well as his servants knew of the arrival of armed men in the town. He rose from the table, his strength renewed for the ordeal ahead of him.

Dusk had now settled over the cathedral town, but only in the palace had candles been lighted. The servants were reluctant to have them, feeling there might be security in darkness. The hymn of grace over, their master repaired to his own room and seated himself on the side of the bed, where he conversed with a small group of his closest adherents, including John of Salisbury, his chaplain William Fitzstephen, and a visitor named Grim from Cambridge, a Saxon monk.

The knights reached the court before the hall, and here they dismounted and left their weapons. The outer court was crowded with the usual beggars, and the four men pushed their way through them, wearing over their chain mail long white cloaks. They were escorted to the room where the archbishop sat.

Reginald Fitzurse, in his role of leader, said, "We bring you the commands of the King."

It was an unfortunate opening. If the King had sent commands it was unfitting that they should be delivered by messengers of such comparative unimportance. It was worse if they were assuming royal sanction for their visit. Thomas à Becket, his brow drawn into a frown, refused to look at them and, at first, to address them. It was only when Fitzurse began to recite the wrongs which the primate had heaped on the King that his one-time leader took a part in the conversation. The excommunications laid on the bishops, declared Becket, were from the Pope and had been uttered with the knowledge and consent of the King. Fitzurse was thunderstruck. "What is it you say?" demanded the knight. "Do you charge the King with treachery?"

Becket turned then and looked at his former aide. "Reginald, Reginald," he said, "I do no such thing."

The tone of the altercation rose to greater heat. The archbishop, unable as usual to control his high temper, became involved in sharp rebuttals to the charges they made. Fitzurse then took it upon himself to say that the King demanded the departure of the archbishop and his servants from the realm, never to return.

A silence fell on the room at that. Thomas à Becket rose to his feet. He towered over the four stocky knights in their white cloaks, making them look insignificant and as futile as schoolboys debating with their master. He spoke in even tones at first. "Never again shall I leave England." There was no mistaking the finality of the words. "Do you think I will fly?" His voice rose suddenly in a burst of scornful laughter, then subsided again. "Not for living man, not for the King, will I fly!"

Then his voice dropped lower to a mystical note. "You cannot be more willing to kill me," he said, "than I am to die."

Fitzurse and his companions realized now that nothing but violence was left to them. The man who had once served under the Becket banner turned a face distorted with deep passion to the group about the primate. "We command you," he said brusquely, "to see that this man does not escape."

The dusk had deepened into darkness, and the knights stumbled as they left the chill of the palace and felt their way across the unlighted courtyard, now deserted, issuing a command to their men, "To arms!" The gate was closed and the armed troops poured inside, shouting, "Reaux! Reaux!" The monks threw aside their cloaks under a sycamore tree and buckled on their swords.

In the meantime two palace servants, Osbert and Algar, shut and barred the entrance to the palace hall. Then they ran frantically from door to door and window to window, bolting them against the aggressors. Thomas à Becket was left alone. He was so deeply sunk in thought that he did not hear the slamming of the shutters, otherwise he would have commanded the servants to stop. He had not moved from the rumpled bed but sat up straight, staring at the solitary candle. When seen in dim light his face always wore an aspect of singular nobility; the fire of the eyes subdued under the finely arched eyebrows, the proud and courageous nose with a generosity of bridge which suggested the soldier, the mobile lips from which the bitterness had departed. What were his thoughts as he sat there? If they were known, the enigma which was Thomas à Becket would be solved. Was he possessed of such pride that he could not recede from a position once taken and so must go on to a tragic death? Was it ambition which activated him, a determination to set himself above everyone, even the King? Was he an actor, a supremely fine one, awaiting the cue for his last great scene? Or was he possessed of such faith, such an overwhelming sense of the greatness of the God he served, that he wanted to fill the earth with voices praising Him and none else?

He was so deeply absorbed that he did not notice the cessation of the bells which had been ringing for vespers.

His people returned to the musing archbishop. They were fairly panting with fear. The knights were arming themselves. What was to be done?

Thomas à Becket, roused from his thoughts, said in an indifferent tone, "Let them arm."

A sound of hammering and broken glass suddenly disturbed the silence of the palace. The knights, finding the doors barred against them, were breaking through the oriel window in a passage between the hall and the private apartments of the archbishop. One of the frightened servants thought of a little-used corridor which ran from the suite to the entrance of the north cloister. By going at once, they could escape into the cathedral, where vespers were now being sung and where they would be in sanctuary.

But Thomas à Becket was not concerned with safety. He preferred to wait for the armed assassins who had been sent, as he had every reason to believe, by the King. They had to take him by the arms and practically drag him to the passage. Once there, he recollected that he had intended to be present at vespers and he then did not hold back. He insisted, however, that someone return for the archiepiscopal cross, and he waited, quite oblivious to the sounds of armed invaders within the palace, until the monk Grim arrived with it. As a result he had not traversed the full distance of the north cloister when the knights issued from the palace and turned into the south passage. Even in the deepening gloom the followers of the primate could see across the garth that the invaders were driving a group of monks ahead of them and that Reginald Fitzurse was brandishing an ax over his head. This was too much. They seized their reluctant master by the arms and hurried him into the chapter house.

He was now in sanctuary, and the men with him sighed with relief, convinced that the pursuers must give up. One servant, however, tugged at the archiepiscopal sleeve and whispered that it would be wise to take refuge in the chapel of St. Blaise. This was a very small chapel above that of St. Benedict and was reached by an obscure door which would not be seen in the dark. If Thomas à Becket heard him, he paid no heed. He knew there were many safe hiding places in the blackness of the cathedral, but he had no intention of concealing himself. He crossed the chapter house and entered the lower north transept.

Pause now for a moment. The tall archbishop was walking to martyrdom for a cause which was lost centuries ago and has been abandoned long since. But this much must be said for the strange man who would die rather than yield; he had always known what the ending must be and in his last moments he was sublime.

The chanting of the monks in the Lady Chapel had stopped with an abruptness which told of panic. Word of an armed intrusion had reached them as they began the fourth psalm of vespers, and the sound died in their throats. Some did not hesitate to scatter and flee for safety, but most of them made no effort to leave, remaining motionless in their stalls behind the high arched screen, their heads lowered, their hands taut on their prayer books.

Can history present a more dramatic and terrifying moment than when Thomas à Becket walked slowly into the transept? The tall figure moved through the gloom of the great church, lighted in small areas only by the candles burning before shrines. He found his way through the pillars, the whole arched space above a void of impenetrable darkness from which faint echoes came; walking without haste, although the clang of armed feet could be heard not far behind on the stone flagging. The courageous Grim carried the cross in the lead, at the same leisurely pace of the man whose fate he expected to share.

As the primate reached the steps of the choir above which the porphyry chair of the archbishops stood (which, clearly, he hoped to attain so they would have to kill him there), his followers swung the gates to and would have locked them if their master had not rebuked them.

"The church of God," he said sternly, "must not be made a fortress!"

His people scattered at that. Having refused this last precaution, he was lost. None wanted to share his fate save the stouthearted Grim, who still stalked ahead, maintaining the cross meticulously at the prescribed level.

Thomas à Becket had not reached the chair when the first of the knights entered heavy-footed into the choir space. The others followed and remained there for a moment, unable to see anything.

"Where is the traitor?" demanded Fitzurse in a voice which echoed from all parts of the cathedral.

No answer came. They began to fear that the man they sought had done what common sense dictated and had found refuge in the crypt or in some dark recess.

"Where is the archbishop?"

An answer came to that without any pause. "Reginald, here I am." Thomas à Becket emerged from the shadows and walked down the steps toward them. Now they saw him clearly, and it is impossible that they could have escaped a feeling of awe and dread. His face had taken on the rapt look of martyrdom.

"Here I am," he repeated. "No traitor, but the archbishop and priest of God. What do you want?"

Word of what was happening had passed from house to house in Canterbury. Disobeying the order to remain indoors, people poured out into the streets, saying to one another, "They will kill our kind father." They moved in a body to the cathedral and began to rush in through the east entrance. Hugh de Moreville detached himself from his companions and ran down the broad dark aisle, waving his sword above his head and calling out in a loud voice that no one was to move a step closer. They could see little, the bewildered citizens, save the faint glow of the candles at side shrines and perhaps the lights of the Lady Chapel far ahead of them. They were aware of De Moreville, however, as he swung his sword and threatened to kill anyone who made a move forward. They were unarmed and so there was nothing they could do, although they were desperately afraid that somewhere ahead of them in the dark their patron and great friend was being done to death.

Many stories are told of what ensued in the space later called The Martyrdom. It is said that bitter taunts were exchanged, that the knights made efforts to seize the archbishop and carry him off a prisoner. It seems of little moment to recount all the conflicting details. Save these: that the first blow, delivered by the sword of De Tracey (whose shield, appropriately, carried two bars gules, as red as blood), was taken by Grim on his raised arm. It shattered the bone, and the sole remaining adherent of the doomed man fell back against the wall. The point of the sword, however, had touched the scalp of the archbishop. He took a step closer to them with blood pouring down his lofty forehead.

"I am prepared to die for Christ," he said, "and for His Church."

They were his last words. De Tracey's sword smote him again. Le Breton then struck him, and he sank to the floor. De Broc stepped viciously on the neck of the wounded man and broke his skull open so that the brains were spread on the stone.

Pointing with the bloody end of his weapon at the inert form, De Broc said: "The traitor is dead. We may go."

6

A Saxon monk named Godric, living the life of an anchorite where the Wear River rises in the Cumberland Hills at the far limit almost of the kingdom, knew of the death of Thomas à Becket the instant it occurred. This is the most extreme case on record, but it was amazing how quickly the news spread. A major convulsion of nature —an earthquake, a rain of forty days and forty nights, the appearance of a terrifying comet in the sky—could not have created a wider and wilder interest.

After the killers had left the cathedral and had ridden away in a sudden terror over what they had done (riding furiously with dread at their shoulders all the way to the castle of De Moreville in Cumberland, to find that the hermit Godric had already spread the word of their crime), the monks cleared the cathedral and hastily closed and locked the doors. They knew that Robert de Broc, who did not seem to share the remorse of the others, was ransacking the palace. There was nothing they could do. They waited until the insensitive brother of the brutal Randulf had broken open all the archiepiscopal coffers and taken possession of the state papers of the Church and stripped the place of costly vestments, the utensils of gold and silver, even the books and furniture, and had left. Then they departed from the cathedral, doing nothing about the body.

Later in the night Osbert, the chamberlain, mustered up the courage to return. With slow and reluctant steps he made his way to the north transept, holding a candle above his head, starting at every sound. The body, he found, was lying on its face, the scalp hanging by no more than a piece of skin. Cutting off a bandage from his habit, Osbert bound the head with fingers which had become reverent and tender.

Other monks now followed him into the darkness of the great church. Speaking in the lowest of whispers, they decided to turn the body over. They found that the countenance of their murdered master was strangely full of peace. The eyes were closed, the lips seemed to smile, there was no more than a single streak of blood on the bridge of the nose. They stood about him in awed silence for several moments and looked down at him. All doubts they might have had about Thomas à Becket were gone.

Then, still in the most complete silence, they brought clean linen and bound up the head properly. The body was lifted and carried to the high altar, which was called the Glorious Altar of Conrad, and laid there in state. Candles were lighted around it, and a vessel was placed where it would catch the blood which still dripped from the mutilated head. No longer, then, could their grief be restrained. They stood in a circle, these men who had served under him, and not all of whom had been loyal by any means, and wept bitterly. It was a long time before they turned silently to go back to their dormitories and left Thomas à Becket to his God.

People who have been reared in the Christian faith believe in miracles, and it caused no surprise the next morning when Brother Benedict told the other Canterbury monks of a vision which had come to him as he slept. Without knowing how or why, he had found himself in the choir and had seen the archbishop rise from where he lay and stand before the altar as though to begin mass. The monk, in bewilderment and fear, had approached closer.

"My lord," he asked in a whisper, "are you not dead?"

"I was dead," answered Thomas à Becket, "but I have risen."

While the monk watched in still greater confusion of mind, an invisible choir had begun to chant, and the voice of the primate had joined in with, "*Arise, why sleepest thou, O Lord? Arise, and cast us not out forever.*"

None doubted that what Benedict had seen had actually happened. With reverence and yet a trace of dread, they approached the altar where the body lay. A few of the candles had guttered out during the night. They blazed up again suddenly, and some of the watchers were certain that a hand not of this earth had been responsible. Some of them also declared they had seen the arm of the archbishop raised to bless them.

The good people of Canterbury had not slept. They had lived out the night in groups in their darkened houses, wondering what the assassins might do next and what sublime things might be happening where the body of the martyred man lay. When the word came from the cathedral soon after dawn that miracles had begun already, there was almost a frenzy to visit the spot and see the sacred clay. They swarmed up the aisles and gazed with awe at the calm face on the altar. Suddenly a woman, who had been so ill that she had been carried to the cathedral, cried that she was cured. She walked out with no assistance, her family following and rejoicing.

This started such a wave of fervor that no one in that large assembly seemed human. They laughed and wept, they prayed, they went down on their knees to touch pieces of cloth or handkerchiefs to the reddened stones. Many more who had been afflicted cried that they were cured.

The anti-Becket faction realized at once the danger of allowing this emotional wave to spread throughout the country, and quick steps were taken to suppress it. Sir Randulf de Broc, the perfect model of the brutal tyrant of the law, was preparing to remove the body and dispose of it before it could be given proper burial. Hearing this, the monks hastened to bury their master before the altar of St. John the Baptist in the crypt. They built a wall around it with a small opening through which the sarcophagus could be seen. Even the bloodstained hands of Randulf de Broc did not dare disturb this tomb.

When the news reached London, the Archbishop of York, who was there, went into the pulpit at St. Paul's to declare that the death of Thomas à Becket was an act of divine punishment. The violent man of Canterbury, he cried, had perished like Pharaoh in his wickedness and pride. Other bishops followed his example, and from pulpits all over the land rang out denunciations of the dead man as a traitor. It was even demanded that his body should not be left in consecrated ground.

All this wildness and fury had no effect. The people of England had seen the hand of God in what followed the death of the archbishop, and all the fulminations of all the bishops in the land could not make them change their minds.

Miracles followed in quick succession. People came on crutches, gazed through the opening in the wall, and threw their supports away as they walked out. The miraculous power showed itself most often in the restoration of eyesight. Many blind people stood before the tomb in the crypt and went away, declaring they could see. One of these beneficiaries was a man whose eyes had been put out by the law, and this is a story which should be told.

The man in question, whose name was Aylward, had been sentenced to this most horrible of punishments because he had broken into the house of a neighbor who owed him money and had taken away goods to compensate himself. Perhaps he was a moneylender and a hard creditor. At any rate, he stood in ill repute with the people thereabouts, for they combined to swear against him. Sentence of mutilation had been pronounced and duly carried out. This had happened in Bedford, and one night Thomas à Becket appeared at the bedside of the blinded man and told him to go the next day to Bedford Church and pray to have his eyesight restored. This Aylward did and suddenly cried out in a madness of excitement that it was as the saintly primate had promised, that he could see! To prove it, he left the church alone, without hesitation or stumbling. This, as might be expected, created more of a sensation than anything which had happened up to that time; for where his eyes had once been were dark and gaping sockets, and if ever man was blind for life, it was this unfortunate redeemer of debts.

An investigation followed at once. Aylward was taken before a group made up of priests and citizens who studied his face with the greatest care. While they did this a strange thing happened. All of a sudden they turned to look at each other, to nod their heads in conviction. Each of them was convinced that the sight of the man had been restored as he had sworn! Somewhere in the unsightly folds of scar tissue, far back in the ugly sockets, something could be seen: a light, they thought, a mere pin point of light. This light was not always there, it came and went, but for that one moment at least all of them had seen it.

Aylward went on living thereabouts and declaring he could see.

It would have been impossible for those who wrote of these things at the time, and even more so for those who described them later, to make any accurate count of the miracles which were reported. They ran literally into the thousands. The power to speak and acknowledge sins was granted to dying people who had lost the use of their faculties. People appealed to the Martyr when in peril on the sea. Miracles of all kinds were performed by his blood, which had been saved in some quantity. It was given away in single drops. A receptacle containing no more than a drop would suddenly be seen to have filled, and this fluid would possess the full potency of the original. For centuries thereafter there were in existence quantities of the Water of St. Thomas, as it was called, and the power to create miracles was still in it.

While these miraculous manifestations were going on, and the whole Continent of Europe had united in belief, it remained a crime in England to say publicly that any miracle had occurred. It was at the risk of flogging or worse that a priest prayed for the soul of Thomas à Becket or mentioned his name in service. There were equal penalties for visiting the spot where he died, but in spite of this the roads were black with pilgrims. For a year no services were allowed in Canterbury.

But no official dam, no matter how strongly built or stubbornly maintained, could hold back such a flood. Within two years the evidence was so overwhelming that the Pope issued a bull of canonization, and Thomas à Becket became St. Thomas, the most appealed to, the most talked about, the most revered saint in the calendar.

Now that the sanction of Rome had been given, all doubts about the miracles ceased, all tendency to think or speak ill of him stopped.

He had become so great in the eyes of men that for a time he monopolized all attention. Belief in him was manifested in unexpected ways. William of Sicily, who had married Henry's daughter Joanna, erected a statue to the Martyr in the church of Monreale. Louis VII of France came to England to pray at the tomb of the man he had sometimes supported, sometimes neglected and opposed. He brought a gold cup and a very large diamond as gifts for the shrine of the saint. His visit was a dull excursion and without drama, which is not strange, because Louis was a dull man.

The worship of St. Thomas continued unabated for several centuries. It became the custom for people to make a pilgrimage to Canterbury to pray at the tomb of the Martyr, often donning the gown of the palmer and carrying a staff. The three roads which led into the cathedral city were never free of men, women, and children, walking to the tomb. They came from all parts of the Continent as well, and the inns thereabouts flourished on the trade of guests who spoke no English but displayed their intentions by holding up a vial or the English penny which each pilgrim was supposed to leave. It has been estimated that as many as one hundred thousand pilgrims walked to Canterbury in a single year. In 1220, in the reign of Henry III, who was a great builder (and a bitter failure as a king in every other respect), the new cathedral was finished and a shrine of unexampled beauty was erected on the spot where the archbishop had fallen.

He became to the people a symbol of everything right, a protector always looking down from the heavenly regions and ready to stand between them and aggression.

One hundred years later a weak and dangerous king was building the wharf where the Tower of London fronted on the river in order to combat the action of the tides and to provide entrances from the water. He had no other motive, as it turned out, but the people were bitterly opposed. They suspected everything he did, and it seemed to them that what he was striving to do was to turn the Tower into a great fortress with which he could overawe and control London. They were delighted, therefore, when the silt under the foundations proved too unstable to hold and the walls came tumbling down one night. The King persisted and, with the assistance of a great architect and builder named Adam de Lamburn, began again. One year later to the very day, there was a similar crash. The barbican which had been going up above the wharf toppled over into the high tide-waters swirling about the base. This could not be coincidence, said the people of London to each other. Never before had the hand of God been seen more certainly than in this destruction of the treacherous King's work. And then a story grew out of the incident which was repeated all over the city and then all over England, and was believed by everyone.

On the night of the second crash a priest was passing and saw a figure, dressed in the robes of an archbishop and holding up a large cross, approach the masonry. There was a lack of substantiality about the figure, an unearthly glow, which told the frightened priest he was witnessing a visitation from the world of the spirit. Losing all power of motion, he remained where he was and saw the nebulous visitor approach the walls, asking in a stern voice, "What do ye here?" The cross was raised and then brought sharply down against the masonry. Instantly the walls crumbled and began to fall. There was a loud reverberation, a swirling of waters; the strange figure vanished, and so did the walls, tumbling into the eager current of the Thames.

The priest, regaining his faculties, turned and ran. To the people who came rushing out of the houses and rubbing sleepy eyes, or from the doors of taverns in obscure closes and corners where behind bolted shutters they had been defying curfew, he told what he had seen, saying that he had recognized the spirit at once. It was St. Thomas the Martyr.

The most striking evidence of the sentiment which existed throughout the Middle Ages is to be found in the burial of the Black Prince. This great warrior, who ranks in English history with Richard Coeur de Lion, died at an early age of an incurable disease, and his last days were spent in planning for his final home on earth. He wanted to be buried beside Thomas à Becket and he designed in the most minute detail the tomb he desired built for his bones. His wishes were carried out so far as the tomb was concerned, a handsome sarcophagus with the effigy of the great warrior, and the lions of England combined with the lilies of France. But it was deemed unfitting that so great a memorial should be erected in the crypt, and so it was placed instead near the site of what undoubtedly had been the Lady Chapel, where vespers were being sung on the night of the martyrdom. It is a pity that his last wishes were thus disregarded. There were points of difference between the primate and the prince but also some qualities they shared in common. They would have slept through the centuries in amity.

7

As for the four knights whose rash act of violence thus worked ill for the King they thought to serve, many legends about them have found their way into histories. They are generally supposed to have lived like lepers, that even dogs ran from them, that they could never escape the evidences of a revulsion which all nature had conceived for them. It has been most often told of them, and most generally believed, that they were summoned to Rome to receive sentences of punishment from the Pope, which took the form of going to the Holy Land to fight for the cross. Three of them are supposed to have died in Palestine and to have been buried in the church of the Templars in Jerusalem. The fourth, William de Tracey, because he had struck the first blow, was reserved for a special form of punishment. He was not permitted to reach the Holy Land because a strong wind always blew in his face and drove him back. This legend was believed even by his descendants, about whom it was written that "the Traceys have always the wind in their faces."

The facts, of course, are quite different. Each member of the execrated group remained in seclusion for some time and was then taken back unobtrusively into the royal service. De Moreville had been suspended for the first year from his post of justiciar-itinerant in the north counties but was then reinstated. Reginald Fitzurse certainly went to Ireland with the forces of the Norman barons. He remained there, founded a family which retained the estates he had won with the sword, and became later a branch of the MacMahons. Four years after the dark events which stamped him with the brand of Cain, William de Tracey was made a justiciar in Normandy and lived out the balance of his life there. Le Breton seems to have settled down on his estates in Somersetshire.

From this it is clear that Henry did not try to escape his share of the guilt by laying it all on the shoulders of the men who had heeded his ill-considered words. As will be shown later, he was prepared to assume guilt himself and to seek expiation in his own way. However, his willingness to take the knights back into his service affords

additional light on his motives and his reactions. He must have become reconciled to what they had done after the first reverberations
had died down and the danger of sacerdotal lightnings had been
averted. He felt an increasing relief that the primate, immovable
in life, had been thus cleared from his path. Not then could the
future be glimpsed, and Henry would have no realization of what
this would do to his memory; how his greatness as a king would be
obscured and forgotten and he would be remembered for the shod-
dier aspects of his life, seen against the dark curtain of one of the
worst crimes in history.

8

Henry received word of the death of his uncompromising opponent at Argenteuil in Normandy. Without uttering a sound he turned
and went into a seclusion which lasted for three days, seeing no one
and refusing food. What his thoughts were can well be imagined.
He would be under no delusions as to what this meant to him. The
opinion of the world would be against him, he would be blamed
and condemned, he might expect that the Pope would excommunicate him as the instigator of the murder. He would know this: in
the duel he had fought with his one-time friend he had emerged
the loser, even though it had been necessary for the archbishop to
die in order to score a victory.

The most superficial examination of Henry's character would
leave no doubt, however, that these considerations would not occupy
his thoughts to the exclusion of everything else. It has already been
said that he never completely lost an affection, and it must be remembered that his friendship with Becket had been a deep one.
There is every reason to believe that, as he wrestled with his conscience and his unhappiness through those three long days, regrets
for the death of that strange man were often uppermost in his mind.
Perhaps he would think of the many times he had ridden into the
hall of the chancellery and had vaulted across the board to the seat
reserved for him. It had been a stimulating relationship and it would
have been continued on the same basis if he had not insisted on putting his friend into the higher post where he had ranked next to
royalty. His sharp temper had often made him wish for Becket's
death, of course, but this had been no more than a phase of his

sudden rages. In his sober moments he had not wanted the struggle to end in tragedy. But it had been rash and bitter words of his which had led to the murder, and he knew that nothing he could do would remove the stain.

Deeper than all would be his regrets for the dream, now shattered beyond repair. The star of empire which had always blazed above him had fallen from the sky. He could expect no acceptance of what had been in his mind now that this had happened. Sixteen words, uttered in a sudden fury, had undone all his striving and planning.

When Henry emerged from his tower room at last, he walked out on the narrow space behind the battlements of the keep. It was getting late, and he wondered why the bells of the abbey which he could see just beyond the walls of the town had not sounded compline. This set him to thinking, and he realized then that he had not heard the bells at all that day.

In a sudden panic he raced down the stairs and into the hall, where people were idling about in readiness for supper. He stopped by one of them to ask a question in an urgent whisper. Was it true, then, that the ban had been placed?

The answer was a reluctant affirmative. The Archbishop of Sens, without waiting on Rome for confirmation, had laid all Normandy under an interdict. No bells had rung, no masses had been said. All day people had been coming to the gates, white-faced, asking questions. What would happen to them? Could they no longer be married by the Church? Would there be no chance to confess their sins? Would the dying be allowed to go from the world unshriven?

Although Henry has been called irreligious, this is far from the truth. He shared the faith of all men and, in addition, he had a thorough respect for the power of the Church. The thought in his mind now would be what he might expect if he were placed under the ban himself. Would other men shun a king? Would he be hampered in carrying on the affairs of state? Would he have to sit alone as he had compelled the two bishops to do?

But a few moments of anxious reflection would suffice for Henry. With him a desperate prospect called for action. First he indulged in a large and furiously quick meal, having three days of fasting to make up for, and then he set his mind to ways of repairing this disaster, of facing the whirlwind he had unleashed. The result was that the Archbishop of Rouen, with two other high ecclesiastical officers, was sent off to Rome, where the Pope had now established himself, with explanations of the mistake which had produced the tragedy and a statement of the amends Henry was prepared to make. This done, he realized that the archbishop was an old man and would travel in slow and solemn state. Accordingly he made up another party of younger men, abbots and archdeacons, with instructions to reach Rome as fast as they could and hold matters in abeyance there until the properly authorized trio of older men put in an appearance.

It was well that he took this double precaution. The young men, reaching the Eternal City long before His Grace of Rouen, found themselves in an atmosphere of the most bitter hostility. Alexander had been so outraged that he had gone into seclusion himself for five days, in vain regrets, no doubt, for the vacillating part he had played while Thomas à Becket was alive. Now he was ready to loose the lightning of his wrath, to excommunicate Henry and lay England under an interdict. By a desperate canvass of the whole papal court, the first envoys accomplished what they had been sent to do, however; they persuaded Alexander to suspend judgment until the bishops arrived and had been heard.

When the Pontiff realized that Henry was ready to submit to penalties and also to abate some of the more objectionable clauses of the Constitutions of Clarendon, his hand was stayed. The excommunication of a monarch as powerful as Henry would have been a serious matter, and without a doubt Alexander was relieved that he need not, after all, proceed to this dangerous extreme.

It was agreed that the English King would not hold the Church in England responsible to him in points of law but would again allow appeals to Rome. Infringement of church rights previously established would cease. Henry was to take the cross and fight in Palestine or, if this should prove impossible, he would pay the cost of maintaining two hundred of the Knights Templars in the field for a period of three years. Less important stipulations were made. His son Henry would be crowned a second time in full accord with church practice, the adherents of Becket would be pardoned and left in the posts they occupied, ample compensation would be made for the years of looting at Canterbury, and funds would be provided for the sisters of the murdered man, Mary and Agnes Becket.

It will be seen from this that Henry did not throw himself entirely on the mercy of the Pope. He made concessions, but they were not sweeping enough to have satisfied Thomas à Becket had the primate been alive to pass on them. The King was too tough of fiber for unconditional surrender. He had been guilty of a series of mistakes and of a great sin, but he did not whine for pardon as his son John was to do at a later period. Henry never forgot his responsibilities as King of England.

The penance he took on himself to pay was no convenient gesture, no halfhearted effort. After his journey to Ireland, which will be dealt with in the next chapter, he came back to England for the purpose. It was at the most critical stage of his whole reign. His sons had united in a family mutiny and had allied themselves with the perpetual enemy, Louis of France, in an attack on Normandy. Eleanor was at the side of her beloved Richard, who could do no wrong. The King of Scotland, William the Lion, was invading Northumberland. The Earl of Leicester, espousing the cause of the rebellious sons, had landed with an army of mercenaries in Norfolk. It seemed quite possible that Henry would go down against such a powerful combination.

He landed at Southampton and rode from there to Canterbury without a stop, except to change horses and for hurried meals. He dismounted at the chapel of St. Nicholas outside the city and walked to St. Dunstan's Oratory, where he put on a hair shirt and over that the gown of a pilgrim. With bare feet, with staff in one hand and the essential penny in the other, he walked through the streets of Canterbury to the cathedral. News of his coming had preceded him and the streets were filled with people, awed into silence by the spectacle of the much-feared King walking on bare feet, which had already begun to bleed, to plead like any common penitent.

Henry played the role fully and humbly. He prostrated himself and kissed the stones where Thomas à Becket had fallen. Then he went to the crypt and lay before the tomb. Here he made confession that, although he had not willed the death of the Martyr, he was responsible for it because of the words he had spoken. He begged forgiveness for his wickedness and pride.

Baring his back, he asked that the waxed cord of flagellation be used, that each high officer of Canterbury strike him five times and each of the monks three. The hundreds of strokes he thus demanded bruised and lacerated him so badly that the last ones to wield the

[178]

cord had to be driven to it by royal insistence. Following this extreme measure, the King sat in silence before the tomb for the balance of the day and all of the night which followed. As the doors of the cathedral had been thrown open at his express command, the townspeople ventured in and stood at a distance while their ruler kept his long vigil. This was indeed something to see, the mighty monarch, master of so large a part of the known world, sitting in sackcloth, doing humble penance for his sins.

Henry did not rise until dawn. He again crossed Canterbury on bare feet. At the oratory he dressed and took to horse. On reaching London he went to the Tower, and on his first night he slept soundly in the belief that he had at last purged himself of his fault.

He was awakened before dawn by a loud rapping at his chamber door. A servant entered with word that a messenger had arrived from the north and was waiting outside. Crawling from his bed with the greatest difficulty, for his back was now stiff and painful, the King hobbled to the door. The messenger, he saw, was covered with dust from many hours in the saddle.

"My lord, I am servant to Ranulf de Glanville," said the man, "and I come with good tidings."

The King waited. He was badly in need of good tidings. The thought undoubtedly was in his mind, Can this be a sign that I am forgiven?

"Behold, my lord, he holds your enemy, the King of Scots, in chains at Richmond!"

Henry's mind took fire at this news. William the Lion defeated and captured! A victory indeed! He would confound all his enemies with such a start as this. Painfully he walked to a window, a narrow slit in the thick masonry. All the bells in London were starting to ring for the victory. People were pouring into the streets, shouting to each other jubilantly. The sun was just rising over the river.

In the mood of humility which gripped him still, the King was certain that this was his reward, the proof that he had been forgiven. It must have seemed to him as he watched the rays of the sun gild the waters of the estuary that this would be the finest day he had ever known.

CHAPTER IX

The Invasion of Ireland

I T HAS BEEN CUSTOMARY in writing of the efforts made to conquer Ireland during the reign of Henry II to speak of the country as uncivilized and barbarous. The evidence does not bear this out: conditions there do not seem much different, at least, from what they had been in England a relatively short time before. The Danish invasions had never penetrated far beyond the eastern coast, and the population was divided into two sections: the inhabitants of the cities along the Irish Sea, the Ostmen, as they were called, where living was on much the same scale as in England at the time of the Conquest, and the real Irish who had to themselves the beautiful country of the interior and the west, the Ireland of mountain and lake, of red deer and wild boar, the Ireland of green fields and soft winds. The real Irish people were wild and untamable, but they do not deserve to be described as savage kerns existing in bogs and little better than the beasts they hunted. The historian of the invasion, Giraldus Cambrensis speaks of the people in the most uncomplimentary way and yet allows himself to lapse into references which leave the opposite impression. Nature, he says, "leads each to man's estate, conspicuous for a tall and handsome form, regular features, and a fresh complexion." The priests, he found, were scrupulously regular in the performance of their duties and never allowed themselves more than one meal a day (but were less abstemious in the matter of drink); all the people were musical and played on two instruments, the lute and the timbrel. The Irish were a race of minstrels, as the huge mass of their earliest literature attests, the Ulster cycle of romances and the Ossianic songs which continue of interest to the present day. Irish enamels had already set the mold for all Byzantine and European work.

It must be said that the Irish people were so prone to quarrel among themselves that they were broken up into many small kingdoms, as the English had been before the time of Egbert, but they had developed the beginnings of a democracy of their own. The choice of a king was always, in theory at least, in the hands of the people. Certainly they had never allowed themselves to be held in the iron slavery of feudalism as had the people of Normandy, from whom the criticisms come. The Brehon Code contained some enlightened conceptions of law.

Two excuses for the invasion are generally given. There was the slave trade between the two countries which had existed for centuries. It seems to have been one-sided. The Ostmen bought Anglo-Saxons as fast as they could be shipped across the narrow sea, and the victims of the traffic constituted the servant class along the eastern coast of Ireland. Clearly, however, the odium must attach to the sellers, who were prepared to bargain away their natural children and their dependents, in even greater degree than to the buyers. The second excuse was the independent status of the Church in Ireland. Although the people showed then the same devotion they have continued to display throughout the centuries, no effort had been made to organize the Church along the lines followed elsewhere. They had archbishops but no central authority, and they did not pay Peter's pence to Rome. The bull of Adrian IV, if it had actually been promulgated, was the first tangible evidence of the desire which all pontiffs had shared to see the Irish Church brought into uniformity with the rest of Christianity.

The real reason was that the Norman kings wanted to add Ireland to their possessions. William Rufus would have made the effort if he had lived long enough. Although Morogh O'Brien of Leinster had sent logs of bog oak grown along the Liffey to serve for the roof of the great new hall the Red King was building at Westminster as a gesture of friendship, the latter had boasted he would make a bridge of his ships over which his soldiers could march on their mission of conquest. The motive for the invasion cannot be explained or condoned on any grounds of necessity or expediency. It was the final phase of the roving instinct which had brought the marauding sea dogs to the north of France in the first place.

Perhaps the fact that Irish independence had been maintained in the face of Roman and Danish aggression, while the people of England had succumbed, acted as a challenge to the ironclad warriors who had made themselves the masters of the English. Where the phalanx of Rome and the galley of the vikings had failed, the Norman might would prevail.

2

A quarrel among Irish rulers was what served to set into execution the plans which had been maturing so long in the mind of Henry. Dermod, son of Morogh, sometimes called McCarty-More, was now King of Leinster. He was a hot-tempered, proud, and savage man, big of frame and loud of voice. He cannot have been entirely bad, however, because Giraldus, who accompanied the first expedition and saw everything with his own eyes, says of him, "He became an oppressor of the nobility and began to tyrannize in a grievous and intolerable manner over the great men of the land." The fact that many of the common men rallied around him at the most critical stage of his later troubles might suggest that he had done his tyrannizing in the right place. One of the most grievous and least tolerable things he did was to steal Devorgilla, the wife of Tieghernan O'Rourke, King of Breffny and East Meath. As Tieghernan was nicknamed Monoculus or the One-Eyed, it may have been that Devorgilla was so anxious to be stolen that the full blame cannot be laid on the shoulders of the amorous King of Leinster. At any rate, it was fourteen years after the theft before a confederacy was formed with Tieghernan which drove Dermod from Leinster, and so the assertion of Giraldus that it was his wife-stealing which cost him his throne is not an acceptable explanation. The confederacy was headed by Roderick, King of Connaught, and as many of the great men of Leinster did not like being tyrannized over and deprived of their hereditary rights, they joined in with the enemies of their ruler and saw to it that he was forced to quit Ireland.

At this stage Dermod displayed the worst side of his nature. Prepared to sell the liberty of the people of Ireland to avenge himself on his enemies, he went to Aquitaine, where Henry was stationed at the time, and offered to do homage for his kingdom if the English ruler would aid him in regaining his throne. Henry was unable to undertake an expedition then, but he gave a letter to the renegade which read as follows:

Henry, king of England, duke of Normandy and Aquitaine and count of Anjou to all his liegemen, English, Norman, Welsh and Scots, and to all nations subject to his sway, sends greetings. Whensoever these our letters shall come unto you, know ye that we have taken Dermod, prince of the men of Leinster, into the bosom of our grace, and good-will. Wherefore, too, whosoever within the bounds of our dominions shall be willing to lend aid to him, as being our vassal and liegeman, to the recovery of his own, let him know that he hath our favor and permission to that end.

This was not what Dermod had hoped for, but at any rate it opened a way for him. He betook himself to Wales and found there two men who were willing to provide him with assistance. The first was Rhys, Prince of South Wales, a descendant of Princess Nesta, who had been one of the many mistresses of Henry I. She had later married Gerald of Windsor and, as the Norman patronymic had come into general use, her descendants were variously known as Fitz-Henrys and Fitz-Geralds. They were mostly landless men and ready for an adventure in Ireland. The second was Richard de Clare, the Earl of Striguil and nicknamed Strongbow, who was at Bristol when Dermod came to that city. This Norman nobleman was in worse straits than the Welsh-Norman descendants of Nesta, having a pack of creditors on his trail. He seems to have been curiously different from the typical Norman adventurer, red-haired and with features as fine as a woman's, a high-pitched voice, and the most courteous of manners. His arms were so long that he could touch his knees while standing upright. Dermod had heard of him as a man of desperate courage and great resource, and he was amazed at their first meeting, believing there had been a mistake. He soon became conscious, however, of the power under the almost effeminate manners of this landless nobleman. Strongbow lent a willing ear to the proposals of the dispossessed Irishman. It was agreed between them that Strongbow would get together a large force of volunteers and that, if the venture proved a success, he was to have Dermod's eldest daughter Eva as his wife and come into the overlordship of Leinster in due course.

Not waiting for his confederates to join him, Dermod sailed across the Irish Sea at once, accompanied by one young Norman only, Richard Fitz-Godobert, and a few servants. His arrival created a stir, but he was permitted to stay on condition that he send all members of his party back and that he himself take up his residence in the monastery of Ferns. Dermod agreed and went into seclusion for the winter. He was closely watched, for the Norman escort had served as a warning of what was in the wind. Dermod, however, was as circumspect as he had always before been rash and injudicious, and he gave them no excuse for interference.

Early in the following May the first of his buccaneering confederates sailed across the Irish Sea. Robert Fitz-Stephen was in command with one hundred men-at-arms and three hundred Welsh archers, armed with the great longbow which later was to win so many battles for the English. They landed in a creek called Bannow south of Wexford and encamped there on an island. The deposed King promptly appeared with five hundred of his former subjects who had rallied to his banner. The combined forces so surprised the defenders of Wexford with their shining armor and their caparisoned horses that, instead of giving battle in the open as they had intended, the Irish retreated behind the walls of the city. It took two days of continuous assault to storm the walls, and the defenders then gave in, acknowledging Dermod as their lawful lord again. The conquest of Ossory followed in quick order, and this placed Dermod in full possession of his domain of Leinster. He gave lands along the coast between Wexford and Waterford to his Norman allies in conformance with his promises. It looked as though the Irish adventure had been brought to a successful conclusion before the man whose name was later to be associated with it as leader, the deceptively mild Richard de Clare, had stirred from his English base.

In the meantime, however, Ireland was stirring. The return of Dermod, obnoxious enough in itself, had been rendered triply distasteful by the presence of his former allies. Roderick of Connaught, who was recognized as the High King of Ireland, called a conference of national leaders, with the result that a large army was assembled for a drive against the renegade King of Leinster. Before a battle could be fought, however, the politic Roderick reached an agreement with Dermod by which the latter would remain in possession of Leinster and would promise that no more Norman mer-

cenaries were to be allowed in the country. This was not as pusillanimous on the part of Roderick as it may seem, for the Irish had
begun to realize it was impossible to face men arrayed in heavy
armor, who advanced and wheeled in well-trained columns, with
undisciplined levies in the Irish *wambais,* a quilted linen jacket
which offered no real protection. The Irish spear, lacking in temper
and weight, was a poor weapon to combat the deadly Norman
sword.

It was now impossible, however, to keep the Normans out of the
country. No sooner was the treaty signed than another band arrived
at Wexford, avid for spoils. It occurred then to Dermod, who never
forgot an injury, that the time had come to punish the people of
Dublin. They had murdered his father, the kind and just Morogh,
and had buried him beside the body of a dog. The new allies were
sent to attack Dublin, and the future capital of the country was
forced to yield after sustaining heavy losses.

Dermod should have been satisfied at this stage. He had his kingdom back, he had tasted the sweetness of revenge, he had sacked
part of the unfriendly city on the Liffey. But that man of ill intent
was becoming ambitious. If he could reconquer Leinster with the
help of these steel-clad mercenaries, why should not all Ireland be
brought under his sway? The *fili* (an Irish term for poet) came out
in him when he sat down and indited a letter to Strongbow. "We
have watched the storks and swallows," he wrote, "and the summer
birds have come; come, aye, and flown again before the ocean blast.
Neither easter breeze no zephyr's breath wafts to us your longed-
for presence. Let the prompt fulfillment of your promise cure this
malady of delay."

The admonition was not needed. Strongbow had been getting
ready. Early in August he began his march to St. David's with a
picked body of men. Recruits flocked to him and, when he finally
embarked at Milford Haven, he had two hundred men-at-arms and
a thousand foot soldiers under his banner with its three crosses.
With this force, much the largest to engage in the campaign, he
landed north of Waterford. The great man had come, forerunner of
a greater, as an old prophecy had it, who "would set his heel on
Desmond's neck and bruise the head of Leinster."

Waterford fell, and then the combined forces of Strongbow and
Dermod marched against Dublin again, that city having shown

further signs of resistance. The earlier arrivals had given a good account of themselves, but it remained for Richard de Clare to complete the work of aggression. He carried Dublin by storm and expelled the Ostmen. When they gathered their forces off the Isle of Man and came back with a fleet, the last demonstration Ireland was to see of viking strength, Strongbow promptly dispersed it.

The following year Dermod died with no one to mourn him. In the *Annals of the Four Masters* it is said that this man "who had made a trembling sod of all Ireland became putrid while living, through the miracle of God, Columcille and Finnan and other saints of Ireland, and he died without penance, without unction, as his evil deeds deserved." The Brehon Code left the choice of a successor in the hands of the people, but this was not the Norman way. Strongbow had married Eva in the meantime and he announced himself the new ruler in her right, although he took the title of earl instead of king.

If Henry had not been so engrossed in his struggle with Thomas à Becket, he would have taken a hand in Ireland long before this because it was clear now that the island was ripe for conquest and permanent occupation. He became alarmed when the news reached him of Strongbow's seizure of power and he promptly wrote to his ambitious subject, demanding that all knights who had gone to Ireland should return on pain of losing their possessions in England. This threat had no effect on the leader of the invasion who had no lands in England to lose. He answered his monarch's command as follows:

Most puissant prince and my dread sovereign: I came into this land with Your Majesty's leave (as far as I remember) to aid your servant MacMorogh. What I won was with the sword. What was given me, I give you.

I am yours, life and living.

This made it clear to Henry that he must act at once if he expected to benefit by the operations in Ireland. The next year he crossed the Irish Sea with a considerable force.

He found on arriving that there was little for him to do. The Ostmen had been driven from the eastern cities, the Irish kings were in a humble mood and prepared to swear allegiance to him as the best way out of their desperate plight, Strongbow had come to heel

IRELAND
at the Time of
the Invasion

ATLANTIC
OCEAN

SCOT-
LAND

NORTH CHANNEL

IRELAND

THE PALE

Dublin

Wexford

Waterford

IRISH
SEA

ST. GEORGE'S CHANNEL

WALES

ST. DAVID'S

Milford Haven
Pembroke

ENGLAND

Bristol

palacios

and had submitted to him. He remained in the country for the winter, making Dublin his headquarters. The city had been badly battered in the incessant fighting, and much of it had been burned. Henry lived in a house of some size but of no pretensions to anything but utility, all on one floor and with a high wattled palisade about it. He dined at a trestle table at which his officers joined him with little regard to rank and title, and he slept on a bed made by stretching a bearskin between four posts.

He had not yet made his penance at the tomb of the Martyr and he was still in doubt, therefore, as to the attitude of Rome. Before leaving England he had renewed his orders that every port must be watched and every man searched before he was allowed to land, so that no papal emissaries could get into the country with bulls of excommunication or interdict. Equal care was being shown along the Irish coast, and no one was permitted to approach the King, particularly priests, until his mission had been ascertained. In the face of all his difficulties, which seemed to be mounting as he grew older, Henry did not change. He was thorough, methodical, farseeing, alive to every need as he had been at the start of his reign, when England was in such dire straits.

He occupied himself while in Ireland with establishing order and setting up an administration along the sound lines of his reforms in England. Officers trained in his ways were put in charge of justice and the raising of taxes. It had been the same everywhere, in sunny Aquitaine, in Anjou, and in Brittany. Always he had proceeded to codify the laws and set the wheels of justice to turning. Always it had been done in the face of bitter opposition from the nobility, who saw their feudal advantages reduced by a system which took the law out of their hands.

He did much to establish what was later known as the Pale, a strip of territory along the eastern coast and centering at Dublin, in which the supremacy of the invaders was acknowledged and English ways of living were introduced. The Pale changed in shape and size in the centuries which followed, sometimes shrinking, sometimes growing, but it remained the core of Anglo-Saxon occupation and the one part of the country where the imprint of the invaders was never wiped out.

3

More than ten years later, after Strongbow had died and various governors had followed him, Henry formally declared his son John King of the country. John, now seventeen years of age, was well loved by Henry, although he was beginning to show the traits which were to make him later the most execrated of all rulers. He had, moreover, been a sorry failure in some military operations in France. Henry was determined that his youngest son was to be a king in his own right, and so to Ireland sailed the smiling, indolent, false John with a considerable force to make good his claim to the full suzerainty of the island. By his side was Ranulf de Glanville, the shrewdest lawyer and administrator in England and the general who captured William the Lion. Henry never allowed his sons out of leading strings. He might make them kings and dukes, but always beside them were long-nosed Normans who knew exactly what Henry himself would want under any circumstances and who had authority to see that things were done his way.

All the skilled officers Henry had trained since the days of the magic chancellorship of Thomas à Becket would have failed to keep John in control. That young man discovered that the Welsh-Normans who had conquered the coast and who were in the main well disposed to the Irish people had become to some degree assimilated. These tall, fair knights had married Irish wives (adopting the native custom of a trial marriage of one year from the Feast of Samhain but liking their mates well enough to put the relationship on a permanent basis) and had settled down on their lands with no more desire for destruction or conquest. This was all the excuse the amiable John needed to shove them aside for the men he had brought with him. They were Normans fresh from France, as rapacious as the adventurers who had followed the Conqueror into England, looking for spoils and ransoms. They started the trouble all over again, burning, slaying, making little distinction between the native Irish and the men of Strongbow.

John himself behaved like a malicious schoolboy, pulling the long beards of the Irish kings and chiefs when they bent the knee to him in submission. He allowed his men to commit the final offense, which was to break open churches and to despoil them of their sacred vessels.

Glanville could do nothing in the face of the bloody and yet farcical turmoil which John created about him. He seems to have given up in despair. Anything he accomplished would, in any event, have been swept aside in the fury of resentment which brought all Ireland raging about the Pale.

It had been arranged that John would be crowned on Christmas Day of the following year. The Pope, who seems to have remained blind to what was going on, sent a crown of gold in the form of peacock feathers to be used at the coronation. Neither could His Holiness have had any realization of the peculiar fitness of such a crown for the vain and arrogant youth on whose brow it was to rest.

But the crowning never took place. John had not lived up to Merlin's prediction of him, "Born of the fell fire-king, a sparklet prince shall dart his bolt of icy fear to Erin's quaking heart." There was no trace of icy fear in the kings of Limerick, Connaught, and Meath when they met his forces at Tegas and scored a decisive victory over them. In the chronicle of Benedict it is said that most of the prince's troops had deserted and gone over to the natives. At any rate, John found himself in a most precarious position and decided that personal safety was better than a coronation. He sailed back to England.

After this reverse Henry gave up his efforts to reduce Ireland. The Pale remained the only part of the country where English rule was maintained.

CHAPTER X

The Sin of Absalom

ENRY'S TROUBLES came upon him when his power was at its height. In 1171 his third son Geoffrey was married to Constance, the heiress of Brittany, and assumed the title of duke of that rugged corner of France, with its rocky shores and tumultuous streams, jutting out between the Sleeve (as the French always called the Channel) and the Bay of Biscay. Now all of northern France was included in the Angevin empire, as well as the west and some of the south. Henry was titular head of the Norman dynasty in Sicily and through his marriage to Eleanor occupied the same suzerainty to the Aquitainian kings of Antioch. England stood higher in the Christian world than at any time before. In London there were always special ambassadors (though that term for them had not yet been coined) from other countries to negotiate military or trade agreements. Englishmen were playing prominent parts on the Continent. As a final step in fitting the futures of his children into his dream of empire, Henry arranged a marriage for John with the heiress of Maurienne.

This mountainous province, lying south of Lake Geneva and extending almost to the Gulf of Genoa, was of much greater importance than its relatively small size would suggest. It controlled the approaches to Italy. With a foothold here, the English King would be able to gaze across the Alps at Frederick Barbarossa with a sense of equality. Nay, at the moment the elements in Germany opposed to their red-bearded Emperor were secretly negotiating with Henry

[191]

to take his place, and so the English ruler had every reason to see himself as another and greater Charlemagne.

The little heiress of Maurienne would not live long enough to play any part in the designs of the ambitious King, but this was in the future and no premonition of it placed a damper on the good spirits of the scheming fathers when they met in the city of Limoges to settle the details of the match. Henry had brought his whole ménage with him: Eleanor, young Henry and his French wife Marguerite, the younger French princess, Alice, who was to marry Richard when she was old enough, and, of course, the youthful John, who undoubtedly derived a sense of importance from the role he was playing.

Limoges had never seen since the days of the Roman occupation, when it had been a large place, such an assemblage of the great of the earth within the walls of the Château, as the more ancient half of the city was called. In addition to the English royal family and the nobility of Aquitaine, who always flocked around when Eleanor appeared, there was the Count of Maurienne and a train of Italian noblemen and, to the excitement of everyone, Raimund of Toulouse. This important and elusive feudal figure had come to pay homage for the first time to Henry for his rich and extensive domain which included all of the southwestern corner of France. The arrival of Raimund was the capstone in Henry's arch of glory, for now at last his sway extended from the farthest north corner of the British Isles to the southernmost part of France.

Limoges was to see the beginning of one of the strangest situations in history. This ancient city, the capital of Limousin, had grown up on the banks of the Vienne and was built solidly of stone, which gave it a notable air of permanence in the eyes of the visitors familiar with the precarious state of wooden London. It was of a great quaintness and charm, a cluster of fine slate-topped spires and much rich-stained glass. Here the bellows of the apprentices blew hot fires for the making of the new champlevé enamel, and here came the pilgrims, who had never heard of St. Thomas the Martyr, to pray at the tomb of St. Martial, filling the narrow streets with their processions on donkeys. The visitors had been taken in at the castle of the viscounts of Limousin, and they were even sleeping up under the battlements.

It was in the hall of the castle that Raimund of Toulouse paid

homage to Henry. He was a man of proud and unstable humors, as were most of the rulers of south Gaul, and his decision to acknowledge the suzerainty of the English King instead of the French was a matter of policy, from which at this particular moment he expected to reap some benefit. He swore the usual oath, which contained a promise to reveal any information he might have of machinations against the King. When he came to this part the tall count paused with deliberate intent.

"It becomes my duty," he said in a whisper meant only for the ears of the King, "to warn you. Make safe your fortresses in Poitou and Aquitaine. Distrust your wife and sons."

The hands of the new vassal were in Henry's when he said this. The King's hands tightened their grip instinctively, but he said nothing to indicate he had heard. The ceremony was carried through and the incident seemed to have ended there.

Supper that night was a sumptuous affair of many courses with "warners" in between which usually consisted of feathered and roasted peacocks or figures done in pastry. There was, of course, a succession of the finest wines of the south. Seated between Eleanor and Raimund of Toulouse, the King imposed enough restraint on himself to stay in his chair and not get up for his usual jaunts around the room. He had little desire for food and his hand seldom raised the jeweled wine cup to his lips. Although not a man of subtle mood, Henry was conscious of a tension in the room. He stole many side glances at Queen Eleanor, who also appeared to have lost her appetite. Ordinarily she talked easily and beguilingly, and much; but this evening her eyes were lowered and she had little to say. She had passed the fifty mark and was no longer the radiant beauty who had once scandalized Europe, but Henry as usual was aware that she had remained a woman of great charm. Her dark eyes made light of the lines at their corners and they were as animated, or nearly so, as when she and her sister Petronille had been queens of the Courts of Love. Her hair, still dark and still lustrous, was held in a gold net called a crespine, over which she wore a small and severely plain circlet of gold. The tight fit of her upper tunic, under which was a bodice strengthened by bone, showed that she was almost as slender as when he had first seen her.

What Raimund of Toulouse had told him was not new to Henry. He had realized for some time that his sons were turning against him and he knew that Eleanor was the chief cause of it. He had hoped this triumph would quiet them down, that they would perceive at last the greatness of what he was striving for and be content to have shares in it. The rift with Eleanor was, of course, an entirely different matter. He allowed his eyes to stray down the table to where the fifteen-year-old Princess Alice was sitting. She also was feeling the tension in the air. At any rate, he had not heard her low-pitched voice all evening. He could not see much of her now, only the blackness of her hair beyond the gold circlet of her sister Marguerite. Eleanor, who always seemed to know everything which went on, was well aware of the interest he took in Princess Alice.

Distrust your wife and sons, Raimund had said! That suave and scornful man was enjoying the good food and wines with the discrimination of a gourmet and was conversing with an ease which irritated his suzerain. Henry had little liking for men of this particular stamp, intellectual triflers who took their duties lightly and considered the details of administration beneath them. At the moment his anger was all for the Count of Toulouse who had dared put into words what he, Henry, had known for some time. Many, in fact, had known of it, but none had shown the audacity to speak of it.

Unable to contain himself any longer, Henry got to his feet and strolled down the length of the dais. He could now see his son Henry, *Li Reys Josnes,* as they called him in Normandy, the Young King. Neither as tall nor as goldenly handsome as Richard, the eldest son was still large and regal enough to cut a good figure. Surely he could have no part in this family discontent, his eldest son! It would not matter as much about the others if he could only be sure of the loyalty of *Li Reys Josnes.*

He stopped beside one of his officers and whispered in his ear. The man, too startled for words, looked up at this strange master, asking himself if this meant the King was going back to his old habit of racing from town to town and making his people live in their saddles. It had been understood there would be a long and pleasant stay at Limoges in order to take full advantage of the presence of Raimund of Toulouse and the Count of Maurienne. Why, then, was the King ordering a start for the north in the morning?

Henry's decision to leave at once was a wise one, even though it ruffled the temper of the proud Count of Toulouse, who thought himself slighted. If trouble was in the wind, he could face it best

behind the strong stone fortresses of Normandy. There was a flurry
of packing that night, and in the morning—soon after dawn, in fact
—the court moved on, striking up the Vienne for Chinon.

The castle of Chinon was one of the three which Henry's father
had willed to Geoffrey, his brother. Geoffrey being dead, it had
come to Henry. Everything seemed to come to Henry: castles and
lands and provinces, wives with duchies in their hands for his sons,
kings as husbands for his daughters. But the castle of Chinon was,
of all the things which had come to him, the one tangible possession
which gave the English King the greatest pleasure. It stood in the
very center of his continental possessions and seemed to him a
symbol of his power. It raised its multitude of towers above a hill
which completely dominated the town. From the Tour de Boissy or
the stout Tour de Moulin it was possible to look far down the lovely
valley of the Vienne. Never before or since, perhaps, has there been
such a tangle of battlements and roofs of blue slate and spires of tall
chapels as were to be seen at Chinon.

It had one unique feature, a hall circular in shape instead of
oblong, arching up into a dome supported by huge beamed nerves.
This hall was lighted by very tall and narrow windows set in em-
brasures, and it was here that the court assembled for supper. The
King had heard of desertions during the day, but he was not prepared for what he saw when he entered the hall behind his pipers
and drums. There were many empty seats around the board, and the
most conspicuous absence was that of *Li Reys Josnes!*

Henry sank into his chair. He glanced up and down the table. All
faces, save that of the Queen, were carefully averted. She returned
his accusing gaze steadily and coolly. If she knew the reason for the
absence of their oldest son, she was not disturbed by it, nor did she
fear how he might deal with the situation.

The Young King, he was informed when he girded himself to the
repugnant task of asking questions, had ridden away from the main
party just as they turned in at Chinon, followed by the members of
his household and his bodyguard of young knights. The truant had
not taken his wife and her attendants, however, because to do so
would have caused too much confusion. The French court was at
Paris, and it was to this city that Henry was on his way, striking out
first for Alençon.

The next night, at a point more than twenty miles north, an earl was missing at the supper table. The night after, three knights. On the third night the chair beside the King was empty! Eleanor had ridden off for the south and, presumably, was hoping to reach Aquitaine, where she could join her favorite son. Henry had done nothing yet, but Eleanor's departure stirred him to action. He sent off parties of armed men in all directions with instructions to overtake her and bring her back.

The Queen had disguised herself as a man, but her predilection for getting into masculine attire (which suggests she possessed certain advantages) did not bring her better luck than on the first occasion when she rode to the Crusades at the head of her amazonian guards. She was caught within a few hours and brought back, her well-turned legs still in male hose but concealed under a long cloak.

Henry refused to see her. She was taken to her quarters and kept there as a prisoner. When the journey was resumed the next morning, the Queen was surrounded by an armed guard. From that time on she was watched so closely that she might as well have been in a cell with iron chains and anklets.

Arriving at Rouen, the King was greeted with the worst of news. The provinces of the west were in arms against him. A knight of the Limousin named Bertran de Born, who was acknowledged to be the greatest minstrel of the day, had written a *sirventes* calling on all subjects of their rightful ruler Eleanor to rise against her English husband. The song was sweeping across Aquitaine. Richard and Geoffrey had declared their intention of allying themselves with their brother in a defiance of parental authority. From the French court King Louis issued a blast. "Here at my side is Henry, King of England," he declared. As for Henry II, the French monarch continued, he was dead as King of England from the moment his son first assumed the crown; and if he still harbored the delusion that he was King, the matter would in good time be righted! Louis had waited many years for revenge on the man who had stolen his wife and taken away so much French territory and now he was enjoying it in full measure.

The Young King was behaving himself in a boastful and juvenile manner which promised little for the day when he might rule England in his father's stead. He had a new seal struck so he could issue writs and pronouncements in his own name. Armed with this, he was proceeding to give England away in huge parcels in return for promises of support against his father. The King of Scotland was to have Northumberland; the Count of Flanders, Kent; the Count of Boulogne, Lincoln. The English people, innocent bystanders in this family strife, were to suffer a second conquest. In a letter to the Pope the Young King declared that the murder of Thomas à Becket was the main cause of his intent to oust his father. "Such has been the origin of our dissension," he wrote to Rome. "Hearken to me, then, most holy father, and judge my cause; for it will be truly just if it shall be justified by thy apostolic authority."

The Great Hall in the royal palace at Rouen was completed when Henry arrived there. It had taken more than sixty years in the building, for Henry I had begun the work. It was enormous and as handsome and stately as the finest of cathedrals. High arched pillars held up a magnificent dome, and the gallery for the minstrels was screened by beautiful stone tracery. Henry had counted on having it ready for the time when his plans would mature. To find it finished now, when everything seemed to be crashing about him, was an ironic reminder that man's destiny was in greater than kingly hands.

He was a grim and morose man these days. Of all his family, only young Prince John was with him. John had already succeeded in making himself thoroughly disliked by his arrogance, his selfishness, his cruelty to servants as well as animals, but this was not apparent to his father. The partiality for John which the King showed in his final years started from this period.

Henry did not change his ways. He still remained constantly on his feet, but in his pacing about he never paused to have speech with anyone. His head was bent forward, he frowned incessantly, the high color of his cheeks suggested that his mind was filled with a perpetual smolder of anger. When attendance at mass compelled him to sit, he was never quiet. He hitched about in his seat, he muttered and grumbled under his breath. The King who had nearly succeeded in knitting together the glittering fabric of a new empire was the unhappiest man in the whole length and breadth of his dominions.

But he broke up the coalition formed against him. With an army made up largely of mercenaries hastily recruited in Brabant, he caught a division of his foes under the command of the Count of Boulogne and smashed it utterly. The count was killed in the action, and so his reward for supporting the Young King was not the rich county of Lincoln but six feet of French soil. Then Henry led his troops to Verneuil in search of the invading forces of Louis of France. "Go tell your King," he cried fiercely to French heralds, "that I am at hand as you see!" Louis of France, the fumbling, ineffective, and unready King, who had never been able to get the better of Henry of England, received the message with fear. Although his army was big enough and strong enough to shove the English out of Normandy, he ordered a retreat instead! Henry did not follow. He struck at the west and captured the army of Brittany at Dol. The old lion he was called (although barely into his forties), and he was now roused and roaring, striking here, striking there, always unexpected and always victorious. Louis gave up in despair. Recommending that the disobedient sons make peace with their father, he retreated so far that the campaign could be considered at an end. The sons conferred with their father at Gisors, but the meeting did not bring about a settlement. The handsome face of Richard was as angry at the finish as at the start because his mother was still a prisoner and no promise of her release had been wrung from the King.

Eleanor was packed off to the royal castle at Winchester. She was not confined to a cell, but under the watchful eye of Ranulf de Glanville she was kept within close bounds. Here she remained, with brief intervals of freedom under the closest of observation, for sixteen years while the furious struggle within the family continued, having no direct part in it, but her plight serving as one of the chief causes of its continuance. Richard, the eagle she had brought into the world, could not be reconciled to his father as long as she was kept in captivity.

The struggle was resumed the following year, but Henry's star went into the ascendant again. The King of Scotland had been captured and the French fleet, assembled for the invasion of the island, had been scattered by adverse winds. The King next struck with all his vigor at the rebellious barons assembled against him in England. Their opposition went to pieces quickly. Before a month was over the King held a council at Northampton, where he had the supreme pleasure of seeing William the Lion stand before him in chains. The now well-tamed barons came there one by one, Mowbray, Bigod, Ferrers, the Bishop of Durham, Gloucester, Clare. They all humbly swore to obey him as their liege lord and to dispute his authority no more.

Then he hurried to Normandy, where Louis was closing in on Rouen with a large army. Poor, feeble Louis, always at the beginning of something and never at the conclusion of it! As soon as he heard that Henry was back and marching down the Seine he turned like a thief caught with stolen goods in his hands and indulged in the most hasty of all his retreats. The three English princes had been marching under the banner of France, and they now came again to Gisors. This time their submission seemed complete.

Henry's real triumph, however, had not been over Louis nor over his own three sons. They were all ready in their minds to oppose him a third time if the opportunity presented itself. His victory was complete and final in another quarter. The English baronage had been thoroughly humbled. The King took advantage of his victory over them to reduce their feudal powers still further. They had to give up most of their castles. These proud and wealthy noblemen, who had considered themselves kings within their own spheres, were made to realize that they were no more than subjects. Thus out of evil came good. Feudal power, always a more direct threat to the safety and happiness of common men than kingly tyranny, was the last reminder of the Conquest, for it had been the arrogant barons of Normandy who had introduced it into England.

2

The picture which history draws of Henry II in his declining years is that of a David beset by a trio of Absaloms who had been urged on to rebel against him by his faithless and vindictive wife. The picture of Queen Eleanor, which was knit early into the tapestry, has never been changed. A false wife and a treacherous queen she remains in history.

But was all the right on Henry's side in this long period of family struggle? Could the four sons (for John, the pampered one, was to join in at the finish) have rebelled repeatedly, sometimes together, sometimes singly, without any justification at all? Was their only motive an unwillingness to wait for their share of his power and possessions?

History has adopted the obvious and conventional view. A son in arms against his father is an unnatural son, fit only to hang by the hair of his head like Absalom and perhaps to die as David's son did. A woman who has been guilty of adultery in her passionate youth is a bad woman and nothing good is to be expected of her, and certainly nothing good must be said of her. She can never be a decent wife and mother and, if in her later years she becomes tolerant and wise, no reliance is to be put in the evidence of these qualities. A portrait of incontinence can never be altered.

This is not a true picture of what was happening in France during these stormy years. There is much to be said for Eleanor and the disobedient sons.

For one thing, Henry had not been faithful to Eleanor. Nothing else could be expected, of course, for he was a man of lusty appetites and nearly twelve years younger than his wife. The real consideration which had led them to marry, apart from the first passionate attachment between a beautiful and unsatisfied woman and a great, husky youth, had been their mutual ambition. Eleanor felt that what she had contributed to the Angevin empire was of such importance that she was a partner, not a mere wife to wait at his beck and call. Certainly she was not willing to accept the slight he put upon her in the most spectacular of his infidelities. It becomes necessary at this point, therefore, to deal with the amorous performances of the otherwise admirable King.

There is that favorite fairy story of history, his romance with Rosamonde Clifford, who lived in a secret bower in the maze at Woodstock and was poisoned by the wicked Queen. This fable has been told so often and believed so long, and it is such a beguiling story, that one hesitates to destroy it by telling the real facts of the case.

Some of the early historians said the bower was so well concealed in the maze that the only way to find it was to follow a thread of silk which Henry alone knew about. If this had been true, she would have become very hungry, living all alone in her romantic bower, because no servants knew the secret and it could hardly have been expected that the King would come with dishes of hot food in his hands. Another version was that the middle-aged King had been visiting his pretty mistress and that a ball of silk thread became caught in his spur and was still attached to his heel when the Queen saw him emerge from the winding green paths of the maze. She followed the clue back through the paths and discovered the bower and its fair occupant. All versions agree on the outcome, that the wicked Queen immediately visited the girl, taking a dagger in one hand and a glass of poison in the other. When she found the Fair Rosamonde was the loveliest creature in the world, envy hardened the heart of the Queen and she told her rival she must choose which way she would prefer to die. The girl, as brave as she was fair, chose the poison, drank from the cup, and soon thereafter was dead.

And now for the less romantic facts. Henry met Rosamonde Clifford on his first visit to England while his mother was contending with Stephen for the crown. He was about seventeen years of age and she was younger. Her father was Walter Clifford, a vavasor of Herefordshire. The term vavasor has meant different things at different times, but at this period it denoted a man who had more land than a knight's fee but had not attained the stature of a baron; and so it can be assumed that the girl had been raised in a rather humble way. Her father was fighting on the side of the Empress, and it is probable that Henry first saw Rosamonde at Bristol, which was the base of operations. She was a beautiful girl. No description of her has been left, but the few things known suggest that there was a sweetness and a spiritual quality to her loveliness. Henry fell in love at once.

The chronicles say he went through a pretended marriage service with her and that she did not know who he was. This is far from credible. The son of Matilda, who might someday be King of England, would have found it next to impossible to conceal his identity from the daughter of one of his supporters. Subsequent happenings indicate that she went with her eyes open into the relationship which resulted in due course in the birth of a son. This first son, who was named William and who later bore the nickname of William Longsword or William *Long-Espée,* was born after Henry had returned to Normandy. When he came a second time and made the Treaty of Wallingford with Stephen, he had already married Eleanor. However, he and Rosamonde resumed their relationship and another son was born, who was named Geoffrey. When Henry came back as King, he placed the girl in a small stone house just outside the wall of the royal park at Woodstock, and here for a short period he paid her visits. Nearly two hundred years later, Edward III, in repairing the palace at Woodstock, gave written instructions that *the house beyond the gate in the new wall, known as*

The Sin of Absalom

Rosamonde's Chamber, should be carefully restored. This, then, was the bower. Just inside the wall, against which the house stood, was the garden maze; and so some small justification exists, after all, for the fantastic shape the story took.

The Fair Rosamonde, however, did not occupy the House Beyond the Gate long. She repented of her way of living soon after Henry's crowning and retired to the convent of Godstow, where she remained for the rest of her life. That Henry had been sincerely in love with her was made clear by what he did for her and her two sons. He liberally endowed Godstow. He gave lands to the first son. The second, Geoffrey, who seems to have been a great favorite with the King, was reared at court with his legitimate sons. Rosamonde remained at Godstow twenty years, and after her death Henry saw to it that her body was placed in the choir under a silk canopy and that candles were kept lighted and prayers said constantly for her soul. This continued until Hugh of Lincoln, deciding it was not wise to keep alive the story of an illicit romance, had the body interred in the regular burying ground of the convent with a modest stone containing only two words, *Tumba Rosamondae*.

Henry was deeply attached to his second illegitimate son, Geoffrey. He not only reared him and had him educated well under his own eye, but he saw to it he was appointed Bishop of Lincoln at the age of twenty. Geoffrey had not wanted to take holy orders, and for a time he refused the post, saying repeatedly, "*Nolo episcopari!*" He wanted to be a soldier, and when Henry was raising an army for service against the Scots, he arrived at camp with one hundred and forty knights he had recruited and equipped at his own expense.

The son of Fair Rosamonde was lucky enough to have an immediate opportunity of showing what a good soldier he would have been. His company was sent to check Roger de Mowbray, who was advancing from the coast with a force of recruits from Normandy. The lavish offers of land that the Young King was making in Paris had put it into the heads of these greedy Normans that all the country was to change ownership again. As the foot troops tramped along the roads behind the belted knights, they looked enviously at the fine green meadows dotted with fat sheep and sang a new song:

> *"Hoppe Wyllykin! Hoppe Wyllykin!*
> *Ingland is myne and thyne!"*

The young bishop led the charge of his mounted troops against these grasping mercenaries. The invaders were unable to withstand the fury of the onslaught and ran away in a great panic, with Geoffrey and his men riding after them and shouting, "Ingland is myne, not thyne!"

It was on this occasion that Henry made clear how much he cared for Rosamonde's son. He met Geoffrey after the latter's return from his triumph and threw an arm affectionately around his shoulders.

"Thou art my true son!" he said in a tone loud enough for many to hear. Then in a lower tone he added, "The others, they are the bastards!"

In the year 1181 the question of Geoffrey's fitness to remain Bishop of Lincoln came to an issue. The Pope demanded that he take holy orders or resign the see. Geoffrey refused and, accordingly, was removed from his high post. Henry thereupon made him chancellor, and he continued to sit in the chair once occupied by Thomas à Becket until the King's death.

3

Despite the emphasis which has been laid in history on the story of the Fair Rosamonde and the wicked role played in it, supposedly, by Eleanor, it is certain that the Queen was never much concerned over Henry's affair with the daughter of the Cliffords. If she had known of the existence of the House Beyond the Gate, she had been allowed little time to feel any resentment, for the record shows that Rosamonde entered Godstow shortly after Henry became King. If the Queen had felt any bitterness, it is unlikely that Henry would have reared the boy Geoffrey at court.

It has always been necessary for queens to accept the fact that kings have mistresses. This has been one of the almost inevitable consequences of unlimited power. Henry did not belong in the ranks of the extremely rare exceptions. He had a son by the daughter of one Sir Ralph Blewitt. She was succeeded by a handsome girl at Stepford who was not of the nobility; her name, therefore, is not recorded. In Normandy he enjoyed the favors of a daughter of Eudes of Porrhoet. The greatest beauty in England, a sister of the Earl of Clare, refused the King's advances, much to his surprise, no doubt.

The Sin of Absalom

There is nothing to indicate that any of these matters disturbed Eleanor unduly. The romance which led to serious trouble came much later, and the circumstances of this affair were such that all the sympathy must be given the Queen. Mention has already been made of the second daughter of Louis of France, who was betrothed to Prince Richard. She was sent to England at the age of five to be brought up and educated there. A pretty and bright child, she seems to have been a general favorite at first. Henry saw little of her, it being the rule to rear royal children in households of their own, with tutors and confessors and almoners and whole droves of servants. The little French girl was stationed perhaps at Tower-Royal or at Woodstock, where the air was supposed to be particularly healthful. When he did see her, sitting impatiently at her lessons or romping with children of her own age, he must have been aware that she was an unusually lively child.

She was brought to live at court at an early age, for the most important part of her education was to learn how to conduct herself as a princess or queen, and the King must have seen much of her whenever he returned from his long sojournings abroad. She does not seem to have been a beauty, but the vivacity of her girlhood had matured into traits in which he took a pleasure—a witty tongue, a gift for wearing clothes, a grace in walking and dancing, an equipment of little mannerisms all her own. Richard was seldom in England while she was growing up, and when he did come he showed no interest in the girl he would have to marry someday. His interests were confined to fighting and hunting and drinking. To Richard the fine edge of a well-balanced sword or a horse of high mettle was of much more concern than the light in a lady's eyes. His father was more observant.

The wedding should have taken place when the princess reached her fifteenth birthday. Henry found some good reason for postponing it, probably the fact that he was under the necessity of traveling continuously about his unsettled dominions. Eleanor, of course, knew the real reason.

Kings had advantages over other men in the pursuit of romance, but they suffered from one serious handicap. They had no privacy at all and so could not conceal their illicit maneuverings. Henry's dalliance with Alice must therefore have followed along the usual lines. He spent longer hours with his officials in the chancellery, presumably in the preparation or revision of writs. Actually he was engaged much of the time in writing notes to the princess, a habit she found rather provoking, as she was not a good scholar and had the greatest difficulty in deciphering them. The humblest kitchen knave or scullion would know about these notes. The King was addicted to the chase, but sometimes he would develop a sudden desire to return to the castle. He would leave his horse with a groom conveniently stationed at the rear, slip in at a back postern, and hurry on tiptoe along halls which had been cleared in advance, reaching finally a room adjoining the apartments of Alice. He thought he was being clever and that no one guessed what it was all about; but the groom, the custodian of the postern, the servants who kept watch over the halls, and the ladies of the princess talked it over and snickered and speculated. Sometimes he would summon a conference of his advisers and would keep them an unconscionable time in an anteroom while they were supposed to be with him. In the meantime a door would open behind the King, he would hear a rustle of silken skirts and feel a hand touch his sleeve. A voice would whisper, "My sweet lord and King!" And all over the palace that evening there would be gossip and guessing as to how long the princess had stayed with him.

Eleanor did not need to be told. She had known all about such tricks as this before Henry was born. She was one of the first to realize that her husband was being guilty of the serious offense of toying with the affections of his daughter-in-law-elect. This was different from his earlier affairs. The Queen could forget about the Fair Rosamonde, but she could not pass over or condone anything as gross and dangerous as this. She knew with what zest this tidbit would be rolled over gossiping tongues in every court in Europe. She, the once fascinating Eleanor of Aquitaine, would become known as a neglected and deceived wife. This was not to be borne in silence.

Eleanor took her distress over the outrageous conduct of Henry to her sons. Their anger can be imagined, particularly that of Richard, who was the one directly injured. He had not shown any interest in the girl, but he was not willing to find himself decorated with antlers on his forehead even before he was married. All of the sons were fond of their mother, and their sympathies were entirely with her in this unsavory mess. When she was taken back to England a prisoner, their opposition to Henry became irreconcilable.

The Sin of Absalom

Curiously enough, the gossip in England at this point was not of Henry and Princess Alice but was all about the Fair Rosamonde. It had happened that the imprisonment of the Queen followed closely on the death of Rosamonde Clifford at Godstow, and the chance to link one event with the other was too good to be missed. It was taken for granted that Henry had remained faithful to his early mistress, that she had assumed the veil to escape the vengeance of the Queen but had been tracked down and poisoned nevertheless. The fact that Eleanor was kept a prisoner so long nourished the legend, and after that it could not be stopped. A ballad was evolved from the story, with all the imaginary trappings of maze and bower and ball of thread, and the wicked Queen and the cup of poison. Improvements were made in the ballad of *Henry and the Fair Rosamonde* as time rolled on. It was a favorite with minstrels for centuries after, the most often clamored for when a wandering crowder arrived at a tavern with his cithara over his shoulder. The final version was that of one Thomas Delone, written perhaps in the fifteenth century, in which some sweeping innovations appear, including a fanciful description of the House Beyond the Gate.

> *Most curiously the bower was built,*
> *Of stone and timber strong;*
> *One hundred and fifty doors*
> *Did to the bower belong,*
> *And they so cunningly contrived*
> *That none but with clue of thread*
> *Could enter in and out.*

The House Beyond the Gate, to return to earth after this not too poetic flight, was quite small. It was a single-story huddle of gray stone with one door, two or three windows, and perhaps a chimney.

In the meantime Louis of France had caught some echoes of the scandal involving his daughter, and he clamored indignantly for the wedding with Richard to take place as arranged, as a means of stopping the stories. Richard, prompted by a desire to put his father in a false position rather than a wish for his long-promised bride, joined in with the same demand. Henry found reasons for a further postponement.

This went on year after year. Henry showed all the resourcefulness of his one-time friend and chancellor, Thomas à Becket, in the contrivance of excuses. When Louis died in 1180 and was succeeded by his son Philip, the situation had not changed. Alice was still going wherever the King went, and Henry was more openly infatuated with her than ever. He was making covert advances to the Pope in the matter of a divorce from Eleanor. If he had succeeded in this, he would unquestionably have married the French princess at once and let the world say and think what it liked. But the Pope refused to consider the granting of a divorce.

On one occasion, when embarrassed by the embittered attitude of all his sons, Henry made a suggestion which obviously he had no thought of carrying out. He declared that, inasmuch as Richard had been a false and disobedient son, he would not allow him to marry the princess but that John, freed by the death of the heiress of Maurienne, should wed Alice as soon as he grew old enough. This served the same purpose of every suggestion Henry had made in the matter. Letters had to be exchanged and several months were wasted. As the idea found no favor, it was finally dropped, just as the King had intended.

The second Henry was finding himself, in fact, in much the same position as the last of the Henrys in the matter of Anne Boleyn. With a wife on his hands and no legitimate reason for a divorce, Henry VIII went to the extreme of separating England from Rome and then promulgating his own divorce. Henry II lived in an age when such a solution was unthinkable. All he could do was to play for time and hope that Eleanor would die. The few things known about Alice suggest that she had some qualities in common with Anne Boleyn. She was ambitious, clever, an aid to the King in planning the devious excuses which kept her from the nuptial couch of Richard. She must have been deeply attached to Henry or she would never have acquiesced in the highly unenviable position this created for her.

With Eleanor in captivity at Winchester, there was no longer need for the King to cover up his movements. His court became convinced that he and the princess were living together as man and wife, and so the whole world came to believe the same. Henry stood out in this matter against all counsel, all pressure, all the misfortunes which could be traced directly to his ill-advised course.

After Richard became King, Philip tried to force him to carry out the old arrangement and marry Alice. Richard refused on the ground that she had been his father's mistress and had borne him a son. If such were the case, the child was born abroad, for there are no records of it in England, and must, moreover, have died in infancy. Philip did not dispute the statement. He finally agreed to a cancellation of the betrothal, and Richard married Princess Berengaria of Navarre instead. Philip then gave his unfortunate sister in marriage to a nobleman of France; a sorry conclusion for her, but not as grim an ending as that of Anne Boleyn, who succeeded in making herself Queen and laid her head on the block because of her success.

But this was after the death of Henry. As long as he lived, he refused to give Princess Alice up. She was thirty-two when he died and for seventeen years had been the object of his infatuated attachment.

4

Another reason the sons had for their continuous efforts to free themselves of parental control was the stern and unchangeable nature of that control. Although Henry and Richard and Geoffrey were granted the outward semblance of authority, they were puppets in the fullest sense of the word. Henry always selected the men to work with them. He saw to it that these advisers and administrators had been thoroughly trained in his own ways of doing things. These stern Norman officials were under orders to see that nothing was done of which Henry would not have approved. If one of the sons differed from his advisers and decided to take matters into his hands, they would produce papers which showed they had the power and the son no more than a make-believe authority. If the son appealed to his father, the latter would side with the officials.

In 1168, when the people of Aquitaine had been on the point of rebellion, Henry had sent Eleanor to Bordeaux to assume the rulership of her own duchy. All Aquitaine was delighted. At last their beautiful Eleanor, to whom they had always given their full allegiance and with whose peccadilloes they had been rather pleased than otherwise, was back again. It seemed like a perfect arrangement, and the Queen approached her task with a deep sense of pleasure. But she soon found herself in the position which would later irk her sons. The Earl of Salisbury had been sent with her and also a whole corps of officials from the English *Curia* and chancellery. When Eleanor wanted to make changes to meet the demands of her people, the earl said no. She was unable to alter any of the laws and regulations which had caused their dissatisfaction. She sent passionately angry appeals to Henry to relieve her of these stern and heavy-handed men. Henry paid no attention. She was frustrated at every turn, and because she was doing nothing for them the people began to lose some of their affection for her, and this galled her high spirit.

The result was that the nobility of Aquitaine staged a palace revolution and murdered the Earl of Salisbury and all his seneschals in one day. The uprising had been badly planned and was soon suppressed. Eleanor was recalled to England, and the old methods of administration were continued thereafter without any change or amelioration.

The laws which Henry had established in England and which he was now enforcing in his continental dominions were better laws for the people than those which had existed before. It was the nobility who objected. They saw their feudal power being pared, they were forced to pay heavier taxes, they found themselves subjects under these new laws instead of rulers. They had for Henry nothing but hatred, these chivalrous knights of Aquitaine and Poitou. But Henry was right and they were wrong.

Unfortunately his sons lacked the insight which Henry possessed in such a great degree. It seemed to the three princes that their father was wrong and the barons who resisted him were right.

5

The struggle between Henry and his sons covered a period of sixteen years. It was very much confused and mixed up. At one time all the princes would be against their father. At other times they were fighting among themselves. At several stages the princes turned on their own allies in Aquitaine and Brittany and put them down with fire and sword.

In 1175 the king and *Li Reys Josnes* made a tour of England together. They visited the tomb of the Martyr. They made a close inspection of the Welsh Marches. They traveled as far north as York. This joint processional had a purpose, of course: to show the people of England that at last the differences between father and son had been adjusted and that once again there was amity in the royal family. Perhaps at no time in his life had Henry been happier.

In the full flush of this peacemaking he began to apply himself again to judicial reform. He defined more clearly the bounds of the six circuits and for the first time gave the *justiciarii itinerantes* power to deal with all cases, with questions of property and wardship and inheritance as well as crime and punishment. Henry remained two years in England, one of his longest stays. Around him at this time were the finest minds England had produced, historians, poets, lawyers. The lawyers were particularly noteworthy. The machinery of the state had created a new class, men of the law who had great ability and learning. Their equal was not to be found in any other country.

But in 1177 the trouble started afresh. The princes flew to arms again and Henry hurried back to Normandy. There seemed no way of pacifying his passionate brood. They hated him and they were at odds with one another. "Is it to be wondered at," asked Richard once, "that we live on such bad terms with one another, having sprung from such stock? From the devil we came, to the devil we must return."

The lionhearted prince was referring to a story about the Angevins which had been widely circulated and believed. The grandmother of Henry's father, the handsome and futile Geoffrey, had gone to mass so seldom that doubts had arisen about her. It was observed that she never remained for the consecration. Her husband decided to make a test and took four men to mass with them with orders that the countess was to be kept in her seat by force if necessary. When the moment came she sprang up as usual and they tried to lay hands on her. However, they only succeeded in retaining her cloak. The countess had flown out of the window, leaving behind her a frightened congregation and a strong smell of brimstone!

The third son, Geoffrey of Brittany, had the same fatalistic streak in him which Richard had displayed. "It is our proper nature," he declared, "planted in us by intention, that ever brother should strive against brother, and son against father."

There was so much switching of sides and betraying of allies that to recite the whole sequence of events would be repetitious and would, moreover, serve no useful purpose. Henry was not able to

fight against his rebellious cubs with his usual spirit. On two occasions he sent envoys to them to discuss peace, but they butchered
the unfortunate go-betweens by way of answer. Another time he
went to Limoges, and a shaft was launched at him from the battlements of the castle. It came close enough to its mark to kill his horse.
With tears streaming down his face the saddened King asked his
son Geoffrey, "What hast thy unfortunate father done to deserve
being made a mark for thy archers?"

These events were to have a sequel which involved Henry in the
greatest sorrow of his life. A message reached him in 1183 that his
eldest son was dangerously ill at Château Martel near Limoges and
wanted to see him. It looked like a trap. The King could not be sure
the message had come from his son and so paid no attention to it.

But the heir of England was even more ill than the message indicated. He was dying. A malignant fever had taken possession of
him, and he seemed to be burning away to nothing before the eyes of
his attendants. His sins weighed heavily on his mind and he talked
incessantly of the need for repentance. Finally, it being clear that
the end was at hand, the stricken young man asked that a bed of
cinders be made on the floor beside his couch and that a rope noose
be tied around his neck. He then ordered his servants to drag him
to the bed of cinders by the end of the rope. This was done, and in
a very few seconds the heir of England breathed his last.

The King had not loved anyone as much as his son Henry. The
news of his death was a loss from which the rapidly aging monarch
never recovered. It was clear to all about him that he had received
a mortal blow. He brooded continuously, his temper was short, he
took no interest in what went on about him. The Young King was
dead. Nothing else seemed to matter.

6

All through the harrowing struggle the hand of Bertran de Born
could be detected. This famous knight and troubadour, who was not
a rich landowner but the lord of a single castle in Périgueux called
Hautefort, had it firmly fixed in his mind that the only hope for the
people of the west and south was to keep the English and the
French at war. As long as Henry and Louis continued to fight, they
would not be free to disturb the peace-loving people of Aquitaine

and Limousin and Auvergne. To accomplish his purpose he proceeded to sow enmity between Henry and his sons. He was always at the shoulder of the Young King or of Richard, implanting suggestions and ideas which would keep the feud alive. Everything that happened was grist to his mill. He made capital of Henry's overtures to Rome in the matter of a divorce. He disturbed the minds of the naturally suspicious princes by surmises as to what was behind the appointment to the chancellery of Geoffrey, the bastard son of Fair Rosamonde. Did the King harbor any idea of giving preference to Geoffrey at his death?

When Eleanor was made a prisoner he wrote a song of lamentation which struck sorrow to the hearts of Aquitaine. "Return, poor prisoner!" he declaimed in verse. "Return to thy people, if thou canst. And if thou canst not, weep and say, 'Alas, how long is my exile!' Weep, weep again, and say, 'My tears are my bread, both day and night!'"

When the Young King first threw in his lot with Richard and the Aquitainians, a coalition which the machiavellian knight himself had done much to bring about, he wrote his most famous *sirvientes, Pois Ventadorns e Combor ab Segur.* This song reverberated throughout Aquitaine, and it brought armed men riding in with Eleanor's colors on their lance tips and a fever in their blood to sever the tie with the Angevin empire. As has already been told, however, the coalition proved an unhappy one. The first hint of reverse sent a cold chill down the spine of Louis, and so the Young King felt compelled to abandon his allies.

Bertran de Born seems to have had a great affection for *Li Reys Josnes*. He was always ready to forgive his vacillations and prepared to trust him again, even after it became abundantly clear that the English prince was unstable and treacherous. The death of the prince at Château Martel caused him genuine grief which he vented in two beautiful songs. With Richard, however, he was continually on his guard. He it was who coined the phrase *Richard Oc e No* for that war-loving prince, Richard Yea and Nay.

The activities of the knight of Hautefort were maintained after the death of the oldest son, and they involved him finally in a struggle for his existence against the King and Richard, the latter having decided for some unexplained reason to support his father against his former friends and associates in rebellion. King Henry had been aware of the activities and plottings of Bertran de Born and had marked him for punishment. The chance to deal with the fearless troubadour seemed to have arrived. Henry marched his forces down the Loire and into Limousin and invested the castle of Hautefort.

It was not one of the strong feudal castles which could resist attack indefinitely. Originally no more than a motte and bailey, a central court surrounded by a line of fortification, it was built with some thought to comfort and the possibility of gardens and flowers under the warm southern sun. However, the uncertainty of the times had persuaded the owner to the addition of bastions and to raising the walls. He defended himself, therefore, with such spirit and success that the King was finally compelled to use a *malvoisin*. It was a "bad neighbor" in every sense of the word, for it was a wooden tower which rose above the level of the walls of the castle and thus turned the tables on the defenders. Bertran and his men were no longer in a position to shoot arrows and hurl stones and pitch on the besieging army from a superior height; instead they were exposed to bombardments from the top of the *malvoisin*. It was impossible for the garrison to hold out, and the troubadour knight surrendered.

He was certain, when he was summoned to appear before Henry in the lower level of the temporary tower, where the King had settled himself, that he would not have long to live. Accordingly he laid aside his battered hauberk and arrayed himself in his best attire. The men of the south went in much for fine silks and velvets and the most pleasing colors, and the cloak which the vanquished knight wore into the presence of his victorious foe was of a rich blue with trimmings of white and gold. He had curled and perfumed his hair and was wearing rings on his fingers.

The interior of the *malvoisin* was dark, as there were only a few slits in the wooden walls for light and ventilation. Ladders had been built up into the high belly of the tower, and there were piles of shavings and empty sacks and a peasant's bed in one corner which the head of the Angevin empire had been using. Richard, his face set and unfriendly, was sitting on a pile of saddles. The King, as usual, was pacing up and down.

Henry came to a stop in front of the captive and ran a bitter eye over the fine plumage of the man who had caused him so much trouble.

"Bertran, Bertran, you used to say you never had occasion for half your wit," he said. Then he threw back his head and laughed. "The time has come when you'll need more wit than you ever possessed."

The knight returned the King's glance with complete ease. He had made up his mind to death and so was beyond fear. "My lord, it is true," he said. "I spoke even so; and what I said was the truth."

The light back of Henry's eyes could be clearly seen, spelling danger for the man who faced him so easily. "I think your wit has failed you at last," said the King.

Bertran de Born nodded his head slowly. "Yes. It failed me on the day when the valiant Young King, your son, expired. On that day I lost sense and knowledge as well as wit."

Henry had known, of course, of the deep affection the knight felt for his son. Silence took possession of the room and then, to the surprise of everyone, it was seen that the King was weeping. He walked slowly to one of the narrow apertures in the dusty wall, his thoughts bitterly concerned with the vision of his beloved son, a rope around his neck, dying alone on a bed of cinders. Suddenly he reached out a hand to the wall but toppled back before he could stay himself. He fell to the floor in a dead faint.

When the King regained his senses, it seemed to him that no more than a second of time had elapsed. Bertran de Born had not moved from his position, and his hand was still on his belt of silver links which he had been fingering when the King collapsed. Richard was still sitting on the saddles, his reddish-gold head bent over deliberately and his hands tightly clasped, as though they desired a chance to close around the neck of this impudent knight. A servant, who had been washing the royal face with cold water, immediately betook himself out of sight when it was apparent that the King had recovered his senses.

Henry got slowly to his feet. He rubbed a hand over his eyes. "Sir Bertran——" he began. His mood had changed completely, and it was clear that all hostile purpose had left him. "You had good reason," he went on in a sad tone, "and good right to lose your wits for my son. He wished you better than any man in the world." Better than he had wished his father! Henry knew this. He sighed deeply. "For love of him, I give you your life, your castle, and—and all you have."

Turning to leave through the open door of the dark shed, the King nodded once to the knight, muttered that he would be paid five hundred silver marks for the losses he had suffered, and shuffled slowly out. Richard followed, with a scowl which made it clear he did not share his father's willingness to forgive.

The part played by Bertran de Born has been debated down the ages and has been variously interpreted. In his own country, where men knew the need which had driven him, he was regarded as a hero and even a statesman. Too many refused to remember anything save that he had incited the sons to rise against their father. Dante heard the story of the man who sowed dissension and proceeded to insert the troubadour knight in the *Inferno*. In Canto 28 he describes a headless figure stumbling through the gloom of the nether regions and carrying his severed head in his hands. "Bertran de Born am I," declared this specter, "the man who gave such evil counsel to the youthful King. Father and son I set against each other."

The inspired Italian should have looked more carefully into the records of that day.

That the troubadour's actions were inspired by a patriotic motive was proven during the last stages of the struggle between Henry and his remaining sons. He took the side of Richard, the son who had not forgiven him, against the father who had been so magnanimous! He did this because Henry was still bent on keeping Aquitaine under his own stern control, while Richard had been won over to the idea of letting the gay and carefree people do as they pleased.

7

The death of Louis provided Henry with a harder and much more resourceful opponent. Philip was only fourteen years old when he ascended the throne of France, but he was soon to give proofs of his mettle.

Several references have been made to Gisors as the scene of peace conferences. It had been selected for the purpose because it possessed a remarkable oak tree, a magnificent specimen so large that it took four men to span the trunk with their arms. The branches extended out and touched the ground and thus, like the banyan tree, made a cool and well-shaded arbor where many men could assemble in comfort. On one of the occasions when Henry and Louis had met under the oak tree to settle their differences, the latter had brought his son with him. Henry was conscious from the first moment of the steady regard of the youthful prince, an unfriendly and unblinking look. Not until the parleys had ended did the boy venture to speak. Then, planting himself in front of Henry and pointing an accusing finger, he addressed the King of England.

"My lord," he said, "you do my father wrong. I perceive you can always get the better of him. I can't hinder you, my lord, but I tell you now that, when I am grown up, I will take back all of which you have deprived him."

From the moment he became King, Philip set himself with a fierce determination, which seemed strange in a boy of his years, to carrying out his threat. He made a point of winning the friendship of the three remaining sons of the English King and became particularly close to Geoffrey, the Duke of Brittany. Geoffrey was the most difficult of all the English princes, and so his liking for Philip was certain to cause trouble. The tie was soon broken, however, in a way which caused the tired King still more grief. Geoffrey, who was the handsomest member of the royal family and almost as adept with arms as the mighty Richard, entered a tournament in Paris. He was thrown from his horse and trampled to death.

The tragedy was an even greater blow to Eleanor, who had loved Geoffrey next to Richard. She received the news of his death at Winchester, and it caused her to fall into a long period of deep melancholy. She had been addressing letters to the Pope with complaints of her plight, and in one of them she wrote, "The Young King and the Duke of Brittany both sleep in dust while their wretched mother is compelled to live on, though tortured by the irremediable recollections of the dead."

Before the French King could set his coalition in action against Henry, Archbishop William of Tyre came through Europe, preaching a new crusade. The Christians in Palestine had not been able to maintain themselves against a great leader who had arisen among the Saracens named Sallah-ed-din, which later was corrupted to Saladin. The royal house of Jerusalem had ended in a girl named Sibylla, and the man she married, Guy of Lusignan, had been declared King. He was not capable of contending against Saladin. Tiberias fell to the infidels, and the capture of Jerusalem itself followed soon after. As a result the Holy Cross was taken by the Saracen forces.

William of Tyre, depicting the cross in the hands of unbelievers, fired the minds of the people of western Europe with the same fervor which Peter the Hermit and Bernard of Clairvaux had created for the First and Second Crusades. Philip and Richard decided they would take the cross and go together. Even in Henry's old veins the blood began to pound. He could not go himself, but he promised to back the effort with all his resources. A truce was declared which was to last until the concerted attack of the west had wrested the Holy Land once more from the paynim. The Church, naturally, was anxious to keep the peace, and Archbishop Baldwin of Canterbury issued an automatic writ of excommunication against anyone who might initiate strife during a period of seven years. Henry's approval of this measure had been secured in advance. It was all in his favor, for what he desired above everything was peace with his sons and with France. He had welcomed the preaching of the Crusade as a diversion which might keep these passionate young men busy. Philip and Richard were furious, and the latter said openly he would pay no heed to the writ if events made it necessary for him to break again with his father. Except in moments of intense emotional strain, Richard had small regard for the Church. The irreligious streak which had always been exhibited by the Angevins was particularly noticeable in the prince of the lion heart.

Henry returned to England to raise the funds needed for the army he had promised. He levied a tax of ten per cent on all property and was stern and unrelenting in the collection. He went from city to city himself, talking to his subjects and questioning them as to their ability to pay. He does not seem to have been particularly happy over the need for this sharp assessment. The fervor inspired by William of Tyre was beginning to evaporate, and he did not like to draw so deeply on the wealth of his kingdom. He became irritable, and any suggestion of criticism caused his temper to flare. "If they curse me now," he retorted to the wife of a baron who had said the people were turning against him, "it is without just cause. If I live to see the end of this, they shall curse me again—and with just cause!"

Soon after this he learned that Philip had disregarded Baldwin's writ and broken the truce. He had invaded Auvergne and captured many castles. Aquitaine was rising to help him, and it was said that Richard would be in the French camp.

Henry crossed hurriedly to France. The army he took with him was small, and his movements lacked the speed and sureness he had always shown in his campaigns. He had little stomach left, it was clear, for this continuous family warfare. He said repeatedly that he did not expect to see England again.

The Church, fearing that war in France might end the plans for the Crusade, did everything possible to settle the differences. Philip was persuaded to meet Henry under the oak of Gisors. Perhaps his willingness to see his aging rival was due to memory of that occasion when he had threatened the great Angevin monarch. It was time for retaliation to begin. They met, as a result, in a mood of mutual animosity. Old wrongs filled the mind of the French King, while Henry soon realized that he had already conceived a greater dislike for the aggressive youth than he had ever felt for the ineffective father. It was impossible for anything good to come out of such a meeting. The two monarchs argued bitterly for three days and then parted without reaching terms.

Later they met at Bonmoulins, again on the urging of the Church, and here Henry was subjected to the greatest humiliation he had yet experienced in life. He saw his son Richard bow the knee to Philip and swear homage for all the lands he ruled in his mother's right. It developed later that the Lionheart had thus belittled himself because he had heard Henry was planning to thrust him aside and declare John his successor. Perhaps Henry had been moving in that direction. He had suggested again that the way to settle the long squabble over Princess Alice was to make her John's wife—a little later. This could easily have aroused suspicions in the mind of Richard.

A troop of French men-at-arms had come into the Council Room and had stationed themselves between the English King and his son. They were not needed, however. Henry was too stunned to make any move. A very sick and weary man, he watched his son and the scornful young King of France walk out together, their arms on each other's shoulders. It had not taken Philip long to carry out the threat he had made as a boy.

The Crusade was forgotten and war began at once. The French came up to Le Mans where Henry had stationed himself with his small army, burning the towns and laying the country waste. Henry was in no position to meet the thrust. Most of his troops were mercenaries and they were few in number. He had made no effort to recruit a large army in England to oppose this threat to his continental possessions, knowing that the English, even the barons of Norman extraction, were weary of the continual struggle and unwilling to take any further part. He was too old and too ill to triumph over the difficulties which now faced him or to improvise ways of averting military disaster as he had done so often before. No longer was he opposed by a weak opponent. Without making any attempt to protect Le Mans, Henry retreated north. It is said that, looking back at the flames of the city which the French had proceeded to destroy, he cried out bitterly against the God who thus heaped humiliation and misfortune on him in his old age.

The final stages in the life of this remarkable man had one redeeming note only. His illegitimate son Geoffrey had come over to France to be beside him. They rode stirrup to stirrup, and the son did everything in his power to raise the spirits of the sick monarch. He tried to anticipate his wants and to take all responsibilities on his own shoulders.

Richard pursued them from Le Mans. He had set out in such haste that he was without armor. Overtaking the English rear guard, he suddenly realized that he had outridden his own men and that the English marshal was in a position to either kill him or take him prisoner. Reining in sharply, he called attention to the fact that he was without his hauberk.

William the Marshal lacked the resolution of Joab, that stout Hebrew warrior who disregarded David's orders and drove his darts into the suspended form of Absalom. Much as he would have preferred to end the family strife by killing the prince, he launched his lance instead into the neck of Richard's horse and turned to ride away.

"I leave *you* to the devil!" he said.

Keep this knight William Marshal in mind. He will play a great part in later events.

By nightfall the royal party was close to the borders of Normandy, and Geoffrey urged his father to ride on to safety. But the old lion was recovering some of his former resolution. He said no, he would stay where he was for the night and in the morning he would strike back for Anjou. Anjou was his own country, he declared, and nothing could compel him to abandon it. Geoffrey, in a panic, pointed out that to reach his Angevin provinces he would have to ride through territory now in the hands of the French. He would be killed or captured if he attempted anything as foolhardy as that. Henry's answer to his son was an order to ride on into Normandy himself and to raise whatever forces he could. He was to come back as soon as possible, and in the meantime the King would stay where he was.

Geoffrey followed his instructions and returned with more troops in a few days. He found his father as determined as ever to ride to Anjou. Shaking his head in despair, the young chancellor organized their scanty forces and led the way south.

To the surprise of them all, they succeeded in reaching Chinon, which lies south and west of Tours, without encountering any opposition. This was the last thing the French had expected them to do, and so to the sheer insanity of the move they owed their success.

Henry decided to remain at Chinon. Perhaps he did so because it was in this huge hilltop castle that all the trouble had started. Here his son Henry had left him the first time; here, then, the last act of the tragedy should be played out. He was a different Henry from the keen and farseeing King who had always known the right thing to do, this silent man who thus sat down in the midst of his enemies and waited for them to strike. A fatalistic mood had taken possession of him. He did not fear them. Let them do their worst!

He had not long to wait. Word reached the castle that Philip was marching down the Loire with his victorious troops. In the south and west the provinces were in revolt. Henry had no more chance of standing out against the clamoring forces of rebellion than had Canute when he faced the tidal waters. Nevertheless, he refused to move. Better to die where he was than to run away!

The triumphant youth who now wore the crown of France summoned the deserted King to meet him at Colombières near Tours. Henry, after much unhappy thought and against the advice of Geoffrey, decided to go. He managed to get into his saddle but soon became too weak to complete the journey. Geoffrey sent word that the King was seriously ill and would not be able to reach the plains selected for the conference.

Philip discussed the situation with Richard and his own military advisers. What was to be done under these circumstances? Should they wait until Henry recovered his strength or should they go to him and tell him the humiliating terms they had decided upon? The eyes of the youthful monarch had a resentful glow as he propounded the problem. He was thinking of those earlier conferences when it had been clear even to a boy that the King of France was being circumvented and forced into distasteful concessions and even hoaxed by the King of England. He did not want to wait any longer for the roles to be reversed.

Richard's opinion, spoken with no trace of filial anxiety, was exactly what the French King wanted to hear. He was sure that his father was not ill. He, Richard, knew all about the wiles he resorted to, his sly maneuverings, when he faced defeat. Demand that he appear at the appointed place and see how quickly he would come to heel: such was the advice of this dutiful son. It was accepted gladly, and a peremptory message was sent to the sick old man. He must present himself at Colombières the following day.

Henry rose from his couch when this word reached him. His face was a sickly gray, his eyes were dull and full of distress, his hands trembled as he fumbled with his sword. He still had a little of his indomitable spirit left, however, for he muttered as his squires lifted him to the saddle, "I will win my land back in spite of them!" Geoffrey had wanted him to ride in a litter, but the suggestion had been brushed aside impatiently.

Even Philip felt some compunction when Henry arrived at Colombières. The mark of death was on the gray face and the stooped back of his father's foe. He asked Henry to take a comfortable seat. The English King refused. He remained in his saddle and demanded, with the sharp impatience of physical suffering, that he know their minds at once. So weak that he had to grip the horns of the saddle, he was hearing a boyish voice say, "When I am grown up, I will take back all of which you have deprived him." The same voice, not yet having achieved a full mature note, was proceeding now to tell him the bitter terms on which he might have peace.

First he must do homage to Philip for all his possessions in France. The sick man straightened instinctively in his saddle when he heard this. He had always refused to recognize Louis as his suzerain. Could he swallow such a bitter pill? He glanced at the circle of hostile faces about him. Pay homage to France? He would do so, he said finally in a low voice, if the oath were so phrased that his honor would not be compromised, nor the dignity of his kingdom.

The words were scarcely out of his mouth when a roar of laughter went up from the followers of the French King. Richard and his men joined in. Henry was startled and glared about him at the guffawing crowd. Ah, if he were only younger! He would teach these jeering fools to show him respect. Then the reason for their amusement flashed into his mind; his answer had been almost identical with that which Thomas à Becket had given him when he demanded the obedience of the servants of the Church. What was it his recalcitrant primate had said? *Saving our order.* Yes, the meaning was the same. He had not realized it when the words rose to his lips. No wonder they were laughing at him.

A disturbing thought entered his mind perhaps. Was this, then, a part of his punishment? Would the evil he had done pursue him as long as he lived?

The French King was going on with the rest of the terms. He, Henry, must acknowledge Richard as his successor and see that the prince received homage at once from his future subjects. Henry nodded his head to this. Granted.

Princess Alice must be placed in the care of the Archbishop of Canterbury or His Grace of Rouen until the Crusade was over, at which time her future would be decided. There was silence for a moment and then a slow nod of the head. Granted.

Philip and Richard were to hold all the lands they had conquered, Touraine and Le Mans and Maine, as pledges that the terms of the peace would be carried out. Granted.

Henry was to pay France as compensation for the costs of the campaign the sum of twenty thousand marks. Granted.

It must be agreed that the barons of England would force him to compliance if at any time he showed a tendency to repudiate the treaty. Henry's face flushed angrily. The barons, his own subjects, were to force *him* to live up to these terms? He said nothing, however. Even this humiliation, he realized, must be borne. Granted!

Finally, he must forgive all his subjects who had thrown in their lot with Richard against him. Granted.

He had given in and accepted these debasing terms without a protest. His spirit was so broken, in fact, that he said nothing when

Geoffrey ordered his squires to lift him from the saddle and place him in a litter. He seemed glad that he would not have to endure again the agony of the long ride.

At Chinon they found the terms already there in writing for the King's signature. Geoffrey, on his father's request, read them out. He read slowly and reluctantly, still finding it hard to believe that the great King had suffered a complete defeat. When he came to the list of those who had conspired with Richard and who must now be forgiven, his voice dropped to a note of disbelief.

"My lord," he exclaimed, "it is impossible!"

The dying King expressed no interest. When there had been so much treachery and breaking of vows, did it matter about the names on this list?

"My lord," whispered Geoffrey, "I must tell you that the first name given is—John, Count of Mortaigne!"

The King's eyes opened. "John?" he cried hoarsely. "John, my heart, my loved son! It can't be! He for whose sake I have suffered all this! Has he also forsaken me?"

"My lord, the name is here."

The broken man turned his face to the wall. "Let the rest go as it will," he whispered. "Now I care not what becomes of me!"

For seven days he lay on his couch, growing weaker with each hour, his eyes fixed on the wall. Once his strong spirit roused from the lethargy of approaching death. "Shame!" he was heard to mutter. "Shame on a conquered king!"

He died with his head on Geoffrey's breast, after speaking for a moment rationally and affectionately and giving him a ring of great value from his finger. Perhaps he said again, "Thou art my true son." Certainly the last days of his life had made the truth of that abundantly clear.

The body was removed to the Abbey of Fontevraud, and here Richard came to look on his father as he lay in state before the altar. All the chronicles of the day agree that blood flowed from the nose and mouth of the dead King and that Richard fell to his knees and began to weep, denouncing himself as the cause of his father's death.

It has always been the way of court officials and servants, when they hear the solemn cry, "The King is dead: long live the King!" to lose no time in bowing the knee of submission to the new occupant of the throne. There have been many instances in history when the body has been left alone while the lickspittle crew rushed to curry favor, and in some cases thieves took advantage of the chance to rob the royal clay.

It is said that the corpse of Henry II was plundered in this way and that the officials responsible for the funeral arrangements found it necessary to resort to sorry expedients; that they used an old and battered scepter and a ring of small value for his finger and even had to take a strip of gold fringe from a lady's undergarment and twist and flute it into a semblance of a crown, so that the great monarch went to his final rest as grotesquely arrayed as a street mummer.

This is denied in other versions. It is asserted that Henry was properly prepared for his lying in state, that a dalmatic of crimson, powdered with gold flowers, covered him to his ankles, that over this was a mantle of deep chocolate with a gold brooch fastening it at the shoulder in the accepted fashion, and that his hands were covered with elaborately jeweled gloves while his feet were in boots of green leather with spurs of gold.

The second version is the easier to believe. It is certain that Geoffrey remained with the body to prevent any indignities being perpetrated. Nor should any belief be put in the story so often told that the face of the dead King was contorted with the feelings of rage and hatred which had filled his mind while he breathed his last. The medieval custom of exposing the bodies of kings and queens for long periods of time so that all their subjects who so desired might see them was dependent on the making of wax replicas for the purpose. It was done secretly, however, and the people always believed that they had seen the actual bodies. It is related that when the effigy of a much-loved queen was surrounded by four thousand wax candles it began to show the effects of so much heat and had to be hastily removed.

It is probable that the body which lay in state in the Abbey of Fontevraud was not that of the King who had striven so hard to be a good king. All that was left of the real Henry had almost certainly been at rest long before the last of his curious subjects had filed by the bier. The expression they saw on his face may have been of their own beholding or a proof of the art, or lack of it, of the one who fashioned the wax.

CHAPTER XI

The Milch Cow of the Third Crusade

ALTHOUGH historians have done their best to present Richard I as a bad king and a man of extraordinary selfishness and cruelty, it has been impossible to shake the popular view which places Coeur de Lion on the highest pedestal. That he was a sagacious general as well as a great fighting man has more than balanced in the scales of public opinion the fact that he was worthless as a ruler.

It is not surprising that he lacked most of the qualities which made his father so outstanding. Henry II was raised in an atmosphere of struggle and dissension and of continual uncertainty as to the future. This toughened his mental fiber and at the same time lent him resolution and a practical and realistic viewpoint. When he ascended the throne he faced conditions which called for the exercise of wisdom, determination, and courage. Richard grew up as the Angevin sun mounted ever higher in the sky, and all his years he lived in an atmosphere of adulation and glory. He was the handsomest of men, or so those who flocked about him said; he was the greatest fighter, the deadliest wrestler, the fastest runner, the finest poet, and the most beguiling troubadour in the whole wide world. His mother worshiped him, and this confirmed the sycophantic chorus of the court. Richard was taught to believe in his own omnipotence. He knew victory only and was ready to pay any price for it.

Still more fatal to the development in him of the qualities needed in a ruler was the Code of Chivalry which guided him throughout his life. Chivalry was a shield of two sides, the outer a shining promise of high honor and courage and self-sacrifice, the hidden side a hideous picture of darkness and superstition and cruelty. The exultant glow of the one has triumphed over the reverse, and the word chivalry has come to mean everything fine and loyal and brave. But time has been a false interpreter. Richard was the perfect product of the code, and all his life he was base and cruel to those under him and willing to be dishonest in his dealings with his subjects in order to achieve a few moments of high triumph on the field of battle. Such was chivalry, such was Richard.

Efforts have been made to judge the King separately from the knight and to keep the callousness of the former from sight by thinking only of the exploits of the crusading leader. But Richard was in everything the knight. It was always the knight who sat at the head of the *Curia* and passed on matters of state. The King did not make a belated appearance when the knight laid aside his heavy iron helmet and unlaced his body armor. It was the knight who lavished the gold of the kingdom on his Palestine adventure and sold everything for which a buyer could be found from a royal castle to a decision in a lawsuit. It was the knight who came back after his long imprisonment and reinstated the bad minister thrown out by his irate subjects. Richard was always the knight and, except for brief moments near the end when he displayed flashes of statesmanship, never the King.

But the facts of his ten-year reign will speak for themselves.

2

Richard began his reign with a properly filial gesture. He dispatched word from Normandy that his mother was to be released at once and was to act as regent of England until he could arrive. The Eleanor who emerged from the castle on the hill beyond Winchester was different from the rebellious and angry woman who had been placed there sixteen years before. Her captivity had been neither close nor unpleasant. Ranulf de Glanville had been a careful custodian but never unfair or unfriendly. The Queen's household had lacked nothing. They had taken their meals in the Great Hall, a not unmixed advantage because the small, round-headed Norman windows made it gloomy. They had pleasant gardens and were allowed to ride and walk under proper guard. The Queen said good-by to her jailer with every evidence of good will.

She took advantage of her powers as regent to perform acts of moderation and mercy. She went from town to town, writes Tyrrell, "setting free all those confined under the Norman game laws which in the later part of Henry's life were cruelly enforced. When she released prisoners, it was on condition that they prayed for the soul of her late husband. She likewise declared she took this measure for the benefit of her soul."

Richard landed at Portsmouth on August 12, 1189. He was almost a stranger, having spent practically all of his life in the south. In a hurry to greet his mother, and learning that she had returned to Winchester, he rode there at once. It was so long since he had seen her that no doubt he wondered if he would be able to recognize her. But Eleanor had not changed much. She was close to seventy now and her hair was white, but the vitality she had always possessed had kept her erect and well. She still had beauty.

Richard himself was now thirty-two years old and at the peak of his physical powers, a vigorous and handsome man. Eleanor's delight in their reunion did not blind her, however, to the faults in what he was planning to do. He was especially bitter about Ranulf de Glanville. "That rogue shall be thrown into the dungeons," he declared, "and loaded with fetters of a thousand pounds!" Some historians say that his mother succeeded in convincing him that her jailer had been considerate and that it would be better to load him with responsibilities than a thousand pounds of chain. Richard of Devizes declares, however, that Glanville had to ruin himself by paying a fine of fifteen thousand pounds of silver, but for reasons which will develop later this seems unlikely.

There was a set pattern about the assumption of kingly power, and a new ruler's first official act was to get his hands on the royal treasure. William Rufus, Henry I, Stephen, Henry II, each of them had come on the gallop to find what the vaults contained. Richard was no exception. Knowing how much gold he was going to need, he was fairly panting with impatience.

The result of the first search was disappointing, for only the relatively small sum of one hundred thousand marks was located. The new King had opened the vaults himself, assisted by some of his closest servants, and without the presence of Ranulf de Glanville. When Richard came in a rage to his mother and said that, by God's feet, he knew there had been looting, Eleanor calmed him down. Had he consulted the chief justiciar in the matter? The late King, she pointed out, had been a man of much discretion and without a doubt had taken special precautions to protect the royal stores. If such were the case, the only man who had shared the secret was Ranulf de Glanville. Richard acted on this suggestion and summoned Glanville to his presence. The latter confirmed what Eleanor had suspected. The late King *had* installed new vaults, the existence of which had been a closely held secret. The keys were produced at once.

The second search revealed a treasure of magnificent proportions, no less than nine hundred thousand pounds, an enormous sum in those days, and much valuable jewelry as well. Richard was amazed at the size of his father's savings. He had believed that the emptiness of the treasury had made it impossible for his father to raise an adequate army for his final bout with the French. Why had Henry refused to use the gold in his secret vaults? Had a miserly streak taken possession of him at the last? Or had it been a sense of responsibility, a feeling that this surplus constituted a national asset and should not be dissipated?

Personal relationships played considerable part in the first discussions that mother and son had together. Richard had seen Geoffrey, the illegitimate brother, in Normandy and had informed him he was no longer chancellor. He had agreed, however, to make Geoffrey Archbishop of York for a substantial sum, three thousand pounds, on the understanding that he was to take holy orders at once and stay out of England for three years. His reason for the last stipulation was easy to understand. The new King did not want anyone as clever and ambitious and popular as Geoffrey in the kingdom while he was away on the Crusades. However, he had been less careful in connection with John. He had brought that dangerous young man with him and had given him six earldoms and eight castles. John, making no promises and divulging none of the schemes which filled his covetous head, was likely to prove a contender with so much power. Richard would have been better advised to keep John out of England and allow Geoffrey a free hand.

For her part, Eleanor was concerned over the marriage plans of the bachelor King. She was determined he was not to marry Alice, and to make sure of this (and to satisfy a somewhat natural grudge) the Dowager Queen had already installed her rival in the role she had played so long herself, the prisoner of Winchester. Richard was not disturbed. He had no desire for secondhand goods and, in any event, he had decided to select his own wife. His choice, he told Eleanor, was Princess Berengaria of Navarre.

His mother must have been shocked at this announcement. The new head of the Angevin empire could have any wife he desired. Why should he be content with the daughter of a third-rate king? What advantage would there be in an alliance with Navarre? But Richard's mind was made up, and Eleanor loved him too well to stand in the way of his happiness. It was agreed that she would go to Pampeluna, the capital of Navarre, and see to the necessary arrangements.

The crowning of Richard was the most dramatic and tragic of all coronation ceremonies held at Westminster. There had been much shaking of heads about the date selected, September 3, which astrologers had always considered one of ill omen, calling it Egyptian Day. To lend substance to the apprehensions, a bat found its way into the abbey and circled around during the ceremony. It showed a preference for the coronation chair and wheeled and flapped about it persistently. Still more startling was a loud peal from the bell tower at the conclusion. The bell ringers swore they had not been responsible, and everyone was convinced that the hands which pulled the ropes had not been mortal. These were small matters, however, compared with what came later that day.

The ceremony itself was carried through with great pomp. Richard walked to the palace between the bishops of Durham and Bath, and for the anointing he fulfilled the letter of the ritual by allowing himself to be stripped to his shirt and drawers. It was felt by everyone in that immense interior that never before had a more kingly-looking ruler taken the oath.

The massacre of the Jews with which the coronation of Richard is associated in history did not begin until the banquet was under way. The King had issued a proclamation the day before, forbidding the attendance of Jews and witches at the ceremony. When a crusade was being preached feelings ran high against the first named, and it had probably been wise to keep them away from a public occasion. But why had witches been included in the prohibition? Was it, asked wags in the taverns, because the King remembered his great-grandmother who had flown out of the window of a church on a broomstick?

No witches tried to attend (unless the bat was one in disguise), but unfortunately a few of the wealthy Jews of London came to Westminster Palace as the banquet started, thinking the order no longer applied and bringing handsome gifts for the newly crowned monarch. Some of the barons resented their presence and had them forcibly ejected. The grounds around Westminster were still filled with people, and the word circulated through the crowd that there had been a plot against the life of the King. Any excuse, even one as feeble as this, was all that was needed. The unwanted gift bearers were knocked about and kicked and beaten. A few were killed and many were badly injured. Their appetite for blood whetted, the people marched back to the city, shouting, "Death to the unbelievers!" Once rioting had started there, nothing could stop it. Most of the houses in the Jewry were burned or wrecked and many lives were taken.

It happened that a deputation of two men named Baruch and Jossen had been sent to London by the Jews of York. Baruch was caught by the mob and severely beaten. He was given the choice of accepting the cross or being hanged to the nearest signpost, and decided to save his life by pretending to abjure his faith. When word of this reached the King, he insisted that Baruch be brought to him for questioning. He asked the old man if he really believed Christ to be the Messiah. The victim of mob violence, recovering his courage, had the fortitude to answer, "No."

When pressed for an explanation, he told the truth, that he was not a convert and would never give up the faith of his race. Richard turned to Baldwin, the Archbishop of Canterbury, and asked what punishment should be inflicted on the self-confessed rogue. The latter replied that he thought the unfortunate man had been punished enough already. The primate was right. Baruch died within a few days from the injuries he had received.

Jossen returned alone to York, discovering as he progressed northward that the riots were spreading throughout the country. He found it necessary to travel by side roads, and only by the exercise of the greatest caution was he able to reach York alive.

The Jewish people living in York were numerous and unusually wealthy, but, as they had gradually drawn into their hands all the banking of the north counties, there were plenty in the city glad of a chance to despoil them. Almost immediately after the return of Jossen a mob broke into the Jewish quarter, looting the shops, burning the houses, and killing all they could get their hands on. Those who survived, more than a thousand in all, took refuge in the King's palace, where, under the leadership of Jossen, they defended themselves with great courage. The rioters sought assistance from prominent members of the baronage and did not find it difficult to interest all who owed money to any of the victims of the purge.

Seeing they were in a hopeless position, the defenders decided to kill themselves rather than surrender to the bloodthirsty mobs. They dispatched their wives and children first and then cut their own throats. The small minority who offered to give themselves up were promised terms but were butchered as soon as they opened the gates. The palace had been set on fire by the more resolute ones, and much of their wealth was destroyed by the flames.

It was a violent beginning to the ten violent years of Richard's reign.

3

During the last visit he paid to England before becoming King, Richard had been in the offices of the chancellery; briefly, because of his dislike for his bastard brother Geoffrey, who was then in possession of the Seal. As he walked down the stone hall he chanced to glance into one of the small rooms where the clerks were employed, and his eyes encountered those of the occupant. People are always staring at royalty, and Richard was so accustomed to it that he would not have paid attention if the appearance of the man in his gloomy little cell had not been so unusual. He was small—a dwarf, in fact—and a most unpleasant-looking one, with a twisted back and dead, unblinking eyes. This curious official was to play a spectacular part in English history under the name of William de Longchamp, a fictitious name according to some historians who deny him noble birth. Nothing much is known about him in reality, except that Richard saw him first in the chancellery offices and that later he was moved to Rouen at the insistence of Henry, who did not trust him. It must have been in Rouen that Richard had his first talk with the man, for soon after his transfer to that city he became chancellor of Poitou.

It developed in the course of the first talk that Longchamp was one of those clever and observant officials who are often found in administrative departments. They are the Flambards, the Thomas Cromwells, who poke their noses into state papers, who study furtively by candlelight, who ferret out secrets they are not afraid to use. When opportunities arise they offer plans more daring and more susceptible of success than anything their superiors have dared advocate. Longchamp had something new to offer Richard, an original method of raising money which would be helpful when the latter assumed the crown. Richard was impressed, as the appointment of Longchamp to an executive post under him makes clear.

And now Richard was King and needed all the money he could get his hands on. Soon after his arrival in England, Westminster heard something which caused a wave of disbelief, astonishment, and horror to spread. William Longchamp, the misshapen little man with the cold dead eyes of a fish, had been appointed chancellor!

At the same time Longchamp was made Bishop of Ely and chief justiciar for the south of England, with the Tower of London as his official residence. He was to divide responsibility for the government of the kingdom during Richard's absence with Hugh de Puiset, who held the palatine bishopric of Durham. Hugh de Puiset was first cousin to Richard and also to Philip of France, and he was as different from Longchamp as any human being could be: a blond giant and a fine soldier (palatine bishops had to be), with courtly manners and a graciousness which made all men his friends. All men, that is, except William Longchamp. That stealthy climber, not content with his spectacular rise to power, was already full of a cankerous jealousy of the man of high rank with whom he must share the control of the country.

Longchamp lost no time in demonstrating that his theories on the raising of money were practical. Everything in the possession of the Crown which could be sold went under the hammer. The King of Scotland, who had sworn homage to Henry after his capture, was permitted to buy back his independence for a large sum; and thus at one stroke of the pen the top of the Angevin empire was lopped off. Every officer of the Crown, every high official of the Church, had to purchase his appointment. The new chancellor set the example by paying three thousand pounds for the chancellery seals (although a higher bid had been put in by one Reginald the Italian) and a thousand marks as chief justiciar of the south. Hugh de Puiset, who was made Earl of Northumberland at the same time, paid two thousand marks for that honor and a thousand more as chief justiciar of the north. Richard was asked why he had taken money from such a close relative and, being of a jocular turn like William Rufus, he replied that he considered the price small for the miracle he had wrought by turning an old bishop into a young earl. As for the general policy of selling appointments instead of giving them to the men most capable of filling them well, the new King was completely frank. He needed the money for the Crusade. Did it matter how it was obtained? Did anything matter, even the welfare of the kingdom, as long as the infidels were driven out of the Holy Land and the cross was recovered?

Longchamp was thorough in his methods. Attended by an imposing train of men-at-arms and clerks, he made a procession of the country. He held court in every city and town and in every castle and turned the proceedings into an open auction. Every post, even the most humble, was put up for bids. Decrees in equity and patents were sold. Lawsuits were settled in favor of the party offering the largest bribe. Royal manor houses and lands and forests were knocked down to the highest bidder.

It was an open scandal. When advisers of good intent approached the King and protested, Richard laughed. "By God's feet!" he cried. "Find me a purchaser and I'll sell London itself!"

England had become the milch cow of the Third Crusade. Every penny which could be taxed out of the pockets of the unfortunate people, or tithed or extracted by threat or promise, was being accumulated for one purpose only, to provide Richard Coeur de Lion with the most powerful and best-equipped army which had ever carried the cross. England could wallow in debt and suffer the most venal government. That was of no consequence.

He hurried to France as soon as he saw that in Longchamp he had a man who would do what he wanted, who would sell *his* everlasting soul in the service of a master he understood.

The Milch Cow of the Third Crusade

With the King gone, the new chancellor began to find posts for all his family. His brothers Henry and Osbert were put in charge of the royal forces at home. Mathew de Cleres, who had married Longchamp's sister Richenda, was made constable of Dover, which was tantamount to putting the key to England's front door in his pocket. Deals were made with men in authority and power and with certain high officers of the Church. A new order was being established, with new men at the head, and a new conception of government; a conception which left everyone else, baron and chapman and socman alike, gasping with astonishment and dismay. As soon as he was solidly entrenched and had back of him a party of office-holders whose tenure depended on his favor, the spider which had taken possession of the Tower began to spin a web for the undoing of Hugh de Puiset.

4

Richard had established himself in the ducal palace at Rouen, eating his meals in the Great Hall and giving audiences there at the same time, devoting no thought to the certainty that the hall would not witness now the consummation of his father's grandiose schemes. He did not care about that kind of glory. He had decided, quite wisely, not to march overland as the men of the First and Second Crusades had done, knowing this would result as before in half of his men dying on the way. Instead he had made up his mind to take the army direct to Palestine by water, and this meant finding a fleet of ships and planning accommodation for the thousands of horses which would be taken and accumulating supplies. He was the busiest man in all Christendom. He consulted Philip in some matters, and it was decided between them that the two armies would meet at Vézelay and then separate, the English sailing from Marseilles, the French from Genoa. The English were to wear the white cross, the French red, and the Flemings green.

The English King was seen to considerable advantage at this stage. He was so concerned with his preparations that he gave little thought to anything else. Even his need of a wife seemed to mean less to him than the proper method of stabling the horses on the voyage. He was thorough and painstaking about every conceivable detail. He drew up a special code to enforce good conduct during the time when his troops would be confined on board ship. As might be expected, he was unnecessarily severe in the matter of penalties. A soldier convicted of slaying another on board ship was to be cast into the sea, lashed to the body of his victim. If the killing occurred on shore, the offender was to be buried alive with the body. The loss of a hand was the penalty for drawing knife on a comrade. Striking with the fist but not drawing blood was to be punished by dipping the offender in the sea three times. A thief was to be shaved on the top of his head and boiling pitch poured on the bared poll, after which a feather pillow would be shaken over it. Richard, as will be recognized, was a disciplinarian.

Much to the surprise of the harried monarch, William Longchamp put in an appearance at Rouen. As Hugh de Puiset was with the court at the time, England had been left without either of the heads Richard had appointed. The visit of the misshapen chancellor was not due, however, to any trouble at home.

He became angry because Hugh de Puiset sat close to the King while he, Longchamp, was seated a very short distance above the salt. To watch his rival talking to the King with the ease of complete intimacy while he, Longchamp, dipped his fingers in the dishes of meat so far away that he could not hear a single syllable of what was being said disturbed the spleen of the lowborn minister and ruined his appetite. He was realizing that Richard would make use of him but would never overlook his vulgarity of origin.

After the meal, while Hugh de Puiset lingered over the wine with his friends, the King summoned Longchamp to the royal apartments. Here was another distinction which the King would always draw between his two lieutenants and which should have eased the mind of the jealous chancellor. When affairs of state were to be settled, he would be summoned to share the royal confidence. Hugh de Puiset would be allowed to stay at table and enjoy his wine.

Longchamp had two matters on his mind. First, he saw a way of using the York massacre in raising funds, a very great deal of money. Second, he was disturbed by the fact that England was to be left without a church head, since Archbishop Baldwin was going on the Crusade and Geoffrey of York was barred from his native shores. Note the order in which the two matters were introduced to the attention of the King. The scheme to make money out of bloodstained York was explained first and won the royal approval. While

the mind of the warrior King was still filled with the pleasant prospect of a further fattening of the war chest, the wily chancellor
proposed his solution of the church problem. Apply to the Pope for
legatine powers for him, Longchamp, so that he could act when
necessary in lieu of the Archbishop of Canterbury. Not realizing that
this would place Hugh de Puiset under the thumb of Longchamp, or
not caring, Richard agreed to the plan and promised that the request
would be sent to the Vatican at once.

And then the chancellor came to the crucial point. He explained
first that York was in the northern half of the kingdom, over which
the Bishop of Durham had jurisdiction. The good bishop might not
agree to the proposal. Even if he agreed, he would hardly be
thorough enough in carrying it out. He, Longchamp, was the only
one—if his royal master would forgive him for thus tootling his own
horn—who could extract the last ounce of gold out of the already
bleeding veins of the northern capital. How, then, could the plan be
put into operation?

Bowing his head over his shrunken chest and nervously twining
and untwining his fingers, this man of low degree who aspired to
rule all England by himself began to explain what was in his mind.
Perhaps he would be accorded the royal permission to return at
once—that very night, in fact—to set the wheels turning. If, on the
other hand, the King in his wisdom saw fit to detain Hugh de
Puiset for several weeks more, the draining of York could be attended to in his absence. The worthy bishop would undoubtedly be
disturbed when he realized what had happened, but even the anger
of so great a man could not undo a *fait accompli*.

Richard nodded his head in assent. Longchamp had obtained
everything he had crossed the Channel for, and he lost no time in
starting back.

The dwarfish chancellor was missed at the royal table the next
day. Hugh de Puiset, a man of decency and honor, was probably not
disturbed at all. He would have no suspicions of the devious reasons
which had brought his co-administrator to Normandy so unexpectedly and had then taken him back so suddenly. Certainly he was
pleased when Richard said he wanted him to stay for several weeks
more. Was this not an evidence of kingly esteem and confidence?

In the meantime Longchamp reached London, where he hastily
assembled a considerable force under the command of his two pre-

cious brothers. A march to York followed. His mission, he announced on arriving, was to inquire into the massacre and take such steps then as the facts would seem to make necessary.

His first move was to depose the royal officers, all of whom were appointees of the bishop, and to put in his own men. His brother Osbert was made sheriff. The clergy were bludgeoned into a stunned silence when he announced himself papal legate, although he did not produce his letters patent.

Having thus seized complete control, this skillful ferret began to follow out the plan he had proposed to the King. He imposed fines right and left, giving consideration only to the size of a man's purse and none at all to his share, if any, in the riots. The last penny which could be squeezed from the citizens was taken in these levies. The lands of the barons who had assisted in the massacre of the Jews were confiscated to the Crown. Up to this point Longchamp had done nothing which might not have occurred to any equally unscrupulous administrator, but he now proceeded to display his genius for despoliation. He announced that the Crown was the heir of the slaughtered Jews. To protect the interests of the King, therefore, he had a search made for the ledgers of the victims and found legal evidence here and there of large sums which had been owed to them. These debts were rigorously collected. Those who had taken a hand in the riots to escape payment of money they owed found that they had spilled innocent blood to no avail. Flambard himself had never thought of a more ingenious scheme than this.

The relatives of the dead *ockerers,* as moneylenders were called in the north, were not allowed a penny of what was collected on these debts.

Again the indispensable Longchamp had demonstrated that the schemes he hatched in his oversized head could be carried out. Not only had he scooped up more money than he had dared to estimate, but he had successfully checkmated his rival. When word of what had happened reached Normandy, Hugh de Puiset asked at once that he be allowed to return to investigate. Richard was graciously pleased to consent. It did not matter now. The money was in the royal coffers, and there was nothing the good bishop could do about it.

It would have been better for the well-intentioned but not very aggressive Bishop of Durham if he had not returned to England at this point. He met Longchamp on the latter's invitation at the royal castle of Tickhill in Yorkshire. The bishop had a letter from the King which had seemed, when handed to him, to establish his authority clearly enough. When he came face to face with Longchamp, however, he began to doubt if it would suffice. The venomous little man said, "It is now my turn to talk." He had papers also; a commission, in fact, to represent the King with full power in all England. The commission carried the Great Seal.

The bishop, puzzled and reluctant, had to give in. He was told he must relinquish everything, his properties as well as his offices. On pain of his life he must not take any further part in state affairs.

Longchamp's flag was hoisted over the keep at Windsor.

5

Power thrust into new hands is almost certain to go to the head. Never in all history has there been a more spectacular demonstration of this than in the case of Richard's upstart deputy. The one-time clerk at the chancellery began to behave as though he thought himself King of England. He imposed his will in everything, he assumed all the trappings of royalty, he tossed men out of office to make room for his own relatives and creatures. Even harder to bear was the way the little man conducted himself. He strutted, he threw out his puny chest, he stormed, he glowered, he snarled. He attired his meager body in the handsomest of clothes and rode on a magnificent charger, looking like one of the monkeys Thomas à Becket chained to the saddles of his horses on his famous ride to Paris.

He pursued his beaten rival with a peculiar degree of malignance. Hugh de Puiset had done him no harm, but he was punished by being sent to a small monastery at Howden. Here he remained in seclusion as long as Longchamp's power lasted.

With no one to stand in his way, Longchamp proceeded to rule like a king, and a very absolute and arbitrary king. He issued dooms and writs, signed with his own signet ring instead of the Great Seal of England. Governing from Windsor Castle, he had a corps of guards of his own who wore a special uniform. Anyone seeking audience of the haughty manikin had to pass through many files of these guards, who questioned them sternly, before they reached a magnificent apartment where Longchamp sat in all his glory. When he made a journey he was accompanied by fifteen hundred armed men, most of them mercenaries from abroad. He would quarter himself in a castle or monastery and demand the best of everything and the utmost deference. He summoned the nobility of the district to attend him. There were expensive jeweled rings on his skinny fingers when he dined in state, and the sons of the local baronage fetched and carried for him as pages.

The hatred he created in the country was so great that he needed his guards about him at all times. No one, from the haughtiest baron to the meanest fripperer on the streets of London, could swallow the insult of his pre-eminence. Everyone seemed to be waiting for a signal, in readiness to spring to arms and deal with this treacherous ape in the guise of a man. Longchamp realized this and, being of some learning, he took a leaf from the book of the Roman emperors. To mask their tyranny, the heads of the Roman state built amphitheaters and amused the people with spectacles and the death grapple of gladiators. Longchamp imported singers, jesters, and jugglers from France and sent them around the country to give the public free entertainment. He thought that, if these mummers were to sing his praises at the same time, the people would come to admire and love him.

At this point Queen Eleanor appears on the scene. The mother of the King had been watching things with eyes which had learned much in seventy years of living. She realized that her beloved son had made a great error and that all the glory he might win at the Crusades could be dimmed by the extraordinary behavior of this deputy he had left in England. Richard was still camped back of Marseilles, waiting to get his fleet assembled and his army loaded. Eleanor went to him and finally convinced him that he must curb the power of the malicious Longchamp. The King responded by instructing Coutance, Archbishop of Rouen, to visit England and study the situation, giving him sealed authority to take any steps he found necessary. In addition he appointed a committee of four barons to act as advisers to Longchamp. This did not satisfy the Queen. She felt that Geoffrey of York should be freed of the three-year prohibition which Richard had laid on him and allowed to return to England so that the Church would have proper leadership in Baldwin's absence. This suggestion, coming from his mother, who had never felt anything but antagonism for the son of the Fair Rosamonde, surprised Richard. The King had a robust dislike for Geoffrey, and it took a great deal of persuasion to make him give in on this point. However, he finally agreed and signed a paper, releasing his half brother from the three-year arrangement. Eleanor then saw to it that Pope Clement sent the pall for Geoffrey's consecration and that the ceremony was performed promptly by the Archbishop of Tours.

Content with what she had done, Eleanor set out for Navarre to arrange the marriage with Berengaria. It had been planned between them, mother and son, that she would bring the princess back with her so the wedding could take place before the ships sailed for the East. Failing this, the Queen and the princess would go by sea and join Richard at Messina. The mountainous road across the Pyrenees and on to Pampeluna, where Sancho the Wise, Berengaria's father, held court, was a long and fatiguing one for a woman of her years, especially as the sea voyage to Sicily seemed the inevitable sequel. Eleanor set off without a moment's hesitation, her back as straight and her spirits as high as when she herself had ridden to the Crusades some fifty years before. Nothing her golden son could need or desire was too much for the silver-haired woman who had been once the toast and the scandal of Europe.

Longchamp had his spy system, of course, and he learned that Geoffrey of York was returning to England. He decided to prevent him from landing.

His sister Richenda, whose husband was constable of Dover, was the feminine counterpart of the chancellor, a small, dark, determined, and vituperative creature. Longchamp sent instructions to her, ignoring her easygoing husband, that the Archbishop of York was to be stopped at any cost. When Geoffrey arrived off Dover in an English smack, he was met by a boat filled with troops from the garrison.

"Deliver him up to us, Master Skipper," shouted the officer in charge.

The captain of the smack knew what was meant and pointed out the archbishop. The latter demanded to know what this was about.

"It means that you go with us," declared the officer. "Madame de Cleres will answer your questions."

The recurrent appearances on the scene of the son of the Fair Rosamonde have made it clear that he was a man of courage and resolution. He now proceeded to demonstrate that he possessed these qualities in a high degree. On reaching shore, he sprang into the saddle of the horse on which he was to have been taken to Dover Castle and made a dash for the road to Folkestone. There was a loud hue and cry at once. When one of his pursuers drew up abreast of the fugitive, Geoffrey kicked his spurred heel into the flank of the man's horse. It shied and then reared away from the road. The rest came thundering along after him, however, and he had no recourse but to turn into St. Martin's Priory, where he could claim sanctuary. It was a close-run thing at that. As he sprang from his saddle the pursuing horsemen poured into the courtyard and he was compelled to race for the chapel. A service was being held, and he heard the monks chanting as he entered:

"He that troubleth thee shall have his judgment . . ."

This sounded reassuring. The troops made it clear, however, that he would not be allowed to escape. A cordon was thrown around the priory while the officer in charge waited for instructions from the shrill little woman in Dover. They were not long in coming. Richenda demanded that they drag the archbishop out by force and bring him to the castle. She did not care what happened to him in the execution of these orders; bring him, dead or alive.

But the memory of the martyrdom of Thomas à Becket was still too vivid in people's minds for orders like that to be followed out. The soldiers refused to obey the command. The best they could be made to do was to stand on guard outside.

There ensued a stormy exchange of messages between the indignant prelate and Longchamp's termagant sister. He reminded her that his person was sacred and that, moreover, he was in sanctuary. To this she replied that others must be the judge of such matters. She insisted that Geoffrey swear an oath of allegiance to the King and produce his papers to prove his right to enter the kingdom. The archbishop responded that he had already sworn allegiance to his brother, the King, and that the papers he carried were not for her eyes. Richenda's final word was that, if her brother so ordered, she would burn down the castle of Dover and St. Martin's Priory as well, and even the city of London.

Richenda, making good her threat, demanded that the archbishop be made a prisoner without any more delay. The soldiers poured into the chapel to carry out these instructions but retreated again in haste when they saw that the churchman had donned the alb and stole of his office and was holding a large cross of gold in his hand. The situation began to resemble too closely the tragedy of Canterbury, and they left the chapel as hurriedly as they had entered.

Two days passed, and then the determined Richenda sent some of her own servants to direct the capture. To their surprise they found that Geoffrey was still sitting at the altar and arrayed as before. His stern eyes dared them to come any closer. They turned and left. However, the cordon outside was maintained, and shrill messages still came from the castle, demanding action.

Two more days went by, while the cordon remained around the priory and the resolute archbishop sat at the altar in his consecration robes. On the night of the fourth day a large body of soldiers, who had been bribed and supplied with a great deal of drink, invaded the chapel. Seizing Geoffrey by the arms, they began to drag him down the aisle. He was a man of considerable strength and he resisted stoutly, beating his assailants with the gold cross. His resistance could not continue long against such numbers, however, and he was finally taken out of sanctuary and to Dover Castle, where the exultant Richenda ordered him placed in one of the dungeons.

Geoffrey was held prisoner in a dark cell for eight days, a long enough time for word of what had happened to spread over England. The storm which arose then decided Longchamp that he would have to give way. With many explanations and apologies, placing the blame on his sister, he had the prelate released. When Geoffrey rode into London, he received a tumultuous welcome. Men by the thousand came out to meet him, and the church bells rang as though for a great victory. Observing the warmth of the demonstration from his secure nook in the Tower, the not too courageous chancellor decided he would be better elsewhere. He departed hurriedly for Windsor, his guards galloping after him.

Shortly before this Coutance had arrived in England together with the four advisers the King had appointed. They presented their papers to the chancellor, but, insisting that their mandates were forgeries, Longchamp had dismissed them curtly. "I, and I alone," he declared, "know the King's mind!" His audacity in taking this stand was due to the fact that the King had embarked at last and could no longer be reached.

The Conquerors

This action had threatened to precipitate a national uprising and, with the imprisonment of the archbishop, Longchamp's cup of iniquity ran over. John, who had been biding his time, summoned all right-thinking men to help him in driving the miscreant from office. Geoffrey joined the prince at Reading, and from there word was sent to Longchamp to meet them on a field near Windsor. Longchamp disregarded the summons. He saw now, however, that he had played for too high a stake and that he had lost. Leaving a lieutenant in command of the royal palace, he decamped and made his way back to London, where he hid himself in the Tower.

His only hope now was to gain the support of the citizens of London. He went out to harangue them on their duty, which was to close their gates and hold out for their rightful King. He had never thought it necessary to learn English and so his vehement speech was delivered in Norman French, which did not please a citizenry already bitterly opposed to him. They laughed, they told him to go back where he belonged, they shouted that the ill-treatment of English bishops was an affront which would never be forgiven a foreign monkey like himself. Longchamp beat a hasty retreat and immured himself again behind the thick and impregnable walls of the Tower. Soon thereafter he received terms from John. All power was to be taken from him, and all his property save three castles. He would have to give a brother and the husband of his scorpion of a sister as hostages. He assented, but his acceptance of defeat was accompanied by a vicious diatribe.

"I yield to force!" he shrilled. "You, being of great numbers, have overpowered me. I, the King's chancellor and his chief justiciar, am condemned against all law and justice. I yield to force and nothing else!"

The final scene in this tragicomedy was enacted at Dover. The once overbearing minister arrived there, disguised as a female peddler, with voluminous skirts and a veil and carrying a bolt of cloth on one arm. He had been ordered to remain in the kingdom where an eye could be kept on him, but his one thought now was to get to Normandy, where he had a large supply of gold hidden.

When he visited the harbor to make arrangements for a ship to take him across the Channel, a group of fishwives saw him and expressed an interest in his wares. Again his lack of English stood him in bad stead. Saying nothing and struggling to get away from them, he aroused their suspicions, and one strong-armed female took hold of his neck while she tore off his veil. Some of them recognized him, and a great uproar was the result.

Knowing that Madame de Cleres was still in possession of the castle, the people of Dover whisked their prisoner out of sight quickly. He was put in a cellar and kept there under strict guard while word was sent to London of his whereabouts.

The upshot was that he was given permission to leave the country, but the three castles were taken from him. He was in no position to refuse these terms and left Dover as soon as a boat could be found for him. And thus ended, or so it seemed at the time, the curious story of the hobgoblin chancellor.

CHAPTER XII

The Lord of the Manor and the Villein

THE BRITONS which the knightly King was fleecing by such barefaced means numbered perhaps as much as four million. Their country had great agricultural wealth, although the inhabitants had not yet shown the genius for production and manufacture which was to manifest itself later. Most of the four million lived on the land—for the towns were neither numerous nor large—and thus they existed in small villages or scattered over manorial estates, tilling the soil with exactitude and raising the sheep which grew the much-sought-after wool. Before telling the story of Richard's adventures in the Holy Land, it will be interesting to take a closer look at this green and fertile country which was providing the blood and bone as well as the gold he needed in his quest for glory.

First it must be said that Englishmen were not free. There were a certain number of native socmen with property of their own, but the great majority belonged to a much lower station. They were called villeins and, as writers of the day seemed pleased to point out, they owned nothing but their bellies and were compelled to pay for the use of land by a curious assortment of labors and obligations.

The nature of the life the villein lived can be most easily gathered from a description of a typical village, and the best glimpse of such a village was to be had on a day of rest—a Sunday or a saint's day, but not one of the holidays when youths cut boughs of hawthorn before daybreak to decorate the Maypoles and the women wore flowers in their hair in readiness for the faddy-dancing.

It is a day in mid-August, without a rain cloud in the sky and the grain in the fields well headed up and beginning to turn yellow. The men, having tended their stock, stand about in small groups; a brawny lot, brown of face from life in the open, eyes friendly, mouths ready enough to grin at a good jape or a song. The women are still busy with household tasks, sticking their heads out of door or window occasionally to call a greeting. There is a festive air to the place, but actually the villagers are arrayed as usual, the women in kirtles which touch the ground and their hair in linen wimples to prevent the wind from blowing their braids about, the men in banded tunics which do not reach the knees, and hose which fit the legs tightly enough to display their fine muscles. The hint of gaiety can be traced to the colors used. They stick to primary reds, blues, and yellows and to bright greens, and in the use of these they are not afraid. There is ease and comfort as well as a primitive beauty in the way they dress.

The village is a huddle of small houses, quite small, in fact, with no more than two rooms, a door, two windows, a chimney seldom. The plastered walls are in two colors which blend picturesquely. Each house has, of course, its garden or *toft*, and these are filled with fruit trees. The church stands in the center, a solid little edifice with a square tower as stoutly proportioned as the men's legs, a bell with a clear high note which can be heard in the farthest spinney on the horizon; built of coarse grit stone which, like the worshipers, turns gray early, the door framed in long-and-short masonry, the windows with well-turned baluster pillars. Next to the church is a tavern which essays a note of hospitality with benches on each side of the door but cannot escape a hint of slyness in such company; not that the priest is likely to protest its proximity because he is thus enabled to keep an eye on his flock. There is a cross on the widening of the road, standing perhaps ten feet high, which is used as a shrine by passers-by, and beside it, as though offering a choice, the stocks. At the nearest pond, but not in sight, is the cucking stool for women offenders, the wantons, the walking morts, the scolds.

But seldom are there passers-by to bend a knee at the weather-beaten cross. The road ends here, and what business could bring strangers? When strangers do come they are eyed with dread, for always they are bearers of bad news, of wars, of approaching pestilence, of taxes. The world does not come here, and the peasants do not go to the world. The law binds them to the land; they cannot go away without the consent of the lord of the manor; they are transferred with the land and the livestock when there is a change of ownership; their children are equally bound. Few of these sturdy men and women have ever been more than five miles away from the village. Is it any wonder that their eyes have a shut-in look, that often they pause to gaze at the wooded horizon, wondering what lies beyond, what the great world is like? There is little difference between a cell and a few miles of walking space when it is known that bars stand just beyond the dip of the land. Yes, they are in reality a sad lot, these men who own nothing but their bellies, whose children are spoken of as litters, whose feet move at the command of a master.

Someday they would go, when leaders arose to tell them this was not God's divinely appointed rule of life. But this was still two centuries off, and freedom would not be won even then, not all at once.

Immediately around the village are the commons, the Lammas lands, now closed in to keep the stock from the fields where the crops are standing. The leaders among the men gather in a group and study the grain, which is so high that the twisting road can be seen for no more than a few perch at most. The harvesting is a community affair, even though the land is divided into individual strips, and there are decisions to be reached. It can be read in the eyes of these more or less self-appointed *secutors* that they see promise of plenty—*if* the lord of the manor does not demand too much of their time for his land—some *love-boons* as well as the three days out of each week. Uneasy speculation remains in every eye on this day of rest. In the midst of talk they turn continuously to study the sky and then to look at those long strips of ripening grain, running as straight as an arrow, in the first stage of flight, to the green shaws in the distance, each third strip lying fallow, each man's share marked with a balk of unplowed ground. A miracle of husbandry, this. If only they could consider their own needs first and get the crops in and threshed before the wet weather came!

The one subject which always came up when villeins got together was the possibility of paying rent in money instead of labor. How could any man hope to save twenty shillings, which was the equivalent of the labor he was assessed at the leet in case he worked as much as a hide of land? Of course there was always a chance of making something extra with assart land. The ambitious villein could venture out to the edge of the ever-encroaching forest and break in as much as he cared to, on which there would be no rent to pay. He might make enough on assart land to become in course of time a free man, even perhaps a socman or thane.

The amount of money in circulation was, of course, very small. A cow was worth no more than four shillings, a sow one, a sheep tenpence (if the wool was of the best variety); a horse might bring as much as a cow.

On a day of idleness the muscles are at rest but the mind never. It was not until the time came for a test at the archery butts that the villagers were able to relax. One of the sons of the manorial lord came by on horseback and paused to watch the activity in the vacant strip of land behind the churchyard. He was an arrogant young fellow, with a demanding eye and a scornful manner. If they thought he had stopped to watch the archery—which was well worth a pause, for there were men in the village who could lodge an arrow in the clout every shot—they were mistaken. He had taken off his perfumed gloves and was fanning himself with them, and all the while kept an eye on the girls, some of whom were as well worth observing as the play. If his real reason for pausing had been noted, there would have been some uneasiness. There was not in England, however, the French custom known as *droit du seigneur* (which compelled a bride of common birth to spend the first night in the bed of the lord of the manor), and a girl could defend her virtue if she so desired.

As the idle day wore on, there would perhaps be a game of football on the common from which the men and boys would emerge with plenty of bruises and some rips in tunics and hose. There would probably be a community supper cooked in large pots on the square (practically all meat was boiled, that being the easiest method with their meager facilities), and that would mean special food, chickens and perhaps a chine of pork. Ordinarily the evening meal consisted of soup and bread and ale, with a bit of cheese. There would be a service at compline in the little church. Then, as the sun sank below the trees on the western horizon, the men would gather about the cross, sitting close together; and they would talk of this and that, of the news which came faintly to them from the world outside, of wars and of kings and queens and of bringings to bed, of death and treachery and the sweep of diseases, and always speculation as to how soon the world would end and what they, poor sinners, could do about getting themselves ready. In spite of the collars around their necks, they were of a sturdy spirit, quick to resent an injustice or to repair a wrong. There would be nothing obsequious in their talk.

This was not the kind of life men of the land would bear for long. Already there were the first signs of a stirring. Itinerant monks sometimes preached strange things on the open space in front of churches. Men would meet at night in forest glades to whisper of this new gospel of equality. It would come to a head in course of time, and there would be much bloodshed and the oak trees would blossom out with a sinister crop of hanged men. Gradually the demands of the common people would be heard and these wrongs would be done away with, in part, at least; and the kind of exactions which Richard had laid on his kingdom of England would no longer be recognized as the right of a king.

2

On the land the common man had certain rights and privileges, but in the forests he had none. The cruel forest laws were unbearable because nearly three quarters of the people lived on the land and so were in close contact with the woods. To know that in the cover of the trees were beasts of chase and warren was a temptation which few of the bold English, with their skill at archery, could resist. It was no wonder that the branding iron and the hangman's rope were in such constant use, and that the woods were full of outlaws.

There has been a general belief that the Norman kings had set aside only the New Forest as a royal preserve, and on that account to exaggerate the extent of the wooded land known by that name. The New Forest covered a little less than one hundred thousand acres of land (and still less than that today), running north from the Solent to the Avon. There had been fewer ejections of residents than the records suggest. The tract had, in fact, been a hunting preserve of the West Saxon kings and so had been a logical choice for William the Conqueror. However, the Norman kings, in their great greed, had expropriated all forest land on principle, thus making it a criminal offense to hunt or trap. The punishments they established were severe in the extreme, ranging from long terms of imprisonment to the loss of eyes or death on the gallows. The verderers, who had been put in charge of the forests as far back as the reign of Canute and had held their swain-motes ever since, had become under the Normans the instruments of a cruel oppression.

But all the laws and prohibitions which could be conceived in the minds of callous kings and written down by court clerks could not keep the natives from venturing into the woods to shoot a buck or snare a rabbit. Forest life came natural to them; they loved the high, arching trees, the calm of a shaded glade, the wild flowers and the animals. It was men of the villages lying close to the New Forest who discovered that the waters of a pond close to the spot where William Rufus fell turned a vermilion shade at certain times, as a hint that Wat Tyrrell had washed his hands there before riding away for the coast and safety. Men in green were to be found at all hours of the night in Mark Ash and Vinney Ridge and the Badger's Wood, keeping the woodwards and the agisters on the watch and providing plenty of work for the justice in Eyre, on whose shoulders fell the responsibility of protecting the King's deer. They sometimes entered this forbidden territory to enjoy the lovely green shades of the forest, and the purples and golds, and perhaps even to collect the many unusual flowers to be found—the oblong sundew, the bog pimpernel, the rampion-bell, the skullcap, the small teasel, and the gold samphire. Most often, however, it was a fondness for venison and for succulent stews of rabbit and squirrel. Sometimes they risked their liberty and their lives for the thrill of demonstrating their skill with that mighty weapon which was coming into its own in England, at last, the longbow.

It was not only in the New Forest or in Sherwood, which witnessed the feats of Robin Hood, that the men in green hose and jerkin poached on the King's land. They haunted the woods in all parts of the kingdom, and everywhere could be heard the twang of the string as it left the nock, the sound of running game.

In the previous reign legends had grown up around three men whose names were William of Cloudesley, Adam Bell, and Clym o' the Clough. They lived somewhere in the wild counties north of

York and had broken the law because of their love of venison meat. They had taken shelter in the woods and had behaved with such audacity that the people of England made heroes of them. A ballad was written which continued to be sung, with much revision and addition, for many centuries afterward. It makes them out to have been supermen in the fullest sense of the word.

> *The baylyes and the bedyls both,*
> *And the sergeaunts of the law,*
> *And forty fosters of the fe,*
> *These outlaws have yslaw.*

They were credited in this earliest of forest ballads with many a daring trick which later would be added to the Robin Hood saga. They even paid a visit to the King and demanded a chance to become law-abiding citizens again. The King looked over their records and found them very black indeed. He saw no reason to pardon them unless they could prove themselves capable of extraordinary things in his service. This sounds much more like Richard Coeur de Lion than that hardheaded man, Henry II, but it is Henry who belongs in the ballad. To give the King the proof he needed, William of Cloudesley proceeded to shoot an apple off the head of his own young son! As William Tell was not born until after the date assigned to the ballad of the three English outlaws, a question arises as to the origin of that famous story.

There have always been doubts about Robin Hood. Did he actually live? Or was he a myth, growing out of the many legends of the greenwood? If he lived and became an outlaw, how many of the exploits credited to him did he actually perform?

There seems every reason to believe that a man named Robin Hood existed and that he was forced into outlawry by his political activities. He did not, however, live in the time of Richard (despite his appearance under the name of Locksley in Sir Walter Scott's *Ivanhoe*) but appears first in the reign of Edward II, more than a century later. He was an outlaw for a relatively short time, too short to make possible all the adventures in which he is supposed to have taken a leading part. He had few associates, and none of them would bear any resemblance to Little John, Friar Tuck, or Maid Marian, most particularly the last.

The name Robin Hood seems to have been an adaptation from

The Lord of the Manor and the Villein

Robert Fitz-ooth, the ballad singers having changed it into the more euphonious form in which it has reached modern readers. This means that he was of Norman extraction. If Fitz-ooth was his real name, a valuable part of the saga is lost, for he has been depicted generally as an Anglo-Saxon gentleman fighting against the oppressive laws of the invaders. That he was of Norman stock and still became an outlaw is, however, interesting evidence of the close mingling of the two races which was manifesting itself in many ways.

Robin Hood was born between the years 1285 and 1295 in the neighborhood of Wakefield and belonged to a good family. He was not, however, the Earl of Huntingdon, as some versions have it, nor does he seem to have been connected with the higher nobility. When Edward II put so much power into the hands of his favorite, Piers Gaveston, that the people rose in protest under the Earl of Leicester, Robin Hood was bold enough to join the forces of dissent. The insurgents were defeated, and so the famous archer (his skill with the bow is the one sure point of identification with the hero of the legends) had to take to Sherwood Forest. He remained an outlaw from April 1322 until December 1323, at which time he was captured. The King was well impressed with the daring young man and not only pardoned him but took him into the royal household as a *vadelet*. Now a *vadelet* was something in the nature of a servant of the royal bedchamber—the word might even be a variant of varlet—and that kind of life became most irksome to the high-spirited ex-outlaw. He disappeared within a year and is supposed to have gone back to forest life, although this cannot be stated with any surety. It is said that he died in the convent of Kirklees, where he went for surgical help when wounded, the prioress being a relative. Out of this version grew a belief that the prioress, knowing him to have a price on his head, allowed him to bleed to death.

The Robin Hood saga comes from gathering together tales of the woods into one colorful series of annals. Robin Hood himself is a combination of William of Cloudesley, Adam Bell, Clym o' the Clough, and all other bold spirits of that ilk. The result is the favorite legend of all time, one which will live forever. It is of no importance that so little of it is true. Robin Hood, as the symbol of resistance, the Tyll Eulenspiegel of the English, has become a figure of historical greatness.

3

Robin Hood did not live in the time of Richard the Lion-hearted, but it was in this reign, at least, that the English mastery of the bow began to manifest itself. It is not known when the yeomen realized the lesson of Hastings and turned their attention to archery. It was probably a gradual process. Although the English became the supreme archers of the world, they did not themselves evolve the longbow. The credit for this must be given the men of Wales, who first discarded the crossbow or arbalest and began to use the longer weapon in their border warfare with the English. The advantages of this powerful bow were seen and, by the time Richard became King, it had come into general use. It was employed in Palestine and was a factor in some of the King's greatest successes.

Though they did not conceive this mighty weapon, they soon demonstrated that they had been designed by nature to make the best use of it. The English eye seemed perfect for sending the arrow off truly from the nock; the English arm and back could best manipulate this lethal instrument. Making it their own, they studied it and experimented with it, bringing it gradually to the perfection of performance demonstrated at Crécy. They made it still longer, and they worked over it lovingly, finding in time the right materials to use. They discovered that yew was the best wood for the bow and that hemp, rubbed with water glue, made the strongest string. Thus they had a weapon which would send an arrow through the strongest armor and was capable of launching three messengers of death while the crossbowman was sending one. It is no exaggeration to say that the longbow made the English armies invincible through most of the period of the Hundred Years' War.

His bow became the chief pride of the Englishman. He was never parted from it. When he worked in the fields, he left it against the trunk of a tree within easy reach. When he visited a tavern, he kept it over his shoulder. It stood at the head of his bed when he went to sleep. They were inseparable, the Englishman and his mighty longbow, and it was no wonder that he became so skillful in the manipulation of it.

It may seem farfetched to claim that only the English eye and back and arm were capable of using this deadly instrument of war and chase to best advantage. The French tried it, however, with no success at all. During the Hundred Years' War an effort was made by the rulers of France to train their foot soldiers in its use. A law was passed making practice mandatory, and rich rewards were offered for proofs of efficiency. The results were so meager that the French military authorities were compelled, most reluctantly, to conclude that in this one respect they could not compete with their island enemies. The French archer went back to the crossbow, and French armies continued to lose battles.

The longbow sent an arrow, tipped with the gray goosefeather of England, straight into the heart of chivalry. There was little left of that high-flown nonsense for the cannon to finish off later.

CHAPTER XIII

Melech-Ric

RICHARD met Berengaria of Navarre through his friendship with her brother. Sancho the Strong, as the brother was called, was the son of Sancho the Wise, King of that picturesque little country on the Spanish side of the Pyrenees. He was about Richard's age, and they possessed many interests in common, a love of conflict and battle, of everything pertaining to the use of arms, of horses and dogs, of music and minstrelsy. Richard was being reared in Aquitaine and he was often in Gascony, which lies across the mountain range from Navarre. It was natural for these two fine young animals to get together as much as possible, to splinter lances, to exchange buffets, to ride and hunt and, in the evenings, to drink and troll a ballad together.

It was while attending a tournament in Pampeluna that Richard first saw Berengaria. He was a guest at the royal palace and took an immediate interest in the young princess, who could not conceal the very great interest she took in him. The information available about Berengaria is quite meager, but it seems that she was small and dark. She had dusky hair which she parted in the middle so that it lay smoothly on her head, and her eyes were full of intelligence as well as gentleness. She read poetry and was more likely to be found alone in one of the palace gardens than gossiping with the young ladies of the court. The impression left of her is of a slender figure flitting about quickly and unobtrusively. She was diffident and even perhaps a trifle fey; the very opposite of the earthy and magnificent

Richard, although they shared one interest in common, a love of music.

He saw little of her at the royal table, but sometimes he would see her briefly during the day, standing on a stair far above him and looking down, or strolling in the gardens with a book, and seeming lonesome and perhaps a little pathetic. She must always have worn a rapt look when the stringed instruments were brought in after supper and Richard took his turn with a vigorous ballad of his own composition, rolling it out in his fine baritone voice.

No reports have come down of this particular tournament, but only one assumption is possible about it: that Richard was the winner and it became his privilege, therefore, to select the Queen of Love; and further, that it was to Berengaria he raised the chaplet of gold on the tip of his lance, and that she involuntarily clapped her hands once with delight before taking the crown and placing it on the smooth dark strands of her hair. No other result is thinkable in view of what came about later.

It is almost certain that he saw her once only. He did not correspond with her, not being a scholar, and being committed, moreover, to marry Princess Alice of France. But clearly he had taken away the impression that, as it was his duty to marry the daughter of some royal family, he would find this reserved and oddly pretty little creature less objectionable than any other. Berengaria had fallen deeply in love with her brother's friend. She was so much in love with him that, as the years rolled by and Richard remained unmarried while his reputation as a wielder of sword and battle-ax became greater all the time, she refused to consider a match with anyone else. How she managed to stand out against the pressure which is continuously exerted to rush princesses into matrimony is a mystery. Perhaps Sancho the Wise was an affectionate as well as a wise father.

When Richard became King of England he was in a position to choose his own wife. He would not marry Alice, having no desire to make his father's mistress Queen of England, even if he had to go to war with Philip because of his refusal. His mind kept turning back to the girl he had seen so many years before, that little sister of his great good friend Sancho. She had not married; he had been sufficiently interested to know that. Berengaria! A lovely name, well suited to a queen. Seeing that now he must take a wife and beget a

The Conquerors

son to succeed him, he knew that he would prefer her to anyone else. The outcome was that his mother, with an imposing train of knights and ladies in waiting and servants by the score, set out for Navarre. She was not only to ask the hand of the Navarrese princess in marriage but was to bring her back without delay. Richard liked to get things done in a hurry.

Berengaria was agreeable, of course. This was what she had waited for, longed for, prayed for, all these years. Sancho the Wise was equally amenable, as he might very well be, for Richard was the greatest catch in the world, the new ruler of the powerful Angevin empire, the most famous of knights, and a friend of the heir of Navarre. It was in every respect a most desirable alliance.

No princess was ever made ready for marriage in quicker time. The seamstresses of the kingdom were called upon, and all over Navarre needles began to fly. The oriental influence which was showing itself in feminine dress as a result of the Crusades was, of course, reflected in the clothes made for Berengaria, but not as much as if she had been French or Italian or English. Navarre was a quiet little kingdom and lay far from the great roads which bound civilization together. However, her dresses were properly long and flowing in line, elaborately embroidered with pearls and thread of gold, and made of the marvelous materials which reached even Navarre behind the Pyrenees, the heavy golden samite and rich baudekin. She had cloaks which were held together with cords at the neck, and all manner of headdresses and veils which showed the unmistakable influence of the East. All her shoes were of the softest leather, fitting the feet closely, and without heels.

And no princess was ever wedded under more unusual circumstances. Eleanor would have been glad to see the marriage solemnized and be finished herself with all this fatiguing travel. The English fleet had left Marseilles, however, when they reached that port, and there was no alternative but to continue overland. They climbed the steep trails of Maurienne into Italy and finally came to Naples, where further embarrassment met them. Richard felt he must be declared free of his undertaking to marry Princess Alice before he could wed Berengaria. It would not be seemly for them to meet, in fact, until this trouble out of the past had been settled. Certainly he was not playing the part of an impetuous lover, and a shadow began to grow in the eyes of the bride who had come all the way from her native land.

Eleanor's gentle daughter Joanna met them at Naples. She had married the Norman King of Sicily and was now a widow and dispossessed by Tancred, the successor to the throne. The three ladies went to Brindisi, where they spent the balance of the winter and part of the next spring. It was fortunate that Joanna took an instant liking to Berengaria. They became, in fact, the closest of friends and continued so through all the stormy times ahead of them. Berengaria was in great need of friendship and comforting. She had not yet laid eyes on her lover and prospective husband, and she was growing more and more disturbed as the warm days passed and she had nothing to do but sit by the shore and wait and hope. As Piers Langtoft says in his rhyming chronicle,

> *The maiden Berengare,*
> *She was sore afright,*
> *That neither far and near,*
> *Her king rode in sight.*

She had every reason to feel concerned. At Messina, Richard and Philip were holding bitter disputes about the matter of the déclassée Alice and finding it impossible to agree. If the French King remained obdurate and refused to free Richard from his obligation, what would happen to her, the bride the English King had summoned with one imperious gesture? Would she have to return home and spend the rest of her days in a nunnery, hiding her shame and her face from the world?

As Richard and Philip did not seem to be making any headway, the old Queen decided she would not wait to see the culmination of the romance. Perhaps she was finding the Italian ports too reminiscent of the days so long before when she herself had ridden to the Crusades, with her own corps of guards, and had been known as the *Golden-booted Dame.* Perhaps she felt that the course of events in England needed watching at closer range. At any rate, she said to her daughter, "Take this damsel for me to the King, your brother, and tell him to espouse her speedily!" Eleanor also had become fond of her charge. Without waiting further, however, the Queen started on her long ride homeward.

Having failed to reach an understanding with Philip, the English King decided he must proceed with his plans in disregard of his difficult colleague. Philip set sail for the East in high dudgeon, and

The Conquerors

Richard at last allowed himself the privilege of greeting his bride. Where or when the meeting occurred, history does not deign to tell. It is unfortunate that the doggerel chronicles of the period were so concerned with the bickering between Richard and Tancred over the return of Joanna's dowry that nothing else seemed to matter. They speak with meticulous care of the golden table twelve feet long, the silk tent, the twenty-four golden cups and twenty-four golden plates, the sixty thousand mules' burden of corn and barley and wine, which Richard insisted must be returned, and how he contented himself finally with forty thousand ounces of gold. But never a word do they tell of the scene when the little princess from Navarre found herself at last in the presence of the tanned giant for whom she had waited so long.

Richard's attitude to his wedding, and to Berengaria, was one of complete detachment. Strangely enough, he was not of a romantic disposition, not the impetuous knight-errant to fight his way through fire and water and a storm of steel to win his bride. He was completely bound up in the great task ahead and in the responsibilities weighing on him. The plan he had evolved for a new order to be called the Knights of the Blue Thong, because they would wear bands of blue leather on their left legs, concerned him more than love passages with Berengaria. He was always the great captain, never the great lover. Berengaria would be his Queen but not the passion of his life.

He even saw reason for postponing the marriage until after Lent, a curious excuse for one as little religious as he showed himself on many occasions. Off he went in his great ship *Trenc-la-Mer*, leading his fleet of more than two hundred vessels with an immense lantern on the poop deck which was lighted up at night to show the way. Berengaria, puzzled and more worried than ever, followed in one of the others.

Richard must have been pleased with the lady of his choice, however, for he made up his mind when he reached Cyprus that this state of affairs could not continue any longer. Accordingly on Sunday, May 12, which was the feast day of no fewer than three saints, Nereus, Achilles, and Pancras, and a beautiful day to boot, King Richard arrayed himself in a rose-colored tunic of satin and over that a mantle of striped silver tissue covered with half-moons, and placing on his head a scarlet bonnet embroidered in gold (looking so handsome, without a doubt, that poor little Berengaria's heart turned over when she saw him), he led her before Bishop Bernard of Bayonne, and the wedding vows were sworn and a choir sang over them. What the bride wore was not considered important enough to set down.

The wedding feast lasted for three days, and it may be assumed that the new Queen was happy at last. Her bliss was short-lived, however. Duty beckoned the bridegroom. The French army had joined the Christian forces which had been besieging Acre for more than two years with the intention of making it a naval base for all crusading operations. While they besieged that strong walled city, Saladin came up with an even larger army and encamped around *them*, so that it was no longer possible to tell who was the besieged and who the besieger. In fact, it became clear that, unless the English arrived soon, the French would be in a very bad way. Richard cut short his honeymoon and was off again in *Trenc-la-Mer*, walking the deck and crying to his captain to clap on more sail, so great was his impatience to be having a hand in the excitement around Acre. His bride of three days and his sister followed in the same vessel which had brought them to Messina.

When the English fleet arrived in the Bay of Acre and Philip found that his brother king had taken matters into his own hands about the marriage, he decided to put the best face on it. He even met the boat which brought the bride ashore and carried her to land in his arms.

2

The fleet had reached Acre just as night was falling. It was still possible to see the Holy Headland, as Mount Carmel was called, on the south side of the bay, lifting its rugged heights above the water and filling the mind with thoughts of Elijah and the Chariot of Fire. Directly east was a faint suggestion against the darkening sky of the distant hills of Galilee. To the left was the beleaguered city, a mass of high white walls on a long promontory stretching out into the sea. For a few minutes it was possible to notice red and yellow roofs and the peaks of mosques over the tops of the walls, even a trace of green gardens. The night closed in then and nothing was left but the fires of the crusading forces which encircled the city.

Richard was given a frenzied welcome. Military bands blared, trumpets rang out, voices were raised in the songs of the Crusades, particularly the first marching song (the air of which is still used to the words of *The Bear Went over the Mountain*), and thousands thronged down to the shore to get a glimpse of the great warrior. This was incense in the nostrils of the English King. He rode through the torchlighted camp to meet his fellow monarchs on his tall and spirited Cyprian horse Fanuelle, which pranced and pawed and tossed its mane as though aware that greatness sat in the jeweled saddle on its back.

As Richard talked with Philip of France, Leopold of Austria, Conrad of Montferrat, and other crusading leaders, the noise suddenly died down. The time for the nightly ritual of the camp had arrived. Richard had heard of this custom, designed to keep up the morale of the troops, but he had not seen it, and he watched intently when a herald stepped into the open space in front of the huge red pavilion of the French King.

A trumpet sounded and, after a moment of silence, the herald cried in a loud voice:

"Help, help, for the Holy Sepulcher!"

Richard could see by the light of the lantern suspended over the pavilion entrance that the soldiers of all nations had raised their arms above their heads while they repeated the words in unison:

"Help, help, for the Holy Sepulcher!"

The sound came from all parts of the semicircle which the crusading commanders had drawn around the city. Three times it was repeated, then each man of the many thousands crossed himself and said a prayer. Sharp orders to retire for the night sent them back to their tents. Nothing more impressive could have been conceived as a welcome than this outward expression of the crusading spirit.

The picture next day was not so impressive. Acre had been surrounded by vineyards and small fruit farms, an orderly belt of green. Now, after nearly three years of siege (for the Germans under Barbarossa had arrived there early and most of them had remained after the death of the red-beard by drowning), the terrain resembled a place visited by earthquake or swept by fire. The litter, the filth, the desolation that three years of careless soldiering can create are beyond description.

Richard did not mind the ugliness of the picture. There was beauty for him in the roughly constructed "bad neighbors" which Philip's engineers had created to tower over the walls of Acre. These had been countered by others inside the walls, so that to modern eyes there would have been the look of an oil camp about the place. Richard walked up and down, studying the approaches, instinctively selecting the best spots to strike. He considered the disposition of the forces with a critical frown. It was clear that Philip of France had little knowledge of military matters. If the Saracens had struck! He glanced off to the east where, between the hills and the sea, clustered a dense thicket of tents under the black flag of Saladin. He could feel the power of these silent watchers.

The Saracens, however, had missed their opportunity. With the addition of the English army, the Crusaders were now at their maximum strength. The garrison of Acre would not hold out long.

Richard's first active step was to inspect the advance force of five hundred men he had sent ahead under the command of Archbishop Baldwin. He found them camped between the Flemish troops and the Florentines, the lions flying above them and carrying the name of Thomas à Becket. The King took no umbrage at this evidence of the worship of all Englishmen for the Martyr of Canterbury. He had known that every sailor in his fleet had prayed each night to St. Thomas.

But Baldwin was no longer in command. He had been an unhappy man when he reached the camp before Acre. Believing that he had come in his old age to fight with an army of inspired soldiers, of militant saints, he had been disillusioned and disheartened by what went on around him, the drinking and profanity, the revelry in the tents of the women—those persistent trulls who had come to Palestine on the crusading ships and their dark-skinned eastern sisters who had managed to reach this splendid market—the cruelties, the brutal killing of spies, the flogging and mutilating of offenders against discipline. The gentle soul of the archbishop had sickened at his realization of war in practice. He strove fiercely to put an end to such things but failed. Finally, his health breaking, he had said a prayer to the God on whose service he had come, ending with a cry of anguish: "O Lord, I have remained long enough with this army!" He had passed away soon after, and if ever a man died of a broken heart it was Baldwin of Canterbury.

The advance force was now in command of an able Englishman named Hubert Walter. Richard was delighted with the vigorous discipline he had imposed. Walter had been educated in the house of his uncle, Ranulf de Glanville, and in spite of this connection, which would have blackened anyone less valuable in Richard's eyes, he had been nominated to the bishopric of Salisbury. He had been consecrated before sailing, but there was no suggestion of the clerical about the aggressive man in an English jack, a coat of canvas laced over breastplates of iron, who met the King now. He gave his sovereign a thorough report on the military situation and told of the arrangements he had made for the disposition of the army. Here, thought Richard, was a man after his own heart, by God's feet! He complimented Walter, said he expected great things of him and would make the rewards equal the achievements. He was as good as his word, for later he made Walter archbishop and put all power in the kingdom in his hands.

The English King had not failed to notice the tension in the welcome extended by Philip of France. There was, of course, the matter of Alice between them and the unforgivable quip of the Griffins of Sicily (a term Richard had coined) who had said that the English King was a lion and the French King a lamb! Finally the rousing welcome given Richard had been to Philip like salt in a raw wound. He was not alone in this. The proud Duke of Austria, the ambitious Conrad of Montferrat, the clapper-tongued Duke of Burgundy had been equally annoyed. They sat apart this first day in a sulky group.

The leaders might remain aloof, but the rank and file had been encouraged and heartened. For this one day, at least, they ceased calling the English *The Tailed men,* an illusion to the mutilation of the mule before the murder of Thomas à Becket, which was considered on the continent the most biting of insults. Even the Knights of St. John, wearing their black cloaks over coats of mail with five white crosses in memory of the five wounds of Christ, shared in the enthusiasm; and the Templars in long white mantles with red crosses on the shoulders and their banners of black and white, which were meant to show that they could be cruel to enemies of the Church even though dedicated to goodness.

Melech-Ric

Almost immediately after this splendid first day Richard took sick. It was one of the fevers which killed off at least as many of the Crusaders as the swords of the Saracens, and it did not warrant the claims made in some chronicles that he was no better than a hollow shell from his excesses as a young man. Some went so far as to say that he was dying of a quartan ague which racked him with paroxysms every fourth day, but, if this had been true, he would have been unable to endure the rigorous campaigning which lay ahead or to perform the prodigious feats with which he became the proclaimed hero of the world. He was so ill, however, that he could not assume any share of the command, even though he had his servants carry him to the front line on a mattress, where he was able to direct the fire of the mangonels. Things did not go well while he was incapacitated, for Philip of France was lacking in the qualities of military leadership. That monarch's detestation of Richard, moreover, was making it impossible for him to maintain any degree of co-operative effort. There was always fresh food, it seemed, on which his hatred could feed. He was getting short of money while Richard was well supplied (Longchamp had seen to that) and inclined to throw gold around him with a total disregard of future needs. Whereas Philip had been paying three *aurei* as a gift for bravery, Richard began to pay four, and the French King's face became saffron with mortification when his own men complained of *his* miserliness, particularly when he found that some of them were deserting to the English ranks.

If Richard had not recovered quickly, the crusading armies would have remained for the balance of the summer around the white-walled city. But he did get well, and immediately there was a stir in the trenches, and the mangonels began to hurl great stones against the walls with a deafening regularity, and the arrows arched into the beleaguered town from the "bad neighbors" so thickly that the garrison, which had been getting shorter of supplies all the time, decided no help could now be expected from the turbaned army sulking impotently along the foothills. Receiving Saladin's consent, they hauled down their flags.

Richard unfortunately took no pains to placate his fellow monarchs. When he found that the Duke of Austria had planted his flag on the walls of Acre beside that of England, he indignantly ordered it torn down, thus making a mortal enemy of the proud Leopold.

It must be said that he made it hard for his allies to work with him, and they have that much justification for what happened later.

While he toiled in the suffocating heat of early summer to get the army ready for the march on Jerusalem, his fellow commanders sat about together in the comfort of loose linen gown and sandals on the flat top of a city palace, sipping the chilled wine which was made possible by the efforts of that most courteous of foes, Saladin —who sent runners every day to the mountains to bring back snow and ice for his august opponents—and eating the pears and grapes from Damascus which came from the same source. From where they sat they could see the flag of England, floating above everything, and the tents of the infidels, which had shrunk in numbers since the capture of the city; and this made them doubly aware that most of the credit for the victory was being given to the English King. As one chronicle puts it, "they bit their gloves." If the conversation of these arrogant and incompetent men could have been preserved, it would have become very clear that their main purpose now was not to drive the paynim out of Jerusalem but to be sure that Richard's glory suffered an eclipse.

The success they had in this was small. In the end they further enhanced his glory and raised his historical stature far above his deserts.

Philip, it developed, had lost all stomach for crusading. He could see for himself nothing but a secondary role, and it was not in his nature to accept that. He had no intention of exhausting his treasury and suffering incredible hardships in order to forward the efforts of the overbearing English King. Accordingly he took most conveniently sick, and dispatches began to reach him of difficulties at home demanding his presence there.

One day a deputation of French nobles arrived at Richard's pavilion. It was stiflingly hot under the canvas, and the King, laboring over an Arab map (Christian maps were always bad while the Arabs had excellent ones), was in his shirt and drawers. It was not the way to receive emissaries from a brother king; but, after all, it was the same garb in which he had been crowned. The deputation did not take any offense, being so sick at heart that they did not notice. At first none of them could speak a word, and when Richard observed the tears in all their eyes he realized what had brought them.

He rose to his feet and threw the map aside angrily. "It will be an eternal disgrace!" he said. "But let him go! I shall fight on alone!"

It became evident later that Philip was ill enough to lend him some excuse. He departed as soon as he had recovered sufficiently, leaving ten thousand of his troops to continue under the command of the Duke of Burgundy. The latter was not a fortunate choice, for he had fallen into the habit of singing lampoons on Richard throughout the city and the camp, and Richard had been retaliating in kind. The Duke had been instructed to see that any drive against Jerusalem would fail. Such, at least, is the charge made against the French monarch, and the subsequent behavior of Burgundy made it clear that at best he had no heart left for the Crusade.

The darkest mark on Richard's reputation resulted from the capture of Acre. Nearly three thousand prisoners had been taken, and it was arranged that they were to be exchanged for the Holy Cross and an equal number of the Christian prisoners who were being held in captivity throughout the East. Whether or not Saladin intended to carry out his part or whether, like more recent exponents of oriental diplomacy, he thought he could wait his opponents out and gain some advantage from it, the Christian prisoners were not produced, nor was the cross forthcoming. Richard waited a long time and then, in a sudden and characteristic blaze of fury, he gave orders for one of the blackest deeds recorded in history. All the prisoners were to be killed without further delay.

This dreadful affair, one of the most barbarous executions the world has seen, was carried out on a large field under the walls of Acre. The captives were assembled *en masse,* thinking, no doubt, that this was their day of liberation. The King's orders had been that all were to be beheaded. This method proved too slow, however, and so the soldiers charged in and struck the cringing Easterners down with lance and sword and mace. It was many hours before the last turbaned figure fell and the last piteous cry for mercy had been stilled. The soldiers, weary and, no doubt, ashamed of the part they had played in this orgy of slaughter, returned to their encampments, and the blood-soaked field was left to the great mounds of the dead and to the birds of prey which came on slowly flapping wings from north and east and south.

The killing of the prisoners of Acre caused such fury throughout

the desert country that most of the Christian captives were wiped
out in retaliation. The feeling in Europe, when news of it was received, was one of regret for the fate of the Christian prisoners rather
than revulsion over the execution of the Saracens. The Crusaders
had gone to Palestine to kill unbelievers, and it did not matter, seemingly, how they went about it.

Richard took the episode in his stride. It had been to him a
military necessity, a way of letting the Saracens know that the invading armies were not to be trifled with any longer. He did not
appear at the field of slaughter, being too busy with his final preparations for the march. It may be assumed that the shrieks of the
dying prisoners did not cause him any loss of sleep.

Berengaria and Joanna had been lodged in regal comfort in one
of the great marble palaces of the city. The interrupted honeymoon
may have been partially resumed, but it is certain that Richard
saw little of his bride. He left her in Acre when the march started,
riding in the van himself with his banners flapping proudly in the
blazing sunlight. He had issued orders, most wisely, that the only
women to accompany the army were the washerwomen!

3

Melech-Ric was born on the march of the Crusaders down the
coast roads of Palestine. Here the unconquerable hero emerged, the
warrior who could not be daunted by odds, the leader who carried
victory in his saddlebags and glory on the elevated tip of his spear.

The march was a daring one, as the terrain was not friendly to
troop movements. First, it was necessary to cross the Holy Headland.
Once the great sanctuary of the Jewish people because it was impas-
sable in places and heavily wooded and, moreover, pitted with caves
which made concealment easy, it provided the Saracens with everything they needed to harass the advancing Christians. They would
emerge from the caverns with their shrill invocations to Allah and
send flights of arrows into the toiling ranks and then disappear.
They ambushed the Crusaders from the thick cover of oak and pine.
They rolled rocks down on them and blocked the roads which, at
best, were winding goat trails.

In the face of all this, Richard's army had to moil up the steep
slopes and along yawning precipices and down through the flint-

CYPRUS

Famagusta

Limasol

MEDITERRANEAN

SEA

ANTIOCH

CALIFATE of TRIPOLI

LEBANON MTS.

Damascus

Sidon

Tyre

Acre

SEA of GALILEE

THE HOLY HEADLAND

Arsouf

JORDAN RIVER

Jaffa

Jericho

Jerusalem

Bethany

Ascalon

DEAD SEA

KINGDOM OF JERUSALEM

CALIFATE of CAIRO

The
NEAR EAST
at the Time
of the
THIRD CRUSADE

S

palacios

bottomed wadis, dragging their heavy equipment with them, their mangonels and supplies. Hardest of all to move was the Great Standard of the Crusade, which was like the mast of a ship, made of solid ceiled work bound with iron and so heavy that it had to be drawn on wheels.

The roads beyond Mount Carmel, if such a term could be applied to the winding paths the Crusaders followed, were steep and rough and stony. The underbrush was thick. The Arabs, accustomed to fighting under such conditions, hung on the flanks and rear and not only captured and flayed alive every straggler, but kept the ranks in turmoil with charges and threats to charge.

The heat was unbelievable. Encased in iron and steel, which weighed them down and increased their sufferings, the brave men who had dropped the handles of the plow or had left the bench of the hatmaker to embrace the cross staggered along and suffered miserably and died by the side of the road under the knives of the unbelievers. The heat drove many of them mad, and they foamed at the mouth and shouted wildly as they fell out of line.

At night they endured almost as much from the cold. As soon as the sun dropped, the heat would evaporate and the sandy encampments would seem as frigid as the space between the worlds. But still each evening the heralds would raise their cry, and the men who were to die on the morrow, or the day after that, or certainly in a very short time, would lift up their arms, and their eyes would fill with tears of faith as they intoned in answer, "Help, help, for the Holy Sepulcher!"

This march, carried out in the intense heat of the summer months, seemed likely to end in disaster when the staggering ranks reached Arsouf early in September. Here Saladin, who had been waiting for the right moment, decided to give battle. He swooped down on the left flank and the rear of the Crusaders, driving back in utter confusion the French contingent under Burgundy and the Knights of St. John. Defeat looked certain until the new battle cry, which the followers of Richard had evolved from the Aquitainian "St. George for the puissant Duke!" was heard from the van. The English King wheeled and came thundering down on the Saracens. Richard himself led the charge, shouting, "St. George for England!"

Richard fought like a man possessed. Wherever he went, no matter what the odds or how unfavorable the situation, the Arabs broke before the fury of his onslaught. He fought for hours, driving the enemy back here, crushing them there, wheeling and charging and changing ranks to charge again, his eyes never losing sight of the battle as a whole and his keen tactical sense telling him where the next blow was to be struck. Perhaps never before had such fighting been seen.

The Arabs retreated finally and left the Crusaders in possession of the field. At Arsouf a new legend had been born, the story of the terrible knight with the reddish-gold hair and the gleaming eyes, the Melech-Ric who would be used for centuries thereafter to discipline children and admonish Arab horses.

Having thus brushed the army of Saladin from his path, Richard finished his march down the coast to Jaffa. Here the crusading forces halted, what was left of them, and spent some weeks repairing the fortifications of the city which the Saracens had destroyed. Jaffa was to serve as the base of operations in the drive to Jerusalem, and it had to be in strong and secure condition. It was not until New Year's Day, therefore, that the advance on the Holy City began. The obstacles encountered were greater than ever, and the advance slowed to a stop at Ramle, a few days' march inland from the coast. The Duke of Burgundy and the Grand Masters of the Templars and Hospitalers were a unit in believing that to penetrate farther would be to court disaster. Their advice was to go south to Ascalon and leave a garrison there to cover their southern flank. Richard was averse to this, but he finally gave in, and the army swung down the coast. They found Ascalon dismantled, and so once again the slow task of repair began. Richard realized that every day counted now, and he wielded a pick himself in his anxiety to get the work done. He demanded, moreover, that every man in the army, from king to foot soldier, should do the same.

Leopold of Austria responded sulkily, "I am not the son of a carpenter or a mason." One historian asserts that the English King responded with a blow. Whether he was as injudicious as that or not, the fact remains that Leopold left camp next day with all his men and returned forthwith to Austria. He became Richard's most bitter enemy, as subsequent events will show.

It was becoming clear that Jerusalem could not be captured. The defenses of the city were very strong, and Saladin had brought up new forces. Richard did not give up hope, however. He ordered

another advance, and his somewhat reluctant battalions resumed the
march. They penetrated as far as Bethany this time. Here, however,
the final blow fell. Burgundy, announcing that he considered the
quest hopeless, ordered the remnants of the French force to turn
and follow him to the coast. The hand of Philip, reaching back from
the West, had stopped his rival at the only moment when success
conceivably could have been won.

There was nothing for the rest of the army to do but retreat also.
Sadly and reluctantly, Richard gave the order.

Contrary to his usual custom, which was to ride in the van, the
English King dropped back to a place with the rear guard. Fanuelle
had been killed and he was mounted on an Arab charger sent to
him by Saladin. He rode with lowered head, his eyes brooding when
not actually filled with tears. He had failed in the only thing in life
which counted. For no purpose at all, it seemed, he had impoverished
the people over whom he ruled and disposed of his own possessions.
Once only on the first day of the retreat did he rouse himself sufficiently to speak. One of his youngest knights came galloping back
to him with a suggestion he thought might bring some relief to the
downhearted leader.

"My lord King," said the knight, pointing with the tip of his lance
at a high elevation of land around which the army was winding. "If
you will ride up there, my lord, you will be able to catch a glimpse
of Jerusalem in the distance."

Richard did not answer immediately. His head had turned instinctively in the direction of the rocky hill. It was several moments
before he could control his voice sufficiently to speak.

"Those not worthy to win the Holy City," he said, "are not worthy
to behold it!"

This glimpse of Richard is one that history should preserve, for
it shows the lionhearted King at his best. Here is proof of the inten-
sity of his desire to drive the infidels out of the Holy City and to
rescue the cross. There had been something deeper than personal
pride and military ambition to urge him on. There were depths to
his character, clearly, which make it easier to feel sympathy for him
in the violent role he was playing. Two events group themselves in
the mind: Richard in his burnished armor on which the fierce sun
glinted, riding slowly down the flinty trail and refusing to turn back
for a sight of the walls and towers of Jerusalem against the sky line

because he had failed; and his passionately ambitious father, dying amid the ruins of his shattered glory and crying, "Shame, shame on a conquered king!"

Father and son shared one trait: they could be great in defeat.

4

There was at this time an extraordinary personage in the East known as the Old Man of the Mountain. He was the ruler of a small racial group called by the outside world Assassins (from which the modern use of the word derives), a corruption of the real name which was Hashashim, the eaters of hemp leaves. Their country was a mere eyrie in the mountains of Lebanon, an almost inaccessible spot, from which the Old Man waged his peculiar kind of war on the rest of mankind without any danger of reprisals.

The subjects of this paranoiac king may have been the forerunners of the dervishes. They were, at any rate, a fanatical race who practiced fantastic rites and indulged in furious dances. Certainly they were original practitioners of kamikazi. Their ruler would send them out to kill anyone in the world he might name, and they would proceed about the task with such single-mindedness, such painstaking attention to detail, that they would accomplish their purpose in the end, if it took months or years. Their method of assassination invariably led to the death of the agent as well as the designated victim, but the mad Assassins were happy to die because they thought they were assured of a place in paradise. They were prepared for murder by being taken into a green garden filled with every form of luxury and many beautiful women. They were told this was paradise, to which their souls would wing after they had died in the service of their master. It sounds very fanciful, but it was the explanation generally believed at the time. This much is certain, that the young Assassins went out to find their victims, and to their own inevitable deaths, with a fervor which betokened a belief in a happy future life.

It was told also of the Old Man of the Mountain that his favorite method of entertaining guests was to lead them out to a garden surrounded on all sides by high cliffs on which a number of guards were stationed. A motion of his hand would cause one of the sentries to hurl himself, without a trace of hesitation and with a shout which had a note of gladness in it, into the air and die on the rocks at the foot of the declivities.

Why this daemonic old man thus waged war on the world has never been explained satisfactorily. However, he existed and it is also a matter of record that his subjects did come down from their eyrie in the Lebanon Mountains to kill people of note at his dictate.

Mention has already been made of Conrad of Montferrat. This proud and difficult member of the crusading band had married Isabella, the second daughter of the last King of Jerusalem. Sibylla, the eigne daughter, had married Guy of Lusignan, and the latter had acted as king in her right. But Sibylla died and Conrad promptly claimed the title because *his* wife survived. The pretensions of the two husbands split the camp of the Crusaders into factions. Richard supported Guy of Lusignan. The majority favored Conrad, however, and so the English King had been compelled to give in. He had promised Guy the throne of Cyprus as consolation.

As the Saracens held the Holy City, the title of King of Jerusalem was an empty one, but Conrad had a real overlordship in Tyre. It so happened that some subjects of the Old Man of the Mountain were killed in Tyre and, when the mad ruler sent messengers to Conrad to demand compensation, the latter treated them with disdain and paid no heed to their complaints. This was all the pretext needed. Two dusky emissaries of death were delegated to leave the mountaintops and accomplish the murder of the so-called King of Jerusalem.

Conrad must have known the danger in which he had placed himself, but he does not seem to have taken the matter seriously. Even when his servants found one morning a curious kind of cake beside his couch, which was a signal the Assassins used to tell where they intended to strike, he refused to become concerned. He was careless enough, in fact, to appear with only a few guards on the streets of Sidon. One of the murderers sprang through the line of guards and stabbed the King mortally. The Assassin and his companion were tortured, but they kept ecstatic expressions on their faces until the very moment of death: they had accomplished their purpose and would soon be tasting the delights of paradise.

In the East there was general understanding of the reasons for the killing of the German Conrad. The poorest beggar on the street could have explained the nature of the offense which had stirred the Old Man to action. Conrad had disliked Richard, but he commended his widow to the protection of the English King before he died, which should have absolved the latter from any suspicion of complicity.

It remained for the truant in France to blacken the name of the former comrade he now hated more than anyone in the world. Since abandoning his part in the Crusade, Philip had found himself the target of criticism. He felt the silent scorn which even his own subjects had conceived, and the resentment this caused in him was heightened by the reports coming from the East of the amazing exploits of the man who had stayed. When the French King heard of the killing of Conrad, he saw the chance he wanted. He gave it out that the assassination had been planned by Richard, basing the accusation on evidence of the flimsiest, which, moreover, had been invented. To lend weight to the story, according to one contemporary writer, "he no longer went abroad without being escorted by armed men; and, for his greater security, he instituted bodyguards from among those who were the most devoted to him, and armed them with great iron or copper maces." The idea of Philip's being in danger in Paris from the agents of the Old Man of the Mountain is a peculiarly absurd one, but there were many in France who believed the slander, or pretended to, and still more in Germany.

That strange madman who ruled in the Lebanons would never have received any mention in English history if it had not entered the spiteful mind of the Man Who Came Back to fasten the crime on the brother-in-arms he had deserted. By the lie he set into circulation, Philip created a situation which was to extend Richard's absence from England for two years after his departure from Palestine.

5

When Richard turned back from Bethany the Third Crusade was over. The fighting continued for some time after, and the English King gained even greater laurels by his bravery and resource at the relief of Jaffa, but there was no longer any thought that the purpose of the invasion could be accomplished. Richard sent Hubert Walter to negotiate a truce with Saladin, and the Eastern potentate took a fancy to the brisk young Englishman. They talked of Richard and of his magnificence as a warrior, and Saladin said that the English King had one fault only, a tendency to rashness. Later a peace was made between East and West for a term of three years, three months, three weeks, three days, three hours, three minutes, and three seconds; and by it Acre and Jaffa were left in the possession of the Christians, while the right of Christians to make pilgrimage to Jerusalem in safety was assured. All the fighting and bloodshed of four years, the terrible losses on both sides, had accomplished no more than that. It was a poor substitute for the purpose which had inspired the nations of Europe to join in this, the most spectacular of all the crusading efforts.

Saladin then met the European captains at Damascus, where they dined together in complete amity. He died in a short time, and his last act was a characteristic display of humility. "Go," he said to those about him, "carry my shroud through the streets and cry with a loud voice, 'Behold all that Saladin, who conquered the East, bears away of his conquests.'"

Richard, thoroughly disheartened, sailed from Palestine in October. It was impossible for him to go by way of France, for the feud with Philip was growing more bitter all the time. He decided, therefore, that he would return by the Adriatic and across Germany, a most unwise decision in view of the hostility of the German rulers. Perhaps it was the need for haste which dictated the route. He had received reports, of course, of John's activities at home and realized no time should be lost.

Under these circumstances he concluded that Queen Berengaria would be safer if she returned separately. This, at least, was the reason given when the royal pair left Palestine on different ships. There were other reasons, of course. It was no secret that the marriage had not been a success. Berengaria had seen little of her warrior husband and, though this might have been due to Richard's preoccupation with the business of fighting, there is every evidence that a coolness had developed. The fault was with Richard. Berengaria had been a good wife, self-sacrificing, obedient and loving, and both puzzled and hurt at the aloofness of her lord.

Berengaria returned, therefore, with her devoted friend and sister-in-law, Queen Joanna, arriving safely at Messina and deciding to proceed overland the rest of the way. When they reached Rome they were horrified to find that the jeweled baldric of Richard was being offered openly for sale in that city. Their alarmed inquiries elicited no information. None knew how it came to be there, nor had any reports been received of the movements of the English King. There could be no mistake about the baldric; they had both seen him wear it many times, a handsome thing of blue velvet with the royal insignia and the letter *R* embroidered on it in gold thread. They became convinced that his ship had gone down in crossing the Mediterranean and the baldric had been among the possessions saved.

If they had known the truth, they would have found it hard to believe. Richard had landed on the coast of Istria and, disguising himself as a pilgrim, had ridden north into the territory of his most bitter and active enemies, the new German Emperor, Henry VI, and Leopold of Austria. He had penetrated as far north as the small village of Eedburg just outside Vienna when the rumors of his presence, which had been spreading throughout Germany, brought the hue and cry down on him. The King was sitting before the fire in the kitchen of an inn when the mayor of Vienna, after placing guards around the building, strode in and said: "Hail, King of England! Thy face betrays thee for who thou art!"

Richard was taken to Vienna and held there in the closest confinement until the Emperor claimed him. For a long time after that he vanished from sight. It was known that he was being kept in imprisonment by the perfidious German rulers, but no acknowledgment could be obtained of this nor any hint as to where the hero of the Crusade was incarcerated.

The sensation created by this was world-wide. The valor of Richard had made him an international hero, and no general belief had been placed in Philip's charge of his complicity in the assassination of Conrad. In England the indignation was so deep that the country would gladly have gone to war for his release. The Council sat day and night considering ways to effect his freedom. Queen Eleanor, who was in England keeping a watchful eye on the ambitions of her youngest son, was like a lioness robbed of her favorite cub. She addressed letters to the Pope in which she passionately demanded that the papacy compel the Emperor to release his prisoner and to which she signed herself, *Eleanor, by the wrath of God, Queen of England.* In other letters at this period she subscribed her name, *Eleanor, humbly, Queen.*

[277]

In the meantime the Emperor had sent word to Philip of France about his plans for the royal captive which, says one of the chronicles, "was to the eye of that king more pleasing than gold or topaz." The Man Who Came Back promptly advised that Richard should not be released, declaring that the world would not know peace if he were. Later Philip tried to buy the person of the English monarch and boasted that "if he once had Richard in his hands, that king would never again see the sun shine on his own possessions." Failing in this, he offered an enormous sum if the Emperor would refuse to release the prisoner. He hastily sent envoys to the King of Denmark, with promises to back him if he would assert his ancient claim to the throne of England because of his relationship to Canute. This scheme was too farfetched even for the proposed beneficiary, and nothing came of it. At the same time—although this did not become known until later—he was making proposals to John which fell on more fertile ground. Philip promised the English prince that he would ease his subjects of their oaths not to make war on Richard and would then attack Normandy. For his part John was to declare himself King in place of his brother and was to assume also another obligation of Richard's, the hand in marriage of Princess Alice. It happened that John had a wife already, having espoused Avisa, the beautiful daughter of the Earl of Gloucester, at the time of Richard's coronation. Both parties to the conspiracy took it for granted that this unfortunate lady could be disposed of without any difficulty.

The negotiations between the precious pair had to be carried on by special messengers, for John was in England at the time. The French King wanted the English prince to visit Paris in order to get the matter settled, but Queen Eleanor, who suspected what was in the wind, saw to it that her youngest son (who had always been afraid of her) was not permitted to cross the Channel.

Later it was learned that John not only agreed to act with Philip against his brother but also expressed his willingness to do homage for the throne of England and to give away a large part of Normandy. He seems to have been prepared on all points to play Roger the Counter to Richard's Bohemund, and steal his brother's crown as Roger had done in Sicily when the great Bohemund went on the First Crusade.

Philip assembled an army and struck at Normandy. Meeting with little resistance, he swept up the Seine, and his troops spread out, capturing town after town and castle after castle. Gisors, Ivry, Neufchâtel fell to the French arms.

Word of all this was carried to Richard in his cell. He did not seem much disturbed. "My brother John," he said with a sigh to the jailer who had been the bearer of the news, "was not made to conquer kingdoms." The captive King was quite right. It developed that John's mission in life was to lose them.

Philip soon thereafter was taught a lesson which his fumbling father had learned early, that Normandy was a hard nut to crack. After his early successes he met with stout resistance on the part of the Norman people headed by the English Earl of Leicester, who had taken command on his way back from the Crusades. Leicester was a good soldier and he quickly organized the strength of the duchy. Philip found himself faced by a wall of steel he could not break, and finally he agreed to a truce, as his father had so often done.

The mystery of Richard's whereabouts had remained unsolved up to this point. The story generally accepted is that he owed the happy chance of his discovery to an old troubadour friend from Aquitaine, one Blondel de Nesle. There is no reason to believe the story—in fact, every reason to set it aside as apocryphal—but it is a highly imaginative yarn and so must be told.

Blondel, so the story goes, was depressed over what had happened to the hero of the Crusade and set out to find him. Once he and Richard had collaborated in the writing of a ballad, each of them doing one verse. Wandering through Germany in the guise of a common minstrel, Blondel sang this song under the windows of every castle he passed. He was rewarded finally for his courage and resourcefulness. After singing the first verse, which was the one he had written, he heard a voice from within take up the air and sing the second verse, which had been the King's contribution. He had found the cage which held the Lion of England.

So great has been the desire to believe this story of the discovery of the chained King that serious efforts have been made to find the *tenson* which Blondel sang; without success, it is hardly necessary to state. Richard, however, proved his ability as a poet and troubadour by composing a lament on the length of time he had been held in confinement. "Two winters am I bound" was the refrain running through it and, when this appeal for the aid of friends reached England, the demand for his release became nationwide.

The Emperor finally threw aside pretense and openly avowed his jailership. He summoned Richard before the Diet of the empire which met at Hagenau and there charged him with a long list of crimes, renewing the absurd story of the murder of Conrad and actually having the effrontery to claim that the English King had betrayed the cause by making a truce with the Saracen. Richard defended himself with vigor and eloquence, throwing the blame on the pusillanimous leaders who had deserted him within sight of the Holy City. He spoke so convincingly, in fact, that the electors of the empire, who were antagonistic to Henry VI, welcomed the chance to accept Richard's version. Henry concluded after the sessions were over that the best he could get now was a large ransom. He agreed to accept the sum of one hundred and fifty thousand marks.

Hubert Walter, who had been placed in command of the army after Richard's departure from Palestine, had succeeded in getting the men back to England. He now crossed to Germany and was allowed to confer with his imprisoned master. Richard put in his hands the formidable task of raising the money for the ransom. That his deputy might have the needed authority, he appointed Walter chief justiciar and expressed his desire that he be elected to the vacant post of archbishop.

Philip of France tried desperately to prevent the release of Richard. He decided to double the ransom figure if the Emperor would refuse to let his captive loose. When this failed because of the clamorous opposition of the German princes, Philip made another proposition. He would pay twenty thousand marks for each month that the departure of Richard was delayed.

Back in England, Hubert Walter proceeded to carry out his instructions with great ability and resource. He had been elected Archbishop of Canterbury on the King's urgent demand. With control of both Church and State in his hands, he set to work to raise the huge sum of money needed. It was a hard task, for England had not yet recovered from the drain of the Crusade. Walter even found it necessary to make a radical experiment, placing a tax on the land. The amount assessed was twenty shillings on each knight's fee, and the landowners groaned at what seemed a ruinous exaction. In addition, demands were made on the Church, even on the monastic institutions, which had always been exempt from taxation. The heads of the Church responded by contributing a quarter of all their rents, and the local clergy agreed to give a tenth of their tithes. A few of the richest monasteries voluntarily melted down their plate and thus raised a sum of thirty thousand marks. Three times the new primate had to go back with additional levies before the first payment of one hundred thousand marks was available.

Eleanor could not wait in England to greet her beloved son. Although she was now seventy-two years old, she accompanied Walter of Rouen, who had been deputed to deliver the money in Germany. Berengaria also would have walked on foot through the mud of Flanders and the snows of the Black Forest in order to see her long-lost husband. But the little-wanted Queen was not invited to go and remained at the home she had found for herself somewhere in Anjou, waiting anxiously for word of his release.

It was a good thing that Eleanor accompanied the English party. When the money had been handed over at a ceremony in the city of Mentz and the sixty-five hostages demanded as security for the payment of the balance had been taken into German custody, an intuitive sense of peril warned the Queen that there must be no delay in getting the ransomed King out of the country. She kept her eyes fixed on the Emperor, realizing that he was acting against his own wishes. He was a man of delicate appearance, with nicely chiseled features and beautifully formed white hands, and seemed on the surface of a gentle humor and the highest honor. The long years had made Eleanor a good judge of men, however, and she was certain this monarch in his scarlet cloak and ermine-trimmed cap had reservations to which he was not giving expression. She was quite right. Henry was inwardly against letting his captive go. The indecision of his mind was shown every time he lifted his eyes and in the way his hands tugged at his well-waxed beard.

It was learned later that he had received further propositions from Philip and would have repudiated the agreement if there had been a loophole. There was none, however, none that the prince electors would recognize. Richard accordingly was released and started immediately for Antwerp, where a ship was waiting to take him to England. The Queen Mother would permit of no delay. It was well that she allowed her sense of distrust to dictate their movements. Soon after they left, the Emperor changed his mind and sent orders that Richard was to be apprehended and brought back. When the imperial officers reached Antwerp, however, the English had already embarked and were on their way down the Scheldt.

The French King fell into the deepest rage of a lifetime spent in umbrage when he learned what had happened. Now he would have Richard to deal with and, from long experience, he knew it was going to be neither easy nor pleasant. John in England, certain that the treacherous diplomacy of the French King would succeed, was in a perilous position. Philip sent him a brief message of warning:

Take care. The devil is loose.

CHAPTER XIV

While the Devil Was Loose

THE REMAINING YEARS of Richard's life were an anticlimax, the twilight of a somewhat tarnished god. Richard himself, fighting continuously in France, demanding more and ever more money, does not seem actually to play a large part. Three other men dominate the scene, the first being, of course, John.

The second was Hubert Walter. This able, thoroughly practical, and always realistic man provides the final scene, in a sense, in the tragedy of Thomas à Becket, for he shows what could have happened if Becket had followed King Henry's orders when he became Archbishop of Canterbury. Walter had been elected archbishop first, and when he accepted the post of chancellor, Hugh Bardolph said to him: "By your leave, my lord, if you really well consider the power of your name and the dignity of your position, you would not impose upon yourself the yoke of slavery. For we have never before seen or heard of a chancellor being made out of an archbishop, though we have seen an archbishop made out of a chancellor."

England had suffered years of strife when the Chancellor Becket was made archbishop. Now, when a chancellor was made out of an archbishop, the country settled down under an efficient but stern administration. Becket had tried to put Church above State. Walter always put the state first, subordinating Canterbury to Westminster.

His first concern on returning to England, after his visit with the glum royal captive, had been to raise the ransom money. While the purses of the people were being emptied and the treasured stores of the monasteries converted into money, the new archbishop had also on his hands the problem of John. He was acutely conscious of that thoroughly unscrupulous member of the royal family moving under the surface, of approaches being made to members of the baronage, of the spinning of a great web. The matter came to a head rather unexpectedly. The story of how things fell out should be told because of the light thrown on the devious character of John and, still more, on the courage and decision of Hubert Walter.

John was a believer in the power of the bribe. Why should he not be? He had accepted many bribes himself in his time and he had successfully dangled them before other men. He was sure, therefore, that the businesslike chancellor could be corrupted. As a first step in that direction, he sent a creature of his to sound out the primate.

The man selected to make the approach was an oily specimen named Adam of St. Edmunds. John was not discerning enough to realize that this fat and unctuous clerk would be wax in the hands of the archbishop-justiciar-chancellor, that Hubert Walter would see through the maladroit Adam at one glance.

This was exactly what happened. Walter had a large company for supper at Westminster in the same hall where Becket had dined in such state and had so often attracted King Henry to the table by the fascination of his talk when Master Adam of St. Edmunds put in an appearance. The primate knew him at once for a spy, an informer, a stalking horse for John. It went against the grain to set him down to supper with his own honored guests, but there was nothing else to be done. So through the course of a long and elaborate meal Walter sat in silence while the uninvited visitor proceeded to make the nature of his mission clear to everyone. His beady eyes roving from face to face, Master Adam discoursed of the generosity of his *sweet and puissant master,* the great Count of Mortaigne, of the wealth and power he was getting into his hands and his willingness to share it, of the closeness of the alliance he had formed with the King of France. Filling his mouth the while with fried eel and peppered leg of capon, and sloshing them down with great gulps of the archbishop's finest imported wines, the suet-bellied clerk tried to do more than drop hints in the ear of the primate. He went far beyond his instructions and endeavored to seduce the whole company as well to the side of England's Roger the Counter.

The wry-faced Walter listened to all this attentively and without interrupting. Once he motioned to his state secretary, who sat at table some considerable distance away. When the latter came and stooped behind his back, the primate whispered in his ear at length, after which the assistant vanished unobtrusively. When the last *tranchoir,* a slice of bread which served the double purpose of plate and final mouthful, had been consumed with smacking lips and the last swallow of wine had trickled down the throats of his guests, Hubert Walter rose. He pronounced the blessing, thanked his guests, and saw them away. Adam of St. Edmunds, a little inclined to stumble and blissfully certain in his unsteady mind that it had been a successful evening, went with them.

The archbishop did not match guile with guile. That was not his way. He met guile with an open and quick display of the authority vested in him. While Master Adam had bumbled over his wine cup, the mayor of London, on instructions delivered by the secretary, had paid a domiciliary visit to his lodgings and had seized all his papers. They were lying now in the *Curia* offices, awaiting the primate's attention. When the adipose Adam had tumbled into his bed and fallen asleep, guards stood outside the doors and windows of the inn, with instructions that he was not to be allowed to leave.

Walter went at once to his cabinet and examined the papers with the thoroughness he brought to every task. Adam was wakened later and subjected to a questioning which left him limp of body and damp of brow.

In the morning a meeting of the Council was held, with the primate presiding. His manner, as he placed a hand on the pile of letters and notes in front of him, was grave and concerned. He told the members of the Council that he had at last the proofs of John's guilt, of his treasonable plotting with Philip to seize the throne and then to give away a large part of the overseas dominions. In the seized papers were orders to the seneschals of John's castles to prepare for resistance to the home-coming King. Going further, the primate pointed out the gravity of the situation in which they now stood. Richard was not yet free, so far as they knew at this point. There might still be a slip in the negotiations. He might, in fact, be done away with by the bitter enemies in whose power he lay.

In the latter event, John would become King and the treasonable course on which he was now launched would be cleansed by success. In spite of this possibility, Richard was King and they were his servants.

To the credit of the Council thus called upon to gamble their lives in the execution of their duty, the decision was unanimous in favor of taking immediate steps against John. He was pronounced a traitor, and a writ was issued for the seizure of all his castles and lands. The primate, as fearless and ruthless as Becket had ever been, went further and excommunicated the rebel brother.

England, it developed, was fiercely and exuberantly against John and in favor of the course followed by the ministers of the absent King. The fame Richard had won in the Holy Land had endeared him to his English subjects, in spite of the way he had robbed and mistreated them. They wanted to see the stay-at-home brother punished.

It became a relatively easy matter to capture the castles which the prince had garrisoned with small bodies of unpaid mercenaries. The only one to hold out was Nottingham, where the defenders retired into the keep and refused to yield. Walter was directing the siege in person when on March 20, a blustery day, Richard landed at Sandwich in a mood as blustery as the weather.

The King was wildly acclaimed in London. The church bells rang out, the people shouted their delight, and there was such a richness of pageantry and so much sumptuous feasting that the agents of the Emperor, who were to stay until the last of the ransom had been paid, were glumly convinced that they had been weak in not demanding a larger sum from a country as prosperous as this. Two days of feasting and drinking were all that Richard could stand, however. He had been so long inactive that his hands itched for the feel of a battle-ax. He took to horse and galloped off to share in the excitement at Nottingham.

Richard's tactics brought the garrison to their knees in quick order. He had a large gibbet set up outside the walls and proceeded to hang the men who had been captured earlier. The inference could not be missed: unless the garrison surrendered at once they would all share the same fate. The flag was hauled down.

John made his submission just as quickly. Queen Eleanor brought him into the presence of the King and asked that his transgressions be overlooked. She was, after all, his mother and had always felt compassion, without a doubt, for her landless young chick. He was now a thoroughly plucked bird and needed her support against the bright-plumaged fighting cock at the head of the family.

Richard had always been fond of his small brother, even though he understood him thoroughly. This was apparent when he told the kneeling John to get up. "I forgive you," he said. "I wish I could as readily forget your offense as you will my pardon."

The King then had himself crowned a second time. This was his opportunity to have the Queen crowned also. Berengaria, naturally, wished nothing so much as to stand beside her husband at Westminster and be confirmed as his consort. But she was not invited to cross the Channel for the purpose. The breach had not been healed.

Perhaps he followed the course of being anointed again to convince the people of his right to take certain ruthless steps. He relieved Walter of the chancellorship and gave that post back to Longchamp, who had accompanied him from Germany. By this action he flew straight in the face of public opinion, for the weazened Longchamp had been expelled on the almost unanimous demand of the country. This, however, was no more than the beginning of the King's recklessness. He proceeded to annul the sale of his lands and castles, by which he had raised money for the Crusade, asserting that the transactions had been in the nature of loans. His statement of claim read as follows:

What pretence have you for keeping in your hands that which is mine? Have you not completely reimbursed yourselves for your advances by the revenues of our possessions? . . . If, after reckoning what you have paid and what you have received, there justly remains any balance in your favor, we will supply the deficit from our treasury, and so leave you no cause for complaint.

Naturally there were no complaints. The unlucky purchasers swallowed the loss in grim silence. It would have done no good to demand a refund, as it happened. The royal treasury was as bare as a bleached bone.

If Longchamp expected to assume more authority for himself, as he had done before, he was soon disillusioned. The primate had retained the post of chief justiciar and so was the chancellor's superior. He had no intention of yielding as much as an inch to the ambitious man under him, and he was not another Hugh de Puiset to be hoodwinked and pushed aside. Walter's stern eye never relaxed its vigilance, and all maneuvering on the part of the reinstated hobgoblin to extend his authority was promptly detected and squelched. Longchamp had to content himself with routine, and he spent his days preparing writs and stamping them, not airily as before with his own signet ring, but properly with the Great Seal.

One step which stemmed directly from the chancellor was the distribution of a letter which purported to have been received direct from the Old Man of the Mountain! This extraordinary document read as follows:

To Leopold, Duke of Austria, and every prince and people of the Christian faith, greeting; Seeing that several kings in the country beyond the sea impute the death of the marquis to Richard, King and lord of England: I swear by the God who reigns eternally, and by the law which we observe, that Richard had no part in that murder. . . . Be it known to you that we have given these presents at our house and castle of Messiac, in the middle of September, and have sealed them with our seal, in the year after Alexander 1505.

This communication was sent to all courts and to the monasteries, where the chronicles of the day were written. It seems absurd to credit this statement to the Old Man of the Mountain, to whom the spires of Notre Dame and the battlements of the Tower of London were as remote as the spots on the sun, but no one challenged the authenticity of the document.

And now the King, having nothing more to detain him in England, hurried off for France to settle accounts with Philip the Truant. He never saw his native land again. Except that he kept demanding more and ever more money from Hubert Walter, he gave his kingdom no further thought. It is stated that within the space of two years he drained the country of the enormous sum of one million and one hundred thousand marks, and that the primate had to devise more and more exactions in wringing revenue from the groaning people. Although the amount stated is an obvious exaggeration, there can be no doubt that England, once the milch cow of the Crusade, was to continue playing that part to the demanding king.

The primate contrived new laws which, though drafted for no other purpose than extortion, contained the germ of an important principle. He realized that taxes could not be levied so continuously save by consent and representation. In all counties juries were chosen by a committee of four elected knights to pass on the amounts assessed against each owner of property. He then took another step forward and in 1195 issued an ordinance for the election in each "hundred" of four knights to act as keepers of the peace. In 1198 he accomplished his final piece of legal pioneering by putting a carucage tax on land which was to be assessed by a sworn and elected jury. This was done to satisfy Richard, who was growing more arrogant and unreasonable all the time.

This new form of tax was, however, a failure. The people were no longer capable of carrying on their weary backs these more and more excessive burdens. The money secured by the juries was too small to suit the rapacious King. At the same time the Council refused to raise an army to assist him in making war, and the primate received the blame for that as well. Although he had served his master with conspicuous success, he was forced to resign his secular office. It was a thankless task to serve a chivalrous king.

2

The third man to share in the domination of the last years of Richard's reign was a citizen of London named William Fitz-Osbert. As the leader and the very heart and soul of a secret society which planned an uprising of the people, Fitz-Osbert was the symbol of resistance to the King's oppression.

The man himself has been presented by most of the writers of the period, who considered any change to be evil, as a demagogue, an irresponsible troublemaker. His appearance is derided and he is said to have worn a beard for the sole purpose of concealing the peculiar vulgarity and villainy of his features. It is difficult to obtain a real look at this twelfth-century leader under the diligently applied coating of abuse, but his actions stamp him definitely as a man of great courage and character and a patriot.

Fitz-Osbert is spoken of as an Anglo-Saxon in most of the chronicles, but his name makes it certain that he was, at least, of mixed blood. He was a lawyer and he had followed Richard to Palestine; a tall man with a beard so long and black that, when he stood up to speak, he looked like a prophet out of the Old Testament. The

Norman authorities set him down on their records as Guillaume Longe-berde. In history he is mostly referred to as William Long-beard.

The citizens of London had many grievances, but the one which weighed most heavily on them at the time when Longbeard played his tragic role was a tax called taillage. A certain sum had been levied on the city and, in line with the theories which Walter was fathering, the amounts to be contributed by each citizen had been left to a jury. This jury was made up of the wealthier merchants (not all Norman, by any means), and they arranged it so that the rich paid a small share and the poorer people the greatest part of the burden. The men of London had never remained silent under injustice, and the whole city seethed and rumbled with dissatisfaction. The leader who rose to lend voice to the unrest was Fitz-Osbert. He fought the division before the London Council and, when they called him a traitor to the King, he declared, "The traitors to the King are they who defraud his exchequer by exempting themselves from paying what they owe him, and I myself will denounce them."

As good as his word, he traveled to Richard's headquarters in France and was granted an audience. Kneeling before the King, he poured out the grievances of the people in impassioned words. Richard's head was full of his campaigning and he paid little attention to Longbeard's plea. He promised to consider the matter, and promptly forgot all about it.

Hubert Walter, who was still in full control when this happened, was enraged that a mere citizen had dared go direct to the King. He promptly issued an ordinance that any Londoner who left the town would be guilty of treason. What is more, he put this arbitrary enactment into practice, throwing into prison some merchants who went to Stamford to sell their goods at a fair. This was the seed which yielded fruit of sedition in the great city on the Thames.

The people of London were ripe for rebellion. Meetings were held in secret in all parts of the town. Groups got together in the cellars of inns, in cemetery corners behind the hospitals, most frequently in the warehouses along the river. A revolutionary society was formed in which the membership, it is estimated, reached a total of fifty thousand. All the members, obviously, were not from London. Many belonged in nearby towns where the heavy hand of the tax extortioner was being felt also. Few details of this girding for action are available, but it is safe to assume that the stout burghers of London followed the usual procedure: district leaders, passwords, means of secret communication between districts, and behind all this a general plan.

One detail only survives in the records. They were collecting arms and storing them in the city. Weapons were brought in, concealed in bales of hay and wool and under straw in farm conveyances. Members from outside carried small arms into town under their tunics or cloaks. In addition to the regular weapons such as battle-axes, swords, and bows and arrows, they collected everything which might be used in an emergency—hatchets and iron crows and even quarterstaves. These stores were concealed at strategic points throughout the city.

There was a tension in the air while this was going on. Men refused to make way when the nobility appeared on horse or foot on the streets, and sometimes there were loud altercations and the men of blue blood beat at the rabble with their whips. While thus preparing for a resort to arms, if forced to that extremity, the citizenry continued to agitate in the open for reform. Meetings were held in the markets and on the streets. Longbeard, the acknowledged leader, was always the speaker.

A report has come down to us of one such gathering. The spot where it was held is not mentioned, but it would probably be in the western end of town where more space was available, perhaps not far from St. Paul's Cross. It was at night and, when William Fitz-Osbert rose to speak, he could not see far in front of him, but he knew that every foot was occupied with men who were heart and soul for action. He knew also that scattered throughout the packed audience would be a few informers and spies for the man who was ruling England for the absent King, Hubert of Canterbury.

Longbeard began his speech with a text. His eyes burning with zeal, he gave it out in a loud voice, "With joy shall ye draw water out of the wells of salvation." He looked about him and raised a hand above his head. "I am the savior of the poor! Do ye, O Poor, who have experienced the heaviness of rich men's hands, drink from my wells the water of knowledge and salvation. I will separate the people who are humble and faithful from the people who are proud and perfidious. I will divide the elect from the reprobate, as the light from the darkness."

There was the rant of the demagogue in this, but, when he went on to deal with their grievances in specific terms, he carried their breathless interest with him. It might then have been John Ball talking to the people, that humble but divinely eloquent monk who led the peasants to London for redress of their wrongs two hundred years later. There is something of the same flavor about his words, the same approach to incoherence which can be the very essence of eloquence. He was above everything direct and outspoken, telling the truth and sparing no one. There was not any hint of forces gathering under the surface, any threat of immediate action, in what he said; but the men of London returned to their small homes with the assurance that the day was near.

Hubert Walter was certain of this also. His spies had discovered all about the secret meetings and the smuggling in of arms. He probably could have made a very close guess as to the number of men involved. Always a believer in direct action, the archbishop decided he must lose no more time. The first step he took was to get his hands on William Fitz-Osbert. Longbeard was stopped on the streets when accompanied by a few only of his close followers. A scuffle ensued in the course of which he drew a dagger and killed the leader of the squad. He and his friends then succeeded in getting away and taking sanctuary in the church of St. Mary le Bow. Here they barricaded the doors and refused to give themselves up. Longbeard expected, without a doubt, that his peril would serve as the signal for a general uprising in the city, and that soon a large part of his fifty thousand followers would be marching to his rescue.

But the shrewd primate had laid his plans with too much care. The streets were filled immediately with armed troops who had been brought in secretly from other parts of the kingdom. They took possession of all street corners and saw to it that no one issued out from the houses. The plans that the men of London had hastily improvised for the uprising fell to pieces in the face of this quick coverage.

Although they soon realized they could not count on help, Longbeard and his friends decided to fight to the end. They paid no attention to repeated demands that they drop their arms and surrender. They battled on with the greatest bravery for hours.

Walter then proceeded to take steps which cost him the respect even of those who wanted the disturbance quelled and the spirit of the stirring masses broken. The right of sanctuary, for which Thomas à Becket would have laid down his life, meant so little to this iron-willed archbishop that he sanctioned a plan to heap straw around the church and set it on fire as a means of forcing Longbeard into the open. The plan succeeded. There was still some fight in the doomed men as they came out from the church, but, when their leader went down with a sword-thrust in the stomach, they gave in and surrendered.

All London, and later all England, was aghast at this violation of sanctuary. The cool archbishop, who had taken up his quarters in the Tower, was not concerned at all. He ordered that the prisoners be put on trial at once. This was done, and the members of the party were found guilty of fomenting rebellion and sentenced to death on the gallows. The next day the sentence was carried out. Impotent to aid the unfortunate prisoners, the people of London looked on in stunned grief while Longbeard was stripped to the skin and tied to the heels of a horse. He was dragged to Tyburn. The sharp stones of the road cut his bare frame to pieces, and he was in a dying condition when his mangled body was trussed in chains to hang on the Tyburn elm. All of his party died at the same time and in the same way.

Then London came to life. During the night the bodies were cut down and carried away. The chains were broken into small pieces which people kept as relics of the brave leader who had given his life for them. By the end of the first day there was a deep hole under the tree where Longbeard had swung, made by the scooping hands of those who felt the ground had become sacred. The secret society no longer existed, and the chance to assert themselves had been lost, but London continued to flock to the site of the hangings in such numbers that Walter had to station his soldiers around Tyburn with orders to allow no one near.

The news of what had happened threw all England into loud protest. The outcry against the action of the archbishop was not directed, however, at the summary execution of the leader of the people. The primate was condemned instead because he had violated sanctuary, and it was on this ground that Richard agreed to dismiss his minister from his secular posts.

Walter's plan of taxation, by which a fixed sum was levied on a community and the apportionment of the payments was placed in the hands of the people concerned, had been the direct cause of the trouble and bloodshed in London. He probably did not realize the importance of the principle he had evolved and the form it would take later, when all control of taxation became the sole function and the chief weapon of the House of Commons. The method was no more than a sop to still some of the opposition to the ever-mounting tax burden. That great good would come out of it ultimately had not entered the mind of the man who devised it and set it into operation.

No pair of shoulders loaded with the cares of the kingdom ever carried them with more ability and decision, but Hubert Walter was at the same time a man of the coldest calculation, with neither scruples nor humane impulses, and even of questionable honesty. The sentiments he stirred in other men were never more openly stated than by Hugh of Lincoln, who was then a very old man. He had repeatedly spoken out against the arbitrary actions of the primate but he reserved the final barb for the last moments of his life. Hubert Walter came to his bedside and declared that he forgave him all the harsh criticisms of the past.

"Indeed, Your Grace," said the dying man, "there have been passages of words between us, and I have much to regret in relation to them. It is not, however, what I have said to you for which I should now be pardoned but for what I have omitted to say. I have more feared to offend Your Grace than to offend my Father in Heaven. I have withheld words which I ought to have spoken and have thus sinned against you. Should it please God to spare my life, I purpose to amend that fault."

3

The Bishop of Beauvais, who happened to be a near relation of Philip of France, got into armor to fight against the English. He was captured and thrown into prison, where he was loaded down with chains. The Pope heard of the bishop's plight and sent a request to the English King for the release of his son, as he called His Grace of Beauvais. Richard's answer was to send the bishop's shirt of chain mail, which was covered with blood, to the Vatican.

With it went a letter: "This have we found. Know thou if it is thy son's coat or not?" The prisoner was not released until he paid his ransom the same as any other man who had taken the sword, a substantial one in this instance, for the revenues of Beauvais were fat.

This incident is typical of the spirit displayed on both sides in the war between the two embittered kings. They harried and burned and took castles and lost castles. The only way they had of venting their mutual spleen was, seemingly, to render thousands of each other's subjects homeless and to kill as many as they could catch.

A peace was patched up finally—which neither of them meant to keep—and then Richard, instead of going home and giving some attention to the sorry condition of his people in England, proceeded to carry out one of the pet plans of a lifetime. On the Seine River, south of Rouen, there was an ideal spot for a great castle which would provide perfect protection against invasion. Here, where the river bends sharply and the valley of Les Andelys breaks the high line of the banks, a spur of rock juts out into the water. A minor Gibraltar, six hundred feet long, two hundred wide, and three hundred above the level of the water, it commands the river and all the surrounding country. Here the English King built his famous Château Gaillard, which has been considered the masterpiece of the age.

At the lip of the rock he erected an octagonal fort with walls ten feet thick and a ditch hewed out of the solid stone. Behind this was the main fort, a tower-flanked structure with a great citadel which followed the conformation of the spur. Fortresses are sometimes said to frown. This one scowled, a belligerent scowl, as though daring the French King to lead his forces up against Normandy. The walls rose so unexpectedly and sharply from the river that they seemed to reach up endlessly into the sky, their impregnability obvious at a glance.

Richard took a year in the building and poured money into it as fast as it could be squeezed out of the English people. His pleasure in what he was doing had some of the naïve delight of a boy piling up a high tower of blocks. When it was finished, he walked to one of the ogive windows at the top of the dungeon tower in the citadel, from which he could see up and down the river and well out over the high chalk cliffs. His eyes lighted up. "How pretty," he cried, "is this child of mine, this child of one year!"

Philip was enraged over the erection of Château Gaillard because there was a clause in one of their many treaties forbidding the fortification of this particular point. Hate flared up between them.

"I will reduce this castle of his," cried Philip, "if the walls are of iron!"

"I could hold my castle against *him,*" answered Richard scornfully, "if the walls were of butter!"

Soon after this Richard became seriously ill of a distemper. It was natural that he should begin to think of his sins. One of the priests about him pointed out that he had been very unfair to his consort. The ailing King agreed that this was so and he issued orders at once for Berengaria to join him. She came with the greatest gladness and helped to nurse him back to health.

When his health had been sufficiently restored, they went together to Aquitaine and spent a Christmas there. The weather was perfect, which means it was warm enough for troubadours to come from all over the golden provinces to amuse the King and his lady, and for gleemen to sing in the gardens. If Richard and Berengaria ever achieved any degree of happiness in each other's company, it was during this short Christmas celebration; short, because Richard was off again almost as soon as the new year started. The struggle with Philip had broken out in its final phase.

The King allowed Berengaria to accompany him on his campaigning this time. This did not mean that she saw much of him. It meant staying in the manor houses of small nobility some distance back from the line while Richard was directing the movements of his troops. Occasionally there would be a sound of furious galloping and she would see the standard of England and her husband riding in the van, his breastplate and taces flecked with foam, his heaume removed from his head so that the wind carried his great yellow mane behind him like a tawny streamer. This was the greatest pleasure she was able to get from his permission to follow him to the front, a glimpse every now and then of Richard riding by.

Greed was the cause of Richard's death, which came about soon after. His war chest was nearly empty and the justiciar who had replaced Hubert Walter was unable to raise much money. It came to the war-mad monarch's ears that a great treasure had been found near the castle of Chaluz in Limousin. The nature of the find was exaggerated as the story continued to spread, and when it finally reached the avid King it had become a dozen figures of knights cast in pure gold around a table of the same precious metal. As suzerain of Limousin, he was entitled to half of any treasure-trove and so he was both incredulous and angry when the lord of Chaluz reported that what he had found in reality was only a few old coins. Richard decided he would collect by force and he led a band of his Brabançon mercenaries, under a captain named Marcadie, into Limousin. They besieged the castle and Richard, in an ever-mounting rage at the resistance of his vassal, swore that he would hang every man, woman, and child in the place. He would probably have done so if an archer had not aimed well from the top of the beleaguered walls and lodged his arrow in the royal shoulder.

The wound was not deep, nor had a vital spot been touched. The surgeon made awkward work of extracting the bolt, however, and as a result gangrene set in. It became apparent then that Richard was going to die. Realizing it himself, he forgave the archer (but Marcadie afterward flayed the man alive and then hanged him) and tried to make up in penitence and prayer for all his many sins.

Berengaria was with him at the end. She sat beside his couch and saw his strength ebb away and the high color of his cheeks change to the gray of death. She was beside him when he breathed his last. If Valhalla had resounded with toasts when he came into the world, there must have been a stirring in the Elysian fields when his soul departed.

He had been King for ten years, this violent man who died of violence. The tower of blocks had toppled over for good; and with the death of Richard the Angevin empire, left to the care of John, toppled also.

4

It would be pleasant if it could be recorded that Berengaria's life flowed in easy courses after Richard's death, but unfortunately she continued the victim of fate's buffeting. Within a few weeks she lost her only sister Blanche and the friend who had stood by her in all her trials, the King's sister Joanna. The latter had married again, a genuine love match, and her husband, Raimund of Toulouse, became involved in the religious persecutions of the Albigenses in the south of France. In his behalf Joanna came to beg Richard's assistance and arrived soon after her brother's death. The shock caused her to give birth prematurely to a son, and she died herself the following day.

For more than thirty years thereafter Berengaria lived quietly at the city of Mans, where she founded the abbey of L'Espan. While John was King she had continual trouble in getting her pension, which was all she had to live on, and she found it necessary to write letters to Queen Eleanor and Pope Innocent III about it. The Queen, who had always been fond of her, arranged the matter at once. Later the Pope had to threaten an interdict on a number of John's castles and honors to make him pay the poor Queen what he owed her. When John died there was a matter of more than four thousand pounds owing to Berengaria, and the debt was compounded in some way. Thereafter she seems to have received the payments with regularity. She died in 1230 and was buried in the abbey she had founded. It is said she was glad to be rid of the cares of this life.

Few figures in history have been as unfortunate as this Navarrese princess. Poor little linnet wedded to a falcon! Poor little neglected Queen! Of all the royal ladies of the island kingdom, she shared one distinction with none—she never saw England!

CHAPTER XV

The Unsolved Mystery

H ISTORY has depicted John as a monster of wickedness and his reign as an unrelieved record of cruelty and oppression. The once landless prince who succeeded to the throne in spite of being the fourth of Henry II's stalwart and healthy sons was probably as bad as he has been presented, selfish, cruel, shameless, cynical, lustful, dishonorable, and utterly false. The available facts justify this far from pleasant portrait.

He was not one of the fair-haired and handsome Plantagenets. It has already been noted that he was somewhat fattish as a boy, and he had now developed into a broad and heavy man, almost squat, and with a square face which was showing more than a trace of jowl. His eyes were dark and he wore a black beard which avoided stringiness by a process of much curling and waxing. But in spite of not possessing that outward guise of nobility which the rest of the brood had and which sometimes concealed the lack of it within, John had a way of making friends. The facetious strain which had cropped out first in William Rufus had been handed on to him and, when he wished, he could be highly amusing. There is too often about men of the worst character a capacity to compel interest and sometimes admiration. The picture of Satan which has been conceived and developed over the years is proof of the fascination he exerts on most people—the hypnotic eye, the strongly marked features, the polished and sophisticated manner. There was something mephistophelean about the new King. Men enjoyed his company, and he had a definite attraction for women. Those who yielded to this attraction always had reason to regret it. He had so little honor in him that the plucking and crushing of a bud were almost simultaneous, and he was so lacking in what might be termed the decencies of dalliance that he would seduce a woman one night and boast of it openly at supper the next.

He had the same irreverence as Richard, but unlike the lion-hearted brother who could blaspheme freely and refuse the sacrament for seven years without any feeling of penitence or fear, John had such a belief in later punishment that his slips from grace were invariably followed by much frantic seeking for forgiveness. There was in him a noticeable tendency to model himself after the great brother in small ways. "By God's feet!" had been the invocation which Richard had rolled out in his fine voice at moments of stress and anger. John, whose voice could be a little shrill, made his, "By God's teeth!"

Strangely enough, he had more of a turn for scholarship than any of the kings from William the Conqueror down, including that so-called man of learning, Henry I. He was known to have read Hugh of St. Victor on the sacraments, the *Sentences* of Peter Lombard, *The Romance of the History of England,* and *The Treatise of Origen,* which was an extensive browsing into the field of learning for a king in those days. He was a hard worker and a continuous traveler.

Such, then, was the man. There is even less good to be said for him as a king. He ruled as though only his own interests and desires counted. He had no wisdom and not a trace of statesmanship, but on many occasions he showed a degree of political craft. If he failed in the resolution to fight an issue or a battle to a finish, he had some sagacity both in government and generalship. He possessed a keen capacity in money matters. One instance will show how much shrewdness he could show on occasion. The city of Liverpool owes its early rise in importance to a flash of good sense which John had the first time he passed the Mersey and saw that here was the place for the much-needed northern port. There was ruthless management in the way he changed the little collection of mud huts into a flourishing town, planning it himself in the form of a cross with seven side streets, and allowing immunity to runaway villeins and slaves while there (how the lords of the manor protested!) and their freedom if they remained a year and a half. Such episodes, unfortunately, were not frequent.

It must be stated in fairness to this much-derided ruler that history has been too prone to saddle him with all the blame for the breaking up of the Angevin empire. The French possessions formed a ramshackle structure, joined together in the first place by such intangibilities as royal marriage ties, held by nothing more durable than the vows of the ruling families. The brisk people of England had nothing in common with the easier-going inhabitants of Aquitaine. Their interests were as far apart as the tongues they spoke. The English had grown tired of shedding their blood and emptying their pockets in the endless strife of ducal factions abroad. They had reached the point where they flatly refused to shoulder war burdens which brought nothing but a sense of importance to their kings.

The magic of Richard's name had kept the empire intact, even though the tides of separation were rising high in his time. With John came the deluge. The last of the sons made a pitifully poor attempt to hold back the flood, but the result would have been the same if he had been a great military leader and a political genius combined; though perhaps in that case the triumph of the French would have been slower and more costly.

John was the complete tyrant, and the people of the island kingdom suffered injustice and deprivation under him. Inasmuch as his oppression led to Magna Charta, however, he was the first and most noteworthy of the bad kings out of whose evil rule came good. The loss of Normandy and the Angevin provinces, although it humbled the pride of the nation, was another great benefit which grew out of disaster. As will be demonstrated later, it blew away the final trace of racial disunity in England. The Saxon and the Norman merged at last into the Englishman when the King ceased to be a colossus with one foot in London and one in Rouen.

These two developments of such major importance, and the fact that his reign provides history with one of its great unsolved mysteries, make the years of John of the deepest interest, even though they are filled with evidences of a depravity fit to chill the blood.

The story of John begins with his contest for the crown, and this leads at once into the intricacies of the aforesaid mystery.

2

England could boast at this time of a fine knight who has appeared once briefly in these pages: when Richard, pursuing his sick and beaten father from Le Mans, found himself facing a man who treated him with the scorn he deserved. This was William Marshal, so called because he held the high post of marshal of England. He was now the Earl of Pembroke and military commander in the Rouen district. Later a detailed account of this remarkable man will be given, but at this point, with a new-made grave still to be closed and a successor to be chosen with a loud clatter of arms, it will suffice to say that William Marshal was the greatest fighting man of the century (not excluding the doughty Coeur de Lion with his battle-ax) and a fine, human fellow of high character and undeviating principles.

It was in the late hours of the evening that a servant wakened the marshal from sleep with news of the death of Richard. The soldier, who was now in his middle fifties and inclined to sleep heavily, roused slowly and sat up in bed, exposing his bare torso and long muscular arms. He did not at once take in the full significance of what he had been told, then he sprang energetically from bed and struggled into his camise. Over this he hastily dropped the gambeson, a padded shirt to protect the body from contact with the metal. Then came a hauberk of jazerant work which was much used at the time, a coat of steel plates attached to a base of canvas. Sleeveless surcoat and a pair of heavy leather boots reinforced with metal completed his costume.

Rouen was packed to the eaves with the birds of prey who collect at the first taint of blood on the air: mercenaries who swaggered in the streets and swilled in the taverns, announcing themselves as not engaged by a careful absence of color in their clothes, even to a discarding of scarves; heavy-chested Flemings, flaxen Germans and Danes, dark and sallow condottieri from the boot of Europe, all waiting to sell themselves to the highest bidder; tougher and more evil than these, the contractors with supplies to sell, diabolically clever fellows with paid bravoes at their heels; and, of course, spies, informers, secret agents, pimps. Rouen after nightfall could be likened only to the back streets of hell. Here a dagger thrust in the ribs was as common and as little thought of as an oath. Although William Marshal had never known a moment of fear in his life, he was too old a campaigner to risk the blackness of the streets without an adequate guard. The wind and the rain, the oldest of campaigners themselves, were on the attack when he started out, with sudden swoops which made the lantern dance on the brown-bill carried in front of the party and caught the midnight wayfarers full in the face, so that rivulets of water ran down their necks under the open iron pots they wore on their heads and got into the armor where it could not be dislodged. All through the centuries man has devised one absurdity after another in the way of apparel, but never has there been anything to equal the discomfort of body armor in a heavy rainstorm.

The shaven-poll who admitted them into the courtyard of the archbishop's palace turned them over to a brother inside and then ran for the cover of his wicket at the gate, knowing the playful habit soldiers had of beating the buttocks of priests with bill handles or treading on their toes with iron shoes. Those inside were equally expeditious in leading the marshal to the bare apartment where the old primate was still bending over his endless documents.

Walter of Rouen heard the news with such a sense of shock that for several moments he said nothing. Then he pointed out the danger of delay in getting the succession settled, and the two of them fell into a serious debate. The archbishop took the stand that Arthur of Brittany, the heir of Geoffrey, who had been born between Richard and John, had first right to the throne; which was correct, according to the accepted law of primogeniture. Marshal shook his grizzled head in denial. Arthur might have the right, but it would be a bad thing to choose him King. He was a foreigner, this boy named after the great Celtic King, and by report he was as proud and tricky as his father had been (the handsome Geoffrey had always been counted the troublemaker of the family) and as strong-willed as his mother, Constance of Brittany, who hated the Plantagenets. England needed a man, declared the marshal, and it would be better to take John.

They discussed the matter with full consciousness that the succession might hinge on what they decided. Between them they could put the might of Normandy back of their choice. Should it be John, who had been born in England and had friends there in spite of everything? Or should it be the unknown quantity, this boy of thirteen who had never been in England and had scarce a drop of Saxon blood in his veins; whose character, moreover, had not yet formed sufficiently to allow them to reach any judgment?

The marshal stuck aggressively to his selection: John, whose faults were all known and who was wanted by the people of the island with a degree of unanimity hard to believe in view of the reputation the sole surviving son had acquired.

The archbishop sighed finally and gave in. John, then, it would be.

"Nothing of which you have done, Marshal," he declared, shaking his head dolefully, "will you have such cause to repine as this."

Although the archbishop was right about what would happen if John were made King, the marshal's choice was that of England. Across the Channel the feeling against the young prince as a candidate was running high. The evidence on this point is so convincing that it can be taken as fact that Arthur would never have been accepted as King of England, even if all the French possessions had declared for him.

In the meantime the adherents of Arthur had received the news of the King's death, and Brittany had blazed into excited support of the prince. Anjou, Maine, and Touraine threw in on the same side. Philip of France turned against his old partner in perfidy and espoused the cause of his nephew. The French monarch announced his readiness to take the field and summoned Arthur to Paris to live in his household and receive education with his own son and heir. In Normandy, which counted most, the strong stand taken by the Earl of Pembroke was keeping the people from joining in the rather hysterical swing to the heir of Brittany. Aquitaine, that loyal land, was standing behind Eleanor and was ready to accept whatever decision she might make.

Eleanor, naturally, chose her only remaining son. John had been so much the favorite of Henry in the bitter last days that there had been restraint sometimes in her attitude toward him. Now this was all swept away. Although she knew full well that John had great faults, she was prepared to battle for him against the grandson who had been trained to hate her by his high-tempered mother.

Eleanor's support was what John needed at this critical moment. Touraine had declared for Arthur, but the imperious old Queen instructed the seneschal to turn over the treasure of that province to John, and this was done at the castle of Chinon on April 14. At the same time a few of the nobility swore fealty to him. From Chinon, John rode north into Normandy, where he found that William Marshal had kept the old duchy loyal to him. He was crowned duke by Walter of Rouen on April 25.

The coronation was conducted with all the old Norman rites. The ducal coronet, which was made in the form of a wreath of golden roses, had always looked out of place on the heads of the hard-bitten men who had worn it. John had broadened out so much that the dainty circlet made him rather absurd. Perhaps he sensed this himself. At any rate, as he took the spear, which was handed to him in place of a scepter according to the Norman custom, he turned and winked at the spectators. At a later stage of the ceremony he let the spear fall out of his hand, and it crashed loudly on the stone paving before the altar. An uneasy silence settled over the cathedral. This was believed a sign that he was doomed to lose the duchy.

The reception he received in England, where he went immediately after being crowned in Normandy, showed how correct William Marshal had been in his estimate of the temper of the English people. They wanted him to be King, and not a single voice was raised in favor of the young prince. The coronation took place on Ascension Day, May 27, and Hubert Walter officiated. Whether it was done as a sop to the nation in view of the poor caliber of the new King, or whether it was the first of the checks which all men knew would have to be imposed on him, the primate solemnly intoned the words of the old ritual which declared him King by choice of the people. Years after, the archbishop confided that he had used that form of oath because the violence of John's character rendered the solemn admonition necessary. It made no difference, of course, so far as John was concerned.

3

For many centuries before the Normans came, and all through the sanguinary stages of the Conquest, the Welsh people had remained in their mountainous corner of the island, refusing stoutly to be incorporated in the growing nation. They were of the same racial stock as the people of Brittany and with the same traditions and ideals, the same dislike for Saxons and Normans and French-men. One great faith sustained these Celtic peoples in their determination to remain apart and independent, and this was the legend of Arthur, the Pendragon, the most enlightened and chivalrous of men. Out of this faith had grown the belief that someday, when the need would be great, Arthur would come back to earth with his sword Excalibur and lead his people again.

Stories continued to grow around the Arthurian legend as time went on. It was generally believed that Glastonbury, where the old Benedictine monastery stood, was in reality the Avalon to which the body of the King was taken after his last battle. This did not prevent rumors of the finding of his grave elsewhere. Crusaders came back from the East with various stories. Some said he lay at the foot of Mount Etna, others said on Mount Sinai. One belief was universal: that anyone who ventured into the woods at midnight would hear the sound of ghostly horns and see a train of hunters ride by like shadows through the glades with the grave-faced Arthur in the lead. He was as much alive in Celtic minds as any king of the day, and the conviction that he would return was at the core of Welsh resistance to English encroachments.

Toward the end of the reign of Henry II an announcement had been made which stunned all believers in the legend. Henry of Blois, the abbot of Glastonbury, gave it out that, acting on the revelations of a Welsh bard, he had made a search of the abbey vaults. At a considerable distance down had been found a huge coffin of oak containing the bones of Arthur and his Queen Guinevere, who had been buried with him. The unusual size of the bones made it certain that they had belonged to the tall Pendragon. The golden hair of the beautiful Queen was seen when the coffin was opened, but it had crumbled into dust as soon as exposed to the air. The main piece of evidence, however, was an inscription on the side of the coffin:

Hic jacet sepultus inclitus Arthurus in insula Avalonia.

If this was really the body of Arthur, he became a man and could no longer be thought of as a God. After the first sensation had died down and the bones had been reinterred in a magnificent sarcophagus, the people of Wales and Brittany rejected the story as a deliberate imposture designed to destroy their faith in the future of the

Celtic race. There were repeated demands to see the coffin with the inscription, but the abbot failed to produce it. In time it was generally believed that the discovery had been planned for political reasons, perhaps on the insistence of Henry himself.

It was soon after this that a posthumous son was born to Constance of Brittany, the widow of Henry's third son, Geoffrey. Henry was delighted, for this was his first grandson, and he decided the boy should be given his name. This was not acceptable to the mother. Constance did not like the King or his wife (Eleanor reciprocated most heartily) and, in fact, wanted nothing to do with the English royal family. She called in the leading men of Brittany and asked their opinion about the naming of the infant duke. Unanimously they said he must be named for the Pendragon, who would return to earth in his own time in spite of lies and impostures, and so Arthur the boy was called. One troubadour declared that the King who founded the order of the Round Table *had* come back; that his soul had entered the body of the child cradled safely in the ducal palace behind the Mordelaise Gate.

Eleanor had disliked her Breton daughter-in-law from the beginning. There is evidence that she was fond of Berengaria, and no hint can be found in the records that her feeling had not been friendly to the French princess who married her son Henry. She seems to have accepted Isabella of Angoulême, who later married John. But Constance of Brittany she did not like, and it may have been that her antagonism grew out of the attitude of the latter. Henry had felt the same way, believing that Constance urged Geoffrey to dispute his authority and to keep the family strife stirred up. Her insubordination in connection with the naming of the infant son was the final proof. Eleanor was in custody at Winchester when this happened, and so no share of the blame can be charged to her. It was Henry's own decision that the young widow must remarry at once and to a man who would always act in accord with the kingly plans. He was concerned chiefly with the fear that his grandson would fall into the wrong hands, but there was another reason for the speed with which a second husband was found. Young Prince John, who could not resist pretty women, was very much attracted to his Breton sister-in-law, and an end had to be put to that.

The husband Henry selected was one of his close adherents, a certain Ranulf, Earl of Chester, a black-a-vised and generally ill-

favored little man for whom the young widow conceived an immediate dislike. Her feelings were given no consideration at all. Knowing that her son would be taken away from her if she refused,
Constance went through the wedding ceremony with this unattrac-
tive bridegroom. It seems improbable that the marriage was con-
summated, for Constance made it clear from the beginning that she
detested her new spouse. Henry was well enough content; he did
not want any more Breton grandsons to complicate matters later.
Ranulf played his part, literally, to the King's taste. He took the
reins into his own hands and drove Brittany in the straight path of
Angevin policy. It is quite likely that he made no effort to take the
nuptial couch by storm. The people of Brittany hated him, but they
were in no position to get the yoke from their necks. They gave
passive obedience and bided their time.

Arthur, in spite of all efforts to the contrary, was reared as a
Breton. His youthful mind was filled with the past glory of his race,
and the ambition was fostered in him to become another king such
as the great Pendragon Arthur. He was an active lad and showed
signs of proving as skilled in the use of arms as his father had been.
When he was admitted to knighthood at a very early age, he took
as his device the lion, the unicorn, and the griffin, which had been
worn by the illustrious monarch for whom he was named.

When Richard failed to bring a son into the world, young Arthur
became the heir apparent. The quietly fanatical group around him
began to see visions in real earnest. The old prophecy would be
fulfilled when a Celtic prince sat once more on the throne of
England.

When Richard's illness led to his reconciliation with Berengaria
and set him thinking about the future generally, he decided to declare Arthur his successor. With this in mind he asked Constance to
send her son to him, to be raised at the court and educated under
the royal eye. Arthur was then nine years old, and his mother had
introduced him a short time before to the Brittany Assembly and
had won their consent to his being associated with her as head of
the state. She was instantly suspicious of the King's suggestion, fearing that Richard's purpose was to get the boy into his hands. When
she held back, Richard sent her an impatient demand to meet him
at Pontorson to discuss the situation. This made her more hesitant
than ever, and he issued peremptory orders to her husband to make

her a prisoner. The ever-pliant Ranulf obeyed his King by lodging his wife in one of the castles of Brittany.

The people were ready to rise in her defense, but Constance sent secret instructions to their leaders that no time was to be wasted in efforts to release her. One thing only counted: Arthur must be kept out of the hands of the English. They obeyed her by making one of their number, the Sieur de Vitré, guardian of the young prince. The Sieur de Vitré proved a resourceful custodian, flitting about the country from one hiding place to another and defeating all efforts to locate his charge. Ranulf of Chester, finding himself unable to cope with the situation, called for help. Richard answered by sending in a body of his Brabançons, and there was much useless fighting and bloodshed. In the end the prince was spirited out of Normandy and placed in the care of the King of France. Richard then threw up his hands, gave orders for the release of his sister-in-law, and from that moment lost all interest in Arthur as his successor. When he died he named John as his choice for the throne.

The likeliest explanation of Richard's course is that he began with the intention of acknowledging Arthur as his heir and that the antagonistic attitude of the mother stirred him to peremptory methods. Such was Richard's way in everything. It is inconceivable that he intended to get rid of the boy, as Constance feared. He had been given so much reason to suspect the motives of John that he would not have stained his own name with murder to secure the succession of his perfidious brother. The blame for the impasse must at least be shared by the haughty and impetuous Constance.

Now that Richard was dead it seemed certain that the quarrel over the succession would embroil England and France in another long and bloody war. Constance, that intense and bitter woman, was as suspicious of Philip, however, as she had ever been of the English, and with the soundest of reasons. The French King had espoused the cause of Arthur with open professions of disinterest, but it had soon developed that he was thinking of nothing but his own gain. His intention was to incorporate Brittany and the provinces of Anjou, Maine, and Touraine into his dominions and to make Arthur a vassal. The young prince, who was still at the French court, realized the truth after the capture of certain towns in Anjou which had held out against the French forces. Philip proceeded to raze the walls and dismantle the forts, at the same time punishing the inhabitants with the utmost severity. Arthur remonstrated at this treatment of people he regarded as his own subjects. Philip did not think it necessary to dissemble. He answered, "Am I not at liberty to do what I want in my own territories?" The purpose of the French King was now so clear to everyone that a bard at his court addressed a poem to him in which he said, "Thou art bound to plant thy tents and enlarge thy states that thou mayst possess in full the dominions of thy ancestors, that the stranger may no longer occupy ought within our borders, but the white dragon and his venomous brood be extirpated from our gardens!"

Arthur made his escape from the French court and reached his native land. His mother, whose wild flights of passion involved her in one mistake after another, was now convinced that her son could no longer hope to sit on the throne of England. She decided that the only thing left for them to do was to concentrate their efforts on achieving for him his full rights as Duke of Brittany. To accomplish this she handed Arthur over to John! She was, clearly, a woman of faulty judgment and furious impulses, but this move was a mistake of such magnitude that it is difficult to conceive of the reasoning which led her to it, unless she thought that John's one-time liking for her would make him partial to her son. She alienated Philip—a small loss, perhaps, in view of his professed intentions—and by making Arthur swear homage to John as King of England she destroyed the validity of her son's claim. When the prince strove later to regain his rights, he was technically a disobedient vassal, and John was afforded that much justification for the violent course he followed.

The desertion of the Breton prince left Philip without any reason for continuing the struggle. He had suffered some reverses and he was now anxious to terminate the contest. Eleanor took it on herself to seize this golden opportunity. Her wisdom had been increasing with each passing year and, as she had now reached the age of seventy-eight, she was a very wise woman indeed. She had assumed again the government of her own dominions and, as the people of Aquitaine were as loyal to her at seventy-eight as they had been when she was lovely and fifteen, she was having success in establishing order. She did homage to Philip for Aquitaine and she arranged with him for the marriage of his son Louis to her own granddaughter, Blanche of Castile.

To make sure there would be no slip and no delay, this indomitable woman rode all the way to Spain, over many hundreds of miles of bad roads from her Aquitainian home to the high passes of the Pyrenees, and then across the rough trails of Navarre to the arid plains of Old Castile. The weather was unusually warm and the land they passed was baked and the heat was sometimes almost unbearable. Eleanor bore up under the discomforts remarkably, sitting straight in her saddle and never causing any delays. Nature had continued kind to her. She still had most of her teeth, a miracle in an age when many women had to drink spiced wine and hold handkerchiefs in front of their mouths when they reached their thirties and their teeth began to rot. She had not taken on weight and was almost as slender as when she had ridden off to the Crusades. But, nevertheless, time was beginning to tell. The wrinkles were deep about her eyes, and in the mornings it required all her will power to start off again on the endless riding under the hot sun.

The marriage was performed with great splendor at Burgos. A Castilian nobleman acted as proxy for the French bridegroom and later went through the more intimate part of the ceremony, which was to enter the bed of the bride (with plenty of witnesses in the room) and to touch his bare foot to hers, which then constituted a legal and binding consummation.

Eleanor brought the bride back with her as she had escorted Berengaria ten years before, hoping no doubt that the results this time would be happier. It had been the intention of the venerable matchmaker to take her lovely granddaughter (who looked much like Eleanor herself) all the way to the expectant bridegroom, but her strength gave out when she reached her own domain. There she had to stay, and the wedding party journeyed on without her.

Eleanor had scored a full triumph. She had secured the throne of England for the last of her sons. She had brought about peace. The Angevin sun was again high in the heavens, and the Breton cause seemed hopelessly lost through the ill-considered actions of the much-hated daughter-in-law.

4

Almost in the center of Aquitaine, a short distance south and east of Rochelle in the enchanting valley of the Charente, was a small province called Angoumois. The capital city was Angoulême, sitting on a high promontory. Little touched by the feudal wars, it still kept its walls strong, inside which it was a warren of narrow streets about the double-towered château of Count Adhémar Taillefer. It was chiefly famous for its beautiful cathedral, and Count Adhémar was equally famous for a beautiful daughter, Isabella; in fact, Isabella was better known than the three-domed nave of the impressive house of God. At the age of fifteen she was a dazzling little creature with the name of being the loveliest woman in the world.

The parents had betrothed her to Hugh of Lusignan, a handsome young knight who was called LeBrun, or the Brown, son of the formidable Count of Marche. The girl had been sent to one of his castles for the same reason that princesses were conveyed early to the country of the man they were to marry. She was content with her lot, being as much in love with the fine, upstanding Hugh as one of her egocentric nature could be. Hugh the Brown was completely enamored of her and was urging that she had now reached the age to marry.

Having concluded peace with Philip, the newly crowned King of England decided he would follow his mother's advice and make a royal processional through his western dominions. She had mentioned in particular the wisdom of forming an alliance with the Count of Marche. His first stop was Angoulême to receive the homage of Count Adhémar. The count and his wife, an ambitious pair, wanted to make the best possible impression on the new head of the Angevin empire. What better could they do than have their beautiful Isabella there to receive him? Perhaps their purpose ran deeper. At any rate, they arranged for their daughter to pay them a visit during the time that John was there.

He saw her first beside her mother at the ceremony. She was wearing a plain gold circlet on her head from which a cloud of diaphanous veiling fell over her shoulders. He thought perhaps that she was a sprite rising from the mist, but a second glance convinced him she was lovelier than any water sprite could be. Her gown of scarlet and gold had been fitted closely to her fine figure, and it showed considerably more of her white shoulders than was customary. It was not just beauty she possessed; she had ways of her own, ways of carrying her head, of walking so that her long, brocaded skirts did not move. She was in fact, irresistible.

John was thirty-two and she was fifteen. He was married. He

could pick and choose among the best-looking women of his court; and, to do him credit, he did. If there was one woman he should treat with distant respect and nothing more, it was this future daughter-in-law of the Count of Marche. But after one long and breathless look John decided that he would disregard all dictates of policy and decency and common sense, that he would divorce his wife and marry Isabella of Angoulême.

Unfortunately for all concerned, the shrewd parents of the radiant little coquette observed how deeply the King was smitten. They would rather have the King of England as a son-in-law than the comparatively humble Hugh the Brown. Isabella seems to have agreed with this view of things, even though her personal preference was for the handsome Hugh rather than the thickset John.

The upshot was that Hugh of Lusignan and his brother, the Count of Eu, were sent to England to lead a foray along the western marches. It is quite possible that the plotters against his happiness hoped he would suffer the fate of Uriah, but no brand or arrow penetrated the armor of the gallant Hugh. The only purpose the campaign served was to afford time for the wedding arrangements to be made.

John's wife Avisa was a granddaughter of that great leader and knight of the bend sinister, Robert of Gloucester, and so they were cousins a few times removed. There had been opposition to the match on that account, and the Pope had been fulminating about it ever since, even demanded that they separate. It was an easy matter, therefore, to break the bond. The Archbishop of Bordeaux called a synod to consider the problem, and it was solemnly declared that the marriage to Avisa was null. Soon afterward John and Isabella were married in the cathedral of that city.

Hugh the Brown came back from England to find that his Bathsheba had been stolen in his absence. He issued a furious challenge to his successful rival to meet him in mortal combat. John accepted but said he would appoint a champion to fight in his place, his life being too important to risk in a personal quarrel. The slighted Count of Lusignan protested angrily that he would fight John himself or no one. The case split the Angevin world wide open, and it was plain to the least discerning eye that the King's action had shaken the loyalty of the nobility he must depend on in any future trouble with France.

John did not care. He was so infatuated with his girl wife that nothing else mattered. He neglected his duties to dance attendance on her. It was the custom even for kings to retire early and rise at five to begin the labors of the day. It would be noon before the uxorious King would emerge from the curtains of the nuptial couch and call huskily for the royal wine cup. Sluggard was the most complimentary term that his people began to call their liege lord. As for Isabella, they termed her a siren and a Messalina.

The newly wedded pair left for England as soon as possible, and Isabella was crowned Queen at Westminster on October 9. It was a very elaborate ceremony, but it served to bring out a bad trait of John's to which no reference has yet been made, parsimony. Although thirty-three shillings were paid for strewing the abbey with fresh rushes and twenty-five to the choir for the singing of the *Christus Vicit*, the King would allow his wife, whose greatest passion was for fine clothes, no more than three coronation cloaks and one pelisse of gray. There is no mention in the records of gifts of jewelry, although John had chests full of bracelets and rings and chains, the accumulated loot of all the Norman kings. He appeared at the coronation himself like a glittering Eastern potentate, bespangled with rubies and emeralds, and with sapphires sewn on his white gloves. John, in fact, was a dandy and loved to bedeck himself in this way. It was inevitable that the young Queen, thus made aware painfully of another flaw in the character of her royal spouse, would think wistfully of the generosity that Hugh the Brown had always shown.

John's English subjects were pleased with the beauty of the girl Queen, but this did not wipe out unpleasant memories of the way she had been stolen, and they were still distressed at the cavalier setting aside of Avisa of Gloucester. They need not have wasted sympathy on the first wife. She was married twice later and was relieved, no doubt, to escape participation in the kind of life John proceeded to live.

5

It was two years later that the storm broke overseas. The Count of Lusignan and his brother had been stirring up disaffection ceaselessly, and now Arthur, free of his uncle's restraint, came out boldly to assert his rights by force of arms. This was done by prearrangement with Philip, who had veered around again. The French King moved his army into Touraine at the same time. John was quarreling with the barons of England over the laxity and corruption of his rule and he found it hard to raise a large enough force to protect his interests in France. By the time he landed in Normandy, the French had taken many cities and castles, Lyons, Mortimar, and Boutavant. The situation was beginning to look grave. Arthur was now fifteen and had been knighted by Philip and married to his daughter Marie. He came fiercely down from Brittany with an army at his back, dreaming of military fame. John had taken Isabella with him and was as notoriously a lie-abed as before, a habit which the Queen seems to have encouraged. He was slow in organizing the defense of his wide-flung dominions, and his followers muttered more bitterly than ever.

It remained for Queen Eleanor to set fire to the resolution of her slothful son and at the same time to fill the greatest role of her career. She was now eighty, and there was no longer any denying that her end was drawing near. Nevertheless, she was fulfilling her duties and traveling about as necessity dictated. This took her, as it happened, to the town of Mirabeau just as the young prince issued out from Brittany. Arthur had no feeling of loyalty or affection for his grandmother, and he turned aside with unfilial zest to invest the town.

It should have been an easy matter to take a place as unimportant as Mirabeau. It was not strongly held or stocked to resist a siege. What followed, nevertheless, was a triumph for the Queen. Bent and tired, clutching a cane in one hand, she collected as many men as she could and occupied the keep within the town. She took on herself the direction of the defense, seeing to it that the battlements were manned and that the resolution of her little band remained equal to the task of holding off the forces of Brittany. No details of the siege have been preserved, but it is easy to see the frail figure pacing the ramparts, watching the movements of the hostile troops in the streets which hemmed them about, waiting anxiously for results from the messengers she had sent off to her son. Her voice was shrill as she called orders to her tiny garrison. It was certain they could not hold out long; that, in fact, they would not be holding out at all if she had not been there.

John received the message and came to life with a vengeance. He marched his troops the eighty-odd miles to Mirabeau in two days. His arrival was so unexpected that Arthur and his men were trapped inside the town and had to surrender. Among those taken prisoner was Hugh of Lusignan, which undoubtedly added a note of personal pleasure to John's pride in his military achievement.

Eleanor was a proud woman when her son came riding into Mirabeau to greet her. She laid stern injunctions on him, nevertheless, knowing the flaws in his character. If he had a shred of statesmanship in him, she said, he would treat Hugh of Lusignan as a chivalrous foe. If he valued his immortal soul, he would not lay a finger on his captive nephew. John, still submissive where his mother was concerned, agreed on both points.

After another forced march by which he relieved the garrison at Arques, which Philip was attacking, the now victorious King took counsel with himself as to what should be done about the prisoners. He had a vindictive streak which made it impossible for him to carry out the promises he had made his mother. The knights captured at Mirabeau were twenty-two in number, including the brave Hugh. They were sent off to England in the most humiliating manner the King could think of, chained together two and two in oxcarts. Hugh was put in Bristol, but the rest were shoved into Corfe Castle, an immensely strong place on a high cliff on the Isle of Purbeck, which John seems to have favored as a prison. The King observed the letter of his promise to his mother in the sense that no violence was offered the prisoners. No food was sent into their cells, however, and most of them died of starvation. An exception was Savaric de Mauleon, a rics-baron of Poitou and a noted troubadour. This resourceful fellow succeeded in making his guards drunk, broke their heads, and escaped. He afterward turned his coat and became a leader of mercenaries for John. He will be heard of later.

Hugh of Lusignan was spared and finally released, because John feared to estrange his young wife.

The captive prince was taken to Falaise and lodged in a cell of the castle. He was protected by the promise John had made his mother and by every consideration of political expediency, for his death would alienate the sympathy of even the closest supporters of the King and strengthen the forces against him. But, knowing John, people waited with the deepest foreboding.

6

Falaise Castle was familiar to Englishmen, for it had played an important part in the story of Anglo-Norman relations. Here Robert of Normandy had brought the tanner's daughter and here the healthy child had been born to her who became William the Conqueror. Here the Norman kings had gone most frequently when they returned to the duchy. This tall castle stood so high on a boat-shaped rock between heavily wooded country and the Cleft of Val d'Ante that it had not been thought necessary to equip it with the usual aids to defense, moat and barbican. The walls were nearly ten feet thick and in places they were double, with passages between in which two men could walk abreast. All the cells in Falaise, and there were many of them, were sunk into the walls, as was the comparatively cheerful apartment where the tanner's daughter had lived.

John arrived at Falaise and went to his chamberlain, Hubert de Burgh, who was in charge. Hubert de Burgh was a distant relation of the King, being descended from a half brother of the Conqueror, and he was a stouthearted and generous knight. He had been an indulgent jailer to the despondent young prince, and it was with grave misgivings, undoubtedly, that he considered the meaning of the King's visit.

Arthur had been allowed some liberty, and it was in a comfortable and even light apartment on the second floor of the keep that he faced his royal uncle. He had donned a tunic with the loose Breton sleeve, and close-fitting trunks; a tall youth, slender and as pliant as a willow bough, his dark eyes showing no fear at all, though he must have known that his position was desperate.

John had a habit of speaking in an almost gentle voice when his designs were most dangerous. He began to urge his nephew to give up all pretensions to a crown he would never wear, and his tone was friendly and forgiving. The prince was not deceived. He knew his uncle hated him. This did not affect the stand he proceeded to take, which was a bold denial that he had been at fault. In fact, he faced the King as determinedly as though their positions were reversed.

When John offered his friendship the boy cried out, "Better the hatred of the King of France!"

[317]

The King boasted that his power was now supreme and that his towers were high and strong; so high and so strong that no prisoner could hope to escape him.

"Neither towers nor swords," declared the boy, "shall make me coward enough to deny the right I hold from my father and my God!"

John abandoned any idea he might have had of coming to an understanding with the prince. "So be it, fair nephew," he said in the familiar subdued tone as he turned and left the apartment.

Hubert de Burgh knew what the sequel would be and he was apprehensive at once when a party of the King's men arrived at Falaise shortly thereafter. John had decided, it developed, that he could not fly in the face of world opinion by killing the boy. To take his eyesight would, however, eliminate him as a candidate for power; and so the instructions of the party were to make use of the white-hot irons with which this form of mutilation was performed.

Arthur had already demonstrated his courage. When he learned the purpose of his cruel uncle, however, his resolution failed him. He was still a boy in years and he wanted to enjoy the life which stretched ahead of him. He wanted eyes to lead armies, to fight on the field of honor, to see the children he would beget, to enjoy the rich pageantry of royal existence. To go through the long years with blackened holes in lieu of eyes, to be denied all the sweets of life, was a fate he could not face. He dropped to his knees before the executioners and begged for mercy.

Hubert de Burgh was a man of compassion and, fortunately, of stout heart as well. He had become fond of the boy and, moreover, he knew that the claim of the young prince to the throne of England was a better one than that of John. He made, accordingly, one of those decisions which so often change the course of history. He disregarded the royal order and sent the executioners away. Then, being very much afraid that what he had done might endanger his own eyes or even his life, he resolved on a deception. He had the bells in the chapel toll as though for a death and gave it out that Arthur of Brittany was no more.

The storm which broke over France when this became known was greater even than he had feared. The subjects and supporters of John were as angry and horror-stricken as his enemies. Realizing now the enormity of his mistake, John disclaimed any part in the death of his nephew. Hubert de Burgh was forced to acknowledge the deception and to produce his prisoner as proof that nothing had happened to him. The storm died down, but it did not take men long to fit together the ends of this curious train of events and to come on the truth. John's reputation suffered almost as much as though his design had been carried out.

It was said that the King was secretly relieved that Hubert de Burgh had disobeyed him. Nevertheless, he had the prince taken from Falaise and imprisoned in Rouen instead. Here a man named William de Braose, the lord of Bramber, was in charge. He was the King's familiar and confidant, a man of great physical strength and high ambition and, it was believed, of no scruples.

It was generally known that the prince had been imprisoned in Rouen, but after the heavy doors clanged shut behind him he was never seen again. No information could be had from the King's men who garrisoned the place. Apprehensions which had fed on the fiasco at Falaise flared up. What had been done with the unfortunate youth? Had the King dared to do away with him after all?

John does not seem to have said anything. None of the men under him could be induced to talk. It became apparent finally that the disappearance of the prince was as much a mystery to the underlings as to the world outside the walls. The only exception, perhaps, was William de Braose. That bull-necked baron continued to enjoy the King's confidence exclusively, and he was as uncommunicative as John himself.

Then rumors began to circulate. The prince, it was said, had been taken from his cell at night and placed in a boat occupied by the King and one other man. He had been murdered by the King's hand and his body had been weighted and thrown into the Seine. This story contains flaws which make it hard to accept. Why should the victim be murdered in the open, and in a boat where he might resist with more hope of success, when he could have been killed in his cell, where he would have no chance to defend himself or to raise an alarm? This was believed, nevertheless, and it is still the story which is told and accepted.

A deep silence was maintained by the King, and so the disappearance of the brave young prince remained a mystery.

7

But why should it be considered a mystery? The scant evidence, when viewed in the light of subsequent events, points the way clearly to the explanation.

It has already been stated that William de Braose was in charge of the new citadel at Rouen when the prince was taken there from Falaise. One other man would have to know what happened to Arthur besides the King whose orders were carried out, and that would be the lord of Bramber. He returned to England with John and remained in high favor, such high favor that others became jealous of the power and pretensions of this overbearing nobleman. "Braose was with the King at Windsor," says one historian, "with him in the court, and with him in the chase." The emphasis thus placed on the fact that they were always together, the guilty King and the man who, perhaps, had been his instrument, is significant.

Braose was married to a most remarkable woman. She had been Maud de Valeri, although in some versions her name is given as Maud de Hay. At any rate, she was a great heiress and had brought her husband many castles along the Welsh Marches, in the valley of the Usk and along the Nedd and the Wye, Castles Radnor, Hay, Brecon, and Bradwardine. She was a handsome woman of the heroic type, a Lady Macbeth in many respects, bold and unscrupulous and intensely ambitious. When her husband was away she took charge and thought nothing of donning armor and leading troops into battle. In fact, she was as quick to string up a prisoner as her violent lord and master. She is said to have been the original of Moll Walbee, the heroine of several old Breconshire romances.

William de Braose and his amazonian spouse were in such high favor during the first years of John's reign that they married their eldest son to a daughter of the house of Gloucester and their own daughter to the sixth Baron de Lacey, who was also the lord of Trim in Ireland. They were growing wealthy rapidly and, as it was a rare thing for anyone around the King to accumulate money, whispers began to circulate. Braose was believed to have some power over the King. This continued for ten years, an exceptional length of time for anyone to retain the favor of the capricious John.

An end always comes, however, to the tenure of favorites. Perhaps a distaste was growing in the King for this man who was waxing so fat beside him. At any rate, the time came when he needed money himself and he made a bargain with De Braose by which the latter was to buy certain lands in Leinster which belonged to the King. At least the King said they did. It developed immediately that there was some question as to his ownership of the lands in question. Two churchmen, the Bishop of Worcester and a brother of the former Archbishop of Canterbury, claimed ownership of part and they refused, naturally enough, to allow the transfer of title to the prospective purchaser. The price John had set was five thousand marks, a large sum indeed in those days, and the King had no intention of letting it slip through his fingers. Not being able to do anything with the two stubborn churchmen, John brusquely ordered his favorite to pay over the five thousand marks and settle things himself with the other claimants.

De Braose must have been very sure of his position, or of the power he had over the King. At any rate, he refused to do anything about it.

By this time John was experiencing the bitter opposition of the barons. To compel a more complaisant attitude on their part, he had demanded that each member of the nobility place a child in his care as hostage for future behavior. The children were kept at Windsor and Winchester and they waited on the Queen. None of the Braose children had been included, but when the difficulty arose over the five thousand marks, John ordered them to send a son to serve as a royal page. Braose and his wife now sensed that their day of favor was over. In spite of this, the haughty Maud was foolish enough to refuse the royal demand. In the hearing of the King's officers she declared that "she would not deliver her children to a king who had murdered his own nephew."

Many people had said the same thing, of course, but never as openly. The statement, coming from the wife of the man who had been the custodian of the Rouen citadel, was almost like a confession. Maud de Braose knew the enormity of her mistake as soon as she had spoken and she hastened to make amends as best she could. She sent to the Queen a herd of four hundred beautiful cattle, all of them pure white except their ears, which were a reddish brown, hoping that this would be accepted as a peace offering. The cattle were kept, but the gift did the outspoken donor no good at all.

The King declared war. If he had been showing favor to De Braose because of what the latter knew, he now went to the other extreme and persecuted him because of it. Orders were given to seize the castle of Bramber. When this home of the once favored companion was found to be an empty shell, the owner having been warned in time to remove everything of value, the King led a force himself to the border marches and took possession of all the castles there which had been part of the dower of the Lady Maud. The now thoroughly frightened and repentant De Braose waited on the King at Hereford and begged for terms. The King demanded that the purchase price for the lands in Leinster be paid in full and that in addition the castles of Radnor, Hay, and Brecon be thrown in. The lord of Bramber agreed to this, having no alternative. However, in a sudden fit of spleen, he set fire to property of the King and fled to Ireland with his family. Later he made another effort to patch things up, keeping at a safe distance, and was told that the price of peace had risen. Never had terms risen more sharply! He was informed that now he would have to pay forty thousand marks, almost a third of the ransom money for Richard, a sum completely beyond the means of any private man.

The sequel to this is one of the grimmest stories in history. Maud de Braose and her eldest son William were captured while trying to leave Ireland for the Scottish coast and were brought to the King. He had them thrown into a single cell in the keep at Windsor with a sheaf of wheat and a flitch of uncooked bacon. The door of the cell was closed upon them.

John seems to have been a believer in the starvation method of getting rid of prisoners. He had employed it with the unfortunate knights captured at Mirabeau, he was to use it on later occasions, but there was something peculiarly repellent in his treatment of the wife and son of the man he now hated so thoroughly.

After eleven days had passed the cell was opened. The two occupants were found dead, each lying in a propped-up position against the wall. It was apparent that the son had succumbed first, for one of his cheeks had been gnawed.

William de Braose fled to France, where he published a statement on what had happened to Arthur. No copy was ever found, unfortunately, of this report of the only surviving eyewitness. A year later the fugitive died at Corbeil.

The Unsolved Mystery

The death of the unfortunate prince could not have been due to natural causes. In that event the body would have been produced promptly to clear the King of the charge of violence. The young contender was killed, then, and by his uncle's orders.

Although the story that the murder was committed in a boat on the Seine is a highly improbable version, it may have had some bearing on the truth. It may have been that the prince was removed from the citadel for a prison somewhere else and the opportunity was used to kill him on the way. It seems more reasonable, however, that the killing occurred within the citadel and that the body was taken in a boat and thrown into the water of the Seine. The exaggerated form the story took later was due, no doubt, to the additions achieved in the course of endless repetition.

CHAPTER XVI

John Softsword

WILLIAM MARSHAL and the leaders of the mercenaries, for whom a new name was being used, routiers, sat in enforced idleness at Rouen and knew that the war was being lost. Philip was concentrating his forces for a drive on Normandy up the Seine, the path his father had followed so often and so badly. This time, clearly, it would be different. John, agitated, angry, his neck weighed down with the relics hanging around it (a sure sign that he had a guilty conscience), was running about with feverish activity from castle to castle and accomplishing nothing. At intervals he would give up trying to be a leader and devote himself to the enjoyment of life with his beautiful young wife. It would have been hard for his harassed lieutenants to decide which aspect of the King they liked least.

That the Angevin ship was foundering was clear from the stream of desertions. The King's own seneschal, Guerin de Chapion, was the first to go over to the enemy. Every day after that there were reports of men who had left the banner of the much-hated King.

A new symptom of weakness was revealed when the French army invested the castle of Vaudreuil. The garrison was commanded jointly by Richard Fitz-Walter and the Sieur de Quincy. To the amazement of all, the two captains surrendered without striking a blow. William Marshal's handsome face went white with rage when he heard the news, and in London men sang ribald ballads on the streets about the knights who had disgraced their country; for the common people did not like the taste of defeat, although it seemed to sit easily enough on the stomachs of the baronage. It was at this point that the King was first called John Softsword.

It was not entirely the fault of the King. All he had to use in opposing the French and the disloyalty in his own dominions were the few thousands of men scattered in garrisons along the borders of Normandy or gnawing their fingers in idleness about Rouen. No help could be expected from England.

Aware that his hands were tied, John gave up. Isabella, nearing the end of her teens, had blossomed into a woman of ravishing beauty, and he seemed to find in her all the solace he needed for the way the Angevin empire was falling to pieces about him. Nothing his advisers could say roused him from his uxorious stupor.

Once, in a fit of petulance, he answered the urgings of William Marshal by crying out, "Let be, Marshal, let be!" Then in a tone of confidence which carried some small hint of his father, he added, "One day, mark you, I shall take back all that he has won."

With calamity ringing them about, this was an idle boast, as both King and marshal knew. Gradually John was forced to the conclusion that peace must be made with the French. Better to concede something now than to let things drift until everything was lost. Accordingly he instructed the Archbishop of Rouen and William Marshal to go to the French King and discuss terms.

2

The time has come to tell something of this remarkable man, William Marshal. A younger son of a powerful Norman family, he had been given as a hostage to Stephen at a stage of the civil war in which his father fought on the side of the Empress Matilda. When the father's conduct had been such that Stephen was reported to be ready to hang the six-year-old boy in reprisal, the unnatural father had one comment only to make, "I have the anvil still and the hammer to make more sons."

The boy had nothing to hope for from a father of this stamp. Being spared by Stephen, who for all his faults was not a cruel man, young William was sent to Normandy to be reared at the castle of an uncle named Tancarville. Lacking all prospects, he was trained to be a soldier and grew into a tall, handsome, and immensely strong youth with a knack in the use of all weapons. As soon as he had been admitted to knighthood, which was at an unusually early age, he began to cut an amazing swath in the tournaments which, in times of peace, filled the days and thoughts of all proper men. The word tournament had not at that period become limited to the kind of jousting which is most familiar, the formal breaking of lances in the lists, varied by an occasional mêlée in which the contestants took sides and hammered away at each other with sword and mace and battle-ax. The kind of contest in which young William won his spurs was a day of actual warfare, fought in the open and without any blunting of points. It was every man for himself. In the dusk, after ten hours of charge and countercharge, of ambush and sally, of hacking and hewing, in the course of which there would inevitably be some fatalities and a great deal of bloodletting, the judges would get together and decide who had been the winner.

The winner was always William Marshal. The men who rank highest in history—Richard Coeur de Lion, Bertrand du Guesclin, Jacques de Lalain, the Chevalier Bayard—could not in point of achievement compare with this almost forgotten English knight. In his declining years the old lion would often fall into reminiscence. One day he did some reckoning and found that he had fought in five hundred tournaments, or in single combat bouts, and that he had been the winner on each occasion, taking his opponent's horse and armor as his prize.

When he was sixty-six years old and was charged by John with a treasonable utterance, the old man threw down his gauge and offered to settle the matter by the arbitrament of battle. There were plenty of knights about the King who were in the prime of life, but they looked askance at the unbeaten champion and none picked up the iron glove.

His success on the field of honor provided him at first with a certain competence. He could live on the sale of his prizes, particularly as a ransom came his way occasionally. He was in due course assigned by Henry II to serve in the train of the heir of England, the Prince Henry who was later known as *Li Reys Josnes*. The young Henry had a keen appetite for everything pertaining to chivalry and he received with delight the Englishman who had already won such a resounding reputation. William proceeded to teach his royal master all the tricks of the tournament: the angle at which to hold the heaume in order to deflect a lance thrust, the use of the new ball-and-spike spur, how to sit most securely in the saddle, how to conserve his strength in a mêlée and then strike at exactly the right moment.

When *Li Reys Josnes* died, the King took William back into his service and promised him, among other things, the hand of the young heiress of Pembroke and Striguil, one of the wealthiest as well as the most attractive wards in the gift of the monarchy. The death of Henry II occurred before this particular agreement could be carried out. As William had unhorsed Richard in the pursuit from Le Mans, he did not expect anything in the way of favors from the new King. Richard had an eye for martial valor, however, and he not only carried out his father's wishes but appointed him marshal of England as well.

Marriage with the pretty heiress brought William Marshal into the overlordship of that thumb of land which protrudes out from Wales into the South Channel and points directly at Ireland. Pembroke Castle, with its seventy-five-foot tower, stood like a mighty sentinel on the inlet of Milford Haven. All about it clustered Norman castles which had been raised to hold this important stretch of water: the keep of Haverford, Tenby, Castle Martin, Lewhaden, Narberth, Stackpole. There were large land grants also in Ireland, and so the once landless knight came into an inheritance which promised him comfort and dignity for the rest of his days. Fortunately the heiress of Pembroke was well pleased with her very much older but justly famous husband and they lived happily together.

This, then, was the man, now in his sixtieth year or thereabouts, on whom John depended in military matters. If there had been any prospect of proper assistance from the barons of England, William Marshal might have driven Philip out of Normandy and regained the Angevin provinces. But the people of England were tired of this endless fighting, and John had trampled on their rights so often that it was impossible to develop any sense of loyalty to him. The old soldier, unable to serve the Crown in the capacity for which he was best fitted, had little stomach for the errand on which his royal master was now sending him. He was sufficient of a strategist, moreover, to know that John had lost and that the task imposed on him was the distasteful one of asking the victor for terms.

The Conquerors

As the two unwilling envoys entered the courtyard of the castle below Amiens where the King of France had located himself, they were surprised to see that among those seeking audience with the King were merchants in plain woolen tunics and flat caps and humble priests from Picardy and the Dordogne. On the stairway they passed an acrobat with the padded shoulders of his trade and a petition in his hands and an old man escorting a boy who also carried a petition, an orphan being brought to ask a favor. They would not have been surprised at the station of these humble seekers for a word with Philip if they had understood the French tradition that a king must make himself accessible to his people. Anyone with a grievance could have a word with the ruler of the country. The kings lived in full view of their subjects, eating at intervals in the open so that the gaping commonalty could watch the viands carried in and see them vanish down the royal throat. They were attended constantly by court officers who helped them to dress and undress, who slept in the royal chamber and even accompanied their master to the bath and to the cold, dark nooks of the back stairs.

William Marshal had never seen the French King and he eyed him with the closest interest as he made his way across the audience chamber, through the mass of spectators assembled to watch that most grateful sight for Gallic eyes, the humbling of Englishmen. Philip was sitting on a chair which had some of the dignity of a throne. He was a big man, now showing signs of portliness. His hair had been fair once, but there was little of it left (the hot sun of the Holy Land was blamed for his early baldness), and he was rather handsome, with ruddy cheeks, a strong, straight nose, and a mouth which was both determined and petulant. This very capable King was watching the advance of the Englishmen with as lively satisfaction as any of his subjects.

There was probably a craning of necks as William Marshal passed, for few there had cast eyes on this great soldier who had never been worsted, who had unhorsed scores of Frenchmen in his day without losing a stirrup. They were undoubtedly puzzled by the lack of embroidery on his surcoat and the plain quality of his gray tunic, as well as impressed by the length and apparent weight of the sword which clanked against his long legs.

Philip, who had an arrogant way of speech, pretended surprise when they stood in front of him. He asked:

"Where is Arthur of Brittany?"

There was no answer they could give to that, so neither Englishman made any comment. After a moment, however, the marshal countered with a shrewd verbal thrust. He had noticed the great number of deserters in the chamber, the men who had left the Angevin dominions to throw in with the French: counts from Anjou, rics-barons from Poitou, captals from Gascony, bishops from everywhere. He had met the eyes of some of them and had observed that without exception they flushed and looked away.

"My lord," he said in a tone loud enough to carry to all parts of the room, "I see many men with you who have broken their oaths and forsworn their allegiance, for which they would lose their heads or at least their eyes in the country from which I come."

It was a bold speech, but it pleased rather than offended the King. Philip had been glad to detach these men from the English cause, but at the same time he had an open contempt for those who broke their vows; a privilege he reserved for himself.

"It is nothing," declared Philip in a tone of equal distinctness. "I think as little of them as I do of the torch I carry to the *secret* at night and throw inside when I am through."

Having said this, the King burst into loud laughter and glanced about the room at some of the more conspicuous members of the company he had thus insulted publicly. William Marshal laughed with him. It was one of the admirable traits of this English knight that he looked everyone straight in the eye, kings and cardinals as well as the humblest of men, and never hesitated to speak his mind. He felt himself free to laugh when the King did.

The peace negotiations could not be said to have started on a good basis, for Philip then proceeded to a long tirade which made it clear that he was in a belligerent mood. He made it very clear that he had little interest in the errand which had brought them to his court.

This became still more apparent at the discussions held on succeeding days. There was one concrete lesson Philip had learned under the oak of Gisors, and he was now using it. He had been taught the art of making a demand and, when it had been conceded, of finding other conditions which would have to be agreed to as well, so that there was never any end to a discussion. In this way, instead of starting with the impossible and being forced gradually to recede, he built his demands up higher and ever higher until they reached a point where an adversary conceded everything in sheer desperation or broke off the negotiations in disgust.

This was the course he followed with the English envoys. If they agreed to one of his demands, they immediately found that the acceptance entailed other concessions. If he could think of nothing else, Philip would proclaim that as the first essential to peace they must produce Arthur of Brittany. They were forced finally to the conclusion that he had no intention of coming to terms. He did not want peace; he was set on war, and war he intended to make until John and the English-Normans had been driven out of Gaul.

As soon as the two envoys were absolutely convinced that he was playing a game of cat-and-mouse with them, they demanded their safe-conduct and left the court.

4

The decisive stage of the fight for Normandy came with the siege of Château Gaillard, the fair child who had pleased Richard so much on her first birthday. Philip had sworn he would take this fort if the walls were of steel and, during the first stages of the envelopment, it looked as though his boast would be put to a literal test. The walls were as strong as though made of steel and the whole structure perched so high on its rock that it seemed like a castle in the clouds. The conclusion was soon reached that it could not be taken by storm. A group of bold young Frenchmen swam out at night and broke the communications between castle and mainland; and after that the French army settled down to starve out the garrison, which was commanded by a good soldier named Roger de Lacey.

John now proceeded to demonstrate that he had some of the military skill which ran so conspicuously in the family, conceiving an excellent plan for the relief of the garrison. In the execution of this plan William Marshal marched down the left bank of the Seine with a force consisting of three hundred knights, three thousand mounted

RICHARD'S
CHÂTEAU GAILLARD

men-at-arms, and four thousand foot soldiers, with an auxiliary troop of routiers under a man named Loupescaire. At the same time a fleet of seventy river boats, which had been assembled at Rouen in Richard's reign for just such an emergency, were to bring the King down the river to attack simultaneously. The marshal arrived promptly and struck the French such a devastating blow that he drove them across the pontoon bridge the French engineers were building. The bridge broke under their weight, and it looked as though the attack would result in a rout of Philip's forces. But John had not taken the tides into consideration and had found himself unable to get away with the fleet. By the time the tide had turned and the flotilla started, the relatively small army under the marshal had sustained the weight of the whole French army and been driven back. John had been late as usual.

It was clear now that the great castle could not be relieved except by an army large enough to engage the French on something like even terms. The marshal advised that they retire instead of remaining in close proximity to an army capable of demolishing them. This opinion was delivered at a council called to discuss the situation, and an affirmative chorus followed the marshal's speech. John, refusing to accept the inevitable, glared about him.

"Let them who are afraid flee," he exclaimed. "I shall stay for yet a year."

The marshal realized that the time had come for plain speech. It must be accepted as fact, he declared, that no reinforcements would join them. John disputed this. He expected additional forces from England. The old soldier gave him a negative shake of the head. "You who are wise, mighty, and illustrious," he said, "to whom it has been given to rule over us, you have offended too many. You lack friends to rally to you now."

John was amazed at the audacity of the marshal. He stared for a moment in silence and then turned and left the room. The next morning his captains looked in vain for him. He had crossed the river during the night, it developed, and returned to Rouen.

The siege became a test of endurance. Roger de Lacey could have held out indefinitely if there had been any way of getting in fresh supplies. Realizing that no help could be expected now, he decided to conserve his stores, and this led to an episode which has no equal for sheer horror in history.

There were four hundred noncombatants in the two castles atop the high rock, made up of the wives and children of the soldiers, some servants, a few priests, and a handful of the usual hangers-on such as entertainers and prostitutes. The commander decided he could not go on filling these useless mouths and he ordered all of them to pack up their belongings and leave. This they did with mixed feelings, some with relief at thus escaping the rigors of the siege, most of them with fear and trembling.

Philip of France concluded that, if he did not permit them to get ashore, the garrison would take them back and so come more quickly to the point of surrender. As a result the frightened people were driven back with a volley of arrows. They toiled with their bundles on their shoulders up the precipitous path to the castle. Roger de Lacey refused to open the gates to them.

The unhappy four hundred had no alternative but to huddle at the rocky base of the hill. Here they remained for three weeks, sleeping in crannies and feeding on berries and weeds and such few fish as they could catch in the waters of the river rolling by.

The soldiers above were under the strictest orders not to deplete the stores by throwing food down to them. On pain of the most dire punishment they were forbidden to give up their own rations to their starving families. All they could do was stand on the ramparts and watch the misery of their helpless wives and children on the wet and wind-swept rocks. Every day they saw wasted bodies thrown into the river and sometimes were able to recognize them. The voices of the starving reached their ears with piteous demands. They could see arms raised up to them in desperate appeal. All the time officers kept watch on the battlements to prevent any attempt at relief.

While the women and children died, the French remained callous and unchangeable in their determination not to let them land. They even found cause for amusement in the faint sounds of weeping and despairing prayer which reached their ears.

Philip and his advisers were practitioners of the Code of Chivalry. Roger de Lacey and his officers were reputedly gallant knights who had sworn to be gentle, compassionate, and fair. There was no thought at the time that they were false to their vows in thus condemning the unfortunates to a lingering death on the bare rocks. The four hundred were only the wives and children of common soldiers. Let them die! They were not important enough to affect considerations of military expediency. The King of France below and Roger de Lacey above had that much excuse and, in the eyes of those who counted, needed none other.

Two hundred of the people had died of starvation and exposure and their bodies had been thrown into the water before the French relented and permitted the wasted survivors to come ashore. Many of them died as a result of excess in eating their first meal.

Never before had the reverse side of the burnished shield of chivalry been exposed so thoroughly to view. Never before had the cruelty of the code been so callously revealed.

5

Roger de Lacey defended the castle until the last crust had been consumed and then surrendered. He had held out for six months. A month before this happened John had sailed to England and, on the eve of his departure, had entrusted the defense of Normandy to the captains of his mercenaries, Loupescaire and Archas Martin. The royal skitterbrook's advice to the remnants of his army, still holding out in castles and towns along the borders, was terse and characteristic: "Let each man look to himself. Expect no help from me."

Philip now rushed in for the kill. Loupescaire, who had stationed himself in the strategic castle of Falaise, surrendered on demand and then entered the service of the King of France with all his troops. Caen, Bayeux, Coutances were captured, and with them went control of all Lower Normandy. The army of Brittany, inflamed with desire for revenge, swept down on the helpless Normans and captured Mont St. Michel and Avranches. The loss of Château Gaillard, which Richard had realized was the key to the duchy, had thrown the path to conquest wide open. Rouen held out bitterly, but the garrison was compelled finally to agree to capitulation if no aid reached them within thirty days. The messages they sent to John had no effect. At the end of the thirty days, therefore, the capital opened its gates to the French. Normandy had been lost.

Queen Eleanor died soon after the fall of Rouen. Her death was universally ascribed to a broken heart, some stating the cause as the murder of Arthur, others the loss of Normandy. The heart of Eleanor, who had been a queen for sixty-seven years and had suffered continuous sorrow, was too stout to break. She died because she was eighty-two years old. Time, that insatiable victor, could no longer be gainsaid. She was buried at Fontevrauld between her husband and her much-loved Richard.

Because of the circumstances of her divorce and her subsequent marriage to Henry II, and even more because of the silly legend of the Fair Rosamonde and the cup of poison, she has been called ever since the Wicked Queen. Once a verdict has been brought in by history, it becomes almost impossible to have it set aside. Eleanor deserves a second hearing and a different verdict. Following her through these three reigns, observing the moderation of her later years and the unquenchable energy with which she strove to help her sons, one becomes much attached to this foolish beauty who turned into a wise old woman. She made up for the mistakes of her youth and deserves much better of history. Farewell, Eleanor of Aquitaine!

The old Queen had been the richest woman in the world. She left her dower castles and lands in England, the handsome châteaux she had inherited in her native land, the wide fertile fields and vineyards of Aquitaine. There was a huge store of beautiful jewelry. John, who had refused to honor any of the legacies in Richard's will, gave everything left by Eleanor to his own wife. Richard's widow, luckless Queen Berengaria, who was in dire straits at the time, received not a penny.

CHAPTER XVII

With Bell, Book, and Candle

HUBERT WALTER, Archbishop of Canterbury and chancellor, died at Teynham in Kent on July 13, 1205, completely unaware that his death would throw England into one of the most tangled situations in all history. Coming back to power after his dismissal by Richard, he had assumed the reins with a firm hand under John. So firm was his hand, in fact, that John had been chafing under a tutelage suitable only for a younger brother. When he heard of Hubert's death, the King lapsed into his habit of clowning at important and sacred moments. Slapping his thigh zestfully, he cried in a tone of delight, "And now, for the first time, I am King of England!"

Two days later John was at Canterbury and paid a visit to the monks on whom the responsibility of choosing a new archbishop would rest. He talked to them in the most friendly way and seems to have left the impression that one of their number might be acceptable for the high post. Naturally the monks were pleased and became most favorably disposed to this King who had been living and ruling under a cloud of hate and blame. The good he had done, however, was quickly dissipated when it was found that a chest of church plate which Hubert had bequeathed to the cathedral had been carried off and that the King intended it for Winchester. John had a genius for offending people and he always seemed to pick the most harmful occasions.

The younger monks of Canterbury, perhaps because of the hint dropped in their ears, decided to take matters into their own hands. Without waiting for the royal permission to act, the *congé d'élire*, they met secretly at midnight and chose their sub-prior Reginald. Then they slipped into the cathedral in a body and installed him on the archiepiscopal throne. This was as far as they could go, and so they sent their nominee off to Rome the next day to secure the confirmation of the Pope.

Reginald was a fat little fellow who waddled pompously and oozed self-importance from every pore, and he was so puffed up with pride over his selection that he disregarded the urgent warnings of his fellow monks to keep the matter a secret until he reached Rome. As soon as his feet touched French soil he gave it out that he was the new archbishop. The word was brought back quickly to England. John, in one of his towering rages, took prompt action and demanded that John de Grey, Bishop of Norwich, be elected instead. Everyone fell in with his choice, even the young monks who had tried to foist the talkative Reginald on the nation and who were now both ashamed of their action and apprehensive of consequences. Despite the lack of opposition to the King's selection, however, it was recognized that his man was not well suited to the office. The Bishop of Norwich was one of the justiciars and of the same stamp as the deceased archbishop, though falling short of his stature; an able enough administrator, ambitious, unscrupulous, and worldly minded. No one dared to stand out against the King.

In order to clear up the situation created by the rashness of the young monks, twelve of the canons of St. Augustine were hurried off as a deputation to the Pope. They were to give him a present of twelve thousand marks and win his consent to the King's nomination.

Now there was in Rome at this time a great Pope, one of the very greatest of all popes, Innocent III. He had been elected to succeed the fumbling and procrastinating Celestine III, and the contrast between them could not have been more marked. In particular contrast with his predecessor, who had been a tired old man of eighty-five when named Pontiff, Lothario de Conti de Segni, a member of the noble family of Scotti, had been thirty-seven only when he was elevated to the vicarship of Christ. He had proceeded with great energy to repair the mistakes of Celestine and had succeeded

in remarkably short time in removing the Holy See from the domination of the German emperors. This accomplished, he had solidified
the Church and brought all branches of it under his firm administration. Innocent was a believer in action, the first pontiff with the
resolution to use the interdict freely as a weapon for the enforcement
of his decrees. This dangerous thunderbolt had always been available to popes, but always they had hesitated to use it, fearing the
repercussions. Innocent had no such hesitations.

Of all the popes who ever ruled in the Vatican, Innocent III was
perhaps the least likely to be influenced by John's demands and
his offer of a bribe of twelve thousand marks. No bribe could have
swayed this inflexible Pontiff. He and John were thoroughly well
acquainted already as a result of a continuous correspondence in
which the Pope had striven to improve the outlook and conduct of
the English King. There had been in particular the matter of Berengaria's dowry and the fulfillment of Richard's will. More than half
of what the lionhearted King had left had been bequeathed to relatives, notably the Emperor Otto of Germany, a nephew. John had
calmly disregarded his dead brother's wishes and had pocketed
everything himself. A brief summary of the letters from indignant
Pope to callous King* will be useful before entering on the period
of active strife between them.

Letters from Innocent to John:

Dec. 1200, Richard's will.
Nov. 1201, Richard's will.
Dec. An admonition not to starve two abbots.
Dec. Richard's will.
Dec. A demand that abbey lands stolen by the King be handed
back.
Mar. 1202. A demand that one hundred men be sent by John to
the Holy Land and that he build a Cistercian monastery as punish-
ment for his bad behavior to his first wife.
Mar. Richard's will.
Jun. An admonition to stop persecuting the Bishop of Limoges
and compensate him for his losses.
Feb. 1203. A reprimand for interfering with the liberties of the
Church.

*Based on Appendix VI, *Innocent the Great,* by C. H. C. Pirie-Gordon,
B.A.

May. A sharp reprimand for behaving shamefully to the Archbishop of Dublin.

Oct. A reminder that he should appear before his suzerain, Philip of France.

Jan. 1204. Richard's will and Berengaria's dowry.

Sept. 1205. Richard's will.

Sept. 23. Richard's will.

Dec. An inquiry into an injustice done an abbess.

Feb. 1206. Richard's will.

Sept. 1207. Berengaria's dowry.

Aug. 1208. Richard's will. (A partial settlement had been made the year before.)

Jan. 1209. Berengaria's dowry.

Jan. 23. Berengaria's dowry.

Oct. 1211. A strong recommendation that the King go on a crusade.

It is quite clear that the relations between them had not been of a kind to make the selection of a successor to the see of Canterbury an easy matter.

The Pope held hearings on the case at once. The twelve English canons, bred to expect a venerable gentleness in the men who sat in the Vatican, must have been overawed by the vigorous conduct of the case by the third Innocent, who was still in his forties. Well did he become the arms of the family of Conti de Segni, which bore an argent-headed eagle. He had an oval face, a long and thin nose, and a powerful chin to compensate for the smallness of his mouth. His eyes, which were somewhat closely placed, had the deep fire in them of power and ambition.

Innocent disposed of the rival claims in brisk order. The election of Reginald was set aside as having been improperly conducted. That of De Grey was also declared null and void because it had been made before the previous election had been passed upon. Having thus cleared the ground in a thoroughly proper and legal way, the Pope summoned the canons to appear before him on Christmas Day and then presented to them the man he had selected himself.

His choice was an Engishman and a cardinal. The red hat had not yet been designed for cardinals (it came into use soon after, however, in 1245), nor did the members of that powerful group wear the purple cloak. It was an unassuming figure, therefore, who faced the contesting deputations, but it is certain that they were instantly impressed, and perhaps awed, by Stephen Langton; even though they had no way of knowing that here was a great man who would prove himself later one of the most justly illustrious of the long line of commoners who came to the fore at critical moments of English history to save the nation from the mistakes and the tyranny of bad kings.

2

Nothing definite is known about the early years of Stephen Langton except that he was born in England and was of pure native parentage, without any trace of Norman blood. It is generally assumed that he came from either Yorkshire or Lincolnshire, with the former favored for the honor. There was a family of Langtons at Spilsby in the latter county, but Stephen's possession of a prebendary in Yorkshire while he taught at Paris would seem to assign him to that great northern county.

He went early to Paris and became the outstanding teacher at the university, some historians stating that he was chancellor there. The post does not seem to have existed at the time, but it may have been that Langton performed the duties which were later assumed by the chancellors. His teaching of theology was of the most enlightened kind. He inclined to follow the lead of Becket, denying the absolute power of kings and setting above them the higher lordship of God. Some of his students were so imbued with his teachings that they went much farther than he had ever done and were accused of heresy, for which a few of them were burned at the stake.

At Paris he met the young man from Italy who bore the name of Lothario de Conti de Signi and who even at that early stage was stamped for future greatness; a reserved young man with brooding dark eyes and an air of intense determination. The future Pope was struck with the clarity and logic of Langton's teaching. He listened often to the man from England and consulted him on points of theological dispute and church discipline. Lothario de Conti de Signi was raised to the College of Cardinals at the age of twenty-eight, a hasty advance which at the time was ascribed to the nepotism of Pope Clement. The new cardinal soon demonstrated that his selection had been a wise one, and he so impressed his colleagues that on the death of Celestine less than ten years after he was elected to succeed him. He took the name of Innocent III, and one of the first things he did was to bring Stephen Langton from Paris. The Englishman became the most popular preacher in Rome, and it was remarked that Innocent went often to hear him. There was no surprise when Langton was made the cardinal-presbyter of St. Chrysogonus.

The new cardinal was able, in this post, to indulge his tendency to scholarship. Among his achievements were many learned commentaries on the Old Testament and even some volumes of a profane nature, including a heroic poem on the six days of creation entitled *Hexameron,* and histories of Henry II and Richard. The manuscripts of his lighter labors are believed to be in existence still, though they have not been located. His greatest contribution was dividing the Scriptures into chapters, and this monumental labor he accomplished to the general satisfaction, it seems, of the contentious scholars of the day. He wrote a hymn, *Veni, Sancte Spiritus,* which is still sung under the English translation of *Come, Thou Holy Spirit, Come.*

Although much has been written about this priest who was to play such a vital part in the history of England, no information exists about the man himself. Was he tall or short? Was he dark or did he carry the badge of his race in a fairness of locks and complexion? If no conclusions can be drawn on these points, his character at least shows plainly through the pattern of events. He was a benign man, moderate though advanced in his views, calm and fearless in emergency. He was a pure patriot and a zealous Christian, his soundness unflawed by selfish considerations. He never blustered or threatened, and so one conceives of him as a man who spoke quietly and depended more on the substance of what he had to say than on how he said it. The spurious wiles of the orator were foreign to his nature, although he could hold men in thrall by the perfection of his reasoning.

3

English Stephen Langton was a magnificent choice for the primacy. The canons had come to Rome with strict instructions from John to secure the selection of Grey, but there can be no doubt that they were seduced by the bearing and the depth of learning shown by Innocent's candidate; and this made it easier for them to yield to papal pressure. They confided to the Pontiff the nature of their instructions, and he at once absolved them from a promise so improperly extracted. The canons then proceeded to elect Stephen Langton. All voted for him except one Elias de Braintefield, who cast his ballot for the King's choice and then left the chamber. He returned, however, and listened at the door while the *Te Deum* was sung over the new archbishop.

John was not at all mollified by the letter he received from the Pope, informing him of what had happened. Innocent had tried to placate him by a gift of four immensely valuable rings and had indited a homily in his own handwriting on the form of them and the significance of the precious stones with which they were set. The King kept the rings but indulged himself in retaliatory action at once. He dispatched two of his most violent officers to Canterbury to expel the monks and take over the revenues of the see. Fulk de Cantelupe and Henry de Cornhulle entered the abbey with drawn swords and carried out his orders with a thoroughness which fell just short, fortunately, of the violence offered Thomas à Becket. John announced to the world that the action of the Pope had been in contravention of his established rights (which, of course, it was) and that he would never allow Stephen Langton to set foot on *land of mine,* by which he meant England.

The Pope was not to be intimidated. He sent the bishops of London, Ely, and Worcester to inform John that an interdict would be laid on England if he did not give in. All the bishops of the realm were present when this message was delivered. They were frightened, knowing the inflexible will of the young Pontiff, and they fell on their knees before John and begged him to save his people from this dread punishment. John was so enraged that he foamed at the mouth, as his father had done so often when crossed, and swore that if the Pope carried out his threat he would expel from the kingdom every bishop, every abbot, every prior, every priest, and every monk, from the wearer of the proudest miter to the most humble of shaven-polls. He swore that all servants of the Vatican who appeared in England on the Pope's orders would have their eyes burned out and their noses slit.

John was in a poor position, however, to oppose the will and the power of the Vicar of Christ. His relations with the barons had been growing more strained all the time. If he had assembled them at once and explained the unwarranted authority the Pope had taken into his hands, he might have united them behind him for the struggle. He was unwilling at this stage to face the barons in a body, fearing, no doubt, that they would take advantage of the chance to deprive *him* of some of the unwarranted authority he had been seizing. He decided to oppose Innocent alone and thereby compromised his case and condemned himself to inevitable defeat.

Other popes had talked of interdicts when kings were recalcitrant but had contented themselves with threats. Innocent was different. When he made a threat, he carried it out.

John had been given until Monday of Passion week to change his mind. Convinced that nothing would happen, the King spent the day as usual, joking with his attendants, telling them that soon there would be a worse devil at large than he had ever been. There would be a postponement, he was sure, leading to more negotiations and more threats. But he had wrongly judged the temper of the young Pope.

That night the three bishops to whom the papal instructions had been given followed out their orders. Wearing the violet robes of mourning usually reserved for Good Friday, they entered their episcopal churches, escorted by priests carrying torches and chanting the *Miserere.* The bells were tolling a funeral knell and the people stood about in silent masses outside and watched, more than half expecting to see the heavens open and avenging angels swoop down to carry God's punishment over England.

The proper procedure for the occasion was followed inside the churches. The shrines and crucifixes were covered, the relics were removed to places of safekeeping, the Wafer of the Host was burned. In loud voices it was proclaimed that the dominions ruled by John had been laid under the ban of the Church. Instantly all torches were extinguished to denote the withdrawal of light from the land.

England had been laid under the dreaded interdict.

4

None of the common people knew what was happening until the first outward signs of the interdict appeared. Hearing no church bells, they hurried to see what was amiss and found the priests removing the bells from the steeples and packing them away in straw. This was going on all over England. In every town and hamlet in the land, therefore, the same questions were asked by people with bewildered faces: What was this? Was God leaving them to the mercy of the powers of evil? Or were the bells to be melted down to pay the bad King's taxes?

The panic spread when the work of dismantling was carried on inside as well. All the sacred vessels were taken down and packed away, the monstrance was removed from the altar, the candles which had been set alight by reverent hands were snuffed out. The doors were closed and locked in the faces of the frightened watchers.

When the meaning of this became clear to them, the people of England were unhappier than they had ever been before. Had God and the Holy Mother and all the good saints given up the struggle in their behalf against the devil? Would all time and life now belong to the powers of evil? Men who conceived of themselves as walking constantly in the Shadow believed that a moment's relaxation on the part of their guardian angels would deliver them into the hands of the imps of hell with their pitchforks and red-hot pincers. And now they were alone and had no protectors, divine or otherwise.

Then it became known throughout the bewildered country that five of the bishops had already fled from England, that priests were following them in droves, that those who remained behind would celebrate mass in locked and darkened churches for themselves alone. There would be no marrying, no burying in consecrated ground as long as the Pope's interdict held. To make matters worse, it was said that the wicked King, who had brought this curse on the land, was swearing he would banish every priest and hang those who remained. This bad King, cried the people in anguish, must indeed be in league with the devil that such things could come to pass!

Quite apart from this feeling of abandonment, the people knew they would miss the ministrations of the Church. In lives as bare as theirs, the tolling of bells at stated hours was a great pleasure, as was the ritual of matin and compline. They were accustomed to hear the knelling when someone they knew was dying, the slow and measured strokes teaching them the solemnity of death. Some of the sting of separation was taken from death by the customs which wrapped it about. They liked the services and they found a sense of

God's nearness therein, even in the dread moment when the hearse was taken down from the ceiling of the church where it was suspended, a triangular frame of wood or latten. It would be placed in front of the altar and fifteen lighted candles would be deposited on it, fourteen of yellow wax to represent the eleven apostles and the three Mary's, and one of white which stood for the Christ. Then the fourteen psalms of *Tenebrae* would be sung, and at the end of each, one of the yellow candles would be extinguished. And then finally only the white taper of Christ would remain, and this would be carried behind the altar so that darkness descended on the church.

There had never been any fear for the souls of departed relatives and friends when the tolling of bells accompanied the carrying out of the coffin, nine strokes for a man, six for a woman, three for a child; nay, there had been solace and comfort and a complete sense of security. There had even been pleasure in the good cheer of the *arvil*, the funeral feast, and a chance for some amusement out of the sin-eaters, those Old Sires who sat outside the house on low stools called crickets and were ready, on payment of a groat, a crust of bread, and a mazer of ale, to rise up and declare that they would pawn their souls for the ease and rest of the departed.

Death would now become a grim and frightening thing. Would the bodies of those who were unfortunate enough to die be buried or would they be left in ditches to rot away? Certainly bodies would be held for more than the usual three days allowed in the hope that they might come back to life, for would not that be the only hope?

It was feared, too, that the joy would go out of weddings, if indeed they would be possible at all. The mating rites had always been jolly affairs in merrie England: the gay procession to the church, the minstrels leading with their capering and playing, the youths next to carry the bride-cup with its gilt rosemary and ribbons, the bride and her two bachelor attendants preceding the groom and his two maidens who held the dow-purse, in which would be the dowry. Would couples in search of happiness be allowed to kneel before priests at the church door and say the responses while the groom endowed his bride by throwing money into a handkerchief held open by the maids in attendance? Certainly there would be no right now to go into the church and kneel together under the care-cloth (a great privilege which only professed virgins were permitted to enjoy) while the blessing was pronounced.

[345]

Perhaps feasting at weddings would still be allowed, but would the best man throw a plate from a window when the couple appeared (if the plate broke, the marriage would be a success), and would later the oatmeal cake be smacked down on the bride's head? Would the John Anderson dance be performed with as much zestful passing of the cushion and as much happy chanting of

Prinkcam, prankcam is a fine dance:
And shall we go dance it once again?
Once again, and once again?

Later it was found that things would not be so bad as feared. The papal bull had carried with it some modifications. Children could be christened, weddings could be performed at the church door, sermons could be preached in churchyards, priests would be permitted to recite the offices for the dead in private homes. The hardest problem facing the nation was that of burial, for no bodies could be laid in consecrated ground. The result was that they were placed in fields. Later, when the ban was lifted, the bodies were transferred to the churchyards. It is recorded that in one small community as many as twenty had to be exhumed. In London it became necessary to make use of empty lots and of the yards of hospitals. There was a large area around St. Bartholomew's which the authorities enclosed and devoted to the burying of the dead. The hospitals did not object; they charged fees both ways.

Most reports of what happened in connection with burials were exaggerated. It was said that bodies lay in ditches and were gnawed by dogs and rats and that pestilence was spread by the stench of them. The problem was handled, as a matter of fact, with common sense and expedition.

The harm that the interdict did was borne equally by people and Church. Cut off from the consolations and the rites of religion, many men found that they suffered no harm. They began to wonder. Was religion as important as they had believed? Heretical ideas, which had not been spreading in England, received impetus from the conditions which Innocent imposed on the country. There was also the matter of tithes and payments for this and that, the mortuary claims of the Church and deodand. Freed from much of this during the years that the interdict lasted, men would find it hard to accept again their share in the upkeep of the Church.

With Bell, Book, and Candle

The struggle between Pope and King continued much longer than Innocent had expected when he ordered the three bishops to put the land under ban by bell, book, and candle. As the years passed the rift became deeper and the feeling more bitter. Church properties fell into disrepair, the rents were expropriated to the Crown, the ranks of the clergy shrank. It must have become apparent soon to the Pope that, in casting the thunderbolt, he had indulged in a costly gamble. But the step had been taken and there was no turning back.

John fought with fang and claw. He tried to regain the loyalty of the people by conducting campaigns in Scotland and Wales. He went on processionals from city to city, taking in his train a bevy of beautiful hostages who had been put in his hands. They included the princesses Margaret and Isabella of Scotland; the Pearl of Brittany, Arthur's lovely sister, who was to remain a captive in England all her life; and Ada, the fair young countess of Holland. He seems to have respected these hostages of high degree; in fact, he went to great pains to find husbands for some of them. He saw that they were clothed expensively, and there is one item among royal expenditures for the purchase of one hundred pounds of figs for their pleasure and health.

In the meantime John was carrying the war to the enemy. Stephen Langton's father, a humble North Country man, had to flee the country into Scotland. The primate himself had taken up residence at Pontigny, where Thomas à Becket had spent most of his exile, and was addressing letters to the people of England. John had the ports watched to stop all such communications from getting into the country, and it became a criminal offense to possess or read these messages. The property of all churchmen who obeyed the commands of the Pope was confiscated.

The bitter seesaw of invective and retaliation went on interminably between the main actors in the drama. And because of this an innocent nation suffered.

5

The Pope had withheld some of his thunder. When the interdict seemed to be failing of results, the second thunderbolt was launched. Innocent called for his bell and he called for his book and he called for his bishops three. They were given another dangerous and thankless task, the excommunication of the King. They obeyed with an understandable degree of caution. Knowing that John would hang them if they set foot on English soil, they published the decree from their safe sanctuaries.

The effect was felt at once. The interdict was a condition shared by all, but excommunication was a personal ban which cut the victim off from all human relationships, as surely in theory, at least, as a leper was banned in practice. John was marked as accursed, and no one was supposed to speak to him except a few officials whose duties made contact obligatory.

John had been in a smoldering state ever since the laying of the interdict. His own excommunication drove him into an explosive fury. When Geoffrey, the Archdeacon of Norwich, withdrew from the Court of Exchequer with the explanation that it was forbidden to serve a ruler on whom the ban of the Church had been laid, the King struck out viciously. Geoffrey, a man of advanced years, was thrown into prison and a cope of lead was soldered on his shoulders. This form of torture, which slowly broke the bones by the weight of the cope, proved so effective that the archdeacon died within a few days.

Officers of the Church who had remained at their posts up to this time began to desert now. The new Bishop of Lincoln fled the country and betook himself to Pontigny to make his submission to Stephen Langton. Others followed in such numbers that the wearisome business of watching the whole coast line had to be taken up again.

This could not last long, however. The King, realizing that his position was degenerating rapidly, sent an invitation to Cardinal Langton to meet him at Dover, announcing in advance the concessions he was prepared to make. He was ready to have the cardinal installed at Canterbury, to forgive all churchmen who had fled the country or had refused to obey him, and to make financial settlements. The invitation, however, had been addressed to the cardinal and not the archbishop, and so Langton refused to accept it. He stood out, moreover, for an unconditional surrender and the promise of the King to pay for all losses the Church had suffered. John was not yet ready to give in on such terms as these. He snorted, cursed, roared, foamed at the mouth, and sent a venomous refusal.

But the Pope had still another weapon to unsheathe. In 1212 he absolved all subjects of John from their oaths of allegiance, coupling with this the declaration that the ban of excommunication would thenceforth apply to anyone who continued to serve him, who lived in his household, who sat or served at his table, who held the stirrup when he set forth to ride, or who spoke a word to him in public or private.

If the royal staff shrank as a result, it was barely perceptible. By this time men were accustomed to the situation. They had to live in spite of all the banning and fulminating and the rumble of sacerdotal storms. The King held his ground. He was beginning to think that England could be made a self-contained corner where the writ of the Vatican would not run nor the papal thunder be heard.

John, in fact, was more disturbed by the prediction of a hermit named Peter of Pontefract, who had given it out that he had only one year to reign and that on the following Ascension Day he would cease to sit on the throne. The hermit was brought to Windsor, and the King demanded to know what grounds he had for such treasonable utterances. Peter of Pontefract was a slow-witted countryman who fitted a term much used at the time, edmede, meaning humble and gently disposed. There was nothing he could say except that the conviction had been lodged in his mind by an agency he believed divine. It had been like a vision, and a voice had said he must tell what he had heard and seen. The prophet was sent to Corfe Castle to await developments.

Pope Innocent now went to the final extreme. He summoned before him all the cardinals in Rome and solemnly declared the deposition of John as King of England. He then took the desperate step of announcing that the crown would be given to Philip of France, a man more capable of ruling nobly and well than the deposed monarch.

Philip had been consulted in advance, of course, and had agreed to act in accordance with the papal policy. He had been eager to start, for this would be the final stage of the plans which had taken possession of the mind of an angry boy under the oak of Gisors. He held a great council at Soissons on April 8, 1213, and gained the consent of the nobility of France to the invasion of England. Having dismembered the limbs of Angevin power, he was now to strike at the very heart of it. He went jubilantly to work to raise the largest army France had yet seen and to assemble in the ports of Normandy a fleet estimated at seventeen hundred ships. All France rang with military preparations. Once again Englishmen looked across the Channel, as they had done in the days of the Conquest and as they were to do many times thereafter, and waited for the ships of the invader to appear.

It seemed at first that Pope Innocent, in making his last extreme move, had defeated his own purpose. Englishmen, fearing invasion above everything, armed themselves behind their derided and hated King. An army grew along the coast of Kent as if by some kind of magic evoked by national necessity. The main camp was at Barham Down near Canterbury, and here sixty thousand men were soon assembled. Smaller camps were located at Dover, Faversham, and Ipswich. John took up his post at the hotel of the Templars at Ewell, occupying himself largely with the need for money to pay the cost of this great rally. He ransacked the monasteries and the closed churches and emptied the pockets of the Jews. It was at this time that he enforced his demands on one Isaac of Bristol for ten thousand marks by ordering that a tooth be extracted from his jaw each day until the money had been paid. Dentistry was one of the functions of the barbers, many of whom wore strings around their necks containing all the teeth they had drawn. The royal practitioner, into whose hands Isaac was put, had six more teeth to display before the reluctant donor gave in. Everyone was giving in and paying, although not under such extreme pressure. The whole kingdom groaned under the exactions, but in the face of the emergency most men found the means to pay their share.

A blow which might have proved decisive was dealt the French by the eldest son of the Fair Rosamonde who, as was related earlier, was known to men as William Long-Espée. The sons brought into the world by that gentle lady were stout fellows who, on any plane of comparison, measured above the legitimate issue of the great Henry. William Long-Espée had always been a favorite with John. The illegitimate half brother accompanied the King everywhere. There never seems to have been a serious rift between them, which suggests that this son of the unfortunate lady lacked the stanchness of the other, Geoffrey of York. John had made a fine match for William, marrying him to Ela, the heiress of Salisbury. Ela, a lady of beauty and high spirit, had become known as the Mystery Maiden after the death of her father in 1196. She disappeared, and it was generally feared that she had been done away with so that one of her paternal uncles could take the title and the enormous wealth of the family. A young knight-errant named William Talbot followed the example of Blondel, however, and sang English ballads under windows in all the castles of Normandy until he received a response. The rescue of the imprisoned maiden resulted, and the gallant knight had the satisfaction of seeing her restored to her family and her rights. The story did not end in the usual way. Ela did *not* fall in love with the devoted William Talbot and she did become very much attached to the middle-aged husband selected for her by the King; and Talbot had to content himself with remaining a close friend of the happy pair. Assuming the title of Earl of Salisbury, the son of Fair Rosamonde played an important part in national affairs and in his declining years built Salisbury Cathedral. The disconsolate Ela founded Lacock Abbey after his death.

William Long-Espée was of a sufficiently complaisant nature to ride in the train of John. When put in command of the naval forces, however, he showed his real mettle. On May 30 he directed an attack on the French vessels in the port of Dam, now known as Dollart Bay, and scored a complete victory. Many of the French ships were captured and at least three hundred of them were burned. The doughty bastard came sailing back to a wildly jubilant country.

But John lacked the fortitude for as stern a struggle as this. Before the victory had been scored over the French fleet he had succumbed to the arguments of Pandulfo, the papal legate. Pandulfo paid him a secret visit and frightened the King by the description he gave of the might of the French army. John capitulated without waiting to see how the first test of strength would come out.

All credit for this sudden collapse must not be given, however, to the wily Pandulfo. John had been uneasy ever since the hermit of Pontefract had predicted the end of his power. The King of Scotland had added to his panic by informing him that a conspiracy was on foot among his barons to dethrone him. The wife of Leolin, one of the princes of Wales, had whispered the same news in his ear. The conspiracy, it was said, had grown out of the efforts of Stephen Langton, who still occupied much of his time at Pontigny by corresponding with men of importance in the kingdom. John did not doubt the truth of the story. He began to suspect every man who came near him. His temper became more violent with each passing day. His hands played nervously with the relics strung around his neck or gripped with sudden passion the hilt of his beaked dagger. Once he burst out with a furious speech which showed how firmly convinced he was that Stephen Langton was at the bottom of everything. "Never shall that Stephen," he cried, "obtain a safe-conduct from me of force sufficient to prevent me from"—his hands clawed at the air—"from suspending him by the neck the moment he touches land of mine!"

Surrender to the Pope, therefore, carried with it release from such fears. If he hid himself under the wing of Innocent, then all the forces of Europe would be behind him and he could laugh at the efforts of the baronage to unseat him. Perhaps also the mind of this cunning King had cast on into the future and had foreseen other advantages which a close alliance with Rome would bring. If this were true, it was with inner reserve and tongue in cheek that John gave his consent to the humiliating terms the legate had brought from the arrogant man in the Vatican.

The day before Ascension, John appeared in the church of the Temple and a long document was loudly intoned. "Ye know," it read in part, "that we have deeply offended our Holy Mother the Church and that it will be hard to draw on the mercy of Heaven. Therefore we would humble ourselves, and without constraint, of our own free will, by the consent of our barons and high justiciars, we give and confer on God, on the Holy Apostles St. Peter and St. Paul, on our Mother the Church and on Pope Innocent III and his Catholic successors, the whole kingdom of England and Ireland, with all their rights and dependencies for the remission of our sins; henceforth we hold them as a fief, and in token thereof we swear allegiance in presence of Pandulfo, Legate of the Holy See."

It was true that four of the great barons of the realm had been consulted—the earls of Salisbury, Boulogne, Warenne, and Ferrars—but to everyone else this announcement was a complete and over-whelming surprise, a thunderclap which left the nation aghast. England a fief of Rome! It was not to be believed. Why had the King, after rejecting much easier terms, decided suddenly to give everything to the Pope?

These thoughts filled the minds of the barons as they saw Pandulfo, a man of great slyness and, some say, of a mean and slinking appearance, take possession of the royal chair. John knelt before him, lifted up his hands and placed them in those of the legate, and swore fealty to the Pontiff. The King then offered money as a token of submission, and the legate refused to accept it as a sign the Church scorned earthly wealth. When John, who seemed willing to go to the farthest limits of abasement, tendered him the crown the minister of the Vatican (a lowly minister, for Pandulfo was no higher than a deacon) accepted it. He kept it five days, moreover, before giving it back.

Directly after the ceremony it was learned that, in addition to thus surrendering himself to Rome, John had agreed to all the papal terms. Stephen Langton was to be received, all the exiled church-men were to be reinstated, all losses sustained by the Church during the years of the interdict were to be made up in full, and the Vati-can was to be paid one thousand marks a year, seven hundred for England, three hundred for Ireland. It was such an abject surrender that men looked at each other blankly, asking themselves if the King had been under some malign influence.

The amazement grew when it was learned that no promise had been received from Innocent of an immediate raising of the bans.

John had one consolation left him for this bitter moment of capitu-lation. Ascension Day passed and he still sat on his throne. He sent word to Corfe that Peter of Pontefract was to be questioned further. The hermit proved much bolder than he had been before, declaring that the ceremony in the Temple had been the fulfillment of his prophecy, inasmuch as the King now ruled as a vassal. When this was reported to him, John fell into one of his most extravagant rages and ordered that the hermit and a son who had been impris-oned with him be executed at once. Accordingly the two humble men from Yorkshire were tied to the heels of horses and dragged all the way to Wareham. Here the broken bodies were hoisted up to the gallows and hanged.

On July 20 a second ceremony was observed. Cardinal Langton had landed in England to take up his duties as head of the Church. John was at Winchester and sent word to the primate to join him there. It was in early morning when the two antagonists met for the first time. The King rode out with his usual train to Magdalen's Hill, a gold circlet on his head in place of a helmet, a look in his eye which was half defiance, half derision. The archbishop was wearing his full canonicals, with all the bishops of England riding in his train. They studied each other for a moment, the massive, violent King and the spare, composed cardinal. John then dismounted and prostrated himself at the feet of the archbishop. This should have been followed by the kiss of peace, but John was still under the ban of excommunication and so it was forbidden for Langton to embrace him. The King, realizing the difficulty, sprang from his kneeling position, laughed loudly, and threw the primate a kiss with his hand.

There was more to this gesture than John's usual sense of the comic at moments of gravity. The kiss was a token of derision. He was laughing at the farce they were playing in the bright sunshine of Magdalen's Hill. There was defiance in it, defiance of Innocent, of Stephen Langton, of the barons of England. There was in it a hint of future purpose, a message which said, Wait, this is not the end, the time will come when I, John of England, will undo all this which is being done!

Nevertheless, with every outward sign of amity, King and archbishop turned their horses and rode back into Winchester, the bishops and knights following after. All joined in the Fifty-first Psalm, the high voice of the King chiming in with the resonant tones of the cardinal.

"Have mercy upon me, O God, according to Thy loving kindness . . .
Wash me, and I shall be whiter than snow . . .
Hide Thy face from my sins . . ."

6

In Winchester Cathedral, Stephen Langton laid the train for further trouble, for himself and for the whole kingdom of England; but it was done out of his desire to see the country free of her woes and his belief that at last the rift had been closed between Church and State. He absolved John of his sins and then performed the Holy Eucharist in thanksgiving. For this he was never forgiven in Rome. Innocent was a stern victor and a stickler for his own rights. He had humbled John and become the actual head of the kingdom. Only when he, the Pope, saw fit to raise the ban would England be freed. The archbishop had exceeded his authority, and from that moment the face of the Pontiff was turned away from his own appointee, the man for whom he had entered on this bitter struggle. Never again was Stephen Langton to know favor.

Innocent had many things to settle before the interdict would be lifted. First he had to inform Philip of France that, as the insurgency of John had been quelled and England was now a fief of Rome, there could be no invasion of the country. Philip naturally was amazed and outraged. Had he then raised a great army and fleet, at unprecedented expense, and all for nothing? Must he now disband his forces without compensation or reward? He fumed bitterly because he had been sure that the decisive defeat of his English rival had been imminent. He did not enjoy serving as cat's paw to the Pope.

This blow to his ambitions, his dignity, and his purse rankled so deeply that the French King turned like a wounded animal and struck at the nearest victim, which happened to be Flanders. The French armies, equipped for immediate fighting, invaded the provinces of the Count of Flanders, who had allied himself with England. It was to help the count that William Long-Espée was sent to attack the French fleet. The victory he scored saved the Low Country and might also have saved England if it had been won a few weeks earlier, or if John had possessed more fortitude.

The terms of John's capitulation to Rome called for payment in full of all losses the Church had sustained. Pandulfo was replaced as legate by Nicholas, the Bishop of Frascati, to whom fell the task of adjusting the claims. They began to come in at once, and John was horrified when he discovered how large they were. Canterbury alone demanded twenty thousand marks. Every bishop had claims for buildings destroyed, livestock stolen, forests burned. Every parish priest, except those who had disobeyed the Pope by continuing to officiate, had suffered losses. In addition there were the rents on church properties which had been collected by the Crown and spent long since; every penny of this vast sum must now be paid back.

With rising wrath and the painful reluctance of a parsimonious man, the King finally brought himself to the point of making an offer. He would pay a lump sum of one hundred thousand marks and the Church could settle how the money was to be applied and divided. This amount would not cover more than a fraction of the losses which had been piling up over the years. The Church rejected the offer flatly.

And now Innocent III did an extraordinary thing. He disregarded the decision of the Church in England and set the amount of reparations at forty thousand marks! John, delighted, accepted with the greatest alacrity. He perceived that his canny view of future developments had been right. The Pope and he were partners, and it was clear that the Pontiff would not permit anything to happen, even for the benefit of the Church in England, which would weaken the King who had become his vassal.

The new legate proved himself most obnoxious to the people of England. Landing with such a small train that he had only seven horses, the cardinal had demanded at once that he be supplied with fifty. He gathered a stately cavalcade about him and traveled in the greatest grandeur, insisting on the best accommodations and paying nothing. He was like a bailiff who had been put in charge of bankrupt property and who forthwith proceeded to inspect everything, to taste, to pry, to ask impertinent questions.

The offense given thus to the people was small compared to the tribulations he heaped on the churchmen. He took it upon himself to settle all disputes within the Church with ruthless disregard of everything but his own lordly will. He filled vacancies without any thought of the qualifications of the favorites he brought in.

On one occasion this amiable Cardinal Nicholas was mobbed by priests, nuns, and hospitalers as he left St. Paul's. They cried out to him in piteous tones that they had obeyed the Pope and gone into exile and poverty. Those who had not obeyed him had remained at home in comfort and without loss and were still in the full enjoyment of their benefices. Was it fair, they demanded, that now they should be told that nothing could be done for them and that strangers should be put in the posts they had vacated? The legate forced his way through them with impatience. He had no instructions to help them, he said. There was nothing he could do for them, nothing.

For one reason and another the better part of a year passed before the interdict was lifted. It had continued for six years, three months, and fourteen days.

CHAPTER XVIII

Magna Charta

O N AUGUST 27 of the following year, Stephen Langton preached at St. Paul's in London. There was nothing remarkable in that fact in itself, for the archbishops were more often in London and Westminster than in Canterbury, but two things made the service noteworthy. First, John was in France, fighting the last and least creditable of his campaigns for the recovery of his lost possessions and did not know what was going on at home. Second, the cathedral was filled with all the great people in the country, bishops and noblemen of high degree, plain knights, and even some of the rich citizens of London; and such a gathering could not have been brought together unless there was something very important in the wind.

While waiting for John to yield, Stephen Langton had spent much of his time in the study of canon law. He had become convinced of the cruelty and injustice of the feudal system as well as the need for curbs on the power of rulers. The course he followed on reaching England makes it abundantly clear that he had resolved in advance to use the power of his high office to relieve the burdens of the people.

He stood up before his august audience on this warm August day, and his eyes kindled when he saw that not one of the men he wanted present had failed him. He preached with his accustomed clarity, taking his text from the Psalms, *My heart trusted in God and was helped and my flesh rejoiced.* What he said has not been recorded, but it is certain that the message he delivered was a spiritual one and that the political situation was not referred to openly. Later in the day there was a secret meeting. Where it was held is not known, but it must have been in the London house of one of the great barons. Stephen Langton was the speaker and, as he rose, an air of solemnity could be seen on every face. Everyone there knew that what they would do that day would later be construed as high treason.

The dramatic point of this historically important speech came when the primate produced a document, which was yellow with age and badly tattered. Did they remember, he asked, that a charter had been signed by Henry I in the early stages of his reign? Few of his hearers had known of the charter, which is not surprising, for a century had passed since it was signed. Still fewer recalled that one hundred copies had been made for distribution to all parts of the country, and none had heard that these copies had disappeared, presumably on the order of the King himself when his mind changed.

It was true, went on the archbishop, that an effort had been made to call back or destroy all copies. One, however, had not been located at the time and so had continued in existence, and after a diligent search had now been found. He held up the yellowed sheet with a reverent hand, knowing it to be the most important state document in the world at that moment. Where it had been found, he did not tell; which was unfortunate, for had he done so part of the mystery at least would have been cleared up.

The archbishop then proceeded to read the copy of this first written safeguard of English liberties. It must have been with special care that he intoned one brief clause:

"And I enjoin on my barons to act in the same way toward the sons and daughters and wives of their dependents."

A casual enough reference on the surface, this, particularly as it deals with the need for reform in matters of estates and inheritances. Its importance lies in the fact that this was an acknowledgment that common men had rights as well as the nobility and that these rights should be incorporated in the laws of the land. These twenty-two words would help greatly in the fight for freedom over the slow-moving centuries. It was, therefore, a solemn moment when he read

them from the paper in his hands and saw acceptance in the eyes
of the rich and powerful barons.

When the reading had been completed, the cardinal voiced the
belief that this might serve as the basis for the rights to which the
consent of the King must now be obtained. His audience seemed in
complete agreement. When he held the thin sheet above his head
and cried, "Swear it!" every voice in the room joined in with conviction.

In the meantime John was being badly beaten in France. He had
formed a coalition against Philip, consisting of the Emperor Otto
of Germany and Reginald of Boulogne. As he was still under the
ban of excommunication and the other partners to the coalition had
also been cursed by bell, book, and candle, their union might very
aptly have been called the Unholy Alliance. It was a most futile
alliance, at any rate. John made no headway at all in his Poitevin
campaign, and his German allies were decisively defeated at the
battle of Bouvines, both Otto and Reginald being captured. This
brought to an end the Unholy Alliance.

John came back to England, the nickname of Softsword his for
life. He whined at the lack of support he had been given and said
that now he would make the people of England feel the weight of
his anger. He not only imposed a new scutage on all who had not
followed him to France, which meant practically everyone, but he
searched old records to find proof of arrears. He discovered among
other things that Dorset and Somerset had not paid their full share
of Richard's German ransom twenty years before, and he collected
what was due. He even proceeded against two men who had been
fined by Richard for supporting him, John, while the King was in
Palestine, and who had not paid!

His bitter humor manifested itself in smaller ways. The Court
of Exchequer was moved from London to Northampton. This bit of
petty revenge proved costly in the long run, for the anger of the
Londoners was so great that they opposed him from that moment
on. He issued orders that all hedges were to be leveled, with the
result that beasts of the forest found their way into the fields of the
peasants and ate up the crops. Any method he could think of to
vent his spleen he put into operation at once; and soon the murmur

of the people could be heard from all parts of the land like the steady roar of the sea.

John brought back a force of routiers under the command of as callous a crew of cutthroats as the Middle Ages had ever produced: Engelard de Cigogni, Andrew de Chanceas, Geoffrey de Martigni, Guyon de Cigogni. With these he started out to punish his rebellious barons, razing such castles as fell into his hands and burning the countryside. Stephen Langton followed him to Northampton and sharply protested against this violence.

"You break your oaths to the people," he declared.

John broke into one of his whinnying tempers. "Rule you the Church!" he cried. "Leave me to govern the State."

Knowing that the King had said publicly there were three men he hated "like a viper's blood" and that he, Stephen Langton, himself was one of the three, the archbishop still had the courage to protest further. He followed the royal trail to Nottingham and threatened to excommunicate every man who obeyed the King's orders. This brought John to his senses and he ended the purge, returning to London.

On Christmas Day there was a meeting of the barons at Bury St. Edmunds, and it was decided to make a definite demand for a charter based on that of Henry I. A delegation waited on John on Twelfth-night and laid the stipulation before him. He was surprised and dismayed at this proof of their unanimity. After considerable delay and much hedging, he finally said he would give an answer by Easter, and that his sureties in the meantime would be the archbishop, William Marshal, and the Bishop of Ely.

Having thus gained for himself several months in which to strengthen his position, he announced his intention of going to the Crusades. No one seems to have believed him, even though he took to appearing in public in the white robe with a cross on the sleeve. He swore homage to Innocent a second time, sealing his paper of submission with gold instead of wax. With great care and cunning he set about fortifying his castles and bringing in more mercenaries.

The barons were not backward in preparing for the struggle which lay ahead. Two thousand knights and their squires assembled at Brackley after Easter. A document termed "The Articles of the Barons" was sent to the King at Oxford with word that on this they would base their demands. The King brushed the paper aside. "Why don't they ask my crown at once?" he cried. "Do they want to make me their slave?"

The time had passed for promises and threats, however. The barons were in the field in great strength, and it was clear that they meant to have their way. Realizing that he was not strong enough to oppose them, he temporized by making a number of absurd suggestions, as for instance that the matter be left to the Pope to decide as suzerain of England. The barons broke off negotiations. They elected Robert Fitz-Walter as their leader in the civil war which now seemed inevitable. After a defeat at Northampton, the barons marched on London and were received warmly by the citizens. This success convinced John that he would have to grant their terms. He sent word to them to meet him on June 15 at a field called Running-Mead on the Thames within close range of Windsor.

2

John had been in every respect an oppressive king, swayed only by his own desire and will, disregarding his coronation vows and the dictates of decency and statesmanship. All the kings from the time of the Conquest, however, had been ruthless and dictatorial. William Rufus and Richard had been worse in the demands they had made on their subjects. Why, then, did the nation remain quiescent under the others and burst into such fiery resentment over the actions of John?

There were two reasons. The first was that John inherited the resentment of a century, that he reaped where his predecessors had sown. The breaking point was reached when he came to the throne and proceeded to put his own diabolical ingenuity into the performance of familiar tyrannies.

The second reason was personal, the universal contempt in which he was held and the horror aroused by his cruelties. It was one thing for a great knight like Richard to toss aside his vows and make a travesty of government and justice, it was a vastly different matter when the prince, who had humbled England abroad and had made a personal enemy nearly every day of his life, followed the same course. A hero will be forgiven much, a coward and rascal nothing. The silence with which the people accepted the tyrannical acts of Richard Coeur de Lion added, of course, to the prompt and violent resentment they showed to John Softsword.

That John faced a solidly organized baronage was the result largely of the personal hatreds he had stirred up among them. Two of the most active leaders were Eustace de Vescy and Robert Fitz-Walter, and history supplies stories to account for the deep enmity they showed.

Eustace de Vescy was lord of the great castle of Alnwick in Northumberland. He had been with Richard in Palestine and was a brave and honorable knight. His wife was a lovely young woman of high spirits, and it was inevitable that the roving eye of the King would rest on her with admiration. The fact that she was devoted to her husband and that no hint of scandal had ever attached to her name served to fan the flames of desire in the amorous King. Noticing that the husband wore a ring of unusual design which he had brought back from the East, the royal philanderer borrowed it on the pretext of having one made like it. He then sent the ring to the wife of De Vescy with a message purporting to come from her husband that she was to meet him that night at a certain house in London. From this point on the story might well have inspired a tale in the *De-cameron*. The chatelaine of Alnwick was not taken in by anything as transparent as this. She went to her husband and told him what had happened. Eustace de Vescy realized what was back of it and decided to trick the King. He hired a lusty wench to play the part of his wife and, when the King came during the night and insinuated himself into the bed which he supposed was occupied by the lady of Alnwick, he did not find it empty.

Some time later Eustace de Vescy was at the royal supper table. John decided to enjoy his triumph in the usual manner. Combing his hands through his black beard and letting his dark eyes rove about the board with an amused gleam, he said to his guest, "Your lady is a delightful companion in the darkness of the night."

A silence fell on the room. Men kept their eyes down out of pity for the husband whose shame was thus being publicly proclaimed. Eustace de Vescy was noted for the violence of his temper as well as for the warmth of his love for his wife. The Northern baron seemed quite self-possessed, however, and answered in an easy tone.

"What grounds have you for saying that, my lord?"

"Grounds of experience," declared John with a loud laugh. "How else could I know?"

The baron allowed himself at this point the luxury of joining in the royal laughter.

"No, my lord," he said. "It was not my wife. Sometimes, my lord, a harlot is encountered in quite unexpected places."

John's rage at this open flouting was so great that the lord of Alnwick had to flee the country. He remained in exile for several years and was frequently in contact with Stephen Langton at Pontigny. The making of peace with Rome gave him freedom to return, and back he came, to play an active part in the humbling of the King who had tried to dishonor him.

A different kind of story is told to account for the undying enmity of Robert Fitz-Walter. He was the owner of Castle Baynard on the Thames and the father of a beautiful daughter called Maud the Fair. John saw Maud the Fair and decided she must be added to his list of victims, willing or otherwise. The girl would not listen to his suit, however, and John resorted finally to force. He had her seized and lodged in the White Tower and there paid her assiduous court. When her father raised a storm, the royal troops seized Castle Baynard and Fitz-Walter was banished from the kingdom. In the meantime the ardor of the royal lover was being dashed by the most contemptuous of rebuffs. Finally he had his prisoner removed to the round turret on top of the keep, which was unheated and probably the most bleak habitation in the whole of England, hoping that the rigors of existence there would soften her will. Finding that she still repulsed him, he had an egg sent her which had been filled with poison. The girl ate the egg and died in great agony, alone in her dismal cell atop the Tower of London.

One may suspect the authenticity of the story about Eustace de Vescy and his wife and the willing trollop who played the trick on the King, but the story of Maud the Fair can be dismissed as untrue for good and sufficient reasons. Robert Fitz-Walter had a daughter named Matilda, but she was married when quite young to Geoffrey de Mandeville, the son of the head justiciar. The young husband got into trouble with the law over an accidental killing. When he was cited to appear on a charge of murder, his father-in-law declared that "he who dares to hang my daughter's man will see two thousand laced helmets before his door!" The son-in-law was not hanged, but Robert Fitz-Walter drew on himself for his bold defiance an order of banishment. Later Maud the Fair died and John married off the widower to his own discarded wife, Avisa, and charged the bridegroom a fee of eighteen thousand marks for his services!

The fact that such highly spiced anecdotes were told in the chronicles of the day and were generally accepted and believed is an indication of the reputation the King had achieved for himself. He may not have tried to seduce the pretty chatelaine of Alnwick in just this way (but he tried, we can be sure of that!), and it is certain that he did not poison the fair Maud in the turret on the keep, but it is abundantly clear that no woman of the court was free from his attentions and that he did not hesitate to dishonor his most powerful subjects when a wife or daughter filled his eye. The hatreds engendered in this way provided embittered leaders for the forces of discontent.

While John was thus disturbing the felicity of the most influential men in the kingdom, he was having trouble with his own lovely wife. After seven years of childless marriage, the beautiful Isabella presented the King with a son on October 12, 1207. The boy was named Henry and he was to live a long life and earn for himself a front place among the worst of kings. Another son followed who was called Richard and became the richest man in the world and was elected Holy Roman Emperor. Three daughters were then born in rather quick succession, the eldest being christened Joan. This little princess was promptly betrothed to Isabella's jilted lover, Hugh of Lusignan! The match never came to anything for a very unusual reason which will be explained in its proper place. Joan, who was beautiful and angelic in character, was married instead at the tender age of eleven to King Alexander of Scotland to patch up a quarrel with that monarch. Because of this the lovely little Queen was called thereafter Joan Makepeace.

Such a steady succession of children should have been proof of domestic felicity in the royal family, but there seems instead to have been a rift which increased with the years. Isabella's reason for marrying John had been ambition. She had never loved him and she was such a sparkling beauty that every man looked at her with admiration. This provided all the ingredients for trouble, and it is perhaps not surprising that the Queen's eye began to develop a roving tendency also. It is recorded that John became convinced of an affair she was carrying on with a man of the court and that he adopted a characteristic way of having his revenge. One day the Queen found the body of her lover dangling at the head of her bed, the cords of the rich hangings knotted about his neck, his face black and swollen, his tongue protruding from his mouth.

At one stage she was placed in restraint as Eleanor had been. It was, however, for a short period only. John never seems to have recovered from his infatuation for his Queen, who was called the Helen of the Middle Ages.

It will be seen that the private life of the King was not of a kind to win back any of the favor which the infamy of his public career had lost. Hatred and contempt for this man who ruled over them led the barons inevitably to the field which has come down in history as Runnymede.

3

History supplies no report of the weather which prevailed along the Thames on Monday, June 15, 1215, but a beneficent Providence would not have provided anything but a day of bright sunshine for this momentous occasion. Let us assume, then, that the sky was bright and clear, the sun so brilliantly warm that the gray of the water was shot through with gold, and that the wide meadow along the river was lushly green with patches and dots of yellow.

But if the day was bright, there was nothing but blackness in the soul of John. For a month he had been at Windsor, following a visit to London, where he had found the citizens a unit in refusing to back him in his struggle with the barons. He had been trying to discover a way out of his difficulties but without success. How had it happened that after his surrender to the Pope, a brilliant right-about-face which had brought him the support of the Pontiff, his fortunes had dipped so suddenly? He could not understand it. When the interdict was raised, it had seemed to him that the domestic situation was well in hand. He had felt safe in dealing arbitrarily with the barons, who were a quarrelsome lot and incapable, seemingly, of continuing long in one camp or fighting together in one cause. But some malign influence had held them together, after all, and thus had brought him to his present desperate pass. Well he knew who had wielded that influence, the insistent, meddling cardinal at Canterbury. Langton should never have been allowed to come back to England.

On his arrival at Windsor it had been crammed with his supporters. They had filled the First King's House and the Marshal's Tower and even the huge round Norman keep. Their iron heels had resounded in Beauclerc's Passage which ran under the King's House, and they had crowded the jousting grounds between conferences with a willingness for combat which they did not show in the King's cause. Gradually their number had decreased. It was nothing new for John to watch his support dwindle, but each desertion this time had thrown him into a deep and sullen dismay. When the day came that only seven knights remained at Windsor, he gave in and sent word to the Army of God and Holy Church, as the barons called themselves, that he would meet them again.

Runnymede, to give it the modern spelling, was an extensive meadow on the south bank of the Thames near Staines where Oxford Street crossed the river. Here the barons had chosen to camp. Its selection had been deliberate, for this sometimes marshy stretch of land had been used by the Druids for ceremonial purposes and later by the Anglo-Saxons for speech-motes. Opposite it was a wooded island of some size, now called Charter Island.

On the appointed morning and at the time set, John rode out from Windsor and proceeded to a position on the north bank opposite the island. His pride was galled by the smallness of the train which followed him. Stephen Langton was at his right hand as surety for his appearance. The King would have been happy without *him!* On the other side rode Pandulfo, whose seat in the saddle was as bad as most clerks' and who jounced and groaned at the rapid pace set by the King. Behind the papal agent was Amaury, Grand Master of the Templars. William Marshal, whose stout old heart made it impossible for him to desert a king to whom he had sworn fealty, rode behind. His presence was a comfort, and yet it had seemed to the King that Pembroke wore a worried frown as they set out. There had been no doubt of the uncertain mood of the usually loyal half brother, William Long-Espée. The six lioncels of Salisbury flapped proudly in the breeze, but under them the hero of the sea battle at Dam wore a doubtful scowl, as though he did not like the way things were going. Beside the son of the Fair Rosamonde rode a cousin of

THE THAMES
from Oxford to London
Showing Norman Fortifications

LEA RIVER

London

Westminster
Abbey

Windsor

THAMES

WEY R.

Runnymede

Oxford

Wallingford

THAMES

KENNET

N
E
S
W

the King, the Earl of Warenne. There were, farther back, a few bishops and a few knights.

It was a miserable train for a king as arrogant as John.

As they drew near the appointed place, the sound of cheering reached their ears, mingled with the neighing of horses and the loud, clear blast of trumpets. Coming into sight of the shore opposite the island, they saw it was filled with armed horsemen, the sun shining on helmets and breastplates and on lances held erect to display the proudest pennons in England: the colors of Bigod, of Bohun, of Percy, of Lacey and Mowbray and De Vere. The King reined in suddenly, his face red with mortification. Here for the first time he saw with his own eyes the tangible evidence of the unanimity of the barons in opposition to him. They had refused to follow him on his continental forays. It had taken hatred of him to bring them out thus in full force!

Robert Fitz-Walter had ridden down close to the water's edge. Beside him was Eustace de Vescy with the cross argent on his shield and Saire de Quincey, whose arms showed eight points azure. The latter was the shrewdest member of the combination and is supposed to have been responsible for the final draft of the Charter. The three leaders watched the small party across the river with anxious eyes, wondering in what mood they would find the savage and unpredictable King.

Every proud name in England was represented in the army behind them. Henry de Bohun was there, which would have amazed his ancestor, Humphrey With-the-Beard, who had been one of the stanchest supporters of the Conqueror. Close by stood a proud baron who was in much the same position, Richard de Percy, whose great-grandfather's nickname had been William With-the-Whiskers and who had been equally unswerving in his devotion. Robert de Vere was probably the proudest participant, being hereditary lord chamberlain of the kingdom. Geoffrey de Mandeville was the wealthiest man there because of the land and riches brought him by Avisa. An unexpected adherent was the oldest son of William Marshal. His appearance was not due to the rather common practice of straddling the fence of allegiance, one member of a family going one way and another serving in the opposite camp. Young William was an enthusiastic partisan of the popular cause and had refused to take his father's advice.

There was only one man in that glittering cavalcade who had no arms or quarterings to show, William de Hardell, mayor of London. He was the first mayor to secure his elevation by popular election and the first also to introduce the trappings which would add so much to the dignity of the post, such as the ridings to Westminster. A bluff and hearty man, he sat his roan charger with ease and pride, being fully conscious of the fact that he represented more real power than any landed baron there.

Most of the men at Runnymede had Norman names, but few if any of them lacked English blood. Few of them owned land in Normandy, few had crossed the Channel. Their thoughts were all of England. They swore Saxon oaths, they worshiped at Saxon shrines. And their concern that day was to compel the granting of a code of laws based on those of the Saxons and modeled on a charter which had been drawn up more than a century before on the insistence of a lovely Saxon princess.

The negotiations were conducted on Charter Island where a fine pavilion had been raised for the purpose. It was clear from the first that the fight had gone out of the King. He agreed to the general content of the document, the forty-eight articles and the *Forma Securitatis,* before the end of the day. It is not true, however, as has often been assumed, that it was written and signed there and then. It took four days of hard work on the part of Saire de Quincey and Stephen Langton to draft it to the satisfaction of all.

They realized, when the royal signature had been scrawled at the end, that it had been surprisingly easy. John had been listless, subject to sudden bursts of impatience, but always ready to concede a point when the barons insisted. It should have been easy enough to guess from his attitude that he was marking time and that, if his fortunes improved, he would not hesitate to break his word later. Langton was shrewd enough to see what was back of the King's complaisance and to make up his mind to a watchful course thereafter.

The leaders had not expected the negotiations to last so long and certain difficulties arose. Not enough food had been provided for as extended a stay, and after the first day the army contractors were out in all directions, bargaining for beef and mutton, and paying handsomely through the nose. At the opening it was a matter of pride for the barons to keep in their saddle in heavy steel under the blazing sun while their leaders sat around in the cool blue-and-gold pavilion and debated with the obese and glowering King of the realm. The second day it became tiresome. The knights dismounted, took from their heads the heavy steel covering called the *chapel-de-fer*, bawled to their squires to slosh them with cold water, and demanded to know among themselves what this cullionly King was doing. The third day many of them had discarded steel and were attired in coats of *cuir-bouilli*, a variety of leather which had been boiled in water until it had almost the resistance of metal but was both lighter and cooler. Some had even come out from their stifling tents without the awkward thigh coverings which made walking so difficult.

On the fourth day it was suspected that nothing in the way of armor would have been found if the rich brocaded surcoats of the knights had been stripped off.

It might have been hard to hold them all through four days of talk, in which they had no part, if the leaders had not been wise enough to arrange for a victory tournament to be held at Stamford after the signing of the Charter.

4

This is the Great Charter, Magna Charta, as it is generally called:

John, by the grace of God King of England, to the archbishops, bishops, abbots, earls, barons, justices, foresters, sheriffs, prevosts ministers, and all his bailiffs and his lieges, greeting. Know ye, that we by the grace of God, and for the saving of our soul, and the souls of all our ancestors, and of our heirs, and for the honour of God, and the safety of holy church, and for the amendment of our government, by the advice of our honoured fathers, Stephen, archbishop of Canterbury, primate of all England, and cardinal of Rome; Henry, archbishop of Dublin, William, bishop of London, Peter, bishop of Worcester, William, bishop of Chester, Benedict, bishop of Rochester, and master Pandulph, sub-deacon of our Lord the apostle, and of our friend brother Anner, master of the order of knights templars in England; and by the advice of our barons, William, earl marshal earl of Pembroke, William, earl of Salisbury, William, earl of Warren, William, earl of Arundel, Alan of Galloway, constable of Scotland, Warin Fitz-Gerard, Peter Fitz-Herbert, Thomas Basset, Alan Basset, Philip d'Aubenie, Robert de Ropelee, John Marshal, and John Fitz-Hugh, and by the advice of other lieges:

Have in the first place granted to God, and confirmed by this our present charter, for us and for our heirs for ever, That the churches of England shall be free, and shall enjoy their rights and franchises entirely and fully: and this our purpose is, that it be observed, as may appear by our having granted, of our mere and free will, that elections should be free (which is reputed to be a very great and very necessary privilege of the churches of England) before the difference arose betwixt us and our barons, and by our having confirmed the same by our charter, and by our having procured it moreover to be confirmed by our lord the apostle Innocent the third. Which privilege we will maintain: and our will is, that the same be faithfully maintained by our heirs for ever.

III. We have also granted to all the freemen of our kingdom, for us and for our heirs for ever, all the liberties hereafter mentioned, to have and to hold to them and their heirs of us and our heirs. If any of our earls, our barons, or others that hold of us in chief by knight-service, die; and at the time of his death his heir be of full age, and relief be due, he shall have his inheritance by the antient relief; to wit, the heir or heirs of an earl, for an entire earldom, C. pounds; the heir or heirs of a baron, for an entire barony, C. marks; the heir or heirs of a knight, for a whole knight's fee, C. shillings at most: and where less is due, less shall be paid, according to the antient customs of the several tenures.

IV. If the heirs of any such be within and in ward, they shall have their inheritance when they come of age without relief, and without fine.

V. The guardians of the land of such heirs being within age, shall take nothing out of the land of the heirs, but only the reasonable profits, reasonable customs, and reasonable services, and that without making destruction or waste of men or goods.

VI. And if we shall have committed the custody of the land of any such heir to a sheriff, or any other who is to account to us for the profits of the land, and that such committee make destruction or waste, we will take of him amends, and the land shall be committed to two lawful and good men of that fee, who shall account for the profits to us, or to such as we shall appoint.

VII. And if we shall give or sell to any person, the custody of the lands of any such heir, and such donee or vendee make destruction or waste, he shall lose the custody, and it shall be committed to two lawful, sage, and good men, who shall account to us for the same, as aforesaid.

VIII.   And the guardian, whilst he has custody of the heir's land, shall maintain the houses, ponds, parks, pools, mills, and other appurtenances to the land, out of the profits of the land itself; and shall restore to the heir, when he shall be of full age, his land well stocked, with ploughs, barns, and the like, as it was when he received it, and as the profits will reasonably afford.

IX.   Heirs shall be married without disparagement; insomuch, that before the marriage be contracted, the persons that are next of kin to the heir, be made acquainted with it.

X.   A widow after the death of her husband, shall presently and without oppression, have her marriage and her inheritance; nor shall give anything for her marriage, nor for her dower, nor for her inheritance, which she and her husband were seized of the day of her husband's death; and she shall remain in her husband's house forty days after his death; within which time her dower shall be assigned her.

XI.   No widow shall be compelled to marry if she be desirous to live single, provided she give security not to marry without our leave, if she hold of us, or without the lord's leave of whom she holds, if she hold of any other.

XII.   We nor our bailiffs will not seize the lands or rent of a debtor for any debt so long as his goods are sufficient to pay the debt: nor shall the pledges be distrained upon whilst the principal debtor is able to pay the debt. But if the principal debtor have not wherewith to pay the debt, the pledges shall answer for it: and if they will, they shall have the lands and rents of the debtor till they have received the debt which they paid for him, if the principal debtor cannot shew that he is quit against his pledges.

XIII.   If any persons have borrowed money of Jews, more or less, and die before they have paid the debt, the debt shall not grow whilst the heir is under age; and if such debt become due to us, we will take no more than the goods expressed in deed.

XIV.   And if any die, and owe a debt to the Jews, his wife shall have her dower, and shall be charged with no part of the debt; and if the children of the deceased person be within age, their reasonable estovers shall be provided them, according to the value of the estate which their ancestor had; and the debt shall be paid out of the residue, saving the services due to the lord. In like manner shall it be done in cases of debts owing to other persons that are not Jews.

XV. We will impose escuage* nor aids within our realm, but by the common council of our realm, except for our ransom, and for the making our eldest son a knight, and for marrying our eldest daughter once: and for these purposes there shall but a reasonable aid be required.

XVI. In like manner shall it be done within the city of London: and moreover, the city of London shall have all her antient customs and liberties by land and water.

XVII. We will moreover and grant, that all other cities, and boroughs, and towns, and ports, have, in all respects, their liberties and free customs.

XVIII. And as for coming to the common council of the kingdom, and for assessing aids (except in the three cases aforesaid) and as for the assessing of escuage, we will cause to be summoned the archbishops, bishops, abbots, earls, and the greater barons, each in particular by our letters; and moreover, we will cause to be summoned in general, by our sheriffs, and bailiffs, all that hold of us in chief, at a certain day; to wit, forty days after at least, and at a certain place; and in our said letters we will express the cause of the summons. And when the summons shall be so made, business shall go on at the day assigned, by the advice of such as are present, though all that are summoned do not appear.

XIX. We will not allow for the future, that any take aid of his freemen, but only to ransom his person, to make his eldest son a knight, and to marry his eldest daughter once; and for these purposes there shall but a reasonable aid be given.

XX. None shall be distrained to do greater service for a knight's fee, or for any other frank-tenement than what is due by his tenure.

XXI. Common pleas shall not follow our court, but shall be held in a certain place.

XXII. Recognizances of novel *disseisin, mordancester,* and *darrein presentment,* shall be taken no where but in their proper counties, and in this manner: We, or our chief justice (if ourselves be out of the realm) will send two justices through every county four times a year; who, with four knights of every county, to be chosen by the county, shall take the said assizes in the county, at a day when the county-court is held, and in a certain place: and if the said assizes cannot be taken upon that day, so many knights and free tenants of them that were present in the county-court that day,

*Taxes for the helmet, or war.

shall stay, as may give a good judgment, according as the concern may be greater or less.

XXIII. A freeman shall not be amerced for a little offence, but according to the manner of his offence; and for a great offence he shall be amerced according to the greatness of his offence, saving his contenement; and so a merchant saving his merchandize; and a villain in like manner shall be amerced saving his wainage, if he fall into our mercy: and none of the said amercements shall be affeered, but by oath of good and lawful men of the vicinage.

XXIV. An earl and a baron shall not be amerced but by their peers, and according to the manner of their offence.

XXV. No clerk shall be amerced but according to his lay-fee, and in like manner as others aforesaid, and not according to the quantity of his churchliving.

XXVI. No ville nor any man shall be distrained to make bridges over rivers, but where they antiently have, and of right, ought to make them.

XXVII. No sheriffs, constables, coroners, nor other our bailiffs, shall hold the pleas of our crown.

XXVIII. All counties, hundreds, wapentakes and tithings, shall be at the antient farms without being raised, except our own demesne mannors.

XXIX. If any that holds of us a lay-fee die, and our sheriffs, or other our bailiffs shew our letters patents of summons for a debt which the deceased owed to us, our sheriff or bailiff may well attach and inventory the goods of the dead, which shall be found upon his lay-fee, to the value of the debt which the deceased owed to us, by the view of lawful men, yet so as nothing be removed till such time as the debt, which shall be found to be due to us, be paid; and the residue shall go to the executors to perform the testament of the dead: and if nothing be owing to us, all his goods shall go to the use of the dead, saving to his wife and children their reasonable parts.

XXX. If any freeman die intestate, his goods shall be divided by the hands of his near kindred and friends by the view of holy church, saving to every one their debts which the dead owed them.

XXXI. None of our constables, nor other our bailiffs shall take the corn, nor other the goods of any person without paying for the same presently, unless he have time given him by consent of the vendor.

XXXII. Our constables shall distrain no man who holds by knight-service, to give money for castle-guard, if he has performed it himself in proper person, or by another good man, if he could not perform it himself for some reasonable cause: and if we lead him, or send him into the army, he shall be discharged of castle-guard for so long time as he shall be with us in the army.

XXXIII. Our sheriffs, our bailiffs, or others, shall not take the horses nor carts of any freeman to make carriage, but by leave of such freeman.

XXXIV. Neither ourselves nor our bailiffs shall take another man's wood for our castles, or other occasions, but by his leave whose wood it is.

XXXV. We will hold the lands of such as shall be convicted of felony but a year and a day, and then we will restore them to the lords of the fees.

XXXVI. All wears shall, from this time forward, be wholly taken away in Thames and Medway, and throughout all England, except upon the seacost.

XXXVII. The writ called Precipe henceforth shall be made to none out of any tenement, whereby a freeman may lose his court.

XXXVIII. One measure of wine shall be used throughout our kingdom, and one measure of ale, and one measure of corn, to wit, the London quart. And there shall be one breadth of dyed cloths, russets, and haubergets, to wit, two ells within the lists: and concerning weights, it shall be in like manner as of measures.

XXXIX. Nothing shall be given or taken henceforth for a writ of inquisition of life or member, but it shall be granted freely and shall not be denied.

XL. If any hold of us by fee-farm, or by soccage, and hold likewise land of others by knight-service, we will not have the custody of the heir, nor of the land which is of the fee of another, by reason of such fee-farm, soccage, or burgage, unless such fee-farm owe knight-service.

XLI. We will not have the wardship of the heir, nor of the land of any person, which he holds of another by knight-service, by reason of any petit serjeantry by which he holds of us, as by the service of giving us arrows, knives, or such like.

XLII. No bailiff for the time to come shall put any man to his law upon his bare word, without good witnesses produced.

XLIII. No freeman shall be taken, nor imprisoned, nor disseized, nor out-lawed, nor exiled, nor destroyed in any manner; nor will we pass upon him, nor condemn him, but by the lawful judgment of his peers, or by the law of the land.

XLIV. We will sell to none, we will deny nor delay to none right and justice.

XLV. All merchants may, with safety and security, go out of England, and come into England, and stay, and pass through England by land and water, to buy and sell without any evil tolls, paying the antient and rightful duties, except in time of war; and then they that are of the country with whom we are at war, and are found here at the beginning of the war, shall be attached, but without injury to their bodies or goods, till it be known to us or to our chief-justice, how our merchants are entreated which are found in our enemies' country; and if our's be safe there, they shall be safe in our land.

XLVI. It shall be lawful for all men in time to come, to go out of our kingdom, and to return safely and securely by land and by water, saving their faith due to us, except it be in time of war for some short time for the profit of the realm. But out of this article are excepted persons in prison, persons out-lawed, according to the law of the land, and persons of the country with whom we are at war. Concerning merchants what is above-said shall hold as to them.

XLVII. If any hold of any escheat, as of the honour of Wallingford, Nottingham, Boloin, Lancaster, or of other escheats which are in our hand, and are baronies, and die, his heirs shall owe to us no other relief, nor do us any other service, than was due to the baron of such barony when it was in his hand; and we will hold the same in like manner as the baron held it.

XLVIII. Men that dwell out of the forest, shall not appear before our justices of the forest by common summons, unless they be in suit themselves, or bail for others who are attached for the forest.

XLIX. We will not make sheriffs, justices, nor bailiffs, but of such as know the law of the land, and will keep it.

L. All that have founded abbies, whereof they have charters from the Kings of England, or antient tenure, shall have the custody thereof whilst they are vacant, as they ought to have.

LI. All the forests that have been afforested in our time, shall instantly be disafforested; in like manner be it of rivers, that in our time and by us have been put in defence.

LII. All evil customs of forests and warrens, and of foresters and warreners, of sheriffs and their ministers, of rivers and of guarding them, shall forthwith be inquired of in every county by twelve knights sworn of the same county, who must be chosen by the good men of the same county. And within forty days after they have made such inquisition, the said evil customs shall be utterly abolished, by those same knights, so as never to be revived; provided they be first made known to us, or to our chief justice if we be out of the realm.

LIII. We will, forthwith, restore all the hostages, and all the deeds which have been delivered to us by the English, for surety of the peace, or of faithful service.

LIV. We will wholly put out of bailiffwicks, the kindred of Gerard de Aties, so that from henceforth they shall not have a bailiffwick in England; and Engeland de Cigoigni, Peron, Guyon, Andrew de Chanceas, Gyon de Cygoigni, Geffry de Martigni and his brothers, Philip, Mark and his brothers, Geffry his nephew, and all their train. And presently after the peace shall be performed, we will put out of the realm all knights, foreigners, singers, serjeants and soldiers, who came with horse or arms to the nuisance of the realm.

LV. If any be disseized or esloined by us, without lawful judgment of his peers, of lands, chattels, franchises, or of any right, we will, forthwith, restore the same; and if any difference arise upon it, it shall be determined by the judgment of the five and twenty barons, of whom mention is made hereafter in the security for the peace.

LVI. As to all things whereof any have been disseized, or esloined without lawful judgment of their peers, by King Henry our father, or by King Richard our brother, which we have in our hands, or which any other has, to whom we are bound to warrant the same, we will have respite to the common term of them that are crossed for the holy land, except such things for which suits are commenced, or inquest taken by our order before we took upon us the cross. And if we return from the pilgrimage, or perhaps forbear going, we will do full right therein. The same respite we will have, and the same right we will do in manner aforesaid, as to the disafforesting of forests, or letting them remain forests, which the Kings, Henry our father, or Richard our brother have afforested; and as to the custodies of lands which are of the fee of other persons, which we have held till now by reason of other men's fees, who held of us by knight-service; and of abbies that are founded in other men's fees, in which the lords of the fees claim a right, and when we shall be returned from our pilgrimage, or if we forbear going, we will immediately do full right to all that shall complain.

LVII. None shall be taken nor imprisoned upon the appeal of a woman, for the death of any other than her husband.

LVIII. All the fines and all the amercements that are imposed for our use, wrongfully and contrary to the law of the land, shall be pardoned; or else they shall be determined by the judgment of the five and twenty barons, of whom hereafter, or by the judgment of the greater number of them that shall be present, or before Stephen, archbishop of Canterbury, if he can be there, and those that he shall call to him; and if he cannot be present, matters shall proceed, notwithstanding, without him; so always, that if one or more of the said five and twenty barons be concerned in any such complaint, they shall not give judgment thereupon, but others chosen and sworn shall be put in their room to act in their stead, by the residue of the said five and twenty barons.

LIX. If we have disseized or esloined any Welchmen of land, franchises, or of other things, without lawful judgment of their peers, in England or in Wales, they shall, forthwith, be restored unto them; and if suits arise thereupon, right shall be done them in the Marches by the judgment of their peers; of English tenements according to the law of England, and of tenements in Wales according to the law of Wales; and tenements in the Marches according to the law of the Marches: and in like manner shall the Welch do to us and our subjects.

LX. As for all such things, whereof any Welchmen have been disseized or esloined, without lawful judgment of their peers, by King Henry our father, or by King Richard our brother, which we have in our hands, or which any others have, to whom we are bound to warrant the same, we will have respite till the common term be expired of all that crossed themselves for the Holy Land, those things excepted whereupon suits were commenced, or inquests taken by our order before we took upon us the cross; and when we shall return from our pilgrimage, or if, peradventure, we forbear going, we will presently cause full right to be done therein, according to the laws of Wales, and before the said parties.

LXI. We will forthwith restore the son of Lewelyn, and all the hostages of Wales, and the deeds that have been delivered to us for security of the peace.

LXII. We will deal with Alexander, King of Scotland, as to the restoring him his suitors and his hostages, his franchises and rights, as we do with our other barons of England, unless it ought to be otherwise by virtue of the charters which we have of his father William, late King of Scotland; and this to be by the judgment of his peers in our court.

LXIII. All these customs and franchises aforesaid, which we have granted to be kept in our kingdom, so far forth as we are concerned, towards our men, all persons of the kingdom, clerks and lay, must observe for their parts towards their men.

LXIV. And, whereas, we have granted all these things for God's sake, and for the amendment of our government, and for the better compromising the discord arisen betwixt us and our barons: we, willing that the same be firmly held and established for ever, do make and grant to our barons the security underwritten; to wit, That the barons shall chuse five and twenty barons of the Realm, whom they list, who shall, to their utmost power, keep and hold, and cause to be kept, the peace and liberties which we have granted and confirmed by this our present charter; insomuch, that if we, or our justice, or our bailiff, or any of our ministers, act contrary to the same in any thing, against any persons, or offend against any article of this peace and security, and such our miscarriage be shewn to four barons of the said five and twenty, those four barons shall come to us, or to our justice, if we be out of the realm, and shew us our miscarriage, and require us to amend the same without delay; and if we do not amend it, or if we be out of the realm, our justice do not amend it within forty days after the same is shewn to us, or to our justice if we be out of the realm, *then the said four barons shall report the same to the residue of the said five and twenty barons; and then those five and twenty barons, with the commonalty of England, may distress us by all the ways they can; to wit, by seizing on our castles, lands, and possessions, and by what other means they can, till it be amended, as they shall adjudge; saving our own person, the person of our Queen, and the persons of our children:* and when it is amended, they shall be subject to us as before. And whoever of the realms will, may swear, that for the performance of these things he will obey the commands of the said five and twenty barons, and that, together with them, he will distress us to his power: and we will give public and free leave to swear to all that will swear, and will never hinder any one: and for all persons of the realm, that of their own accord will swear to the said five and twenty barons to distress us, we will issue our precept, commanding them to swear as aforesaid.

LXV. And if any of the said five and twenty barons die, or go out of the realm, or be any way hindered from acting as aforesaid, the residue of the said five and twenty barons shall chuse another in his room, according to their discretion, who shall swear as the others do.

LXVI.   And as to all things which the said five and twenty barons are to do, if, peradventure, they be not all present, or cannot agree, or in case any of those that are summoned cannot or will not come, whatever shall be determined by the greater number of them that are present, shall be good and valid, as if all had been present.

LXVII.   And the said five and twenty barons shall swear, that they will faithfully observe all the matters aforesaid, and cause them to be observed to their power.

LXVIII.   And we will not obtain of any one for ourselves, or for any other, any thing whereby any of these concessions, or of these liberties may be revoked or annihilated; and if any such thing be obtained, it shall be null and void, nor shall ever be made use of by ourselves or any other.

LXIX.   And all ill-will, disdain, and rancour, which has been between us and our subjects of the clergy and laity since the said discord began, we do fully release and pardon to them all. And moreover, all trespasses that have been committed by occasion of the said discord since Easter, in the sixteenth of our reign, to the restoring of the peace, we have fully released to all clerks and laymen: and so far as in us lies we have fully pardoned them: And further, we have caused letters patent to be made to them in testimony hereof, witnessed by Stephen, archbishop of Canterbury, Henry, archbishop of Dublin, and by the aforesaid bishops, and by Mr. Pandulphus, upon this security and these concessions. Whereby, we will and strictly command, that the church of England be free, and enjoy all the said liberties, and rights, and grants, well and in peace, freely and quietly, fully and entirely to them and their heirs, in all things, in all places, and for ever as aforesaid. And we and our barons have sworn that all things above written, shall be kept on our parts, in good faith, without ill design. The witnesses are the persons above-named and many others.

LXX.   This charter was given at the meadow called Running-Mead, betwixt Windsor and Stanes, the fifteenth day of June, in the seventeenth year of our reign.

JOHN

5

It will be seen that the Great Charter went beyond that of Henry I in its specific mention of the rights of Englishmen. Consider Clause XLIII—the numbering was done later and will not be found in the original document—which says with a precision never before attempted that "no freeman shall be taken, nor imprisoned . . . but by the lawful judgment of his peers, or by the laws of the land." The parliamentary principle, which had been slowly and imperfectly evolved by the Anglo-Saxons, was affirmed in Clause XV, "We will impose no escuage" (generally called scutage, a helmet or war tax) "nor aids within our realm but *by the common council of our realm* . . ."

The rights of common men were dealt with in a more forthright manner than the brevity of Henry's Charter had made possible. Clause XVIII says: "A freeman shall not be amerced for a small offence . . . and none of the said amercements shall be affeered *but by oath of good and lawful men of the vicinage.*"

If Saire de Quincey was responsible for the form of the Charter, he deserves more credit than he has ever been given, and a permanent place among those who have contributed to the liberties of mankind.

When all is said and done, however, the greatest thing about the Great Charter is that it was won by force from a hostile king. When John set down his signature at the bottom of this historic document, he was recognizing the right of the people to make demands and to have a hand in drafting the laws under which they lived and worked and had their being. The clauses are in most respects an amplification of the old laws, but they grow in stature and significance because the laws are here reduced to concrete form and sworn to as a covenant between ruler and people.

CHAPTER XIX

Twilight of a Tyrant

JOHN had been unperturbed, seemingly, while the Charter was being drawn up. Once it had been signed, he returned to Windsor Castle, locked himself in his room, and allowed the mask to drop. He indulged in the most prolonged tantrum of a lifetime, rolling on the floor, foaming at the mouth, bleating curses on the barons collectively and individually. This fit was followed by a period of intense thought and of long discussion with Pandulfo.

On the morning of Friday, June 26, John rode away from Windsor, accompanied by the papal legate. They went to Winchester, where the King stayed long enough to send letters to his agents in various cities, Ghent, Caen, Bordeaux, Naples, Genoa. He wanted these purveyors of flesh and blood, who were paid so much for each man delivered, to get him mercenaries, particularly the stout young men from the Low Countries and the German states around the Palatinate. He would pay well; nay, he would give them rich lands and houses and he would even turn over to their leaders the castles of his subjects when the defeat of the barons had been accomplished. Pandulfo started for Rome to let the Pope know what had befallen in England. This much done, John went to the Isle of Wight and waited there for his plans to mature. His pride had been so affronted that he did not want to face his familiars and the courtiers and their wives until the score had been wiped off the slate.

Pandulfo had no difficulty in convincing Innocent that John should be supported in his struggle with the barons. He was a much misunderstood man, declared this oily and sinister go-between, a king who deserved, in reality, the affection of his subjects. The barons were concerned only with winning back their feudal power and, in resisting John, they were fighting against Holy Church. Thus Pandulfo. The Pope listened and was in complete accord with his agent.

Pope Innocent was a sick man, with only a few months to live. The crowning achievement of a lifetime devoted to the consolidation of the power of the Church had been the submission of John. It had been the first step, or so the Pontiff believed, toward the accomplishment of a great dream, the forming of a Christian empire of which the Pope would always be the head. Innocent conceived himself the temporal as well as the apostolic leader of the English state and saw the uprising of the barons as a repudiation of his authority. Under the circumstances he decided that prompt and sweeping steps were indicated. The hand which had hurled so many thunderbolts was raised again.

On August 24 Innocent issued a bull annulling the Charter. It was sharp in its condemnation of the national cause and ended with the words:

> We can no longer pass over in silence such audacious wickedness, in contempt of the apostolic see, in infringement of the rights of the king. . . . We altogether quash the Charter and pronounce it to be, with all its obligations and guarantees, null and void.

At the same time he promulgated another bull, ordering the barons to lay down their arms in pain of excommunication.

Pandulfo returned with these powerful weapons as Stephen Langton was starting for Rome in the hope of convincing the Pope of the righteousness of the popular cause. The archbishop refused to publish the papal bulls and the agent triumphantly produced another by which Stephen Langton himself was suspended from office for a term of two years. This made it very clear that the waters at Rome had been most thoroughly muddied and that the only hope left was to see the Pope and convince him he had acted on false information. Accordingly Langton boarded the ship which had been waiting for him and started on the two-month journey to Italy.

It was a logical step to take and yet, as events shaped themselves, it brought the cause of the people close to disaster. Langton was unable to make any impression on Innocent. While he kicked his heels in impotence in unfriendly anterooms, the barons in England, lacking his wise leadership, were soon at odds with each other. They permitted John to gain the upper hand in the civil war which ensued. That the King lost in the end was due to his capacity for making mistakes greater even than those for which Robert Fitz-Walter and his badly organized Army of God and Holy Church were responsible.

Langton was coldly received in Rome. His fellow cardinals turned their backs on him, and it was a long time before he was allowed an audience with the Pontiff. Innocent was harsh and accusatory with the man on whom he had once lavished his highest favors. The archbishop faced the torrent of censure with admirable calm and an unbending will to stand by the cause he had espoused and led. They parted in anger, and from that moment the papal doors were closed to the Englishman.

The situation came to a head amid a scene of great magnificence The Fourth Lateran Council, summoned by the Pope, marked the apex of apostolic power which had been achieved during his pontificate and which would never again be equaled. The heads of the Church attended from all parts of Christendom, from as far east as Antioch and as far west as Iceland, coming by ship when possible and laboring over mountain passes and rocky roads to reach the center of the world, the Eternal City. When this brilliant assembly opened, there were present all the cardinals and apostolic officers, 412 bishops, 800 heads of monastic orders, as well as innumerable priors and sub-priors, and representatives from every ruler in Europe. John had sent the abbot of Beaulieu, Thomas de Huntington, and Geoffrey de Crowcombe as his deputies, with very special instructions to look well after his interests. Never before had so many miters been seen at one time, and so many wise and kindly faces under them (and some that were harsh and dictatorial and simoniacal and nepotistic), nor such a combination of the rich vestments of the high churchmen with the simple brown and gray robes of the monkish heads.

Stephen Langton, under the disgrace of suspension, was not allowed to attend as a delegate. He sat among the spectators and, having human weaknesses as well as other men, suffered much distress of mind because of his exclusion. Letters that he wrote at the time to friends in England show how low he had fallen in spirit. He thought seriously of surrendering his high rank as cardinal and archbishop and joining the order of the Carthusians, one of the most rigid of all monastic orders. If he had joined the English Charterhouse at Witham, he would have spent the rest of his life in seclusion and contemplation, existing in poverty and in tattered garb, eating one meal a day and never tasting meat. The opportunity that eremitical life offered for writing no doubt appealed to the disillusioned primate. He was much in the street of the Saxons, where the faces of fellow countrymen were often seen. Here stood St. Mary's Church which a Saxon king had built.

He was present when the situation in England came up for action but was neither allowed to speak nor to introduce any explanation of what had happened. Crowded among the spectators at one side, he heard himself denounced as a troublemaker and the barons scored as disobedient vassals.

The assembled leaders of the Church had come to Rome with certain grave problems to solve, particularly the growth of heretical opinion. The creeds of the Cathari and the Waldenses were to be crushed, the crusade against the Albigenses in southern France to be strengthened, the first development within the Church of a form of inquisition to be declared. With all this on their hands they paid little attention to the trouble in the island over which the Pontiff had assumed suzerainty. They did not have the least inkling that something sublime had happened in England, that the spirit of liberty, after lying in chains through the long, icy centuries of the Dark Ages, had begun to stir. With unanimity they confirmed the suspension of Stephen Langton as Archbishop of Canterbury and voted into effect the excommunication of the barons who had not obeyed the Pope by laying down their arms.

Pope Innocent presided over this famous Council with the mark of death on his face and wasted figure. He was so ill that for many days he had not been able to eat any food but oranges, and it was doubted if his strength would carry him through. The exultation of this official climax to his supreme pontificate, however, enabled him to stand the fatigue. With glowing eyes he voiced his belief in the temporal superiority of the Church, in the words of the prophet, "Lo! I have set thee this day over the nations and over the kingdoms, to pluck up and to break down, and to destroy and to overthrow, to build and to plant." His thin face was transfigured as he thus expressed his faith, and the Council stirred as one man and gave him its fervent approval. It did not enter the heads of the great leaders of the Church that, in their willingness to march behind his blazing chariot, they had stamped on the one constructive movement for the benefit of downtrodden humanity which had been started in centuries.

They created additional monastic orders, they decreed a new crusade, they agreed to pay a tithe of their revenues for this final effort to redeem the Holy Sepulcher, they reformed marriage laws and the rules of pilgrimage and appointment procedure. All this was proof of the firm will for progress which had brought them together. It was perhaps the fault of the age in which they lived that they condemned Magna Charta without any serious consideration.

The excitement of the Lateran Council had been a heavy tax on the small store of strength left in the worn frame of the Pope. He survived the winter months, but when the heat of summer began, he found it necessary to seek some amelioration of his sufferings in the hills. He went first to Viterbo, then to Orvieto, and finally reached Perugia. Here word came to him that Louis of France had landed with an army in England. Perhaps he realized then that the ambitions of kings could not be curbed and bridled by apostolic decree and that the walls of power he had been raising were doomed to tumble as soon as his firm hand was withdrawn. He fell into a coma and died within a few days.

In the meantime the man who had been chiefly responsible for Magna Charta remained under suspension and could not leave Rome. He existed in the shadow of papal disapproval, compelled to watch developments in England from afar. He continued to fret in exile while the cause of liberty passed through many stages of serious crisis.

2

John threw off the mask as soon as his reinforcements began to pour into the country. He came out of his hiding place, roaring for revenge on the men who had humbled him. He struck first at Rochester, which William d'Aubigny, a descendant of beautiful Queen Adelicia, was holding for the barons. The routiers were nominally under the command of John, but the generalship of the siege was supplied by Savaric de Mauleon who, as has been made clear before, was as deft at composing a *chanson* as cracking a skull. The royal force was a rare collection of cutthroats, all of them boasting such names as Mauger the Murderer, Ivo the Ironhearted, and Dennis the Damned. Their work won for them collectively the title of Satan's Guards.

D'Aubigny held out bravely. He stayed the arm of an archer who was aiming at the King and who protested that he wanted to rid the country of "our bloody enemy." "Hold thy hand," said the commander. "Strike not this evil beast whose fate is in God's decision."

The garrison did not give in until the food had been consumed. John, more savage in victory than in defeat, would have hanged them all, starting with the fair Queen's descendant, but Savaric de Mauleon pointed out the folly of such a course. The war had but started and there were many more battles to be fought, some of which they might lose. If the garrison were hanged, the King's own mercenaries might expect the same fate in the event of a reverse. If the King wanted to keep them under his banners, he must not initiate a policy of mutual extermination. Grumblingly the King gave in.

The barons seemed incapable of organizing themselves again. The action of the Pope had been a serious blow to them and had resulted in many defections. The absence of Langton left them as rudderless as a ship adrift. They did nothing to stop the ramping, triumphant King when he swept England from the Channel to the borders of Scotland. John carried fire and sword with him and turned the green countryside into a blackened wilderness. It was his amiable habit to apply the torch himself each morning to the house where he had spent the night. This unbalanced ruler, who had earned the name of John Softsword when fighting the French, became a regular lion when he faced scattered levies. How bold he was, how sharp and vicious the sword he now wielded!

The barons, bold enough as individuals, were a futile lot in combination. Lacking leadership, they were unable to check the monarch they had humbled at Runnymede. The best they could think of doing in this crisis was to appeal to France for help! The request was made to Prince Louis because his wife, Blanche of Castile, was next in line to the English throne if John and his brood were thrown aside. As Louis was heir to the throne of France, the ultimate result of this step would have been the union of the two countries and the further subjugation of the English people. That the barons were able to contemplate and even favor such a result is an indication of the panic into which they had fallen.

This was late in 1215 and Pope Innocent was still alive. He thundered protests and threatened to place an interdict on France if the invitation of the barons was accepted. The young prince listened to his wife, who was urging him to support her pretensions to the throne of England, and refused to listen to the papal threats. King Philip, however, could not afford to antagonize Rome, and a council was called to debate the matter.

The papal legate, Gualo, was invited to attend and he protested against French interference in a country which was a fief of Rome. He made much of the fact that John had taken the cross, declaring that the English King would lead an army to the Holy Land as soon as the trouble with his barons had been settled.

Philip was a model of discretion all through the deliberations. Wearing a surcoat of the sky blue he seemed to prefer, and with his arms crossed on his gigantic chest, he chose his words with the utmost care, keeping a wary eye on the legate the while. He avowed himself a devout subject of His Holiness and unwilling to do anything hostile to Rome. At the same time, he said, his son had an undoubted claim to the English crown and his right to accept the invitation of the barons must be given due consideration.

As though this were a signal, various knights in the train of the prince took the floor in turn and argued that the murder of Arthur had disqualified John and that accordingly the throne of England was vacant. The prince followed with an impassioned speech in which he expressed himself as free in so far as England was concerned to make his own decision. It had already been made, it seemed, for the young man declared his intention of sailing against John with or without his father's permission. This brought Philip into the lists. Father and son had a heated dispute, at the end of which the prince turned and stalked from the council.

The proceedings smack of play-acting, as though the King had decided he must make a show of obeying the Pope while secretly in accord with his son. The chief actors in the farce had been so carefully coached, however, that the breach between father and son seemed real. For a very short time: almost immediately the masks were removed and the work of preparation for the invasion of England began.

Innocent knew he was being tricked. With the signs of death on his face and frail form, he preached in Rome from the text, "The sword, the sword is drawn!" He was bitter in his denunciation of France and equally critical of father and son. Stephen Langton sat in the church and listened to the words which condemned England to more civil war, realizing that the people would be the losers no matter which side won. Perhaps, being human, he felt some sardonic satisfaction at the situation in which the Pope found himself involved.

Louis proceeded to assemble a large army and to gather in the ports of northern France a fleet of nearly one thousand vessels to transport the troops across the Sleeve. Such preparation would not have been possible without the approval and co-operation of the King. The knights of France rallied to the cause, swearing the usual oaths—to abstain from cutting their hair or beards, from bathing, from the favors of women—until the conquest of England had been completed. Eustace the Monk was secured to command the naval operations, and this was a costly appointment. John had never been able to afford his services although he had tried on several occasions. Eustace was a monk turned pirate and a villain of such deep dye that he deserves to rank among the greatest freebooters of all time, with Barbarossa, no less, or with Avery, Morgan, and Madame Ching. The flag of France waved over the camps and fluttered at the mastheads of the ships. The period of play-acting was over.

When Louis landed on the Kentish coast, John retreated from his camp back of Dover. The French by-passed Dover, where stout Hubert de Burgh was in command, and marched up to London. Here many of the barons swore fealty to Louis. His wife rode through the streets as haughtily as though she were Queen already.

England was now in a sorry plight, for the contest offered no choice of sides to the people. They lost either way. The French prince made no effort to conceal the chains he held behind his back. Every castle taken by this worthy son of the grasping, insatiable Philip was promptly given to one of his own followers. He paid no attention to the barons on whose invitation he had come and was quite prepared to confiscate all their holdings. One of his followers, the Vicomte de Melune, confessed on his deathbed that Louis had sworn to drive into exile every man who had been at Runnymede as traitors to a king.

The difficulties of the situation had become painfully clear to Englishmen.

3

It was in mid-October. A wind was blowing from the north and driving the rack across the sky so briskly that the small, hurrying clouds changed shape each moment. Whenever this kind of weather came, people would look up and say, *The Abbot of Abbots is calling the Gray Monks home,* meaning that there would be a storm.

All day long John and his troops had been moving up from Weisbeck with the intention of crossing the sands where the Welland River, then known as the Willestrem, emptied into the Fossdyke Wash. The impatient King, in spite of his gout which made it necessary for him to ride with one leg in a sling, had stayed in the van, waving his followers on to greater efforts and cursing the snail's pace with which they responded. He had forgotten that an armed force can travel no faster than the slowest of its supply wagons. He had not only insisted on a long train of them for the conveyance of arms and provisions and, it was whispered, of his gold and treasure, but he had refused to allow the wagons to be separated from the main body.

As he had grown older the King had become more and more like his father in one respect. He could not stay still. He wanted always to be on the move, never remaining anywhere longer than one night. With his kingdom in danger, he was more restless than ever.

John had some of the qualities of generalship which he called upon when hard pressed. His position now was desperate and he had been attempting its betterment with bold strokes. The proper strategy of defense was to contain the French army within the small corner it held of the southeast. To do this he had broken his army into units and placed them in garrison along the line of the Thames, at Windsor, Wallingford, Oxford. His next objective was to break communications between the invaders and the strong counties of the north, where the opposition to him was most marked. He had daringly struck north of London, leaving the land behind him, as always, black and desolate. He had scored some successes, and now here he was, marching with a relatively small body of troops along the approaches to The Wash.

No matter how insistently the King might ride ahead, he never allowed himself to get out of sight of the lumbering vehicles. He cantered or galloped with his head cocked aslant so that he could keep them in view. Sometimes he waited for them to come up so he could ask questions of the drivers and demand increased vigilance of the rear guard. It was clear that he was uneasy and suspicious.

He had the best of reasons for his uneasiness. Being cautious as well as parsimonious, he had never believed it safe to leave his treasure in one place. His gold and precious jewels had been entrusted to the care of monasteries in different parts of the country. Late in June he had sent letters to sixteen bishops and abbots, instructing them to forward at once everything they had been holding for him. From Rufford and Bindon and Merton and Waltham had come well-guarded stores. The King had carried his treasure with him from that time on, even on his campaigns.

Although the royal regalia was legally supposed to be stored in the vaults at Winchester, John had preferred to keep the outward symbols of his kingship with him; and so, on this raw and windy day as he progressed slowly toward the crossing of The Wash, the crown and scepter and orb of England were concealed somewhere in that long tail of creaking wagons. Also there was the regalia which the Empress Matilda had smuggled out of Germany, including the crown she had worn and the sword of Tristan. It has been estimated from lists supplied by the monasteries that he had in addition a great accumulation of costly articles. There were cups of gold and white silver to the number of nearly two hundred, many of them richly jeweled. There were goblets and flagons and standing cups and mazers. There were rings, jeweled belts, pendants (one containing a pregnant stone, so called because there was a smaller stone inside it), and a seemingly endless assortment of gold crosses, clasps, thuribles (ornamented with towers and castles in the Gothic manner), bedewin stones, unset rubies and emeralds and sapphires.

It is not to be wondered at that his journeyings were a constant torment to the King and that he supervised personally the packing and unpacking of the canvas-covered wagons.

The tide had not started to rise perceptibly when they reached the sandy shallows where the river flowed into The Wash. John was convinced they could cross safely and he was the first to urge his horse into the water. He had decided to spend the night at Swineshead, a Cistercian monastery more than ten miles to the north, and nothing else would suit him. Accordingly he gestured impatiently for his men to follow him. The guards came first, splashing through the water and then galloping up the sands to the higher ground beyond. The rest of the troops crossed as briskly as they could, and it seemed certain that the whole train would get over before the tide imposed any serious barrier.

What the King did not know—and none of his advisers seemed aware of it either—was that the twice-a-day meeting of fresh and salt water sometimes became a struggle of homeric proportions. The pleasant bickering sound of the river would turn into a furious roar when it encountered the inward thrust of the sea. There would be threshing and tossing and angry whirling, converting the ford into a maelstrom.

It was almost as though the forces of heaven and earth watched, as they had done once before at the crossing of the Red Sea by the children of Israel, and waited for the exact moment to strike. Although the tide was on the rise, John shouted an order to the wagon train to come on. The drivers obeyed and the wheels began to grind their way into the wet sand. One by one the wagons entered the water, the horses urged on by loud shouts and the cracking of whips. Then, as they had done when the Egyptians pursued the fleeing Israelites, the waters came rushing in at the outstent line. The swirling flood rose to the hubs, then to the tops of the wheels. It was too late for the wagons to turn. Was it too late for them to get through?

The strong current of the river accepted the challenge of the sea and the jousting began. The King saw his wagons engulfed with a suddenness which seemed incredible. There were mad cries for help from the drivers and the shrill screeching of horses fighting to get free of harness. And then, in a matter almost of seconds, the whole train vanished from sight. Such a thing was impossible—and yet it had happened! The crown and the scepter of England and the regalia of Matilda had been lost to sight and washed away by the furious waters. The fabulous sword of Tristan, minus the splinter of steel which had been left in the skull of the giant Morôlt, would never be seen again.

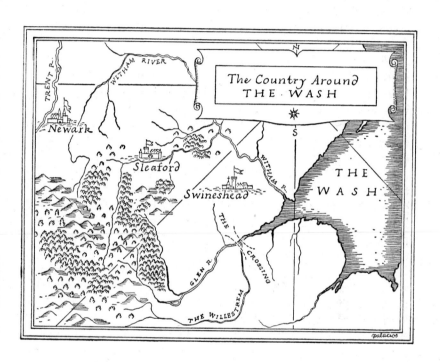

The Conquerors

The blow which nature had dealt him left the King speechless. This, he knew, was the end of everything. What use now the exactions of a lifetime, the endless taxes which had driven his subjects to rebellion, the theft of a brother's legacies, the pulling of teeth from helpless Jews! Every coin which had not been doled out painfully to Mauger the Murderer and Ivo the Ironhearted was gone, tossed about in wagons which would soon disintegrate and scatter the treasure on the bottom of the North Sea. He had no gold left now to pay his mercenaries. He was tired and ill. The uneven struggle could not be continued.

Turning his horse without a word, John rode up the grade to the northern road. In an unbroken silence he galloped to Swineshead. Here he was given a lukewarm welcome, for he was always at odds with the Cistercians over the sums he demanded from them, and proceeded to eat a heavy meal, ending with a dish of late peaches and a tankard of ale. He became ill almost immediately and loudly declared that the monks had poisoned him.

Later the story spread that one of the staff had put the blood of a toad in the ale and, being forced by the King to drink of it first, had gone out to the garden and died immediately, the whole region of his weasand becoming black and corrupt from the virulence of the poison. This was one of the wild stories which invariably grow out of tragedies in high places.

It is true, however, that the King called for a horse litter and went on that night, in a raging fever and acute pain, to Sleaford. It was raining the next morning, but he insisted on continuing the journey. At midday he was so weak that he almost fell from his saddle and had to finish the distance in a horse litter. He groaned and cried out with the pain but would not allow a stop to be made until they reached Newark and he was taken to the palace of the Bishop of Lincoln.

On the way from Sleaford the mind of the King had been constantly on his loss. He had moaned and ground his teeth and cursed the day he was born. But when they laid his sick bones on a bed in a tower from which there was a view of the Trent and of the country beyond, he subsided and had nothing more to say.

The King was dying. The abbot of Croxton, who was a wise man with herbs and bloodlettings, was brought to attend him. After one glance at the inert form and the livid cheeks, the abbot turned to the royal servants clustered in a silent group and shook his head. There was nothing to be done for John of England.

Nature took a most active part in the last hours of the wicked King's life. The storm promised by the scurrying Gray Monks had arrived the day before with flurries of wind and rain. Now it took the form af a gale, roaring down from the north and howling about the tower of the bishop's palace. Everyone knew that such winds were sent for one purpose, to carry off souls, and the servants hastily bolted shutters over the linen frames in the windows. This did no good, for nothing could keep out the sound or conceal the purpose of the blasts from the ears of the dying King. John accepted the inevitable with more resignation than he had ever been known to show, speaking occasionally in a low voice and eagerly welcoming the bishop, who administered the last rites. He dictated a statement which was all he left in the way of a will, the only important clause it contained being the appointment to the guardianship of his son and heir Henry of the only man he thoroughly trusted, William Marshal; a confidence which that stout veteran justified soon thereafter by the expedition with which he relieved England of the French threat.

4

When a king is dying, the world about him stands still. The lashing rain could not keep the curious people of the neighborhood from leaving the counter and bench and plow and gathering at the gates of the bishop's palace. They even wedged themselves into the courtyard and stood about in soggy discomfort, whispering among themselves and staring up at the lights in the tower windows, the wind blowing their horn-peaked caps into fantastic shapes. Respect for death is one of the deepest of instincts, and there was no tendency to decry the man who was passing or speak of his wickedness.

The castle was filled to overflowing. The knights who had arrived in the King's train remained in a body, a grim and uneasy lot. All of them knew the decision they faced, on which their possessions and perhaps their lives depended; whether to remain under the royal banner and fight for a nine-year-old boy or to go over to the other side and fight with the French invader. Each man eyed his neighbor suspiciously; they spoke seldom, and briefly; they watched the door behind which the King was dying, and waited.

There were the captains of mercenaries also, who were in a still sharper dilemma, for it was doubtful if any of them could hope to escape from England with whole skins. Every man's hand would be against Mauger and Ivo and Dennis as soon as the last breath left the body of the laboring King. They should have departed before this, but there was pay owing to them and they perhaps hoped the new King would have need of them. There were churchmen of all degrees, as wary and expectant as the men in arms. The policy of Innocent had chained them to the cause of John, but now the strong Pope was dead, and the future was a void into which even a powerful bishop could not gaze without uncertainty and dread. One thing was certain: this was a case where there would be no demand for *deodand;* unless they wanted to distrain on the waters of The Wash and the Willestrem and the sands of the Fossdyke. It would have been a profitless venture, for the only part of John's treasure which was ever recovered was a round and rusted article on which a peasant stumbled while bowel-deep in the water and later sold to a peddler for a farthing. It was of gold and shaped like a crown but so small that it had certainly never rested on the broad pate of John of England. More likely it was the top of a standing cup. Everything else was lost.

There were droves of men of lesser degree: spies from the northern reaches of Ermine Street (parts of which are now incorporated in the Great North Road) who had come to report on baronial strength and activities; contractors who had arrived in the expectation of selling sheep and beeves to the royal forces; clyster-pipes, as doctors were popularly called because of their method of affording bodily relief, all of them with miraculous cures which would bring recovery to the King and fame to them; and the usual mysterious individuals who refused to divulge anything about themselves. A self-seeking lot: it almost seemed as though every man in England who had reason for wishing John to live had found his way to the tall and glum castle of the Bishop of Lincoln.

None of them had any hope left. They paced about and muttered among themselves and pounced on every royal servant who emerged from the inner rooms. They listened apprehensively to the wind which seemed to be growing more violent. It was after the most demanding blast, which tore at the shutters and roared over the battlements, that the abbot of Croxton appeared in the doorway and made the sign of the cross.

The abbot embalmed the body and it was taken to Worcester. Here John was buried in accordance with his last instructions beside the bier of good St. Wulfstan, clothed in the white robe and red cross of a Crusader. John had had no illusions about himself. He knew how sinful he had been and he believed, as all men did, that the devil prowled about new-made graves for the souls he could claim as his own. The dead King wanted to be well disguised when the odor of brimstone filled his tomb and the long satanic fingers came prying at his winding sheet.

CHAPTER XX

A Nation Again

THE reign of John marks the end of the period during which the effects of the Conquest were felt. In view of the terrible sufferings of the people in the first stages, and the monstrous injustice of the land seizure, it may seem callous to assert that the destructive aspects of 1066 were outweighed by the benefits. Looking back over the centuries, however, it is easy to see that this was so.

In Anglo-Saxon days the land was torn by civil wars. The men of Northumbria were as foreign to the people of Mercia as those of Gaul or Spain. With the coming of the foreign kings, and their stern conceptions of law enforcement, the country drew together; in silence and suffering and under the iron hand of oppression, it is true, but with the corrective speed of the surgeon's knife. What might have taken centuries to accomplish was effected in a little more than one hundred years. Internal peace was a boon the Normans brought.

The towns benefited almost immediately from the Conquest. There had been a change of masters, and the native part of the population had a sense of racial inferiority imposed on them, but prosperity visited them at once. The ships of the world came to their ports, and the wool of England gave back higher standards of living. The Normans were commercial-minded. They were sharp dealers, acquisitive and shrewd. The power of the guilds developed rapidly from the time when Norman merchants and artisans were admitted to the ceremonies of the Craft-box and to a part in electing the portreeves and mayors. In a few generations a man's name meant little. He might carry the Norman patronymic of Fitz and still be three quarters Saxon in blood. What counted was that the towns were spreading out beyond their walls and their power growing so great that kings had to listen to them.

In the country the sufferings of the conquered people were deeper. The castles of the grasping barons, who had come over with steel in their hands and rapine in their hearts, overawed the land and put the stamp of slavery on the men who labored with plow and rake and hoe. In the Saxon days, however, the villein had worn the iron collar of the thrall and had seen his children stolen for the Irish slave trade. Again it was a change of masters, again the greatest suffering came from the sense of inferiority thrust upon them by the lords of the land. Class distinctions were more marked in the agricultural districts, and so the coming of racial unity was slower. But as early as the days of John the lines of demarcation were no longer sharp. The man with the longbow on his back looked the knight on his steel-accoutered horse squarely in the eye and did not hesitate to claim his rights.

The Normans, numerically inferior, had come to a land of settled customs and traditions. Inevitably they were drawn into the life of England. The country and the people remained Anglo-Saxon in spite of everything. The natives took the newcomers into their ways of living and thinking, to the worship of their saints. The proof of Norman absorption is found in the gradual mastery established by the English language, despised though it had been at the start. Historians have cited the fact that in the writings of the native Layamon, when "pen he took with finger and wrote a book-skin," there were few Norman words, although Layamon lived at the end of the twelfth century. Green estimates that he used no more than fifty words in thirty thousand lines. As time went on, of course, Norman terms and phrases were borrowed wholesale but to serve as additions and embellishments only to the noble tongue of the island.

The emergence of English as the sole language of general use was delayed by the tendency of men like Thomas à Becket, Nicholas Brakespeare, and Stephen Langton to go abroad in search of learning, to Paris in particular, and to come back with French and Latin on their lips. Even in the stormy days of the sons of Henry, however, a university was growing up around St. Frideswide's and St. Martin's at Oxford. In less than a century the teaching of eager and poverty-stricken youths in the porches of the churches and in the *hospitia* formed by groups was helping in the gradual establishment of the native tongue.

John's mistakes brought about the two great changes to which may be attributed the final unity of the land. The first was the loss of Normandy. Once the duchy which Rollo had conquered with his sea rovers had been incorporated back into the realm of France, the Normans in England ceased to be anything but Englishmen. This had been coming about gradually before. Few of the barons had continued to hold land along the Seine, the Epte, the Eure, or the Sarthe. The tendency to divide estates among sons on each side of the water had in a generation alienated the possessions in the duchy. English barons crossed the Channel to fight or to journey to the Holy Land, and for practically no other reason. Certainly there had been no visiting back and forth for a century. Navigation was a perilous and hit-and-miss affair, and too often a traveler would wait a month for a favorable wind. The wives and children of the Normans in England had not known their cousins across the Channel. The country along the Seine had become less than a memory.

To complete the division, news traveled slowly, and the echo of events on one side of the water was faint when it reached the other. Take a case in point. After John's death his widow returned to Angoulême, where her daughter Joan was being brought up as the future bride of the man she had jilted herself, Hugh the Brown of Lusignan. Isabella was in her early thirties and at the very peak of her dazzling beauty. Hugh saw her and declared fervently that she must be his bride and not the little Joan. Isabella was happy enough to make the change (probably she had it in mind in going over), they were married forthwith, and Joan Makepeace was sent back to England. Isabella had involved her new husband in trouble with the King of France by her plotting to create an English confederacy, and with his neighbors by her queenly ways, before the news reached England that the old romance had blossomed again.

Thus quickly the two divisions of the once extensive Angevin empire drew apart; and in that drawing apart a great nation was born.

The second change was Magna Charta, which gave back the

Saxon conceptions and laws. The Conquest had interrupted the development of the English idea of justice and the emergence of a workable parliamentary system. By his oppressive rule John brought the Norman part of the population to a realization of the need for the ancient checks and safeguards, for the personal liberties and privileges toward which the English had been working. Not until the Saxon conception had been carried forward so far and so vigorously by Magna Charta could the effects of the Conquest be considered at an end.

2

It is easy now to see that the defeat at Hastings was in the long run a great benefit for the English people. Generations of readers, identifying themselves with the gallant Saxons, have suffered with Harold in his death throes on the spur of Senlac, and with his lovely mistress, Edytha Swannes-hals (the Swan-necked) when she came at night to the battlefield, her fair hair wrapped in a black *couvre-chef* and a lantern in her hand, searching through the piles of dead for his body, and finding it at last, mangled almost beyond recognition, with the head and one leg severed from the trunk. Inevitably they had speculated on what the history of England would have been if right had triumphed at Hastings.

If Harold had won, the English people would have been spared a long period of suffering and oppression at the hands of cruel masters. But there would have been a great loss. The Anglo-Saxons had an instinct for self-government, a willingness to struggle on toward a distantly glimpsed goal. Left to themselves, would they have achieved in time all the objectives which have been reached? Perhaps: but it is impossible to avoid doubts. The Saxons had certain racial weaknesses which would have held them back in other respects. Could they have advanced to greatness in one direction while lagging in so many others?

They were a gross people, dull, sensual, inclined to a degree of drunkenness which the Normans called *a tirelarigot*. They were lacking in ambition, in dispatch, in commercial instincts. These lacks would have handicapped them, particularly as they lived in the racial privacy, amounting almost to a vacuum, which island existence supplies. It is futile to speculate on what the future of England would have been if the Norman invasion had been a failure. This much is certain, however: the city of London would never have been the capital of a great empire. Would the people have been happier in the semi-obscurity of insular life? Would they have achieved sufficient strength to maintain their independence through centuries of pressure from without?

As it fell out, the Normans possessed the qualities lacking in the Anglo-Saxon. They had drive, an instinct for mastery, a never idle ambition. Without the Saxon instinct for political progress, they were as incomplete in their way as the English were in other directions. The mingling of Saxon and Norman blood produced a great race.

If Harold had not lost on the ridge of Senlac, there would never have been the opportunities which sent Drake around the world and Wolfe to the Plains of Abraham. If the smoldering Tostig had not been willing to betray his country to avenge himself on his brother, there would not have been a race of shopkeepers which could lead the world at the same time in political and scientific advance and produce a glittering roster of great names—Roger Bacon, Francis Bacon, Wycliff, Shakespeare, Cromwell, Darwin, Winston Churchill. If the men who died on the ridge had been allowed a glimpse into the mists of the future and had seen great continents reclaimed, an empire built around their little island, the path of freedom won, they might have counted their lives well lost.

Selected Bibliography

So much reading was required in the preparation of this book that a complete list of sources consulted would be unnecessarily long. The books listed have been most useful.

HISTORY

Barnard, F. P. *Strongbow's Conquest of Ireland.*
Belloc, Hilaire. *A History of England.*
Berington, J. *The History of the Reign of Henry II and of Richard and John, His Sons.*
Creasy, Sir Edward S. *History of England from the Earliest Times.*
Davis, H. W. C. *England under the Normans and Angevins.*
Dixon, Hepworth. *Her Majesty's Tower.*
——. *Royal Windsor.*
Eadmer. *Historia Novorum.*
Favyn, André. *Histoire de Navarre.*
Freeman, Edward Augustus. *The Growth of the English Constitution from Earliest Times.*
——. *The History of the Norman Conquest.*
Giles, Rev. J. A. *Mathew Paris' English History.*
Giraldus, Cambrensis. *Expugnatio Hibernica.*
Green, John Richard. *Short History of the English People.*
Hallam, Henry. *View of the State of Europe during the Middle Ages.*
Hayward, Sir John. *The Lives of the Three Norman Kings of England.*
Hume, David. *History of England.*
Jennings, George Henry. *Anecdotal History of the British Parliament.*
Knight, Charles. *The Popular History of England.*
Lagrèze, Gustave Bascle de. *La Navarre Française.*
Map, Walter. *Les Romans de la Table Ronde.*
Maurois, André. *The Miracle of England.*

[403]

Bibliography

Oman, Sir Charles W. C. *The Dark Ages.*

Poole, Austin Lane. *England and Burgundy in the Last Decade of the Twelfth Century.*

Rule, Martin. *On Eadmer's Elaboration of the First Four Books of the Historia Novorum.*

Smith, Goldwin. *The United Kingdom.*

Thierry, Augustin. *The Conquest of England by the Normans.*

Turner, Sharon. *History of England through the Middle Ages.*

Wilkinson, Kosmo. *The Personal History of the Upper House.*

William of Malmesbury. *Chronicle of the Kings of England.*

Yonge, Charlotte Mary. *Cameos from English History.*

HISTORIES OF SINGLE REIGNS

D'Auvergne, E. B. F. *John, King of England.*

Freeman, Edward Augustus. *William the Conqueror.*

————. *The Reign of William Rufus.*

Green, Mrs. J. R. *Henry the Second.*

James, G. P. R. *History of the Life of Richard Coeur de Lion.*

Lyttleton, George (Baron). *The History of the Life of King Henry the Second and the Age in Which He Lived.*

Norgate, Kate. *John Lackland.*

————. *Richard the Lion Heart.*

Salzman, Louis Francis. *Henry II.*

Wilkinson, C. A. *Coeur de Lion.*

BIOGRAPHY

Almedingen, M. E. *The English Pope.*

Biegy, Katherine. *A Medieval Worldling, Eleanor of Aquitaine.*

Brabrook, Sir Edward. *Robin Hood.*

Browning, Charles Henry. *Magna Charta Barons and Their Descendants.*

Burke, Mary Francis. *The Queen of the Troubadours.*

Casartelli, L. C. *The English Pope.*

Campbell, John Lord. *Lives of the Lord Chancellors.*

Chayter, Henry John. *Savaric de Mauléon.*

Clark, George Thomas. *The Earls, Earldom and Castle of Pembroke.*

Clayton, Joseph. *Pope Innocent III and His Times.*

Coulton, G. G. *Two Saints.*

Dark, Sidney. *St. Thomas of Canterbury.*

Froude, James Anthony. *Life and Times of Thomas Becket.*

Gutch, J. M. *On the Veritable Existence of Robin Hood.*

Hook, Walter Farquar. *Lives of the Archbishops of Canterbury.*

Hutton, William Holden. *St. Thomas of Canterbury.*

Jarman, Thomas Leckie. *William Marshal.*

Jones, W. Lewis. *Walter Map.*

Kingsley, Charles. *Hereward the Wake.*

[404]

Bibliography

Mann, Horace K. *Nicholas Breakspear.*
Maurice, C. E. *Stephen Langton.*
Perrier, Joseph Louis. *Bertran de Born, Patriot, and His Place in Dante's Inferno.*
Pirie-Gordon, C. H. C. *Innocent the Great.*
Planche, J. R. *The Conqueror and His Companions.*
Robertson, James Craigie. *Becket, Archbishop of Canterbury.*
Rosenberg, M. V. *Eleanor of Aquitaine.*
Strickland, Agnes. *Lives of the Queens of England.*

Life and Customs

Armitage, Ella S. *The Early Norman Halls of the British Isles.*
Barfield, T. C. *England in the Middle Ages.*
Bennett, H. S. *Life on the English Manor.*
Coulton, G. C. *Medieval Panorama.*
Eyton, Robert William. *Court, Household and Itinerary of King Henry I.*
Fryar, John R. *Old English Burial Customs.*
Hall, H. *Court Life under the Plantagenets.*
Holliday, Carl. *Wedding Customs, Then and Now.*
Hope, W. H. St. John. *English Fortresses and Castles.*
Hunt, Thomas P. *The Wedding Days of Former Times.*
Oman, Sir Charles W. C. *Castles.*
Round, J. H. *The Castles of the Conquest.*
Stuart, D. M. *Men and Women of Plantagenet England.*
Wright, Thomas. *Domestic Manners and Sentiments in England during the Middle Ages.*

Geography

Belloc, Hilaire. *The Historic Thames.*
Besant, Sir Walter. *Early London.*
Bowles, William Lisle. *Annals and Antiquities of Lacock Abbey.*
Brent, John. *Canterbury in the Olden Time.*
Cook, T. A. *The Story of Rouen.*
Cornish, Charles John. *The New Forest.*
Cox, J. Charles. *Canterbury.*
Deville, Achille. *Histoire du Château-Gaillard.*
Dodd, Mrs. Anna. *Falaise, the Town of the Conqueror.*
Evans, Christopher J. *Breconshire.*
Hare, A. F. C. *Walks in London.*
Harries, William Tyndale. *Landmarks in Liverpool History.*
Holbach, Maude M. *In the Footsteps of Richard Coeur de Lion.*
Irvine, H. Douglas. *History of London.*
Lamb, Charles. *The Story of Liverpool.*
Pépin, Eugène. *Chinon.*
Raine, James. *York.*

[405]

Bibliography

Ries, W. *The Medieval Lordship of Brecon.*
Stanley, Arthur Penrhyn. *Historical Memorials of Canterbury.*
——. *Historical Memorials of Westminster Abbey.*
Wise, John Richard de Capel. *The New Forest.*

RELIGION

Adam, G. B. *Pope Innocent III and the Great Charter.*
Bargent, F. J. *On the Martyrdom of St. Thomas of Canterbury.*
Butler, C. C. *Monasticism.*
Capgrave, John. *Lives of St. Augustine and St. Gilbert.*
Cook, G. H. *Medieval Chantries and Chantry Chapels.*
Cooke, Alice M. *A Study in Twelfth Century Religious Revival and Reform.*
Coulton, G. G. *Five Centuries of Religion.*
Cranage, D. H. S. *The Home of the Monk.*
Gavin, Antonio. *A Short History of Monastical Orders.*
Graham, R. S. *Gilbert of Sempringham and the Gilbertines.*
Holland, Cornelius. *The Old English Chantry.*
Knowles, David. *The Monastic Order in England.*
Krehbiel, E. B. *The Interdict.*
Micklethwaite, J. T. *The Cistercian Order.*
Spence-Jones, H. D. M. *Cloister Life in the Days of Coeur de Lion.*
Williams, Watkin Wynn. *Monastic Studies*

THE THIRD CRUSADE

Ambroise. *The Crusade of Richard Coeur de Lion.*
Lamb, Harold. *The Crusades.*
Richard of Devizes. *In Chronicles of the Crusades.*
Vinsauf, Geoffrey de. *Richard Coeur de Lion and the Third Crusade.*

COSTUME

Brooks, Iris and Laver, James. *English Costume.*
Calthrop, Dion Clayton. *English Costume.*
Davenport, Milla. *The Book of Costume.*
Fairholt, F. W. *Costume in England.*
Hill, Georgiana. *A History of English Dress from the Saxon Period to the Present Day.*
Hodgetts, T. F. *The English in the Middle Ages.*
Martin, Charles. *The Civil Costume of England from the Conquest to the Present Day.*
Schild, Marie. *Old English Costumes.*
Smith, C. H. *The Ancient Costume of Great Britain and Ireland.*
Strutt, Joseph. *A Complete View of the Dress and Habits of the People of England.*
——. *The Regal and Ecclesiastical Antiquities of England.*

Bibliography

GENERAL INFORMATION

Ascham, Roger. *Toxophitus.*
Bell, Robert. *Ancient Poems, Ballads, and Songs of the Peasantry of England.*
Belloc, Hilaire. *The Eye-Witness.*
Birch, Walter de Gray. *Domesday Book.*
———. *Notes on the Will of King John.*
Brooke, Z. N. *The Register of Master David of London and the Part He Played in the Becket Crisis.*
Brown, Paul Alonzo. *The Development of the Legend of Thomas Becket.*
Chappell, William. *Popular Music of the Olden Times.*
Coulton, G. G. *Ten Medieval Studies.*
David, Charles Wendell. *The Claim of Henry I to Be Called Learned.*
Ellis, Henry. *A General Introduction to Domesday Book.*
Evans, Sir John. *The Origins of Pounds, Shillings and Pence.*
Farrer, W. *An Outline Itinerary of King Henry the First.*
Ford, Horace A. *Archery.*
Froude, James Anthony. *Short Studies on Great Subjects.*
Halliwell, J. O. *Account of the Death of King John.*
———. *On the Era and Character of Robin Hood.*
Hargrove, Ely. *Anecdotes of Archery.*
Jenkinson, A. V. *The Jewels Lost in the Wash.*
Johnson, Samuel. *A History and Defence of Magna Charta.*
Lamprey, H. *The Story of Weaving.*
Landon, Lionel. *The Itinerary of King Richard I.*
Lethbridge, T. C. *Merlin's Island.*
Lewis, E. *The Romance of Textiles.*
Oman, Sir Charles W. C. *A History of the Art of War.*
———. *The Coinage of England.*
Parker, F. H. M. *The Forest Laws.*
Pauli, Reinhold. *Pictures of Old England.*
Percy, Thomas. *Reliques of Ancient English Poetry.*
Powicke, F. M. *King John and Arthur of Brittany.*
Roberts, Thomas. *An Inquiry and Investigation into Such Extraordinary Feats as Are Said to Have Been Achieved with the English Longbow in Former Times.*
Round, J. H. *Feudal England.*
Russell, J. C. *Attestation of Charters in the Reign of John*
Spurrell, F. *Notes on the Death of King John.*
Thomson, Richard. *Magna Charta of King John.*

Index

Index

of; marriage to King John of England, 312–14, *see also* Isabella of Angoulême

Anjou, attempt of France toward, 309–10; Fulk, Count of, 66; Geoffrey, called Plantagenet, Count of, 69, 74–77, 79, 91, 93; Henry, the Young King, given lordship by Henry II, 156; retained in Angevin Empire, 93

Annals of the Four Masters, quoted, 186

Anselm, Archbishop of Canterbury, 32–34, 45–48, 57, 59

Aquitaine, commerce with, 110; Eleanor of, *see* Eleanor of Aquitaine; extent of, 112; Richard (I) given lordship by Henry II, 156; under suzerainty of England, 191; William, Duke of, 112–13

Arabian resistance in Third Crusade, *see* Saladin

Archas Martin, captain under King John of England, 334

Archery, in Battle of Hastings, 12; English skill at, 249, 251–55

Architecture of London in reign of Henry II, 107

Argenteuil, France, Henry II at, 175

Army of God and Holy Church, barons in time of King John, 366, 384

Arnold of Brescia, 125–26, 127

Arsouf, Palestine, battle during Third Crusade at, 270–71

Arthur, the Pendragon, legend of, 306–7

Arthur of Brittany, 303–10, 314–23

Arthurian legend, 306–7

"Articles of the Barons, The," sent to King John of England, 360

Arundel, William d'Aubigny, first Earl of, 80–81, 92

Arundel Castle, 80–81

Ascalon, Palestine, in Third Crusade, 271

Assassins from Lebanon Mountains, 273–75

Assisi, St. Francis of, 142–43

Aubigny, William d', in war against King John, 386–87; William d', Earl of Arundel, 80–81, 92

Aumale, Count of, 121

Avalon, in Arthurian legend, 306

Avisa of Gloucester, wife of (1) King John of England and (2) Geoffrey of Mandeville, 278, 313–14, 364

Avranches, France, captured by army of Brittany, 334

Aylward, eyesight restored by St. Thomas, 170–71

Badger's Wood, 251

Baldwin, Archbishop of Canterbury, 218, 231, 236, 263–64

Baldwin, Count of Flanders, 14

Baldwin, King of Jerusalem, 72

Baldwin, son of Stephen of Blois, 72, 76

Baldwin, tailor of London, 45

Ballads of forest outlaws, 252

Barham Down, military camp for defense against French invasion at, 350

Barons, acquisition of property by, 17–20; Innocent III, opposition of, 382–86; and Magna Charta, 357–61, 366–70; opposition to King John, 321, 342–43, 365–66; power during reign of Stephen of Blois, 90–91, 94; powers reduced by Henry II, 102–3, 106, 199–200; war with King John, 363, 384

"Barons, The Articles of the," sent to King John of England, 360

Bartholomew de Chesney, lord of Addington, 119

Baruch, Jew of York, 231

Bath, Bishop of, at coronation of Richard I, 230

Bathrooms, in time of Henry I, 49–50

Battle dress of Saxons, 1

Battle weapons of Saxons, 12

Battles: Hastings, in Norman invasion, 10–12; Stamfordshire, in Norse invasion, 7–9; of the Standards, in Scottish invasion, 80; Tegas, Ireland,

Index

in English invasion, 190; Tenchebrai, disciplinary campaign of Henry I against Normandy, 65–66
Bayeux, France, captured by Philip II, 334
Bayeux tapestry, 52
Baynard Castle, 363
Beauchamp Tower, of Tower of London, 110
Beaulieu, Thomas de Huntington, abbot of, 384
Beaumont, Robert de, Earl of Leicester, 153, 178
Beauvais, Bishop of, in war against Richard I, 294–95
Bec abbey, France, 32
Becket, Agnes, 177
Becket, Gilbert, 101, 107, 129
Becket, Mary, 177
Becket, Thomas, see Thomas à Becket
Bedford, miracle at, 170–71
Beds, in time of Henry I, 49
Belfry Tower, of Tower of London, 110
Bellême, Robert de, 63
Benedict, chronicle of, cited, 190
Benedict, Brother, monk of Canterbury, 168–69
Benedictines, Black, monastic order of, 138
Benet the Steward, of London, 45
Berengaria of Navarre, wife of Richard I, 230, 256–98
Bermondsey, palace at, 110
Bernard of Bayonne, Bishop, 261
Bernard of Clairvaux, St., 114, 139
Bertran de Born, minstrel of Limousin, 197, 212–16
Bethany, Palestine, in Third Crusade, 272
Bigod, Hugh, Earl of Norfolk, 368
Black Prince, 173–74
Blanche of Castile, wife of Louis VIII of France, 310–11, 387
Blanche of Navarre, 297
Blanche Nef, La, ship, 66–67
Blewitt, Sir Ralph, 204

Blondel de Nesle, troubadour, 279
Bloody Christmas, 64–65
Bloody Tower, of Tower of London, 110
Bohemund, Prince of Antioch, 278
Bohun, Humphrey de, constable at coronation of Henry II, 119, 121
Bohun, Henry de, at signing of Magna Charta, 368
Bonmoulins, France, meeting of Henry II and Philip II at, 219
Bordeaux, Archbishop of, marriage of King John of England annulled by, 313
Boulogne, Count of, 198
Boulogne, Duchess of, on Second Crusade, 114
Boulogne, Earl of, consulted on capitulation of King John to Rome, 352
Boulogne, Eustace, Earl of (grandfather), 72
Boulogne, Eustace, Earl of (grandson), 86
Boulogne, Matilda of, wife of King Stephen of England, 72–73, 79, 82, 85–87, 89, 91
Boulogne, Reginald of, coalition with King John against Philip II of France, 359
Bouvines, France, defeat of Otto of Germany and Reginald of Boulogne by Philip II at, 359
Bovate, measure of land, 19
Brabant, Fair Maid of, see Adelicia, wife of Henry I of England
Brackley, meeting of barons at, 360
Bradwardine Castle, 320
Brakespeare, Nicholas, see Adrian IV, Pope
Bramber, William de Braose, lord of, 319–22
Bramber Castle, 322
Brecon Castle, 320, 322
Brehon Code, of Ireland, 181, 186
Breteuil, William de, 42
Bricstab of Chatteris, 58

[411]

Index

Brihtric Meau, son of Alfgar, lord of the honor of Gloucester, 14–15, 16

Brindisi, Italy, Eleanor of Aquitaine at, 259

Bristol, Stephen of Blois held prisoner at, 84–89

Brittany, in Angevin Empire, 123, 156, 191; Arthur and the English succession, 307–10, 314–23; attempt of France toward, 309–10; racial stock and legend of, 305–7; revenge against England, 334

Broad Arrow Tower, of Tower of London, 110

Brockenhurst, death of William Rufus at, 40–41

Bulls, papal, *see* Papal bulls

Bur Castle, Bayeux, France, 159

Burgos, Spain, marriage of Louis VIII of France and Blanche of Castile at, 311

Burgundy, Duke of, at Third Crusade, 264–72

Bytham awarded to Norman baron, 18

Cade, William, moneylender, 102, 109–10

Caen, France, captured by Philip II, 334; tomb of Queen Matilda at, 15–16

Caesar's Tower converted to Tower of London, 19–20

Calaroga, Castile, birth of St. Dominic in, 142

Canonical courts, 146–50

Cantarist, post of, 141

Canterbury, Archbishops of: Anselm, 32–34, 45–48, 57, 59; Baldwin, 218, 231, 236, 263–64; Hubert Walter, 264, 280–81, 283–94, 305, 336; Lanfranc, 32; Richard, 142; Stephen Langton, 336–89; Theobold, 92, 100–1, 121, 129–30, 135; Thomas à Becket, 135–74

Canterbury, Archbishop's palace, after exile of Thomas à Becket, 158

Canterbury Cathedral, library of, 142; miracles after death of Thomas à Becket, 168–72; monks expelled by King John, 342; murder of Thomas à Becket in, 160–68; new edifice, 172

Canterbury pilgrims, 172

Canute, King of England and Denmark, 2

Carmel, Mount, Palestine, in Third Crusade, 261, 268–70

Carthusians, monastic order of, 138: English Charterhouse at Witham, 385

Castile, Blanche of, marriage to Louis VIII, 310–11

Castles of England: Alnwick, 362; Arundel, 80–81; Baynard, 363; Bradwardine, 320; Bramber, 322; Brecon, 320, 322; built during reign of Stephen of Blois, 94; Corfe, Isle of Purbeck, 316; demolished by Henry II under Treaty of Wallingford, 103; description of, 48–50; Dover, 243; erection of, 19–20; Gloucester, 83–84; Haverford, 327; Hay, 320, 322; Heningham, 91; Knaresborough, 160; Lewhaden, 327; Martin, 327; Narberth, 327; Northampton, 150–53; Nottingham, 286; Oxford, 89; Pembroke, 327; Radnor, 320, 322; Saltwood, 161–62; Stackpole, 327; Tenby, 327; Tickhill, 239; Windsor, 50–51

Castles of France: Angi, 15; Bur, Bayeux, 159; Chaluz, 297; Château Gaillard, 295–96, 330–34 (picture, 331); Chinon, 93, 196, 221–24; Falaise, 316–17; Hauteford, 213–14; Loudon, 93; Mirabeau, 93, 315–16; Vaudreuil, 324

Cathari, sect of, 385

Celestine III, Pope, 337

Celtic race and legend of, 305–7

Cenwalch, King of the West Saxons, 68

Chaluz Castle, France, death of Richard Coeur de Lion at, 297

Champagne, Eudes de, property awarded to, 18

Index

Chancellor, office of, 63; under Thomas à Becket, 102, 130–31

Chancellors of England: Geoffrey, natural son of Henry II, 204, 220–25, 229, *see also* Geoffrey of York; Hubert Walter, 283–87, 336; Roger le Poer, 74; Thomas à Becket, 101–2, 130–44; William de Longchamp, 233–45, 287

Chantry, custom of, 141

Charter, Great, *see* Magna Charta; of Henry I, 54–58

Charter Island, 366–70

Château Gaillard, 295–96 (picture, 331); siege of, 330–34

Château Martel, France, death of Henry, the Young King, at, 212

Chester, Hugues-de-Loup, Earl of, 19; Randulph, Earl of, 82, 119; Ranulf, Earl of, 307–9; Richard, Earl of, 66

Chinon Castle, France, 93, 196, 221–24

Chivalry, Code of, 53–54, 227, 333–34

Christina, sister of Edgar the Atheling, 44–48

Church in England, claims of losses after interdict, 355–56; in early Middle Ages, 137–43, 344–46; excommunication of English subjects serving King John, 349; excommunication of King John, 348; laxities under William Rufus and Henry I, 59–60; laying of interdict by Pope Innocent III, 343–56; resistance to royal power, 33–34, 142, 145–53, 177, *see also* Magna Charta; *see also* Stephen Langton; Thomas à Becket

Church in Ireland, 181

Church of Rome, Fourth Lateran Council, 384–86; under Adrian IV, 124–28; under Innocent III, 298, 337–86, 388–89; *see also* Papal bulls; Popes

Churches of England: All Hallows Barking, 110; Canterbury Cathedral, 142, 160–74; parish churches of London, 108; St. David's Cathedral,

Wales, 138; St. Martin's-in-the-Lane, 140; St. Martin's le Grand, 110; St. Mary le Bow, 292–93; St. Paul's Cathedral, 110; St. Stephen's, Northampton, 151; Temple, the, London, 352; village churches, 247; Westminster, 4; Winchester Cathedral, 354; Worcester Cathedral, 121

Cistercians, monastic order of, 138–39, 154–55

Cîteaux, France, parent Cistercian house at, 138

Civil war, between King John and barons, 361, 384–96; between Stephen of Blois and Empress Matilda, 80–92

Clarendon, Constitutions of, 148–50, 154, 177

Clement III, Pope, 241, 340

Clerambault, abbot of, St. Augustine's Monastery, 146, 162

Cleres, Mathew de, 235, 241

Clifford, Walter, 202

Cloth, manufacture in London of, 108–9

Clym o' the Clough, forest outlaw, 251–53

Coins, from Henry II to Henry VII, 103–5; *see also* Money

Colchester granted to Eudes the sewer, 52

Colnbrook, lands given to monks of Abingdon, 58

Colombières, France, meeting of Henry II and Philip II at, 221–24

Commerce in reign of Henry II, 110

Confiscation of property by William the Conqueror, 17–18

Connaught, Roderick, King of, 182, 184–85

Conrad of Montferrat, 262–64, 274–75

Constance, Princess, of France, wife of Eustace, son of Stephen of Blois, 82

Constance of Brittany, wife of (1) Geoffrey, son of Henry II, and (2) Ranulf, Earl of Chester, 123, 191, 303, 307–10

[413]

Index

Index

Dress, *see* Costume

Dublin, as headquarters for Henry II, 188; sack of, 185, 186

Duke's Money, coins issued by Henry II, 103

Dunstan, St., at Glastonbury abbey, 23

Durham, Hugh de Puiset, Bishop of, 230, 233–39; Ralph Flambard, Bishop of, 34–39

Earl, meaning of title, 91

Eccles Hoard of old English pennies, 105

Edgar the Atheling, 17, 43–44

Edmer, author of *Historia Novorum*, 46

Edward, brother of Hugues-de-Loup, 19

Edward II, King of England, rebellion against, 253

Edward the Confessor, King of England: accession of, 2; reputation of saintliness, 2–3; successor named by, 3–4

Edwin, earl of the north, at Norman invasion, 6

Edytha, daughter of King Malcolm of Scotland, *see* Matilda, wife of Henry I of England

Edytha, wife of Edward the Confessor, 3

Edytha Swannes-hals, 401

Eedburg, Germany, capture of Richard Coeur de Lion at, 277

Ela, wife of William Longsword, 350–51

Eleanor, wife of King of Castile, 123

Eleanor of Aquitaine, wife of (1) Louis VII of France and (2) Henry II of England, 96–124, 178, 191–335: coronation as Queen of England, 118–21; divorce from Louis VII, 116; imprisonment of, 199–200, 206–8, 227–28; marriage to Louis VII, 113–16; rebellion against Henry II, 194–99; as regent under Richard I, 227–28, 240–41, 258–59, 277–81; as ruler of Aquitaine, 209–10, 310;

on Second Crusade, 114–15; support of son John in contest for throne, 304–5, 310–11, 315

Election, first mayor of London chosen by popular, 369

Elias de Braintefield, canon of St. Augustine, 342

Ely, Bishops of: Eustace, 342–43, 360; Nigel, 100; William de Longchamp, 233

Ely, Isle of, resistance to Normans, 21–23

Emma, wife of (1) Ethelred II of England and (2) Canute of England and Denmark, 2

Engelard de Cigogni, captain of mercenaries under King John, 360

England, kings of: Edward the Confessor, 2–4; Harold II, 4–12; Henry I, 15, 40–70; Henry II, 69, 70, 77, 91–225, 307–8; Stephen, 68, 72–94; William I, 13–29; William Rufus, 15, 28–42; and Normandy, question of union or separation, 70; in reign of Richard I, 246–55

English language, mastery established by, 399–400

English subjects, absolved from oaths of allegiance to King John by Pope Innocent III, 349

Ethelred the Unready, King of the English, 2

Ethelric, daughter of Henry I, *see* Matilda (Empress)

Eu, Count of, 313, 314

Eudes, sewer of Henry I, Colchester granted to, 52

Eudes of Porrhoet, 204

Eugenius III, Pope, 124, 130

Euphemia, daughter of Henry I, 60

Eustace de Vescy, 362–63, 368

Eustace of Boulogne, Earl (grandfather), 72

Eustace of Boulogne, Earl (grandson), 76, 79, 82, 86, 91; coins issued by, 104

Eustace of Ely, Bishop, 342–43

Index

Index

Freteval, France, meeting of Henry II and Thomas à Becket at, 157
Fulford, battle with Norsemen at, 7
Fulk, Count of Anjou, 66
Fulk de Cantelupe, 342
Funeral services of medieval England, 344–45

Gaillard, Château, 295–96 (picture, 331); siege of, 330–34
Garonne, Guillaume de, 18
Gaveston, Piers, favorite of Edward II, 253
Geoffert, Bishop of Hereford, 52
Geoffrey, son of Geoffrey of Anjou, 93, 96, 196
Geoffrey de Crowcombe, 384
Geoffrey de Martigni, captain of mercenaries under King John, 360
Geoffrey of Anjou, Count, called Plantagenet, 69, 74–77, 79, 91, 93
Geoffrey of Brittany, Duke, 123, 156, 191; rebellion against Henry II, 178, 197–200, 209–17
Geoffrey of Norwich, Archdeacon, 348
Geoffrey of York, Archbishop, 202–4, 220–25, 229, 240–44
Gerald of Windsor, 183
Germany, Emperors of: Henry V, 60, 74–75; Henry VI, 277–82; Otto IV, 338, 359
Gernun, Robert, 58
Gilbert, Earl of Gloucester, 278
Gilbert the Weaver, of London, 45
Gilbertines, monastic order of, 138
Giraldus Cambrensis, cited, 138, 180–81, 182
Gisors, France, captured by Philip II, 279; meeting of Henry II and Philip II at, 219; meeting of Henry II with his sons, 199, 200; peace conferences at, 216–17
Glastonbury, as Avalon of Arthurian legend, 306
Glastonbury abbey, coffin of King Arthur and Queen Guinevere found at, 306; Henry of Blois, Abbot of,

306; history of, 23; massacre of monks by Normans, 23–24
Gloucester, charter taken away from, 16; Gilbert, Earl of, 278; Robert, Earl of, 84, see also Robert of Gloucester
Gloucester Castle, Stephen of Blois held prisoner at, 83–84
Godfrey, King of Jerusalem, 72
Godfrey, son of William d'Aubigny, Earl of Arundel, 81
Godobert the white-tawyer, 102
Godric, Saxon monk, 167–68
Godstow, Convent of, 203
Godwine, Earl, 1–2
Golden Book of St. Albans, cited, 61
Gravelines, France, arrival of Thomas à Becket at, 153–54
Gray Monks, 138–39, 154–55
Great Charter, see Magna Charta
Green, J. R., historian, cited, 399
Grim, monk from Cambridge, 162–67
Gualo, papal legate of Innocent II, 388
Guerin de Chapion, 324
Guibert, Pope, 33
Guilds, 109
Gundulph, Bishop of Rochester, 20, 21
Guy of Lusignon, King of Jerusalem, 217–18, 274
Guyon de Cigogni, captain of mercenaries under King John, 360
Gyrth, brother of Harold II, 12

Hackett, Francis, quoted, 104
Hampshire, New Forest in, 39–40
Hanley, manor of, 16
Hardell, William de, mayor of London, 369
Harold II, King of England: as advisor to Edward the Confessor, 2–4; accession of, 4; defense against Normans, 9–12; defense against Norsemen, 1–2, 4–9
Harold Hardrada, King of Norway; claim to English throne, 2, 6; invasion of England, 6–9
Hastings, Battle of, 10–12

Index

Index

Hugh of Lincoln, Bishop, 97, 140, 203, 294

Hugh of Lusignon, 312–16, 364, 400

Hugh of Rouen, Archbishop, 70

Hugh of St. Victor, cited, 300

Hugh the Brown, *see* Hugh of Lusignon

Hugues-de-Loup, property awarded to, 19

Humber River, Norse invasion by, 6

Humbold, archdeacon of Salisbury, 47

Humphrey de Bohun, lord of Hereford, 121

Huntingdon, Earl of, Robin Hood as, 253

Huntington, Thomas de, *see* Thomas de Huntington

Iconium, Sultan of, 115

Inge the Hunchback, Norwegian candidate for Scandinavian archbishopric, 124

Innocent III, Pope, 298, 337–86, 388–89; deposition of John from throne of England and promise of crown to Philip of France, 349; excommunication of English subjects serving King John, 349; excommunication of King John, 348; laying of interdict on England, 342–47; Magna Charta, opposition to, 382–86; raising of ban on England, 354–56; surrender of King John to, 352–53

Innocent the Great, book by C. H. C. Pirie-Gordon, cited, 338n.

Interdict, laid on England by Pope Innocent III, 342–56; laid on Normandy after murder of Thomas à Becket, 176

Invasions of England: Danish, 2; French, during civil war between King John and barons, 389–95; Norman, 9–12; Norse, 6–9; Scottish, 80, 178, 198–99

Ipswich, military camp for defense against French invasion at, 350

Ireland, desecration of churches by Normans, 189; English and Norman invasion of, 184–90; English invasion sanctioned by Pope, 126–27; internal conflict, 182–83; John given lordship by Henry II, 156, 189–90; lands granted to Normans, 184; reasons for invasion, 181–82; at time of invasion, 180–81 (map, 187)

Irish enamels, 181

Irish people, of interior and western country, 180–81

Isaac of Bristol, 350

Isabella, princess of Scotland, as hostage of King John, 347

Isabella, wife of Conrad of Montferrat, 274

Isabella of Angoulême, wife of (1) King John of England and (2) Hugh of Lusignon, 307, 312–15, 325, 364–65, 400

Isle of Man, sea attack of Ostmen launched from, 186

Ivanhoe, cited, 252

Ivry, France, captured by Philip II, 279

Jaffa, Palestine, in Third Crusade, 271, 275, 276

Jerusalem, campaign in Third Crusade for possession of, 268–73; Christian pilgrimages permitted after Third Crusade, 276; kings of: Baldwin, 72, Godfrey, 72, Guy of Lusignon, 217–18

Jettenwald (Giant's Wood) seized by crown, 39

Jews, massacre of at coronation of Richard I, 230

Joan (Makepeace), wife of King Alexander of Scotland, 364, 400

Joanne, wife of (1) William II of Sicily and (2) Raimund of Toulouse, 123, 259–60, 268, 276–77, 297–98

Jocelin, Bishop of Salisbury, 158

John, King of England, 123, 198, 229, 298–397: and Arthur of Brittany, 315–23; betrothal to heiress of Maurienne, 191–92; called Soft-

Index

sword, 325, 359; children of, 364; conflict with Church of Rome, 342–56; conspiracy against Richard I, 278–87; contest for crown, 302–11; death of, 394–97; deposition from throne declared by Pope Innocent III, 349; English kingdom made fief of Rome, 352–53; excommunication by Pope Innocent III, 348; lordship of Ireland given by Henry II, 156, 189–90; and Magna Charta, 360–61, 365–70, 382; marriage to Isabella of Angoulême, 312–14; rebellion against Henry II, 222; subjects absolved from oaths of allegiance by Pope, 349; war with barons, 386–94; war with France, 315–16, 324–25, 328–34, 349–51, 357, 359

John de Grey, Bishop of Norwich, 337–39

John of Oxford, Bishop of Norwich, 97

John of Salisbury, 97, 126, 162

Joseph of Arimathaea in England, 23

Jossen, Jew of York, 231–32

Jousting Grounds, at Windsor, 50

Judicial circuits, origin of, 64, 106

Judicial reform, under Henry II, 211; see also Laws

Jury, trial by, 105, 141

Justiciar, office of, 63

Kent, coast defended against French invasion, 350; promised to Count of Flanders by Henry, the Young King, 198; volunteers to support claims of Stephen of Blois from, 86; William of Ypres, Earl of, 103

Kilburn, priory of, 61

King chosen by common men, 78–79

Kirklees, convent of, 253

Knaresborough, Castle, 160

Knights and the Code of Chivalry, 53–54, 227

Knights of St. John, 264, 270, 271

Knights of the Blue Thong, 260

Knights Templars, 264, 271; Grand Master at signing of Magna Charta,

366; hotel at Ewell as headquarters for King John against French invasion, 350

La Blanche Nef, ship, 66–67

Lacey, Robert de, 100

Lacey, Roger de, 330–34

Lacey, sixth Baron de, 320

Lacock Abbey, founding of, 351

Lady Chapel, in Canterbury Cathedral, 165–67, 174

Lady of England, Empress Matilda elected to be, 85–88

Lambeth, Council of Church at, 45–48

Lamburn, Adam de, architect, 172

Lammas lands, 248

Land, assessment by jury, 289; measurement of, 19, 26; tax on, first, 280

Landowners dispossessed by William the Conqueror, 16–20

Lanfranc, Archbishop of Canterbury, 32, 122

Langtoft, Piers, quoted, 259

Langton, Stephen, see Stephen Langton

Lantern Tower, of Tower of London, 110

Lateran Council, Fourth, 384–86

Laudabiliter, papal bull sanctioning English invasion of Ireland, 126–27

Laws: Brehon Code of Ireland, 181; under Henry I, 54–58, 63–64; under Henry II, 105–6, 188; under William Rufus, 31, 35–36; under William the Conqueror, 24–25

Layamon, twelfth-century author, cited, 399

Le Breton, Richard, 160–74

Legislative system set up by Henry I, 63

Leicester, Robert de Beaumont, Earl of, 153, 178; Simon de Montfort l'Amaury, Earl of, 279; Simon de Montfort, Earl of, 253

Leinster, Dermod, King of, 182–86; Morogh O'Brien, King of, 181, 185

[420]

Index

LeMans, France, destroyed by Philip II, 219–20

Leolin of Wales, 351

Leopold, Duke of Austria, 262–71, 277

L'Espan, abbey of, Mans, France, 298

Lewhaden Castle, 327

Limoges, France, at time of Henry II, 192

Lincoln, battle at, 83; palace of Bishop, death of King John at, 394–97; promised to Count of Boulogne by Henry, the Young King, 198; William, Bishop of, 348

Lions of England, origin of, 101

Liverpool, development of, 300–1

Loefwin, brother of Harold II, 12

Loanland, principle of, 35–36

Lombard, Peter, author of *Sentences*, cited, 300

London, entry of William the Conqueror into, 17; fire of 1132, 76; under Henry II, 107–12; rebellion against taxation under Richard I, 290–93; resistance to claims of Empress Matilda, 87–88; Tower of, *see* Tower of London; in the Twelfth Century (map), 111; William, Bishop of, 342–43

Londoners, in reign of Henry I, 45

Longbow, use of, 184, 251, 254–55

Longchamp, William de, Chancellor, 232–45, 287

Lord Mayor of London, first, 109

Lothario de Conti de Segni, *see* Innocent III

Loudon Castle, France, 93

Louis VI (the Fat), King of France, 113

Louis VII, King of France, 82, 96, 133, 134, 154, 172, 178, 207–8, 216–17: marriage to Eleanor of Aquitaine, 113–17; war against Henry II, 197–200

Louis VIII, King of France: invasion of England, 386, 387–95; marriage to Blanche of Castile, 310–11

Loupescaire, captain at siege of Château Gaillard, 332, 334

Louvain, Count of, 68

Lovell, Lord, support of Empress Matilda's claim to throne by, 82

Luke de Barré, bard, 69

Lund, Sweden, Danish see established at, 125

Lyons Castle, Normandy, death of Henry I at, 69–70

Macbeth, King of Scotland, 44

Magdalen's Hill, Winchester, meeting of King John and Stephen Langton at, 353–54

Magna Charta, 56–57, 357–61; annulled by Pope Innocent III, 382–86; signing of, 365–70; text of, 370–80

Maine, attempt of France toward, 309–10; retained in Angevin Empire, 93

Malcolm, King of Scotland, 121

Malcolm Canmore, King of Scotland, 43–44

Malmesbury, William of, chronicles of, cited, 62

Mandeville, Geoffrey de, 363–64, 368

Mandeville, William de, Constable of the Tower, 38

Mans, France, residence of Queen Berengaria in, 298

Mantes, France, destruction of by William the Conqueror, 27–28

Maps: Angevin Empire, 193; Battle of Senlac (Hastings), 11; Country Around the Wash, 393; Ireland at the Time of the Invasion, 187; London in the Twelfth Century, 111; Near East at Time of Third Crusade, 269; Normandy at the Time of the Conquest, 5; Thames, from Oxford to London, Showing Norman Fortifications, 367

Marcadie, captain under Richard I, 297

Marche, Count of, 312

[421]

Index

Margaret, Princess, of Scotland, as hostage of King John, 347

Margaret, wife of King Malcolm of Scotland, 43–44

Marguerite, Princess, of France, wife of Henry, the Young King, 134–35, 192–95

Marie, Princess, of France, wife of Arthur of Brittany, 315

Mark Ash forest, 251

Marshal, William, *see* William Marshal

Martel, Château, death of Henry, the Young King, at, 212

Martial, St., tomb of, in Limoges, France, 192

Martin, Castle, 327

Martyr, tomb at Canterbury, pilgrimages to, 172

Martyrdom, The, in Canterbury Cathedral, 167

Mary, wife of Eustace of Boulogne, 72

Mathew de Cleres, 235, 241

Matilda (Empress), Lady of England, wife of (1) Henry V, Emperor of Germany, and (2) Geoffrey (Plantagenet), Count of Anjou, 71–93, 137; coins issued by, 103; declared heir to English throne, 68; denied throne, 77–79; married to Count Geoffrey of Anjou, 69, 75–76; struggle for throne, 80–91; as wife of Henry V of Germany, 51, 60

Matilda (Queen), of Boulogne, wife of Stephen of England, 72–73, 79, 82, 85–87, 89, 91

Matilda (Queen), wife of Henry I of England, 43–61; Charter stipulated by, 54–57

Matilda (Queen), wife of William the Conqueror, 14–28, 52

Matilda, daughter of Stephen of Blois, 72

Matilda, wife of Count of Perche, 67

Matilda, wife of Geoffrey de Mandeville, 363

Matilda, wife of Henry of Saxony, 122–23

Maud de Valeri, wife of William de Braose, 320–22

Maude, Queen, *see* Matilda, wife of Henry I

Mauger of Worcester, Bishop, 342–43

Mauger the Smith of London, 45

Maurice, Bishop of London, 42

Maurienne, Count of, 192–95

Maurienne, heiress of, betrothed to John of England, 191–92

Melech-Ric, *see* Richard I

Mellent, Earl of, 82

Melune, Vicomte de, 390

Mentz, Germany, Richard Coeur de Lion released at, 281

Merlin, prophecies of, 99–100, 190

Merrie England, first use of term, 59

Merton, priory of, 129

Messina, Italy, Richard I and Philip II at, 259

Milford Haven, Pembroke Castle at, 327

Militia, established under Henry II, 106

Minstrelsy, 53–54

Mirabeau Castle, France, 93; siege of, 315–16

Mohun, Baron, support of Empress Matilda's claim to throne by, 82

Mold, Queen, *see* Matilda, wife of Henry I of England

Moll Walbee, fictional heroine, 320

Monasteries, in reign of Henry II, 137

Monastic orders in England, 137–43

Money, customs of minting, 64; raised by King John for defense against French invasion, 350; raised to supply needs of Richard I, 233–38, 288–89; reform under Henry II, 103–5; during reign of Stephen of Blois, 94

Mont St. Michel, France, captured by army of Brittany, 334

Montfort, Simon de, Earl of Leicester, 253

Montfort l'Amaury, Simon de, Earl of Leicester, 279

[422]

Index

Mora, ship, 66

Moreville, Hugh de, 160–74

Morkar, earl of the north, at Norman invasion, 6

Morogh O'Brien, King of Leinster, Ireland, 181, 185

Mortagne, Eustace, Earl of, 86

Mount Carmel, Palestine, in Third Crusade, 261, 268–70

Mowbray, Robert de, Earl of Northumberland, 30, 51

Mowbray, Roger de, 203

Mowbray, William, Lord, 368

Murder of Thomas à Becket, 160–67

Narberth Castle, 327

Naval battle between English and French in port of Dam, 351

Navarre, Berengaria of, wife of Richard I of England, 230, 256–98; Sancho the Wise, King of, 256–58; visit of Eleanor of Aquitaine to, 241, 258

Near East, at time of Third Crusade (map), 269

Nesta, Welsh princess, mistress of Henry I and wife of Gerald of Windsor, 77, 183

Neufchâtel, France, captured by Philip II, 279

New Forest, creation of, 39–40; extent of, 250–51

Newark, death of King John at, 394–97

Nicholas, Cardinal, Bishop of Frascati, papal legate of Innocent III, 355–56

Nigel, Bishop of Ely, 100

Norman ambitions toward England, 3

Norman barons, *see* Barons

Norman invasion, 9–12

Normandy, campaign of Philip II of France against, 324–34; and England, question of union or separation, 70; Henry, the Young King, given lordship by Henry II, 156; invaded by Philip II, 278–79; lost by England, 334; Robert, Duke of, 28, 30, 42, 52, 65–66; at the Time of the Conquest (map), 5; William, Duke of, *see* William I, the Conqueror

Norse invasion, 6–9

Northallerton, Battle of the Standards at, 80

Northampton Castle, trial of Thomas à Becket at, 150–53

Northern England, desolation after Norman conquest, 20

Northumberland, returned to Henry II by King Malcolm of Scotland, 121; Hugh de Puiset, Earl of, 234–39; promised to King of Scotland by Henry, the Young King, 198; Robert de Mowbray, Earl of, 30, 51; Tostig, Earl of, 4–9

Norwich, Geoffrey, Archdeacon of, 348; John de Grey, Bishop of, 337–39; John of Oxford, Bishop of, 97

Nottingham, resistance to Normans, 17–18

Nottingham Castle, siege of, 286

Officers of royal household, 51–52

Olaf Tryggvisson, Norse hero, 6

Old Jewry, massacre at coronation of Richard I, 231; London moneylenders of, 109

Old Man of the Mountain, 273–75; purported letter from, 288

Olivia, daughter of William d'Aubigny, Earl of Arundel, 81

Osbert, servant to Thomas à Becket, 163, 168

Osbert de Longchamp, 235–38

Ossianic songs of Ireland, 181

Ossory, Ireland, siege of, 184

Ostmen of Ireland, 180, 181; expelled from Dublin, 186

Otto IV, Emperor of Germany, 338, 359

Outlaws of the forest, 251–53

Oxford, John of, Bishop of Norwich, 97

Oxford Castle, siege by King Stephen of, 89–90

Index

Oxford University, 124, 400; attended by Thomas à Becket, 129; in time of Henry II, 142

Pale, the, English territory in Ireland, 188–90

Pampeluna, Spain, meeting of Richard I and Berengaria at, 256–57

Pandulfo, papal legate of Innocent III, 351–55, 366, 382–83

Papal bull, canonizing Thomas à Becket, 171; declaring William of Normandy's right to English throne, 9; *Laudabiliter*, sanctioning English invasion of Ireland, 126–27

Paris, Matthew, quoted, 83, 93

Parish churches of old London, 108

Pearl of Brittany, the, as hostage of King John, 347

Pembroke, William Marshal, Earl of, 220, 302–5, 324–32, 360, 366, 395

Pembroke Castle, 327

Penny, coinage of, 103–5

Perche, Count of, 67

Percy, Guillaume de, 18

Percy, Richard de, at signing of Magna Charta, 368

Pereric, coins issued by, 104

Perugia, Italy, death of Pope Innocent III at, 386

Peter of Blois, chaplain to Henry II, quoted, 96

Peter of Pontefract, prophecy concerning King John of, 349, 353

Peter the Hermit, 30

Petronille of Aquitaine, 113

Peveril, Guillaume, 18

Philip I, King of France, 27–28

Philip II (Augustus), King of France, 208–9, 216–17, 388–89; conflict with Richard I, 275, 278–82; campaign against Flanders, 355; English crown promised by Pope Innocent III to, 349; support of Arthur of Brittany for English crown, 304, 309–10, 314–16; in Third Crusade, 218, 235, 259–67; war against Henry II, 217–24; war against Richard I, 294–97; war against King John, 315–16, 324–25, 328–34, 349–51, 359

Philip de Brois, 146–47

Pillage by Norman conquerors, 23–24

Pirie-Gordon, C. H. C., author of *Innocent the Great*, cited, 338n.

Plantagenet, Geoffrey of Anjou, first so called, 69

Plantagenet kings: Henry II, 95–225; John, 299–397; nature of, 93–94; Richard I, 226–97

Poaching on King's land, 251–53

Poitou, William de Longchamp as chancellor of, 233

Pontigny, France, Cistercian monastery at, 154–55; residence of Archbishop Stephen Langton in, 347, 351

Poor Clares, order of, 143

Popes: Adrian IV, 124–28; Alexander III, 146, 149–50, 154–57, 171, 177–78; Anastasius, 125; Celestine III, 337; Clement III, 241, 340; Eugenius III, 124, 130; Guibert, 33; Innocent III, 298, 337–86; Urban II, 33–34

Pound, coinage of, 104

Presentment of Englishry, law, 25

Preserve laws, resentment against, 39–40

Property, confiscated by William the Conqueror, 17–18; deeds and registration under William the Conqueror, 25–27; as loanland, 35–36; recording in Domesday Book, 25–27; reversion to crown under William Rufus, 35–36; taxation of, 280, 289; titles confused during reign of Stephen, 90–91

Proxy marriage, ceremony of, 311

Puiset, Hugh de, 233–39

Pulleyn, Robert, Cardinal, 124

Purbeck, Isle of, Castle Corfe on, 316

"Queen," first use of title in England, 15

Index

Index

Roger of Salisbury, chief minister to Henry I, 67–68, 100

Roger of Sicily, King, 278

Roger of Worcester, Bishop, 342–43

Roger of York, Archbishop, 142, 147, 156–59, 170

Rohaise, wife of Eudes the sewer, 52

Rohaise, wife of Gilbert Becket, 129

Romance of the History of England, The, cited, 300

Rosamonde Clifford, mistress of Henry II, 201–3

Rouen, France, captured by Philip II, 334; cosmopolitan character of, 302–3; Hugh, Archbishop of, 70; royal palace at, 198; Walter, Archbishop of, 177, 240, 243, 281, 303–5

Roumara, Baron, support of Empress Matilda's claim to throne by, 82

Royal succession, Saxon conception of, 3

Rumsey, nunnery of, 44–48

Runcone, Norman priest given church at, 19

Runnymede, signing of Magna Charta at, 361, 365–70

Saints, *see* under name of saint

St. Albans, Benedictine monastery at, 124

St. Andrew, monastery of, 150

St. Augustine's Monastery, 146

St. Bartholomew's, Smithfield, cloth fairs at, 108

St. Bartholomew's hospital, London, 346

St. Benedict Chapel, Canterbury Cathedral, 165

St. Blaise Chapel, Canterbury Cathedral, 165

St. David's Cathedral, Wales, 138

St. Dunstan's Oratory, Canterbury, 178

St. Edward's Chapel at Windsor, 50

St. Frideswide's monastery, Oxford, forerunner of Christ Church College, 400

"St. George for England," 270

St. Martin at Battle monasteries, 138

St. Martin's-in-the-Lane church, 140

St. Martin's le Grand church, London, 110

St. Martin's Priory, 242

St. Martin's Vintry, London, 110

St. Mary le Bow church, sanctuary violated at, 292–93

St. Mary's Chapel, Rome, 385

St. Nicholas Chapel, Canterbury, 178

St. Paul's Cathedral, 110, 129

St. Stephen's church, Northampton, 151

St. Swithin, minister of, burial of William Rufus at, 41

St. Swithin's Lane, London, Drapers' Company hall in, 108

Saladin, 217–18, 261–76

Salisbury, Ela of, 350–51; Hubert Walter, Bishop of, 264, 275–76, 280, *see also* under Canterbury, Archbishops of; Jocelin, Bishop of, 158; John of, 97, 126, 162; Roger of, 67–68; William Longsword, Earl of, 202, 350–51, 352, 355, 366

Salisbury Cathedral, building of, 351

Saltwood Castle, 161–62

Sancho the Strong, son of Sancho the Wise, 256–57

Sancho the Wise, King of Navarre, 256–58

Sanctuary, practice of, 139–41; violated during tax rebellion, 292–93

Sandwich, landing of Thomas à Becket at, 158

Saracens in Third Crusade, *see* Saladin

Savaric de Mauleon, 316, 387

Saxon landowners dispossessed by Normans, 16–20

Saxon resistance to Norman conquest, 20–25

Saxons, appearance of, 1; battle dress of, 1; concept of government, 1–2

Scandinavian request for archbishops, 124–25

Scholarship in early medieval church in England, 142

Index

Scotland, Alexander, King of, 351, 364; David, King of, 80, 88; Malcolm, King of, 121; Malcolm Canmore, King of, 43–44; William the Lion, King of, 178, 179, 198–99, 233–34

Scott, Sir Walter, cited, 252

Scottish invasions of England, 80, 178, 198–99

Second Crusade, 114–15

Senlac, Battle of, 10–12

Sens, France, Archbishop of, 176; headquarters of Pope Alexander at, 149; Thomas à Becket in exile at, 155

Sentences, book by Peter Lombard, cited, 300

Serbruge, Queen of the West Saxons, 68

Serlo, Abbot, 40

Sewer, office of, 51–52

Sherwood Forest, 251–53

Shilling, coinage of, 104

Sibyelle of Flanders, on Second Crusade, 114

Sibylla, wife of Guy of Lusignon, 217–18, 274

Sicily, Roger, King of, 278; Tancred, King of, 259–60; under suzerainty of England, 191; William I, King of, 125; William II, King of, 123, 172, 259

Sigurd of the Mouth, Norwegian candidate for Scandinavian archbishopric, 124

Sleeve, English Channel, 191

Soissons, France, invasion of England planned by Philip II at, 349

Soldier's apparel in reign of Richard I, 302

Sovereign, coinage of, 104

Spires, Germany, Emperor Henry V buried at, 74

Sports of villagers, 249

Stackpole Castle, 327

Staller, office of, 51

Stamfordbridge, battle with Norsemen at, 7–9

Standards, Battle of the, 80

State and church, struggle between, *see* Church in England, resistance to royal power; Magna Charta

Stephen (of Blois), King of England, 68, 72–94; accession of, 77–79; coins issued by, 103; successor named by, 92–93; war with Empress Matilda, 80–91

Stephen Harding, St., 138–39

Stephen Langton, Archbishop of Canterbury, 339–89; arrival in England of, 353–54; and Magna Charta, 57, 357–61, 365–70; suspended by Pope, 383–86, 389

Streets of old London, 109–10

Striguil, Richard de Clare, Earl of, 183–89

Strongbow, *see* Richard de Clare

Suffolk, volunteers to support claim of Stephen of Blois from, 86

Superstitions in time of Henry II, 99

Surrey, William Warren, Earl of, 43

Sweden, enmity between Sviars and Gautors, 125

Swen Forkbeard, Norse hero, 6

Sweyn, King of Denmark, 6

Swineshead monastery, illness of King John at, 394

Taillefer, Norman minstrel, 10–12

Taillevent, French royal cook, 131

Tailors of London in reign of Henry I, 45

Talbot, Geoffrey, 82

Talbot, William, 351

Tancred, King of Sicily, 259–60

Taxation, under Richard I, 280, 289–90, 294; under Richard I, rebellion against, 290–94; under William I, 26–27

Tegas, Ireland, battle at, 190

Templars, *see* Knights Templars

Temple, church of the, London, capitulation of King John to Rome in, 352

Tenby Castle, 327

Tenchebrai, battle of, Norman and French against English, 65–66

Index

Tezelin, cook to William the Conqueror, property awarded to, 18

Thames, from Oxford to London, Showing Norman Fortifications (map), 367

Theobold, Archbishop of Canterbury, 92, 100–1, 121, 129–30, 135

Theobold, brother of Stephen of Blois, 78

Thingmen, bodyguard of Saxon kings, 1

Third Crusade, 218–45, 258–76; money raised by Richard Coeur de Lion for, 233–38

Thomas à Becket, St., Archbishop of Canterbury, 101–2, 129–79: acceptance of archbishopric, 135–37; as chancellor, 130–44; exile in France, 153–57; resistance to state jurisdiction, 145–53; return to England and murder of, 157–67

Thomas de Huntington, abbot of Beaulieu, 384

Thorkill the Tall, Norse hero, 6

Throne of England, conferring under Saxons of, 3

Tiberias, capture by Saracens of, 218

Tickhill Castle, 239

Tieghernan O'Rourke, King of Breffny and East Meath, 182

Torfrida, wife of Hereward the Wake, 21

Tortulf, ancestor of Geoffrey of Anjou, 75

Torture, methods of, 90

Tostig, Earl of Northumberland, 4–9

Toulouse, Countess of, on Second Crusade, 114

Toulouse, France, military expedition of Henry II against, 132–33

Touraine, attempt of France toward, 309–10, 315; retained in Angevin Empire, 93

Tournaments, 256–57, 326

Tours, Archbishop of, 241

Toustain, Norman head of Glastonbury abbey, 23–24

Tower of London, additions to, 110; construction of, 19–20, 37; as official residence of William de Longchamp, 233, 244; Ralph Flambard, Bishop of Durham, in, 38–39; as royal residence, 50

Tower-Royal, London, building of, 72; as home of Eleanor of Aquitaine, 110

Towns, benefit from Norman Conquest to, 398–99

Tracey, William de, 160–74

Treasure of English crown, lost at The Wash, 390–92

Treatise of Origen, The, cited, 300

Treaty of Wallingford, 91–92

Trenc-la-Mer, ship of Richard Coeur de Lion, 260–61

Trent River, battle at, 83

Trial, by jury, 105, 141; by ordeal, 105–6

Trim, Ireland, Baron de Lacey, lord of, 320

Tristan, sword of, in England, 71, 391–92

Tyburn, hangings of London rebels at, 293

Tyrrell, Walter, lord of Poix, 40–41

Ulster cycle of romances, 181

Urban II, Pope, 33–34

Vaudreuil Castle, France, surrender to Philip II, 324

Vavasor, title of, 202

Vermandois, Count of, 113

Vesey, Ives de, 18

Village, in medieval England, 246–50

Villein, status and life of, 246–50

Vinney Ridge forest, 251

Vitré, Sieur de, 309

Volfan, brother of Hugues-de-Loup, given church at Runcone, 19

Volmar, brother of Hugues-de-Loup, 19

Waldenses, sect of, 385

Wales, invaded by Henry II, 121;

Index

Nesta, Princess of, 77, 183; racial stock and legend of, 305–7

Wallingford, Treaty of, 91–92

Walter, Hubert, Archbishop of Canterbury, 264, 275–76, 280–81, 283–94, 305, 336

Walter of Coutances, Archbishop of Rouen, 240, 244, 281, 303–5

Warren, William, Earl of Surrey, 43

Warenne, William, Earl of, 352, 368

Wars: between England and France: in reign of Henry II, 197–200, 217–24, in reign of King John, 315–16, 324–25, 328–34, 349–51, 357, 359, 386, 387–95, in reign of Richard I, 294–97; between King John and barons, 361, 384–96; with Normandy and France, in reign of Henry I, 52, 65; of succession between Stephen of Blois and Empress Matilda, 80–92

Wash, The (map, 393), English treasure lost at, 390–92

Water of St. Thomas, 171

Waterford, Ireland, siege of, 185

Wedding services of medieval England, 345–46

Welland River, see Wash

Westminster Abbey, building of, 4; coronation of Richard I at, 230–31; during Becket's chancellorship, 130–31; coronation of Henry II at, 118–21; marriage of Henry I at, 48; sanctuary in, 140

Westminster Palace, 50; Cotton-Hall, 74; White-Hall, 71

Wexford, Ireland, siege, 184

White-Hall at Westminster, 71, 100, 143

White Tower, see Tower of London

Wigmore, Lord of, 121

William I, the Conqueror, King of England, 13–29: children of, 15; claim to English throne, 2, 3–4; conquest of England, 13–23; Domesday Book ordered by, 25–26; invasion of England, 9–12; legislation under, 24–25; successor named by, 28; taxation under, 26–27

William I, of Sicily, 125

William II (Rufus), King of England, 15, 28–42

William II, of Sicily, 123, 172, 259

William, the Lion, King of Scotland, 178, 179, 198–99, 233–34

William, archdeacon of Canterbury, 47

William, of Normandy, Duke, see William the Conqueror

William, son of Henry II, 117, 122

William, son of William d'Aubigny, Earl of Arundel, 81

William Atheling, son of Henry I, 60, 66–67

William Clito, 63

William de Braose, lord of Bramber, 319–22

William de Hardell, mayor of London, at signing of Magna Charta, 369

William de Longchamp, Chancellor, 232–45, 287

William de Tracey, 160–74

William Longbeard, see Fitz-Osbert, William

William Longsword (Long-Espée), Earl of Salisbury, 202, 350–51, 352, 355, 366

William Marshal, 220, 302–5, 324–32, 360, 366, 395

William of Aquitaine, 112–13

William of Aquitaine, St., 112–13

William of Cloudesley, forest outlaw, 251–53

William of Lincoln, Bishop, 348

William of London, Bishop, 342–43

William of Malmesbury, chronicles of, cited, 62

William of the White Hands, Archbishop of Reims, 62

William of Tyre, Archbishop, 217–18

William of Ypres, 82, 86, 88, 103

William Tell legend, possible origin of, 252

Index

Index by Harriet Thompson.